STUDENT SOLUTIONS MANUAL

Cost Accounting
A Managerial Emphasis

Third Canadian Edition

Charles T. Horngren
Stanford University

George Foster
Stanford University

Srikant M. Datar
Stanford University

Howard D. Teall
Wifrid Laurier University

PEARSON

Prentice
Hall

Toronto

ISBN 0-13-039142-5

Executive Acquisitions Editor: Samantha Scully
Senior Developmental Editor: Madhu Ranadive
Production Editor: Emmet Mellow
Production Coordinator: Deborah Starks

3 4 5   08 07 06 05 04

Printed and bound in Canada.

TABLE OF CONTENTS

CHAPTER 1
THE ACCOUNTANT'S ROLE IN THE ORGANIZATION

1-2   **Management accounting** measures and reports financial as well as other types of information that assists managers in fulfilling the goals of the organization. **Financial accounting** focuses on external reporting that is guided by generally accepted accounting principles.

1-4   The business functions in the value chain are:

- **Research and development**—the generation of, and experimentation with, ideas related to new products, services, or processes.
- **Design of products, services, and processes**—the detailed planning and engineering of products, services, or processes.
- **Production**—the coordination and assembly of resources to produce a product or deliver a service.
- **Marketing**—the process by which individuals or groups (a) learn about and value the attributes of products or services and (b) purchase those products or services.
- **Distribution**—the mechanism by which products or services are delivered to the customer.
- **Customer service**—the support activities provided to customers.

1-6   Uses of feedback in a management control system include:

- Changing goals
- Searching for alternative means of operating
- Changing methods for making decisions
- Making predictions
- Changing operations
- Changing the reward system

1-8   *Supply chain* describes the flow of goods, services, and information from the initial sources of materials and services to the delivery of products to consumers, regardless of whether those activities occur in the same organization or in other organizations.

Cost management is most effective when it integrates and coordinates activities across all companies in the supply chain as well as across each business function in an individual company's value chain. Attempts are made to restructure all cost areas to be more cost-effective.

1-10   The SMAC is the Society of Management Accountants of Canada. The CMA (Certified Management Accountant) is the professional designation for management accountants and financial executives. It demonstrates that the holder has passed the admission criteria and demonstrated the competency of technical knowledge required by the SMAC and its provincial societies.

1-12 Steps to take when established written policies provide insufficient guidance are:

(a) discuss problem with the immediate superior (except when it appears that the superior is involved).
(b) clarify relevant concepts by confidential discussion with an objective advisor.

If (a) and (b) and other avenues do not resolve the situation, resignation from the organization should be considered.

1-14 Yes, management accountants have customers just as companies have customers who purchase or use their products or services. Management accountants provide information and advice to many line and staff people in the organization and to various external parties. It is essential that they provide information and advice that line and staff customers and external parties view as timely and relevant.

1-16 (15 min.) Major purposes of accounting systems.

1. The three major purposes are:

(a) Routine internal reporting for the decisions of managers.
(b) Nonroutine internal reporting for the decisions of managers.
(c) External reporting to investors, government authorities, and other outside parties on the organization's financial position, operations, and related activities.

2. Note: In part 2 of the required for 1-18, it should read "Identify a major purpose served by each of the above five reports prepared by Barnes and Noble's management accounting group."

    1. (c)
    2. (a)
    3. (b)
    4. (c)
    5. (c)

3.   1. (a) Planning—decision by shareholder about whether to purchase more stock in Barnes and Noble (B&N).
      (b) Control—decision by bank whether B&N has maintained financial ratios specified in loan agreements.
   2. (a) Planning—decision to increase or decrease local marketing support.
      (b) Control—decision on whether recent sales promotion led to an increase in revenues.
   3. (a) Planning—decision about whether or not to expand B&N's Internet lines of business.
      (b) Control—decision by VP of New Business Development on the performance of an analyst.

1-16 (cont'd)

4. (a) Planning—decision on which books to include in a special chat-room site.
    (b) Control—decision by publisher to pay additional bonuses to authors due to their book being on a bestseller list.
5. (a) Planning—decision by B&N on the amount and type of insurance to purchase next year.
    (b) Control—decision by insurance company to approve a cash payment to B&N.

1-18 (15 min.) **Value chain and classification of costs, pharmaceutical company.**

Cost Item	Value Chain Business Function
a.	Design
b.	Marketing
c.	Customer service
d.	Research and development
e.	Marketing
f.	Production
g.	Marketing
h.	Distribution

1-20 (15 min.) **Scorekeeping, attention-directing, and problem-solving.**

Because the accountant's duties are often not sharply defined, some of these answers might be challenged.

a. Scorekeeping
b. Attention directing
c. Scorekeeping
d. Problem solving
e. Attention directing
f. Attention directing
g. Problem solving
h. Scorekeeping, depending on the extent of the report
i. This question is intentionally vague. The give-and-take of the budgetary process usually encompasses all three functions, but it emphasizes scorekeeping the least. The main function is attention directing, but problem solving is also involved.
j. Problem solving

1-22 (10 min.) **Management accountants and customer focus.**

1. Line managers are the primary customers of the management accounting function. Line managers in each of the six business function areas (R&D, design, production, marketing, distribution, and customer service) use management accounting information in their decisions.

2. Line managers rely on the continued support of management accountants to justify their budgets and headcount approvals. If these line managers do not find the information provided both relevant and timely, management accountants will not receive the resources necessary to continue fulfilling their potential contributions. This is similar to Ford not being able to retain its customers if it does not continue to satisfy (and even exceed) their expectations as to the reliability and performance of Ford motor vehicles.

1-24 (15 min.) **Changes in management and changes in management accounting.**

Change in Management Accounting	Key Theme in New Management Approach
a.	Total value-chain analysis
b.	Key success factors (quality) or Total value-chain analysis
c.	Dual external/internal focus
d.	Continuous improvement
e.	Customer satisfaction is priority one

1-26 (15 min.) **Planning and control decisions; Internet company.**

1. Planning decisions at WebNews.com focus on organizational goals, predicting results under various alternative ways of achieving those goals, and then deciding how to attain the desired goal. For example, WebNews.com could have the objective of revenue growth to gain critical mass or it could have the objective of increasing operating income. Many Internet companies in their formative years make revenue growth (and subscriber growth) their primary goal.

Control focuses on (a) deciding on, and taking actions that implement the planning decision, and (b) deciding on performance evaluation and the related feedback that will help future decision making.

2. **Planning decisions**
    a. Decision to raise monthly subscription fee
    c. Decision to upgrade content of online services
    e. Decision to decrease monthly subscription fee

Control decisions
    b. Decision to inform existing subscribers about the rate of increase—an implementation part of control decisions
    d. Demotion of VP of Marketing—performance evaluation and feedback aspect of control decisions

1-28 (15 min.)   **Management accounting guidelines.**

1.   Cost-benefit approach
2.   Behavioural and technical considerations
3.   Different costs for different purposes
4.   Cost-benefit approach
5.   Behavioural and technical considerations
6.   Cost-benefit approach
7.   Behavioural and technical considerations
8.   Different costs for different purposes
9.   Behavioural and technical considerations

1-30 (15 min.)   **The chief financial officer and the controller.**

1.   As a controller, Rodriguez was primarily responsible for management accounting and financial accounting functions. Typical functions of a controller include:

- Financial planning and budgeting
- Operations administration
- Profitability reporting
- Inventory accounting
- General ledger
- Accounts payable
- Accounts receivable

2.   The chief financial officer's responsibilities include:

- Controllership
- Treasury
- Risk management
- Taxes
- Internal audit
- Information systems (in some organizations)
- Investor relations
- Financial planning

1-32 (30 min.) **Software procurement decisions, ethics.**

1.   Companies with "codes of conduct" frequently have a "supplier clause" that prohibits their employees from accepting "material" (in some cases, any) gifts from suppliers. The motivations include:

(a)   Integrity/conflict of interest. Suppose Michaels recommends that a Horizon 1-2-3 product subsequently be purchased by Mexa. This recommendation could be because he felt he owed them an obligation as his trip to the Cancun conference was fully paid by Horizon.

(b)   The appearance of a conflict of interest. Even if the Horizon 1-2-3 product is the superior one at that time, other suppliers likely will have a different opinion. They may believe that the way to sell products to Mexa is via "fully-paid junkets to resorts." Those not wanting to do business this way may down-play future business activities with Mexa even though Mexa may gain much from such activities.

Some executives view the meeting as "suspect" from the start given the Caribbean location and its "rest and recreation" tone.

2.   <u>Pros of attending user meeting</u>

(a)   Able to learn more about the software products of Horizon.
(b)   Able to interact with other possible purchasers and get their opinions.
(c)   Able to influence the future product development plans of Horizon in a way that will benefit Mexa. An example is Horizon's subsequently developing software modules tailored to food product companies.
(d)   Saves Mexa money. Visiting suppliers and their customers typically costs money whereas Horizon is paying for the Cancun conference.

<u>Cons of Attending</u>
(a)   The ethical issues raised in requirement 1.
(b)   Negative moral effects on other Mexa employees who do not get to attend the Cancun conference. These employees may reduce their trust and respect for Michaels' judgment, arguing he has been on a "supplier-paid vacation."

<u>Conditions on Attending Which Mexa Might Impose</u>
(a)   Sizable part of time in Cancun has to be devoted to business rather than recreation.
(b)   Decision on which Mexa executive attends is <u>not</u> made by the person who attends (this reduces the appearance of a conflict of interest).
(c)   Person attending (Michaels) does not have final say on purchase decision (this reduces the appearance of a conflict of interest).
(d)   Mexa executives only go when a new major purchase is being contemplated (to avoid the conference becoming a regular "vacation").

1-32 (cont'd)

A Conference Board publication on <u>Corporate Ethics</u> asked executives about a comparable situation:
- 76% said Mexa and Michaels face an ethical consideration in deciding whether to attend.
- 71% said Michaels should not attend as the payment of expenses is a "gift" within the meaning of a credible corporate ethics policy.

3.   <u>Pros of having a written code</u>

The Conference Board outlines the following reasons why companies adopt codes of ethics
(a)   Signals commitment of senior management to ethics.
(b)   Promotes public trust in the credibility of the company and its employees.
(c)   Signals the managerial professionalism of its employees.
(d)   Provides guidance to employees as to how difficult problems are to be handled. If adhered to, employees will avoid many actions that are unethical or appear to be unethical.
(e)   Drafting of the policy (and its redrafting in the light of ambiguities) can assist management in anticipating and preparing for ethical issues not yet encountered.

<u>Cons of having a written code</u>

(a)   Can give appearance that all issues have been covered. Issues not covered may appear to be "acceptable" even when they are not.
(b)   Can constrain the entrepreneurial activities of employees. Forces people to always "behave by the book."
(c)   Cost of developing code can be "high" if it consumes a lot of employee time.

CHAPTER 2
AN INTRODUCTION TO COST TERMS AND PURPOSES

2–2 **Cost assignment** is a general term that encompasses both (1) tracing accumulated costs to a cost object, and (2) allocating accumulated costs to a cost object.
Cost tracing is the assigning of direct costs to a chosen cost object.
Cost allocation is the assigning of indirect costs to a chosen cost object.
The relationship between these terms is as follows:

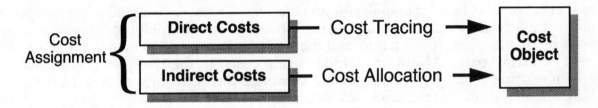

2–4 Managers believe that costs that are traced to a particular cost object are more accurately assigned to that cost object than are allocated costs. Managers prefer to use more accurate costs in their decisions.

2-6 Cost reduction efforts frequently focus on:

1.   doing only value-added activities, and
2.   efficiently managing the use of the cost drivers in those value-added activities.

2–8 **A variable cost** is a cost that changes in total in proportion to changes in the quantity of a cost driver.
    A **fixed cost** is a cost that does not change in total despite changes in the quantity of a cost driver.

Suppose the cost object is a Ford motor vehicle. A dashboard is a variable cost of the motor vehicle. The annual lease of the plant in which the vehicle is assembled illustrates a fixed cost for that year.

2–10 A unit cost is computed by dividing some total cost (the numerator) by some number of units (the denominator). In many cases the numerator will include a fixed cost that will not change despite changes in the number of units to be assembled. It is erroneous in those cases to multiply the unit cost by volume changes to predict changes in total costs at different volume levels.

2–12 No. Service sector companies have no inventories and, hence, no inventoriable costs.

2–14   Direct materials costs: The acquisition costs of all materials that eventually become part of the cost object (say, units finished or in process) and that can be traced to that cost object in an economically feasible way. Acquisition costs of direct materials include freight-in (inward delivery) charges, sales taxes, and custom duties.

Direct manufacturing labour costs: The compensation of all manufacturing labour that is specifically identified with the cost object (say, units finished or in process) and that can be traced to the cost object in an economically feasible way. Examples include wages and fringe benefits paid to machine operators and assembly-line workers.

Indirect manufacturing costs: All manufacturing costs considered to be part of the cost object (say, units finished or in process) but that cannot be individually traced to that cost object in an economically feasible way. Examples include power, supplies, indirect materials, indirect manufacturing labour, plant rent, plant insurance, property taxes on plants, plant depreciation, and the compensation of plant managers.

Prime costs: All direct manufacturing costs. In the two-part classification of manufacturing costs, prime costs would comprise direct materials costs. In the three-part classification, prime costs would comprise direct materials costs and direct manufacturing labour costs.

Conversion costs: All manufacturing costs other than direct materials costs.

2-16   (10 min.) Total costs and unit costs.

1. Total cost, $4,000. Unit cost per person, $4,000 ÷ 500 = $8.00

2. Total cost, $4,000. Unit cost per person, $4,000 ÷ 2,000 = $2.00

3. The main lesson of this problem is to alert the student early in the course to the desirability of thinking in terms of total costs rather than unit costs wherever feasible. Changes in the number of cost driver units will affect <u>total</u> variable costs but not <u>total</u> fixed costs. In our example, it would be perilous to use either the $8.00 or the $2.00 unit cost to predict the total cost because the total costs are not affected by the attendance. Instead, the student association should use the $4,000 total cost. Obviously, if the musical group agreed to work for, say $4.00 per person, such a unit variable cost could be used to predict the total cost.

2-18   (15 min.) Computing and interpreting unit manufacturing costs.

1.

	Supreme	Deluxe	Regular
Direct materials costs	$ 84.00	$ 54.00	$ 62.00
Direct manuf. labour costs	14.00	28.00	8.00
Indirect manuf. costs	42.00	84.00	24.00
Total manuf. costs	$140.00	$166.00	$ 94.00
Kilograms produced	80	120	100
Cost per kilogram	$1.7500	$1.3833	$0.9400

2. Given the unit volume changes for August 2002, the use of unit costs from the past month at a different unit volume level (both in aggregate and at the individual product level) will yield incorrect estimates of total costs in August 2002.

2-20 (15 min.) **Cost drivers and the value chain.**

1.

Business Function Area	Representative Cost Driver
A. Research and Development	Number of patents filed with government agency
B. Design of Products/Processes	Hours spent designing tamper-proof bottles
C. Production	Hours Tylenol packing line in operation
D. Marketing	Minutes of television advertising time
E. Distribution	Number of packages shipped
F. Customer Service	Number of calls to toll-free customer phone line

2.

Business Function Area	Representative Cost Driver
A. Research and Development	– Hours of laboratory work – Number of new drugs in development
B. Design of Products/Processes	– Number of focus groups on alternative package designs – Hours of process engineering work
C. Production	– Number of units packaged – Number of tablets manufactured
D. Marketing	– Number of promotion packages mailed – Number of sales personnel
E. Distribution	– Weight of packages shipped – Number of supermarkets on delivery route
F. Customer Service	– Number of units of a product recalled – Number of personnel on toll-free customer phone lines

2–22 (15-20 min.) **Variable costs and fixed costs.**

1.   Variable cost per tonne of beach sand mined:

Subcontractor	$80 per tonne
Government tax	50 per tonne
Total	$130 per tonne

Fixed costs per month:

0 to 100 tonnes of capacity per day	=	$150,000
101 to 200 tonnes of capacity per day	=	$300,000
201 to 300 tonnes of capacity per day	=	$450,000

2.

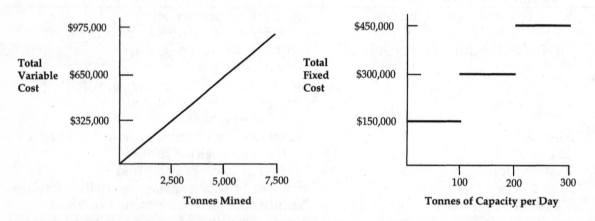

The concept of relevant range is potentially relevant for both graphs. However, the question does not place restrictions on the unit variable costs. The relevant range for the total fixed costs is from 0 to 100 tonnes; 101 to 200 tonnes; 201 to 300 tonnes, and so on. Within these ranges, the total fixed costs do not change in total.

3.

Tonnes Mined Per Day	Tonnes Mined Per Month	Fixed Unit Cost Per Tonne	Variable Unit Cost Per Tonne	Total Unit Cost Per Tonne
(1)	(2) = (1) × 25	(3) = FC ÷ (2)	(4)	(5) = (3) + (4)
(a) 180	4,500	$300,000 ÷ 4,500 = $66.67	$130	$196.67
(b) 220	5,500	$450,000 ÷ 5,500 =$81.82	$130	$211.82

The unit cost for 220 tonnes mined per day is $211.82, while for 180 tonnes it is only $196.67. This difference is caused by the fixed cost increment from 101 to 200 tonnes being spread over an increment of 80 tonnes, while the fixed cost increment from 201 to 300 tonnes is spread only over an increment of 20 tonnes.

2-24   (20-30 min.) **Inventoriable costs vs. period costs.**

1.   *Manufacturing-sector companies* purchase materials and components and convert them into different finished goods.
        Merchandising-sector companies purchase and then sell tangible products without changing their basic form.
        Service-sector companies provide services or intangible products to their customers—for example, legal advice or audits.
        Only manufacturing and merchandising companies have inventories of goods for sale.

2.   *Inventoriable costs* are all costs of a product that are regarded as an asset when they are incurred and then become cost of goods sold when the product is sold. These costs for a manufacturing company are included in work-in-process and finished goods inventory (they are "inventoried") to build up the costs of creating these assets.
        Period costs are all costs in the income statement other than cost of goods sold. These costs are treated as expenses of the period in which they are incurred because they are presumed not to benefit future periods (or because there is not sufficient evidence to conclude that such benefit exists). Expensing these costs immediately best matches expenses to revenues.

3.   (a) Mineral water purchased for resale by Loblaw—inventoriable cost of a merchandising company. It becomes part of cost of goods sold when the mineral water is sold.
        (b) Electricity used at a GE assembly plant—inventoriable cost of a manufacturing company. It is part of the manufacturing overhead that is included in the manufacturing cost of a refrigerator finished good.
        (c)   Amortization on Excite's computer equipment—period cost of a service company. Excite has no inventory of goods for sale and, hence, no inventoriable cost.
        (d) Electricity for Loblaw's store aisles—period cost of a merchandising company. It is a cost that benefits the current period and is not traceable to goods purchased for resale.
        (e)   Depreciation on GE's assembly testing equipment—inventoriable cost of a manufacturing company. It is part of the manufacturing overhead that is included in the manufacturing cost of a refrigerator finished good.
        (f)   Salaries of Loblaw's marketing personnel—period cost of a merchandising company. It is a cost that is not traceable to goods purchased for resale. It is presumed not to benefit future periods (or at least not to have sufficiently reliable evidence to estimate such future benefits).
        (g)   Water consumed by Excite's engineers—period cost of a service company. Excite has no inventory of goods for sale and, hence, no inventoriable cost.
        (h)   Salaries of Excite's marketing personnel—period cost of a service company. Excite has no inventory of goods for sale and, hence, no inventoriable cost.

2-26   (15-20 min.)   **Classification of costs, merchandising sector.**

Cost object: Video section of store

Cost variability: With respect to changes in the number of videos sold

There may be some debate over classifications of individual items. Debate is more likely as regards cost variability.

Cost Item	D or I	V or F
A	D	F
B	I	V
C	D	V
D	D	F
E	I	F
F	I	V
G	I	F
H	D	V

2–28   (20 min.)   **Computing cost of goods manufactured and cost of goods sold.**

(a)

Marvin Department Store
Schedule of Cost of Goods Purchased
For the Year Ended December 31, 2004
(in thousands)

Purchases		$155,000
Add transportation-in		7,000
		162,000
Deduct:		
Purchase return and allowances	$4,000	
Purchase discounts	6,000	10,000
Cost of goods purchased		$152,000

(b)

Marvin Department Store
Schedule of Cost of Goods Sold
For the Year Ended December 31, 2004
(in thousands)

Beginning merchandise inventory 1/1/2004	$ 27,000
Cost of goods purchased (above)	152,000
Cost of goods available for sale	179,000
Ending merchandise inventory 12/31/2004	34,000
Cost of goods sold	$145,000

2-30 (25-30 min.) **Income statement and schedule of cost of goods manufactured.**

Howell Corporation
Income Statement for the Year Ended December 31, 2002
(in millions)

Revenues		$950
Cost of goods sold:		
Beginning finished goods, Jan. 1, 2002	$ 70	
Cost of goods manufactured (below)	645	
Cost of goods available for sale	715	
Ending finished goods, Dec. 31, 2002	55	660
Gross margin		290
Marketing, distribution, and customer-service costs		240
Operating income		$ 50

Howell Corporation
Schedule of Cost of Goods Manufactured
for the Year Ended December 31, 2002
(in millions)

Direct materials costs:		
Beginning inventory, Jan. 1, 2002	$ 15	
Purchases of direct materials	325	
Cost of direct materials available for use	340	
Ending inventory, Dec. 31, 2002	20	
Direct materials used		$320
Direct manufacturing labour costs		100
Indirect manufacturing costs:		
Indirect manufacturing labour	60	
Plant supplies used	10	
Plant utilities	30	
Amortization—plant, building, and equipment	80	
Plant supervisory salaries	5	
Miscellaneous plant overhead	35	220
Manufacturing costs incurred during 2002		640
Add beginning work in process inventory, Jan. 1, 2002		10
Total manufacturing costs to account for		650
Deduct ending work in process, Dec. 31, 2002		5
Cost of goods manufactured		$645

2–32 (25-30 min.) **Income statement and schedule of cost of goods manufactured.**

Chan Corporation
Income Statement
for the Year Ended December 31, 2002
(in millions)

Revenues		$350
Cost of goods sold:		
Beginning finished goods, Jan. 1, 2002	$ 40	
Cost of goods manufactured (below)	204	
Cost of goods available for sale	244	
Ending finished goods, Dec. 31, 2002	12	232
Gross margin		118
Marketing, distribution, and customer service costs		90
Operating income		$ 28

Chan Corporation
Schedule of Cost of Goods Manufactured
for the Year Ended December 31, 2002
(in millions)

Direct material costs:		
Beginning inventory, Jan. 1, 2002	$ 30	
Direct materials purchased	80	
Cost of direct materials available for use	110	
Ending inventory, Dec. 31, 2002	5	
Direct materials used		$105
Direct manufacturing labour costs		40
Indirect manufacturing costs:		
Plant supplies used	6	
Property taxes on plant	1	
Plant utilities	5	
Indirect manufacturing labour costs	20	
Amortization—plant, building, and equipment	9	
Miscellaneous manufacturing overhead costs	10	51
Manufacturing costs incurred during 2002		196
Add beginning work in process inventory, Jan. 1, 2002		10
Total manufacturing costs to account for		206
Deduct ending work in process inventory, Dec. 31, 2002		2
Cost of goods manufactured (to income statement)		$204

2-34 (20-30 min.) **Overtime premium, defining accounting terms.**

1.

	Westec	La Electricidad	BBC
Revenues	$420	$820	$480
Direct materials	250	410	270
Direct manuf. labour	40	100	60
Indirect manufacturing	80	200	120
Total manuf. costs	370	710	450
Gross margin	$ 50	$110	$ 30
Gross margin percentage	11.9%	13.4%	6.2%

2.   The BBC job is the only one with overtime charges. The charge is $20 (2 hours × $10 per hour overtime rate). The exclusion of this $20 from direct manufacturing labour costs will also affect indirect manufacturing labour costs allocated (at the 200% rate) to the BBC job. The revised gross margin is:

	BBC
Revenues	$480
Direct materials	270
Direct manuf. labour	40
Indirect manufacturing	80
Total manuf. costs	390
Gross margin	$90
Gross margin percentage	18.7%

The sizable increase in gross margin for BBC is due to $60 of costs being excluded—the $20 of overtime premium plus the $40 of indirect manufacturing costs allocated using the 200% rate.

3.   The main pro of charging BBC the $30 per hour labour rate is that this is the actual labour cost. The BBC job was, in fact, done in overtime hours.

The main con is that it penalizes the BBC job for a factor unrelated to its manufacture. The job was brought in one week ago, and there was much flexibility when it could be scheduled. It was done in overtime due to the Westec job being a rushed one.

A preferable approach is to assign all jobs with no special "rush" requirements the same labour cost per hour. This means that differences in job scheduling will not affect job profitability. Jobs that have a "rush" requirement ("hot-hot") are given an extra expediting cost to reflect any additional costs the expedition requires.

2-34 (cont'd)

4. The incentive payments would be :

	5% of Revenues	Incentive
Westec	0.05 × $420	$21
La Electricidad	0.05 × 820	41
BBC	0.05 × 480	24
		$86

	20% of Gross Margin	Incentive
Westec	0.20 × $ 50	$10
La Electricidad	0.20 × 110	22
BBC	0.20 × 90	18
		$50

EMI prefers jobs that produce high gross margins rather than high gross revenues. The 20% incentive better aligns the sales representative's incentive with that of EMI.

EMI should define how revenues and costs are to be measured so that ambiguities are reduced. The revenue and cost rules should be known in advance. If a rushed job is requested by a customer, the salesperson should know the rush-job charge so that he or she knows the consequences of accepting the request.

2–36 (30-40 min.) **Fire loss, computing inventory costs.**

1. = $50,000 2. = $28,000 3. = $62,000

This problem is not as easy as it first appears. These answers are obtained by working from the known figures to the unknowns in the schedule below. The basic relationships between categories of costs are:

Prime costs (given)		= $294,000
Direct materials used	= $294,000 – Direct manufacturing labour costs	
	= $294,000 – $180,000	= $114,000
Conversion costs	= Direct manufacturing labour costs ÷ 0.6	
	= $180,000 ÷ 0.6	= $300,000
Indirect manuf. costs	= $300,000 – $180,000	= $120,000
	(or 0.40 × $300,000)	

2–36 (cont'd)

Schedule of Computations

Direct materials, 1/1/2002			$ 16,000
Direct materials purchased			160,000
Direct materials available for use			176,000
Direct materials, 2/26/2002	3.	=	62,000
Direct materials used ($294,000 – $180,000)			114,000
Direct manufacturing labour costs			180,000
Prime costs			294,000
Indirect manufacturing costs			120,000
Manufacturing costs incurred during the current period			414,000
Add work in process, 1/1/2002			34,000
Manufacturing costs to account for			448,000
Deduct work in process, 2/26/2002	2.	=	28,000
Cost of goods manufactured			420,000
Add finished goods, 1/1/2002			30,000
Cost of goods available for sale (given)			450,000
Deduct finished goods, 2/26/2002	1.	=	50,000
Cost of goods sold (80% of $500,000)			$400,000

Some instructors may wish to place the key amounts in a Work in Process T-account. This problem can be used to *introduce* students to the flow of costs through the general ledger (amounts in thousands):

Work in Process			Finished Goods			Cost of Goods Sold
BI	34		BI	30		
DM used	114	COGM 420	——>	420	COGS 400	——>400
DL	180					
OH	120		Available			
To account for	448		for sale	450		
EI	28		EI	50		

2-38 (30 min.) **Budgeted income statement.**

1.

Target ending finished goods, Dec. 31, 2003	12,000 units
Forecasted sales for 2003	122,000 units
Total finished goods required in 2003	134,000 units
Beginning finished goods, Jan. 1, 2003	9,000 units
Finished goods production required in 2003	125,000 units

2.

Revenues (122,000 units sold × $4.80)		$585,600
Cost of units sold:		
Beginning finished goods, Jan. 1, 2003	$ 20,970	
Cost of goods manufactured	281,250	
Cost of goods available for sale	302,220	
Ending finished goods, Dec. 31, 2003	27,000	275,220
Gross margin		310,380
Operating costs:		
Marketing, distn., and customer-service costs	204,700	
Administrative costs	50,000	254,700
Operating income		$ 55,680

Supporting Computations

a.

	Manufacturing Costs for 125,000 units		
	Variable	Fixed	Total
Direct materials costs	$175,000	$ –	$175,000
Direct manufacturing labour costs	37,500	–	37,500
Plant energy costs	6,250	–	6,250
Indirect manufacturing labour costs	12,500	16,000	28,500
Other indirect manufacturing costs	10,000	24,000	34,000
Cost of goods manufactured	$241,250	$40,000	$281,250

b. Direct materials costs = 250,000 kgs × $0.70 per kg = $175,000.

c. The average unit manufacturing costs in 2003 is $281,250 ÷ 125,000 units = $2.25. Finished goods, December 31, 2003 = 12,000 × $2.25 = $27,000.

d.

Variable mktg., distn., and customer-service costs, 122,000 × $1.35	$164,700
Fixed marketing, distn., and customer-service costs	40,000
Fixed administrative costs	50,000
	$254,700

2–40 (30 min.) **Missing data.**

1.   Direct materials inventory, 8/1/2004   90
     Direct materials purchased   360
     Direct materials available   450
     Deduct direct materials used   375
     Direct materials inventory, 8/31/2004 $ 75

2.   Total manufacturing overhead costs $ 480
     Variable manufacturing overhead costs   250
     Fixed manufacturing overhead costs $ 230

3.   Total manufacturing costs $1,600
     Deduct:
       Direct materials used $375
       Manufacturing overhead   480   855
     Direct manufacturing labour costs $ 745

4.   Work-in-Process inventory, 8/1/2004 $ 200
     Total manufacturing costs   1,600
            1,800
     Deduct cost of goods manufactured   1,650
     Work-in-Process inventory 8/31/2004 $ 150

5.   Finished goods inventory 8/1/2004 $ 125
     Cost of goods manufactured   1,650
     Goods available for sale $1,775

6.   Goods available for sale $1,775
     Deduct cost of goods sold   1,700
     Finished goods inventory, 8/31/2004 $ 75

CHAPTER 3
COST-VOLUME-PROFIT RELATIONSHIPS

3–2   The assumptions underlying the CVP analysis outlined in Chapter 3 are:

1. Changes in the level of revenues and costs arise only because of changes in the number of product (or service) units produced or sold.
2. Total costs can be divided into a fixed component and a component that is variable with respect to the level of output.
3. The behaviour of total revenues and total costs is linear (straight-line) in relation to output units within the relevant range.
4. The unit selling price, unit variable costs, and fixed costs are known.
5. The analysis either covers a single product or assumes that a given revenue mix of products will remain constant as the level of total units sold changes.
6. All revenues and costs can be added and compared without taking into account the time value of money.

3–4   **Contribution margin** is computed as revenues minus all costs that vary with respect to the output level.

Gross margin is computed as revenues minus cost of goods sold.

Contribution-margin percentage is the total contribution margin divided by revenues.

Variable-cost percentage is the total variable costs (with respect to units of output) divided by revenues.

Margin of safety is the excess of budgeted revenues over breakeven revenues.

3-6   Breakeven analysis denotes the study of the breakeven point, which is often only an incidental part of the relationship between cost, volume, and profit. Cost-volume-profit analysis is a more comprehensive term than breakeven analysis.

3-8   An increase in the income tax rate does not affect the breakeven point. Operating income at the breakeven point is zero and thus no income taxes will be paid at this point.

3–10   Examples include:

Manufacturing—substituting a robotic machine for hourly wage workers.

Marketing—changing a sales force compensation plan from a percentage of sales dollars to a fixed salary.

Customer service—hiring a subcontractor to do customer repair visits on an annual retainer basis rather than a per visit basis.

3-12   Operating leverage describes the effects that fixed costs have on changes in operating income as changes occur in units sold and hence in contribution margin. Knowing the degree of operating leverage at a given level of sales helps managers calculate the effect of fluctuations in sales on operating incomes.

3-14 A company with multiple products can compute a breakeven point by assuming there is a constant mix of products at different levels of total revenue.

3–16 (10 min.) **CVP analysis computations.**

	Revenues	Variable Costs	Fixed Costs	Total Costs	Operating Income	Contribution Margin	Contribution Margin %
a.	**$2,000**	$ 500	**$300**	$ 800	$1,200	$1,500	**75.0%**
b.	2,000	**1,500**	300	**1,800**	200	500	**25.0%**
c.	1,000	700	**300**	1,000	0	300	30.0%
d.	1,500	**900**	300	**1,200**	300	600	40.0%

3-18 (15-20 min.) **CVP analysis, changing revenues and costs.**

1. $\quad$ USP $\quad=\quad$ 8% × $1,000 = $80
    $\quad$ UVC $\quad=\quad$ $35 ($17 + $18)
    $\quad$ UCM $\quad=\quad$ $45
    $\quad$ FC $\quad=\quad$ $22,000 a month

(a) $\quad$ $Q \quad = \quad \dfrac{FC}{UCM} \quad = \quad \dfrac{\$22,000}{\$45}$

$\qquad\qquad = \quad$ 489 tickets (rounded up)

(b) $\quad$ $Q \quad = \quad \dfrac{FC + TOI}{UCM} = \dfrac{\$22,000 + \$10,000}{\$45}$

$\qquad\qquad\qquad = \quad \dfrac{\$32,000}{\$45}$

$\qquad\qquad = \quad$ 712 tickets (rounded up)

2. $\quad$ USP $\quad=\quad$ $80
    $\quad$ UVC $\quad=\quad$ $29 ($17 + $12)
    $\quad$ UCM $\quad=\quad$ $51
    $\quad$ FC $\quad=\quad$ $22,000 a month

(a) $\quad$ $Q \quad = \quad \dfrac{FC}{UCM} \quad = \quad \dfrac{\$22,000}{\$51}$

$\qquad\qquad\qquad = \quad$ 432 tickets (rounded up)

(b) $\quad$ $Q \quad = \quad \dfrac{FC + TOI}{UCM} = \dfrac{\$22,000 + \$10,000}{\$51}$

$\qquad\qquad\qquad = \quad \dfrac{\$32,000}{\$51}$

$\qquad\qquad = \quad$ 628 tickets (rounded up)

3–20 (20 min.) **CVP exercises.**

	Revenues	Variable Costs	Contribution Margin	Fixed Costs	Budgeted Operating Income
Orig.	$10,000,000^G	$8,200,000^G	$1,800,000	$1,700,000^G	$100,000
1.	10,000,000	8,020,000	1,980,000	1,700,000	280,000
2.	10,000,000	8,380,000	1,620,000	1,700,000	(80,000)
3.	10,000,000	8,200,000	1,800,000	1,785,000	15,000
4.	10,000,000	8,200,000	1,800,000	1,615,000	185,000
5.	10,800,000	8,856,000	1,944,000	1,700,000	244,000
6.	9,200,000	7,544,000	1,656,000	1,700,000	(44,000)
7.	11,000,000	9,020,000	1,980,000	1,870,000	110,000
8.	10,000,000	7,790,000	2,210,000	1,785,000	425,000

^{G} stands for given.

3–22 (10-15 min.) **CVP, income taxes.**

1. Operating income = Net income ÷ (1 – tax rate)
   = $84,000 ÷ (1 – 0.40) = $140,000

2. Contribution margin – Fixed costs = Operating income
   Contribution margin – $300,000 = $140,000
   Contribution margin = $440,000

3. Revenues – 0.80 Revenues = Contribution margin
   0.20 Revenues = $440,000
   Revenues = $2,200,000

4. Breakeven point = Fixed costs ÷ Contribution margin percentage
   Breakeven point = $300,000 ÷ 0.20
   = $1,500,000

3–24 (10 min.) **CVP, margin of safety.**

1. $$\text{Breakeven point} = \frac{\text{Fixed costs}}{\text{Contribution margin percentage}}$$

$$\text{Contribution margin percentage} = \frac{\$400,000}{\$1,000,000} = 0.40$$

2. $$\text{Contribution margin percentage} = \frac{\text{Selling price} - \text{Variable cost per unit}}{\text{Selling price}}$$

$$0.40 = \frac{\text{USP} - \$12}{\text{USP}}$$

$$0.40 \text{ USP} = \text{USP} - 12$$
$$0.60 \text{ USP} = \$12$$
$$\text{USP} = \$20$$

3.

Revenues, 80,000 units × $20	$1,600,000
Breakeven revenues	1,000,000
Margin of safety	$ 600,000

3–26 (15 min.) **Gross margin and contribution margin,
            making decisions.**

Salaries and wages of $150,000 could be variable costs and fixed costs. The answer
assumed they are all fixed costs.

1.	Revenues		$500,000
	Deduct variable costs:		
	Cost of goods sold	$200,000	
	Sales commissions	50,000	
	Other operating costs	40,000	290,000
	Contribution margin		$210,000

2. Contribution margin percentage $= \dfrac{\$210,000}{\$500,000} = 42\%$

3. Incremental revenue (20% × $500,000) = $100,000
   Incremental contribution margin

(42% × $100,000)	$42,000
Incremental fixed costs (advertising)	10,000
Incremental operating income	$32,000

    If Mr. Schmidt spends $10,000 more on advertising, the operating income will
increase by $32,000 converting an operating loss of $10,000 to an operating income of
$22,000.

Proof (Optional):

Revenues (12% × $500,000)		$600,000
Cost of goods sold (40% of sales)		240,000
Gross margin		360,000
Operating costs:		
Salaries and wages	$150,000	
Sales commissions (10% of sales)	60,000	
Depreciation of equipment and fixtures	12,000	
Store rent	48,000	
Advertising	10,000	
Other operating costs:		
Variable $\left(\dfrac{\$40,000}{\$500,000} \times \$600,000\right)$	48,000	
Fixed	10,000	338,000
Operating income		$ 22,000

3–28 (30 min.) **CVP, sensitivity analysis.**

1. USP   = $30.00 × (1 – 0.30 margin to bookstore)
            = $30.00 × 0.70 = $21.00

    UVC   = $ 4.00   variable production and marketing cost
            3.15   variable author royalty cost (0.15 $30.00 × 0.70)

    UCM   = $21.00 – $7.15 = $13.85

    FC   = $ 500,000   fixed production and marketing cost
            3,000,000   up-front payment to Washington
            $3,500,000

Exhibit 3-28A shows the PV graph.

Exhibit 3-28A
PV Graph for Media Publishers

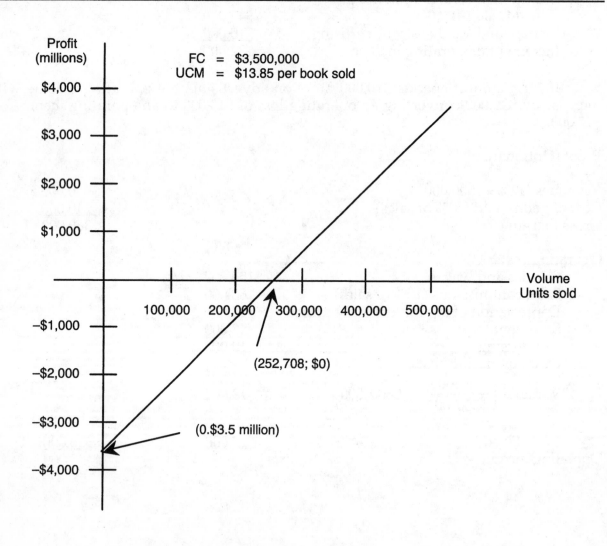

3–28 (cont'd)

2. (a) Breakeven number of units $= \dfrac{FC}{UCM}$

$= \dfrac{\$3,500,000}{\$13.85}$

$= 252,708$ copies sold (rounded)

(b) Target OI $= \dfrac{FC + OI}{UCM}$

$= \dfrac{\$3,500,000 + \$2,000,000}{\$13.85}$

$= \dfrac{\$5,500,000}{\$13.85}$

$= 397,112$ copies sold (rounded)

3. (a) Decreasing the normal bookstore margin to 20% of the listed bookstore price of $30 has the following effects:

USP $= \$30.00 \times (1 - 0.20)$
$= \$30.00 \times 0.80 = \$24.00$

UVC $= \$\ 4.00$ variable production and marketing cost
$= \underline{+\ 3.60}$ variable author royalty cost $(0.15 \times \$30.00 \times 0.80)$
$\quad \underline{\$\ 7.60}$

UCM $= \$24.00 - \$7.60 = \$16.40$

Breakeven number of units $= \dfrac{FC}{UCM}$

$= \dfrac{\$3,500,000}{\$13.85}$

$= 252,708$ copies sold (rounded)

The breakeven point decreases from 252,708 copies in requirement 2 to 213,415 copies.

(b) Increasing the listed bookstore price to $40 while keeping the bookstore margin at 30% has the following effects:

USP $= \$40.00 \times (1 - 0.30)$
$= \$40.00 \times 0.70 = \$28.00$

3–28 (cont'd)

UVC = $ 4.00 variable production and marketing cost
     = + 4.20 variable author royalty cost (0.15 × \$40.00 × 0.70)
      $ 8.20

UCM = $28.00 − $8.20 = $19.80

$$= \frac{\$3,500,000}{\$19.80}$$

= 176,768 copies sold (rounded)

The breakeven point decreases from 252,708 copies in requirement 2 to 176,768 copies.

3-30 (30 min.) Revenue mix, new and upgrade customers.

	New Customers	Upgrade Customers
USP	$210	$120
UVC	90	40
UCM	120	80

Let S = Number of upgrade customers
     $1.5\,S$ = Number of new customers
Revenues − Variable costs − Fixed costs = Operating income
[$210 (1.5 S) + $120 S] − [$90 (1.5 S) + $40 S] − $14,000,000 = OI
$435 S − $175 S − $14,000,000 = OI
Breakeven point is 134,616 units when OI = 0

$260S	=	$14,000,000
S	=	53,846 (rounded)
1.5S	=	80,770
		134,616

Check

Revenues ($210 × 80,770; $120 × 53,846)	$23,423,220
Variable costs ($90 × 80,770; $40 × 53,846)	9,423,140
Contribution margin	14,000,080
Fixed costs	14,000,000
Operating income	≅ $ 0

2. When 200,000 units are sold, mix is:

New customers	120,000
Upgrade customers	80,000

Revenues ($210 × 120,000; $120 × 80,000)	$34,800,000
Variable costs ($90 × 120,000; $40 × 80,000)	14,000,000
Contribution margin	20,800,000
Fixed costs	14,000,000
Operating income	≅ $ 6,800,000

3-30 (cont'd)

3.   (a) $[\$210 + \$120S] - [\$90 + \$40S] - \$14,000,000 = \text{OI}$

$$
\begin{aligned}
330S - 130S &= \$14,000,000 \\
200S &= \$14,000,000 \\
S &= 70,000 \\
S &= \underline{70,000} \\
&\underline{140,000} \text{ units}
\end{aligned}
$$

<u>Check</u>

Revenues ($210 × 70,000; $120 × 70,000)	$23,100,000
Variable costs ($90 × 70,000; $40 × 70,000)	<u>9,100,000</u>
Contribution margin	14,000,000
Fixed costs	<u>14,000,000</u>
Operating income	$ 0

    (b) $[\$210 (9S) + \$120S] - [\$90 (9S) + \$40S] - \$14,000,000 = \text{OI}$

$$
\begin{aligned}
2,010S - 850S &= \$14,000,000 \\
1,160S &= \$14,000,000 \\
S &= 12,069 \text{ (rounded)} \\
9S &= \underline{108,621} \\
&\underline{120,690} \text{ units}
\end{aligned}
$$

<u>Check</u>

Revenues ($210 × 108,621; $120 × 12,069)	$24,258,690
Variable costs ($90 × 108,621; $40 × 12,069)	<u>10,258,650</u>
Contribution margin	14,000,040
Fixed costs	<u>14,000,000</u>
Operating income	≅ $ 0

As Zapo increases its percentage of new customers, which have a higher contribution margin than upgrade customers, the number of units required to breakeven decreases:

	New Customers	Upgrade Customers	Breakeven Point
Requirement 3(a)	50%	50%	140,000
Requirement 1	60%	40%	134,616
Requirement 3(b)	90%	10%	120,690

3-32 (20 min.)   **Gross margin and contribution margin.**

1.   Cost of Goods Sold $1,600,000
     Fixed Manufacturing Costs   <u>   500,000</u>
     Variable Manufacturing Costs   <u>$1,100,000</u>

     Variable manufacturing costs per unit = $1,100,000 ÷ 200,000 = $5.50 per unit

2.   Total marketing and distribution costs $1,150,000
     Variable marketing and distribution (200,000 × $5) <u>1,000,000</u>
     Fixed marketing and distribution costs   <u>$ 150,000</u>

3.   Selling price   = $2,600,000 ÷ 200,000 units = $13 per unit

$$\begin{matrix} \text{Contribution margin} \\ \text{per unit} \end{matrix} = \begin{matrix} \text{Selling} \\ \text{price} \end{matrix} - \begin{matrix} \text{Variable} \\ \text{manufacturing} \\ \text{costs per unit} \end{matrix} - \begin{matrix} \text{Variable marketing} \\ \text{and distribution} \\ \text{costs per unit} \end{matrix}$$

                            = $13 – $5.50 – $5.00 = $2.50

$$\text{Operating income} = \left(\begin{matrix} \text{Contribution margin} \\ \text{per unit} \end{matrix} \times \begin{matrix} \text{Sales} \\ \text{quantity} \end{matrix} \right) - \begin{matrix} \text{Fixed manufacturing} \\ \text{costs} \end{matrix} - \begin{matrix} \text{Fixed marketing} \\ \text{and distribution} \\ \text{costs} \end{matrix}$$

          =   ($2.50 × 230,000) – $500,000 – $150,000
          =   –$75,000

Foreman has confused gross margin with contribution margin. He has interpreted gross margin as if it were all variable, and interpreted marketing and distribution costs as all fixed. In fact, the manufacturing costs, subtracted from sales to calculate gross margin, and marketing and distribution costs contain both fixed and variable components.

4.   Breakeven point in units $= \dfrac{\text{Fixed manufacturing, marketing and distribution costs}}{\text{Contribution margin per unit}}$

                                 $= \dfrac{\$650,000}{\$2.50} = 260,000$ units

Breakeven point in revenues = 260,000 × $13 = $3,380,000.

3-34 (15-20 min.)   **Appendix, uncertainty, CVP.**

1.   King pays Foreman $2 million plus $4 (25% of $16) for every home purchasing the pay-per-view. The expected value of the variable component is:

Demand (1)	Payment (2) = (1) × $4	Probability (3)	Expected payment (4) = (2) × (3)
100,000	$ 400,000	0.05	$ 20,000
200,000	800,000	0.10	80,000
300,000	1,200,000	0.30	360,000
400,000	1,600,000	0.35	560,000
500,000	2,000,000	0.15	300,000
1,000,000	4,000,000	0.05	200,000
			$1,520,000

The expected value of King's payment is $3,520,000 ($2,000,000 fixed fee + $1,520,000).

2.   USP   = $16
        UVC   = $ 6 ($4 payment to Foreman + $2 variable cost)
        UCM   = $10
        FC   = $2,000,000 + $1,000,000 = $3,000,000

$$Q = \frac{FC}{UCM}$$
$$= \frac{\$3,000,000}{\$10}$$
$$= 300,000$$

If 300,000 homes purchase the pay-per-view, King will break even.

3-36 (15-20 min.) **CVP analysis, service firm.**

1. Revenue per package $4,000
    Variable cost per package   3,600
    Contribution margin per package $ 400

Breakeven (units) = Fixed costs ÷ Contribution margin per package

$$= \frac{\$480,000}{\$400 \text{ per package}} = 1,200 \text{ tour packages}$$

2. Contribution margin ratio = $\dfrac{\text{Contribution margin per package}}{\text{Selling price}} = \dfrac{\$400}{\$4,000} = 10\%$

Revenue to achieve target income = (Fixed costs + target OI) ÷ Contribution margin ratio

$$= \frac{\$480,000 + \$100,000}{0.10} = \$5,800,000, \text{ or}$$

Number of tour packages to earn $100,000 operating income:

$$\frac{\$480,000 + \$100,000}{\$400} = 1,450 \text{ tour packages}$$

Revenues to earn $100,000 OI = 1,450 tour packages × $4,000 = $5,800,000.

3. Fixed costs = $480,000 + $24,000 = $504,000

Breakeven (units) = $\dfrac{\text{Fixed costs}}{\text{Contribution margin per unit}}$

Contribution margin per unit = $\dfrac{\text{Fixed costs}}{\text{Breakeven (units)}}$

$$= \frac{\$504,000}{1,200 \text{ tour packages}} = \$420 \text{ per tour package}$$

Desired variable cost per tour package = $4,000 – $420 = $3,580

Because the current variable cost per unit is $3,600, the unit variable cost will need to be reduced by $20 to achieve the breakeven point calculated in requirement 1.

Alternate Method: If fixed cost increases by $24,000, then total variable costs must be reduced by $24,000 to keep the breakeven point of 1,200 tour packages.

Therefore the variable cost per unit reduction = $24,000 ÷ 1,200 = $20 per tour package.

3-38 (20-25 min.) **CVP analysis (CMA adapted).**

1.
Selling price		$16.00
Variable costs per unit:		
Purchase price	$10.00	
Shipping and handling	2.00	12.00
Contribution margin per unit (CMU)		$ 4.00

$$\text{Breakeven point in units} = \frac{\text{Fixed costs}}{\text{Contr. margin per unit}} = \frac{\$600,000}{\$4.00} = 150,000 \text{ units}$$

2. Since Galaxy is operating above the breakeven point, any incremental contribution margin will increase operating income dollar for dollar.

Increase in units sales = 10% × 200,000 = 20,000
Incremental contribution margin = $4 × 20,000 = $80,000

Therefore, the increase in operating income will be equal to $80,000.
Galaxy's operating income in 2003 would be $200,000 + $80,000 = $280,000.

3.
Selling price		$16.00
Variable costs:		
Purchase price $10 × 130%	$13.00	
Shipping and handling	2.00	15.00
Contribution margin per unit		$ 1.00

$$\text{Target sales in units} = \frac{\text{FC} + \text{TOI}}{\text{CMU}} = \frac{\$600,000 + \$200,000}{\$1} = 800,000 \text{ units}$$

Target sales in dollars = $16 × 800,000 = $12,800,000

3–40 (20-25 min.) **CVP, shoe stores (continuation of 3-39).**

1. Because the unit sales level at the point of indifference would be the same for each plan, the revenue would be equal. Therefore, the unit sales level sought would be that which produces the same total costs for each plan.

$$\text{Let } Q = \text{ unit sales level}$$
$$\$19.50Q + \$360,000 + \$81,000 = \$21.00Q + \$360,000$$
$$\$81,000 = \$1.50Q$$
$$Q = 54,000 \text{ units}$$

2.

	Commission Plan		Salary Plan	
Sales in units	50,000	60,000	50,000	60,000
Revenues @ $30.00	$1,500,000	$1,800,000	$1,500,000	$1,800,000
Variable costs @ $21.00 and @ $19.50	1,050,000	1,260,000	975,000	1,170,000
Contribution margin	450,000	540,000	525,000	630,000
Fixed costs	360,000	360,000	441,000	441,000
Operating income	$ 90,000	$ 180,000	$ 84,000	$ 189,000

The decision regarding the plans will heavily depend on the unit sales level that is generated by the fixed salary plan. For example, as part (1) shows, at identical unit sales levels in excess of 54,000 units, the fixed salary plan will always provide a more profitable final result than the commission plan.

3. Let TQ = Target number of units

    a.

$$\$30.00TQ - \$19.50TQ - \$441,000 = \$168,000$$
$$\$10.50TQ = \$609,000$$
$$TQ = \$609,000 \div \$10.50$$
$$TQ = 58,000 \text{ units}$$

    b.

$$\$30.00TQ - \$21.00TQ - \$360,000 = \$168,000$$
$$\$9.00TQ = \$528,000$$
$$TQ = \$528,000 \div \$9.00$$
$$TQ = 58,667 \text{ units (rounded)}$$

The decision regarding the salary plan heavily depends on predictions of demand. For instance, the salary plan offers the same operating income at 58,000 units as the commission plan offers at 58,667 units.

3-42 (30 min.) **CVP analysis, income taxes, sensitivity.**

1a. In order to break even, Almo Company must sell 500 units. This amount represents the point where revenues equal total costs.

Let Q denote the quantity of canopies sold.

$$
\begin{aligned}
\text{Revenue} &= \text{Variable costs + Fixed costs} \\
\$400Q &= \$200Q + \$100,000 \\
\$200Q &= \$100,000 \\
Q &= \underline{500} \text{ units}
\end{aligned}
$$

The calculation can also be expressed as

$$
\begin{aligned}
\text{Breakeven} &= \text{Fixed Costs} \div \text{Contribution margin per unit} \\
&= \$100,000 \div \$200 \\
&= \underline{500} \text{ units}
\end{aligned}
$$

1b. In order to achieve its net income objective, Almo Company must sell 2,500 units. This amount represents the point where revenues equal total costs plus the corresponding operating income objective to achieve net income of $240,000.

$$
\begin{aligned}
\text{Revenue} &= \text{Variable costs + Fixed costs + Operating income} \\
\$400Q &= \$200Q + \$100,000 + [\$240,000 \div (1 - 0.4)] \\
\$400Q &= \$200Q + \$100,000 + \$400,000 \\
Q &= \underline{2,500} \text{ units}
\end{aligned}
$$

2. To achieve its net income objective, Almo Company should select the first alternative where the sales price is reduced by $40, and 2,700 units are sold during the remainder of the year. This alternative results in the highest net income and is the only alternative that equals or exceeds the company's net income objective. Calculations for the three alternatives are shown below.

Alternative 1

$$
\begin{aligned}
\text{Revenues} &= (\$400 \times 350) + (\$360 \times 2,700) = \$1,112,000 \\
\text{Variable costs} &= \$200 \times 3,050 = \$610,000 \\
\text{Operating income} &= \$1,112,000 - \$610,000 - \$100,000 = \$402,000 \\
\text{Net income} &= \$402,000 \times (1 - 0.4) = \underline{\$241,200}
\end{aligned}
$$

Alternative 2

$$
\begin{aligned}
\text{Revenues} &= (\$400 \times 350) + (\$370 \times 2,200) = \$954,000 \\
\text{Variable costs} &= (\$200 \times 350) + (\$190 \times 2,200) = \$488,000 \\
\text{Operating income} &= \$954,000 - \$488,000 - \$100,000 = \$366,000 \\
\text{Net income} &= \$366,000 \times (1 - 0.4) = \$219,600
\end{aligned}
$$

Alternative 3

$$
\begin{aligned}
\text{Revenues} &= (\$400 \times 350) + (\$380 \times 2,000) = \$900,000 \\
\text{Variable costs} &= \$200 \times 2,350 = \$470,000 \\
\text{Operating income} &= \$900,000 - \$470,000 - \$90,000 = \$340,000 \\
\text{Net income} &= \$340,000 \times (1 - 0.4) = \$204,000
\end{aligned}
$$

3–44 (20 min.)   **CVP, cost structure differences, movie production (continuation of 3-43).**

1.   Contract A
    Fixed costs for Contract A:

Production costs	$21,000,000
Fixed salary	15,000,000
Total fixed costs	$36,000,000

Unit variable cost = $0.25 per $1 revenue marketing fee
Unit contribution margin = $0.75 per $1 revenue

(a)   Breakeven point in revenues $= \dfrac{\text{Fixed costs}}{\text{Unit contribution margin per \$1 revenue}}$

$$= \frac{\$36,000,000}{\$0.75}$$

$$= \$48,000,000$$

Box-office receipts of $76,800,000 translate to $48,000,000 in revenues to Royal Rumble.

Contract B
    Fixed costs for Contract B:

Production costs	$21,000,000
Fixed salary	3,000,000
Total fixed costs	$24,000,000

Unit variable cost = $0.25 per $1 revenue fee to Media Productions
$0.15 per $1 revenue residual to directors/actors
$0.40 per $1 revenue

Unit contribution margin = $0.60 per $1 revenue

Breakeven point in revenues $= \dfrac{\$24,000,000}{0.60} = \$40,000,000$

Box-office receipts of $64,000,000 translate to $40,000,000 in revenues to Royal Rumble.

Difference in Breakeven Points

Contract A has a higher fixed cost and a lower variable cost per sales dollar. In contrast, Contract B has a lower fixed cost and a higher variable cost per sales dollar. In Contract B, there is risk-sharing between Royal Rumble and Savage, Michaels, and Martel that lowers the breakeven point, but results in Royal Rumble's receiving less operating income if *Feature Creatures 2* is a mega-success.

2.

Revenues, 0.625 × $300,000,000	$187,500,000
Variable costs, 0.40 × $187,500,000	75,000,000
Contribution margin	112,500,000
Fixed costs	24,000,000
Operating income	$ 88,500,000

Feature Creatures 2 has a higher breakeven point than *Feature Creatures* because FC2 has a higher level of fixed costs and a lower unit contribution margin.

3-46 (20-25 min.) **Revenue mix, two products.**

1. Let Q = Number of units of Deluxe product to break even
    3Q = Number of units of Standard product to break even

    Revenues – Variable costs – Fixed costs = Zero operating income

$$
\begin{aligned}
\$20(3Q) + \$30Q - \$14(3Q) - \$18Q - \$1{,}200{,}000 &= 0 \\
\$60Q + \$30Q - \$42Q - \$18Q &= \$1{,}200{,}000 \\
\$30Q &= \$1{,}200{,}000 \\
Q &= 40{,}000 \text{ units of Deluxe} \\
3Q &= 120{,}000 \text{ units of Standard}
\end{aligned}
$$

The breakeven point is 120,000 Standard units plus 40,000 Deluxe carriers, a total of 160,000 units.

2. Unit contribution margins are: Standard: $20 – $14 = $6; Deluxe: $30 – $18 = $12
    (a) If only Standard carriers were sold, the breakeven point would be:
        $1,200,000 ÷ $6 = 200,000 units
    (b) If only Deluxe carriers were sold, the breakeven point would be:
        $1,200,000 ÷ $12 = 100,000 units

3. Operating income = 180,000($6) + 20,000($12) – $1,200,000
                      = $1,080,000 + $240,000 – $1,200,000
                      = $120,000

    Let Q = Number of units of Deluxe product to break even
    9Q = Number of units of Standard product to break even

$$
\begin{aligned}
\$20(9Q) + \$30Q - \$14(9Q) - \$18Q - \$1{,}200{,}000 &= 0 \\
\$180Q + \$30Q - \$126Q - \$18Q &= \$1{,}200{,}000 \\
\$66Q &= \$1{,}200{,}000 \\
Q &= 18{,}182 \text{ units of Deluxe} \\
&\quad\ \text{(rounded)} \\
9Q &= 163{,}638 \text{ units of Standard}
\end{aligned}
$$

The breakeven point is 163,638 Standard + 18,182 Deluxe, a total of 181,820 units.

The major lesson of this problem is that changes in sales mix change breakeven points and operating incomes. In this example, the budgeted and actual total sales in number of units were identical, but the proportion of the product having the higher contribution margin declined. Operating income suffered, falling from $300,000 to $120,000. Moreover, the breakeven point rose from 160,000 to 181,820 units.

3-48 (15-25 min.)   **Revenue mix, three products.**

1.   Let A = Number of units of A to break even
       5A = Number of units of B to break even
       4A = Number of units of C to break even

Contribution margin – Fixed costs = Zero operating income

$$\$3A + \$2(5A) + \$1(4A) - \$255,000 = 0$$

$$\$17A = \$255,000$$

A	=	15,000 units of A
5A	=	75,000 units of B
4A	=	60,000 units of C
Total	=	150,000 units

2.   Contribution margin:

A: 20,000 × $3	$ 60,000	
B: 100,000 × $2	200,000	
C: 80,000 × $1	80,000	
Contribution margin		$340,000
Fixed costs		255,000
Operating income		$ 85,000

3.   Contribution margin

A: 20,000 × $3	$ 60,000	
B: 80,000 × $2	160,000	
C: 100,000 × $1	100,000	
Contribution margin		$320,000
Fixed costs		255,000
Operating income		$ 65,000

Let A =   Number of units of A to break even
    4A =   Number of units of B to break even
    5A =   Number of units of C to break even

Contribution margin – Fixed costs = Breakeven point

$$\$3A + \$2(4A) + \$1(5A) - \$255,000 = 0$$

$$\$16A = \$255,000$$

A	=	15,938 units of A (rounded)
4A	=	63,752 units of B
5A	=	79,690 units of C
Total	=	159,380 units

3-50 (30 min.) **CVP, nonprofit event planning.**

1.   Computation of fixed costs.

	Golf Club	Town Hall
Rental cost of venue	$2,000	$ 6,600
Chamber administration/marketing	3,500	3,500
Band	2,500	2,500
	$8,000	$12,600

Computation of contribution margin per person:

	Golf Club	Town Hall
Selling (ticket) price per person	$120	$120
Catering cost per person	80	60
Contribution margin per person	$ 40	$ 60

$$\text{Breakeven point} = \frac{\text{Fixed costs}}{\text{Unit contribution margin}}$$

$$\text{Breakeven point for Golf Club venue} = \frac{\$8,000}{\$40} = 200 \text{ tickets}$$

$$\text{Breakeven point for Town Hall venue} = \frac{\$12,600}{\$60} = 210 \text{ tickets}$$

2.   Operating income = Revenues – Variable costs – Fixed costs

Let Q = Number of tickets sold
OI = Operating income

Golf Club Venue

$$\begin{aligned}
\text{OI} &= \$120Q - \$80Q - \$8,000 \\
\text{When Q} = 150\text{: OI} &= (\$120 \times 150) - (\$80 \times 150) - \$8,000 \\
&= \$18,000 - \$12,000 - \$8,000 \\
&= -\$2,000 \\
\text{When Q} = 300\text{: OI} &= (\$120 \times 300) - (\$80 \times 300) - \$8,000 \\
&= \$36,000 - \$24,000 - \$8,000 \\
&= \$4,000
\end{aligned}$$

3-50 (cont'd)

Town Hall Venue

$$
\begin{aligned}
\text{OI} &= \$120Q - \$60Q - \$12{,}600 \\
\text{When } Q = 150: \quad \text{OI} &= (\$120 \times 150) - (\$60 \times 150) - \$12{,}600 \\
&= \$18{,}000 - \$9{,}000 - \$12{,}600 \\
&= -\$3{,}600 \\
\text{When } Q = 300: \quad \text{OI} &= (\$120 \times 300) - (\$60 \times 300) - \$12{,}600 \\
&= \$36{,}000 - \$18{,}000 - \$12{,}600 \\
&= \$5{,}400
\end{aligned}
$$

The Golf Club venue has higher variable costs per person and lower fixed costs. In contrast, the Town Hall venue has lower variable costs per person and higher fixed costs.

3.   Requirement 2 gives the operating income equation for each venue. Setting these two equations equal and solving for Q, gives 230 as the level of ticket sales at which the operating incomes for the two venues are equal:

$$
\begin{aligned}
\$120Q - \$80Q - \$8{,}000 &= \$120Q - \$60Q - \$12{,}600 \\
\$40Q - \$60Q &= \$8{,}000 - \$12{,}600 \\
\$20Q &= \$4{,}600 \\
Q &= 230
\end{aligned}
$$

Above 230, the Town Hall venue will yield higher operating income than the Golf Club venue.

3–52 (30-40 min.) **CVP, Income taxes. (CMA)**

1. $$\text{Revenues} - \text{Variable costs} - \text{Fixed costs} = \frac{\text{Target net income}}{1 - \text{Tax rate}}$$

   Let X = Net income for 2002

   $$20,000(\$25.00) - 20,000(\$13.75) - \$135,000 = \frac{X}{1 - 0.40}$$

   $$\$500,000 - \$275,000 - \$135,000 = \frac{X}{0.60}$$

   $$\$300,000 - \$165,000 - \$81,000 = X$$

   $$X = \$54,000$$

2. Let Q = Number of units to break even
   $$\$25.00Q - \$13.75Q - \$135,000 = 0$$
   $$Q = \$135,000 \div \$11.25 = 12,000 \text{ units}$$

3. Let X = Net income for 2003

   $$22,000(\$25.00) - 22,000(\$13.75) - (\$135,000 + \$11,250) = \frac{X}{1 - 0.40}$$

   $$\$550,000 - \$302,500 - \$146,250 = \frac{X}{0.60}$$

   $$\$101,250 = \frac{X}{0.60}$$

   $$X = \$60,750$$

4. Let Q = Number of units to break even with new fixed costs of $146,250
   $$\$25.00Q - \$13.75Q - \$146,250 = 0$$
   $$Q = \$146,250 \div \$11.25 = 13,000 \text{ units}$$
   $$\text{Revenues} = 13,000(\$25.00) = \$325,000$$

   Alternatively, the computation could be $146,250 divided by the contribution margin percentage of 45% to obtain $325,000.

5. Let S = Required sales units to equal 2002 net income
   $$\$25.00S - \$13.75S - \$146,250 = \frac{\$54,000}{0.6}$$
   $$\$11.25S = \$236,250$$
   $$S = 21,000 \text{ units}$$
   $$\text{Revenues} = 21,000 \text{ units} \times \$25.00 = \$525,000$$

6. Let A = Amount spent for advertising in 2003
   $$\$550,000 - \$302,500 - (\$135,000 + A) = \frac{\$60,000}{0.6}$$
   $$\$550,000 - \$302,500 - \$135,000 - A = \$100,000$$
   $$\$550,000 - \$537,500 = A$$
   $$A = \$12,500$$

3–54   (20-30 min.)   **Appendix, CVP under uncertainty.**

1.   (a)   At a selling price of $100, the unit contribution margin is ($100 – $50) = $50, and it will require the sale of ($200,000 ÷ $50) = 4,000 units to break even. The sales in dollars are $400,000 and there is a 2/3 probability of equaling or exceeding this sales level—that is, that 2/3 of the area under the graph exists between $400,000 and $600,000.

1.   (b)   At a selling price of $70, the unit contribution margin is ($70 – $50) = $20, and it will require the sale of ($200,000 ÷ $20) = 10,000 units to break even. At the lower price, the sales in dollars are $700,000 and there is a 2/3 probability of equaling or exceeding this sales volume.

Therefore, if you seek to maximize the probability of showing an operating income, you are indifferent between the two strategies.

2. $$\begin{array}{c}\text{Expected}\\\text{operating}\\\text{income}\end{array} = \left[\left(\begin{array}{c}\text{Selling}\\\text{price per unit}\end{array} - \begin{array}{c}\text{Variable}\\\text{cost per unit}\end{array}\right) \times \left(\begin{array}{c}\text{Expected}\\\text{sales}\\\text{level}\end{array}\right)\right] - \left(\begin{array}{c}\text{Fixed}\\\text{costs}\end{array}\right)$$

At a selling price of $100:

   Expected revenues   = $450,000 ($100 × 4,500)

   Expected operating income   = [($100 – $50) × 4,500] – $200,000
                             = $25,000

At a selling price of $70:

   Expected revenues   = $750,000 ($70 × 10,715)

   Expected operating income   = [($70 – $50) × 10,715] – $200,000
                             = $14,300

A selling price of $100 will maximize the expected operating income.

3-56 (20-25 min.) **Ethics, CVP, cost analysis.**

1. (a) USP = $55
   UVC = $22 ($14 + $8)
   UCM = $33
   FC = $20,000,000
   $$Q = \frac{FC}{UCM} = \frac{\$20,000,000}{\$33}$$
   = 606,061 monthly treatments (rounded up)

   (b) USP = $55
   UVC = $14
   UCM = $41
   FC = $20,000,000
   $$Q = \frac{FC}{UCM} = \frac{\$20,000,000}{\$41}$$
   = 487,805 monthly treatments (rounded up)

2. Allen believes that $8 per monthly visit should be included in the variable costs per visit. His argument is that a product like "Vital Hair" has a positive probability of attracting product litigation. By excluding any allowance for the possible event, the assumption is that it will be zero.

   Allen faces an integrity issue. His report to the Executive Committee will understate his expected cost estimates when he takes Kelly's advice. His report likely will be seen by those not attending the Executive Committee meeting. Moreover, even those attending the meeting may not remember any verbal comments Allen makes at the meeting.

   One possibility Allen should have explored is reporting the $14 per treatment variable cost in the breakeven computations but also include qualifications in the report about possible product litigation costs.

3. Allen likely has been placed in a compromised situation. He may feel Kelly deliberately set him up to avoid the $8 amount being reported to the Executive Committee. At a minimum, he should directly confront Kelly with his concerns. If she is unresponsive, he faces a very tough dilemma. His options are:

   (a) Stay in his current position and be more determined next time to have his concerns registered.
   (b) Report his concerns to Kelly's immediate superior.
   (c) Resign.

If he selects (a), it would be useful to show Kelly the Code of Professional Ethics and stress how her behaviour has put him in a difficult ethical situation.

CHAPTER 4
JOB COSTING

4-2   In a *job-costing system* costs are assigned to a distinct unit, batch, or lot of a product or service. In a *process-costing system*, the cost of a product or service is obtained by using broad averages to assign costs to masses of similar units.

4-4 The seven steps in job costing are (1) identify the chosen cost object or job, (2) identify the direct costs of the job, (3) select the cost-allocation base(s) to use for allocating indirect costs to the job, (4) identify the indirect costs associated with each cost-allocation base, (5) compute the rate per unit of each cost-allocation base used to allocate indirect costs to the job, (6) compute the indirect costs allocated to the job, and (7) compute the total cost of the job by adding all direct and indirect costs assigned to it.

4-6 Three major source documents used in job-costing systems are (1) job cost record or job cost sheet, a document that records and accumulates all costs assigned to a specific job, (2) materials requisition record, a document used to charge job cost records and departments for the cost of direct materials used on a specific job, and (3) labour-time record, a document used to charge job cost records and departments for labour time used on a specific job.

4-8   Two reasons for using six-month or annual budget periods are:
   a.   The numerator reason—the longer the time period, the less the influence of seasonal patterns, and
   b.   The denominator reason—the longer the time period, the less the effect of variations in output levels on the allocation of fixed costs.

4-10   An accounting firm can use job cost information (a) to determine the profitability of individual jobs, (b) to assist in bidding on future jobs, and (c) to evaluate professionals who are in charge of managing individual jobs.

4-12   Debit entries to Work-in-Process Control represent increases in work in process. Examples of debit entries are: (a) direct materials used (credit to Materials Control), (b) direct manufacturing labour billed to job (credit to Wages Payable Control), and (c) manufacturing overhead allocated to job (credit to Manufacturing Overhead Allocated).

4-14   A service company might use budgeted costs rather than actual costs to compute direct labour rates because it may be difficult to trace some costs to jobs as they are completed.

4-16 (20 min.) **Actual costing, normal costing, manufacturing overhead.**

1. $$\text{Budgeted manufacturing overhead rate} = \frac{\text{Budgeted manufacturing overhead costs}}{\text{Budgeted direct manufacturing labour costs}}$$

$$= \frac{\$1{,}750{,}000}{\$1{,}000{,}000} = 1.75 \text{ or } 175\%$$

$$\text{Actual manufacturing overhead rate} = \frac{\text{Actual manufacturing overhead costs}}{\text{Actual direct manufacturing labour costs}}$$

$$= \frac{\$1{,}862{,}000}{\$980{,}000} = 1.9 \text{ or } 190\%$$

2. Costs of Job 626 under actual and normal costing follow:

	Normal Costing	Actual Costing
Direct materials	$ 40,000	$ 40,000
Direct manufacturing labour costs	30,000	30,000
Manufacturing overhead costs		
$30,000 × 1.75; $30,000 × 1.90 *Ind.*	52,500	57,000
Total manufacturing costs of Job 626	$122,500	$127,000

3. $$\text{Total manufacturing overhead allocated under normal costing} = \text{Actual manufacturing labour costs} \times \text{Budgeted overhead rate}$$

$$= \$980{,}000 \times 1.75$$
$$= \$1{,}715{,}000$$

$$\text{Underallocated manufacturing overhead} = \text{Actual manufacturing overhead costs} - \text{Manufacturing overhead allocated}$$

$$= \$1{,}862{,}000 - \$1{,}715{,}000 = \$147{,}000$$

There is no under- or overallocated overhead under actual costing because overhead is allocated under actual costing by multiplying actual manufacturing labour costs and the actual manufacturing overhead rate. This, of course, equals the actual manufacturing overhead costs. All actual overhead costs are allocated to products. Hence, there is no under- or overallocated overhead.

4. Actual costing reflects the actual results incurred, while normal costing reflects expectations of the amount the overhead should be. Normal costing can be done in advance and thus can be used in pricing and planning decisions.

4-18 (20-30 min.) **Job costing, accounting for manufacturing overhead, budgeted rates.**

1. An overview of the product costing system is:

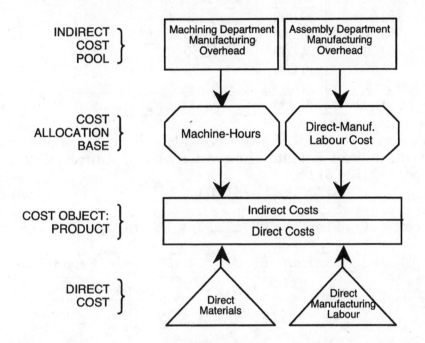

Budgeted manufacturing overhead divided by allocation base:

Machining overhead: $\dfrac{\$1,800,000}{50,000}$ = $36 per machine-hour

Assembly overhead: $\dfrac{\$3,600,000}{\$2,000,000}$ = 180% of direct manuf. labour costs

2.
Machining overhead, 2,000 hours × $36	$72,000
Assembly overhead, 180% of $15,000	27,000
Total manufacturing overhead allocated to Job 494	$99,000

3.

	Machining	Assembly
Actual manufacturing overhead	$2,100,000	$ 3,700,000
Manufacturing overhead allocated,		
55,000 × $36	1,980,000	
180% of $2,200,000		3,960,000
Underallocated (Overallocated)	$ 120,000	$ (260,000)

4-20 (20-30 min.) **Computing indirect-cost rates, job costing.**

1.

a.

	Budgeted Fixed Indirect Costs	Budgeted Hours	Budgeted Fixed Indirect Cost Rate Per Hour	Budgeted Variable Indirect Cost Rate Per Hour	Budgeted Total Indirect Cost Rate Per Hour
Jan.-March	$50,000	20,000	$ 2.50	$10	$12.50
April-June	50,000	10,000	5.00	10	15.00
July-Sept.	50,000	4,000	12.50	10	22.50
Oct.-Dec.	50,000	6,000	8.33	10	18.33
b.	$200,000	40,000	$ 5.00	$10	$15.00

2a. All four jobs use 10 hours of professional labour time. The only difference in job costing is the indirect cost rate. The quarterly-based indirect job cost rates are:

Hansen: $(10 \times \$12.50)$ = $125.00
Kai: $(6 \times \$12.50) +$ $(4 \times \$15.00)$ = $135.00
Patera: $(4 \times \$15.00)$ $+$ $(6 \times \$22.50)$ = $195.00
Stevens: $(5 \times \$12.50) +$ $(2 \times \$22.50) + (3 \times \$18.33)$ = $162.50

	Hansen	Kai	Patera	Stevens
Revenues, $65 × 10	$650	$650	$650	$650.00
Direct costs, $30 × 10	300	300	300	300.00
Indirect costs	125	135	195	162.50
Total costs	425	435	495	462.50
Operating income	$225	$215	$155	$187.50

b. Using annual-based indirect job cost rates, all four customers will have the same operating income:

Revenues, $65 × 10	$650
Direct costs, $30 × 10	300
Indirect costs, $15 × 10	150
Total costs	450
Operating income	$200

3.   All four jobs use 10 hours of professional labour time. Using the quarterly-based indirect cost rates, there are four different operating incomes as the work done on them is completed in different quarters. In contrast, using the annual indirect cost rate all four customers have the same operating income. All these different operating income figures for jobs with the same number of professional labour-hours are due to the allocation of fixed indirect costs.

4-20 (cont'd)

An overview of the Tax Assist job costing system is:

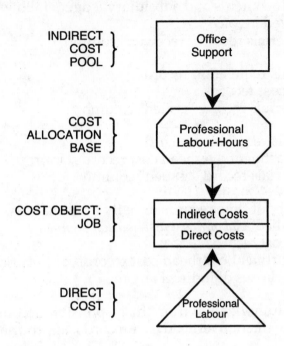

4-22 (20 min.) **Job costing, journal entries, and source documents (continuation of 4-21).**

The analysis of source documents and subsidiary ledgers follows:

1. a. Approved invoice
   b. dr. Materials record, "received" column

2. a. Materials requisition record
   b. dr. Job cost records
      cr. Materials record, "issued" column

3. a. Materials requisition record
   b. dr. Department overhead cost records, appropriate column
      cr. Materials record, "issued" column

4. a. Summary of time records or daily time analysis. This summary is sometimes called a *labour cost distribution summary*.
   b. dr. Job cost records
      dr. Department overhead cost records, appropriate columns for various classes of indirect labour

5. a. Special authorization from the responsible accounting officer
   b. dr. Department overhead cost records, appropriate columns

6. a. Various approved invoices and special authorizations
   b. dr. Department overhead cost records, appropriate columns

7. a. Use of an authorized budgeted manufacturing overhead rate
   b. dr. Job cost record

8. a. Completed job cost records
   b. dr. Finished goods records
      cr. Job cost record

9. a. Approved sales invoice
   b. dr. Customers' accounts (or Cash)
      cr. Sales ledger, if any

10. a. Costed sales invoice
    b. cr. Finished goods records

11. a. Special authorization from the responsible accounting officer
    b. Subsidiary records are generally not used for these entries

4-24 (10–15 min.) **Accounting for manufacturing overhead.**

1. Budgeted manufacturing overhead rate $= \dfrac{\$7,000,000}{200,000}$
$= \$35 \text{ per machine-hour}$

2.

Work-in-Process Control	6,825,000	
Manufacturing Overhead Allocated		6,825,000

(195,000 machine-hours × $35 = $6,825,000)

3. $6,825,000 – $6,800,000 = $25,000 overallocated, an insignificant amount.

Manufacturing Overhead Allocated	6,825,000	
Manufacturing Overhead Control		6,800,000
Cost of Goods Sold		25,000

4-26 (10 min.) **Job order costing, process costing.**

a.	Job costing		l.	Job costing
b.	Process costing		m.	Process costing
c.	Job costing		n.	Job costing
d.	Process costing		o.	Job costing
e.	Job costing		p.	Job costing
f.	Process costing		q.	Job costing
g.	Job costing		r.	Process costing
h.	Job costing (but some process costing)		s.	Job costing
i.	Process costing		t.	Process costing
j.	Process costing		u.	Job costing
k.	Job costing			

4-28 (15–20 min.) **Job costing, unit cost, ending work in process.**

1. Cost of Job M1:

Direct materials	$ 75,000
Direct manufacturing labour	270,000
Manufacturing overhead allocated	180,000*
Total cost	$525,000

*Budgeted rate $30 × 6,000 direct manufacturing labour-hours = $180,000

2. Per unit cost = $\dfrac{\text{Total cost of the job}}{\text{Number of units in the job}}$

    $\qquad = \dfrac{\$525,000}{15,000 \text{ units}} = \$35$ per unit

3.

Finished Goods Control	525,000	
Work in Process Control		525,000

4. The work in process consists of Job M2 only:

Direct materials	$ 50,000
Direct manufacturing labour	210,000
Manufacturing overhead allocated	150,000†
Work in process May 31	$410,000

† Budgeted rate of $30 × 5,000 direct manufacturing labour-hours.

4-30 (20-30 min.) **Job costing; actual, normal, and variation of normal costing.**

1. Actual direct cost rate $\qquad$ = $110 per professional labour-hour

Actual indirect cost rate $= \dfrac{\$2,436,000}{42,000 \text{ hours}} = $ $58 per professional labour-hour

Budgeted direct cost rate $= \dfrac{\$4,000,000}{40,000 \text{ hours}} = $ $100 per professional labour-hour

Budgeted indirect cost rate $= \dfrac{\$2,600,000}{40,000 \text{ hours}} = $ $65 per professional labour-hour

	(a) Actual Costing	(b) Normal Costing	(c) Variation of Normal Costing
Direct Cost Rate	$110 (Actual rate)	$110 (Actual rate)	$100 (Budgeted rate)
Indirect Cost Rate	$58 (Actual rate)	$65 (Budgeted rate)	$65 (Budgeted rate)

2.

	(a) Actual Costing	(b) Normal Costing	(c) Variation of Normal Costing
Direct Costs	$110 × 1,720 = $189,200	$110 × 1,720 = $189,200	$100 × 1,720 = $172,000
Indirect Costs	58 × 1,720 = 99,760	65 × 1,720 = 111,800	65 × 1,720 = 111,800
Total Job Costs	$288,960	$301,000	$283,800

The differences in job costs arise from the different uses of actual versus budgeted rates. The actual costing figure of $288,960 is less than the normal costing figure of $301,000 because the actual indirect cost rate ($58) is less than the budgeted indirect cost rate ($65). The normal costing figure of $301,000 exceeds the variation of normal costing figure of $283,800 because the actual direct cost rate ($110) exceeds the budgeted direct cost rate ($100).

All three job-costing systems use the actual professional labour-hours of 1,720. The budgeted 1,500 hours is not used in the job-costing system. However, it may have been used by Vista Group in budgeting on the Carefree Years job. If Vista quoted a fixed price, it may well have lost money on this job.

4-30 (cont'd)

An overview of the Vista Group job costing system is:

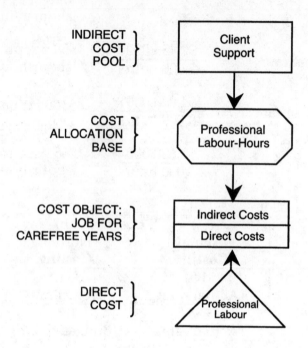

4-32 (15-20 min.) **Job costing, law firm.**

1.

INDIRECT COST POOL }	Client Support
COST ALLOCATION BASE }	Professional Labour-Hours
COST OBJECT: JOB FOR CLIENT }	Indirect Costs / Direct Costs
DIRECT COST }	Professional Labour

2.

$$\text{Budgeted professional labour-hour direct-cost rate} = \frac{\text{Budgeted total direct labour compensation}}{\text{Budgeted total direct labour-hours}}$$

$$= \frac{\$104,000}{1,600 \text{ hours}}$$

$$= \$65 \text{ per professional labour-hour}$$

3.

$$\text{Budgeted indirect-cost rate} = \frac{\text{Budgeted total costs in the indirect-cost pool}}{\text{Budgeted total professional labour-hours}}$$

$$= \frac{\$2,200,000}{1,600 \text{ hours} \times 25}$$

$$= \frac{\$2,200,000}{40,000 \text{ hours}}$$

$$= \$55 \text{ per professional labour-hour}$$

4.

	Richardson	Punch
Direct costs:		
Professional labour, $65 × 100;150	$ 6,500	$ 9,750
Indirect costs:		
Legal support, $55 × 100; 150	5,500	8,250
	$12,000	$18,000

4-34 (20 min.)   **Normal costing, overhead allocation, working backwards.**

1.

$$\text{Manufacturing overhead allocated} = \$3,600,000$$

Manufacturing overhead is allocated at 200% of direct manufacturing labour costs.

$$\text{Manufacturing overhead allocated} = 200\% \times \text{Direct manufacturing labour costs}$$

$$\text{That is,} \quad \$3,600,000 = 2 \times \text{Direct manufacturing labour costs}$$

$$\text{Hence,} \quad \text{Direct manufacturing labour costs} = \frac{\$3,600,000}{2} = \$1,800,000$$

2.

$$\text{Total manufacturing costs} = \text{Direct materials costs} + \text{Direct manufacturing labour costs} + \text{Manufacturing overhead allocated}$$

$$\text{That is, } \$8,000,000 = \text{Direct materials costs} + \$1,800,000 + \$3,600,000$$

Hence, Direct materials costs = $2,600,000

3.   Note the structure of entries made to the Work-in-Process T-account

Work in Process

Beginning balance, 1-1-2003	xxx	Cost of goods manufactured	
Manufacturing costs	xxx	(transferred to finished goods)	xxx
Ending balance, 12-31-2003	xxx		

It follows that

$$\text{Work in Process on 1-1-2003} + \text{Total manufacturing costs} = \text{Cost of goods manufactured} + \text{Work in Process on 12-31-2003}$$

Hence,

$$\text{Work in Process on 12-31-2003} = \text{Work in Process on 1-1-2003} + \text{Total manufacturing costs} + \text{Cost of goods manufactured}$$
$$= \$320,000 + \$8,000,000 - \$7,920,000$$
$$= \$409,000$$

4-36 (40 min.) **Proration of overhead, two indirect-cost pools.**

1.

$$
\begin{array}{l}
\text{Budgeted manufacturing} \\
\text{overhead cost rate for} \\
\text{the Machining Department}
\end{array}
=
\frac{\begin{array}{c}\text{Budgeted manufacturing overhead costs} \\ \text{in the Machining Department}\end{array}}{\begin{array}{c}\text{Budgeted machine-hours in the} \\ \text{Machining Department}\end{array}}
$$

$$
= \frac{\$6,000,000}{100,000} = \$60 \text{ per machine-hour}
$$

$$
\begin{array}{l}
\text{Budgeted manufacturing} \\
\text{overhead cost rate for} \\
\text{the Assembly Department}
\end{array}
=
\frac{\begin{array}{c}\text{Budgeted manufacturing overhead costs} \\ \text{in the Assembly Department}\end{array}}{\begin{array}{c}\text{Budgeted direct manufacturing labour - hours} \\ \text{in the Assembly Department}\end{array}}
$$

$$
= \frac{\$5,000,000}{125,000} = \$40 \text{ per direct manufacturing labour-}\mathsf{h}
$$

2.

Machining Department

Total actual machine-hours = 67,500 + 4,500 + 18,000 = 90,000 machine-hours

Manufacturing overhead allocated = 90,000 × $60 = $5,400,000

$$
\begin{array}{l}
\text{Manufacturing overhead} \\
\text{costs underallocated}
\end{array}
=
\begin{array}{c}\text{Actual manufacturing} \\ \text{overhead costs}\end{array}
-
\begin{array}{c}\text{Manufacturing} \\ \text{overhead allocated}\end{array}
$$

= $6,200,000 − $5,400,000 = $800,000

Assembly Department

$$
\begin{array}{l}
\text{Total actual direct} \\
\text{manufacturing labour - hours}
\end{array}
=
\begin{array}{c}90,000 + 4,800 + 25,200 = 120,000 \text{ direct} \\ \text{manufacturing labour-hours}\end{array}
$$

Manufacturing overhead allocated = 120,000 × $40 = $4,800,000

$$
\begin{array}{l}
\text{Manufacturing overhead} \\
\text{costs overallocated}
\end{array}
=
\begin{array}{c}\text{Manufacturing overhead} \\ \text{allocated}\end{array}
-
\begin{array}{c}\text{Actual manufacturing} \\ \text{overhead costs}\end{array}
$$

= $4,800,000 − $4,700,000 = $100,000

4-36 (cont'd)

2. a. Write-off to Cost of Goods Sold leads to
   (i)   higher Cost of Goods Sold of $800,000 as a result of underallocation of manufacturing overhead in the Machining Department
   (ii) lower Cost of Goods Sold of $100,000 as a result of overallocation of manufacturing overhead in the Assembly Department. Hence,

   Cost of Goods Sold = $16,000,000 + $800,000 – $100,000 = $16,700,000

2. b. Proration based on ending balances (before proration) in Work in Process, Finished Goods, and Cost of Goods Sold.

   Account balances in each account after proration follows:

Account (1)	Account Balance (2)	Proration of $800,000 Underallocated Overhead in Manufacturing Dept. (3)	Proration of $(100,000) Overallocated Overhead in Assembly Dept. (4)	Account Balance (after Proration) (5)=(1)+(3)+(4)
Work in Process	$ 3,250,000 (16.25%)	0.1625 × $800,000 = $130,000	0.1625 × ($100,000)=($ 16,250)	$ 3,363,750
Finished Goods	750,000 (3.75%)	0.0375 × $800,000 = 30,000	0.0375 × ($100,000)=($ 3,750)	776,250
Cost of Goods Sold	16,000,000 (80.00%)	0.80 × $800,000 = 640,000	0.80 × ($100,000)=($ 80,000)	16,560,000
	$ 20,000,000 (100.00%)	$800,000	$(100,000)	$20,700,000

2. c. Proration based on the overhead allocated (before proration) in the ending balances of Cost of Goods Sold, Finished Goods, and Work in Process for each Department follows.

Machining Department

Account (1)	Overhead Costs Allocated to Each Account in Machining Department Using Budgeted Machine-Hour Rate × Actual Machine-Hours (2)			Proration of $800,000 Underallocated Machining Department Overhead (3)		
Work in process	$60 × 18,000	=	$1,080,000 (20%)	0.20 × $800,000	=	$160,000
Finished goods	$60 × 4,500	=	270,000 (5%)	0.05 × $800,000	=	40,000
Cost of goods sold	$60 × 67,500	=	4,050,000 (75%)	0.75 × $800,000	=	600,000
			$5,400,000 (100%)			$800,000

4-36 (cont'd)

Assembly Department

Account (1)	Overhead Costs Allocated to Each Account in Assembly Department Using Budgeted Direct Manuf. Labour-Hour Rate × Actual Direct Manuf. Labour-Hours (2)				Proration of ($100,000) Overallocated Assembly Department Overhead (3)		
Work in process	$40 × 25,200	=	$1,008,000	(21%)	0.21 × ($100,000)	=	$ (21,000)
Finished goods	$40 × 4,800	=	192,000	(4%)	0.04 × ($100,000)	=	(4,000)
Cost of goods sold	$40 × 90,000	=	3,600,000	(75%)	0.75 × ($100,000)	=	(75,000)
			$4,800,000	(100%)			$(100,000)

Account balances in each account after proration of underallocated Machining Department costs and overallocated Assembly Department costs follow.

Account (1)	Account Balance (before Proration) (2)	Prorated $800,000 of Underallocated Machining Department Overhead (calculated earlier) (3)	Prorated ($100,000) of Overallocated Assembly Department Overhead (calculated earlier) (4)	Account Balance (after Proration) (5)=(2)+(3)+(4)
Work in process	$ 3,250,000	$160,000	$ (21,000)	$ 3,389,000
Finished goods	750,000	40,000	(4,000)	786,000
Cost of goods sold	16,000,000	600,000	(75,000)	16,525,000
	$20,000,000	$800,000	$(100,000)	$20,700,000

3.   If the purpose is to report the most accurate inventory and cost of goods sold figures, the preferred method is to prorate based on the manufacturing overhead allocated amount in the inventory and cost of goods sold accounts (as in requirement 2c). Note, however, that prorating based on ending balances in Work in Process, Finished Goods, and Cost of Goods Sold (as in requirement 2b) yields a close approximation to the more accurate proration in requirement 2c. Also note that the write-off to Cost of Goods Sold method (as in requirement 2a) results in account balances in Work in Process, Finished Goods, and Cost of Goods Sold that are not very different from the most accurate method. Furthermore, the Write Off to Cost of Goods Sold method is simpler than the other methods. Depending on the objectives of proration, a manager may prefer any one of the methods over the other two.

4-38 (20 min.) **Job costing, contracting, ethics.**

1.   Direct manufacturing costs:

Direct materials	$25,000	
Direct manufacturing labour	6,000	$31,000
Indirect manufacturing costs,		
150% × $6,000		9,000
Total manufacturing costs		$40,000

Aerospace bills the Armed Forces $52,000 ($40,000 × 130%) for 100 X7 seats or $520 ($52,000 ÷ 100) per X7 seat.

2.   Direct manufacturing costs:

Direct materials	$25,000	
Direct manufacturing labour[a]	5,000	$30,000
Indirect manufacturing costs,		
150% × $5,000		7,500
Total manufacturing costs		$37,500

[a]$6,000 – $400 ($25 × 16) setup – $600 ($50 × 12) design

Aerospace should have billed the Armed Forces $48,750 ($37,500 × 130%) for 100 X7 seats or $487.50 ($48,750 ÷ 100) per X7 seat.

3.   The problems the letter highlights (assuming it is correct) include:

    a.   Costs included that should be excluded (design costs),
    b.   Costs double-counted (setup included both as a direct cost and in an indirect cost pool), and
    c.   Possible conflict of interest in Aerospace Comfort purchasing materials from a family-related company.

Steps the Armed Forces could undertake include:

    (i)   Use only contractors with a reputation for ethical behaviour as well as quality products or services.
    (ii)   Issue guidelines detailing acceptable and unacceptable billing practices by contractors. For example, prohibiting the use of double-counting cost allocation methods by contractors.
    (iii)   Issue guidelines detailing acceptable and unacceptable procurement practices by contractors. For example, if a contractor purchases from a family-related company, require that the contractor obtain quotes from at least two other bidders.
    (iv)   Employ auditors who aggressively monitor the bills submitted by contractors.

4-40 (35 min.) **General ledger relationships, under- and overallocation.**

A summary of the T-accounts for Needham Company before adjusting for under- or overallocation of overhead follows

Direct Materials Control		
1-1-2002 30,000	Material used for	
Purchases	manufacturing	
400,000	380,000	
12-31-2002 50,000		

Work-in-Process Control		
1-1-2002 20,000	Transferred to	
Direct materials	finished goods	
380,000	940,000	
Direct manuf.		
labour 360,000		
Manuf. overhead		
allocated 480,000		
12-31-2002 300,000		

Finished Goods Control		
1-1-2002 10,000	Cost of goods	
Transferred in	sold 900,000	
from WIP		
940,000		
12-31-2002 50,000		

Cost of Goods Sold		
Finished goods		
sold 900,000		

Manufacturing Overhead Control	
Manufacturing	
overhead	
costs 540,000	

Manufacturing Overhead Allocated	
	Manufacturing
	overhead
	allocated to
	work in
	process 480,000

1. From the credit entry to Direct Materials T-account,
    Direct materials issued to manufacturing = $380,000.

2. Direct manufacturing labour-hours $= \dfrac{\text{Direct manufacturing labour costs}}{\text{Direct manufacturing wage rate per hour}}$

    $= \dfrac{\$360,000}{\$15 \text{ per hour}} = 24,000 \text{ hours}$

    $\begin{array}{l}\text{Manufacturing overhead} \\ \text{allocated}\end{array} = \begin{array}{l}\text{Direct manufacturing} \\ \text{labour-hours}\end{array} \times \begin{array}{l}\text{Manufacturing} \\ \text{overhead rate}\end{array}$

    $= 24,000 \text{ hours} \times \$20 = \$480,000$

3. From the debit entry to Finished Goods T-account,
    Cost of jobs completed and transferred from WIP = $940,000

4-40 (cont'd)

4. From Work-in-Process T-account,

$$\text{Work-in-process inventory on } 12/31/2002 = \$20,000 + \$380,000 + \$360,000 + \$480,000 - \$940,000$$
$$= \$300,000$$

5. From the credit entry to Finished Goods Control T-account,

Cost of goods sold (before proration) = \$900,000

6. $$\text{Manufacturing overhead underallocated} = \text{Debits to Manufacturing Overhead Control} - \text{Credit to Manufacturing Overhead Allocated}$$
$$= \$540,000 - \$480,000$$
$$= \$60,000 \text{ underallocated}$$

7. a. Write-off to Cost of Goods Sold will increase (debit) Cost of Goods Sold by \$60,000. Hence, Cost of Goods Sold = \$900,000 + \$60,000 = \$960,000.

    b. Proration based on ending balances (before proration) in Work in Process, Finished Goods, and Cost of Goods Sold.

Account balances in each account after proration follows.

Account (1)	Account Balance (2)	Proration of \$60,000 Underallocated Manufacturing Overhead (3)	Account Balance (after Proration) (4)=(2)+(3)
Work in Process	\$ 300,000 (24%)	0.24 × \$60,000 = \$14,400	\$ 314,400
Finished Goods	50,000 (4%)	0.04 × \$60,000 = 2,400	52,400
Cost of Goods Sold	900,000 (72%)	0.72 × \$60,000 = 43,200	943,200
Total	\$1,250,000 (100%)	\$60,000	\$1,310,000

8. Needham's operating income under the write-off to Cost of Goods Sold and Proration based on ending balances (before proration) follows:

	Write-off to Cost of Goods Sold	Proration Based on Ending Balances
Revenues	\$1,090,000	\$1,090,000
Cost of goods sold	960,000	943,200
Gross margin	130,000	146,800
Marketing and distribution costs	140,000	140,000
Operating income/(loss)	\$ (10,000)	\$ 6,800

4-40 (cont'd)

9.   If the purpose is to report the most accurate inventory and cost of goods sold figures, the preferred method is to prorate based on the manufacturing overhead allocated component in the Inventory and Cost of Goods Sold accounts. Proration based on the balances in Work in Process, Finished Goods, and Cost of Goods Sold will equal the proration based on the manufacturing overhead allocated component if the proportions of direct costs to manufacturing overhead costs are constant in the Work in Process, Finished Goods, and Cost of Goods Sold accounts. Even if this is not the case, the prorations based on Work in Process, Finished Goods, and Cost of Goods Sold will better approximate the results if actual cost rates have been used than the write-off to Cost of Goods Sold method.

Another consideration in Needham's decision about how to dispose of underallocated manufacturing overhead is the effects on operating income. The write-off to Cost of Goods Sold will lead to an operating loss. Proration based on the balances in Work in Process, Finished Goods, and Cost of Goods Sold will help Needham avoid the loss and show an operating income.

The main merit of the write-off to cost of goods sold method is its simplicity. However, accuracy and the effect on operating income favour the preferred and recommended proration approach.

CHAPTER 5
ACTIVITY-BASED COSTING AND ACTIVITY-BASED MANAGEMENT

5-2 Overcosting may result in competitors entering a market and taking market share for products that a company erroneously believes are low-margin or even unprofitable.

Undercosting may result in companies selling products on which they are in fact losing money, when they erroneously believe them to be profitable.

5-4 An activity-based approach focuses on activities as the fundamental cost objects. It uses the cost of these activities as the basis for assigning costs to other cost objects such as products, services, or customers.

5-6 The purpose for computing a product cost is to determine whether unit costs should be based on total manufacturing costs in all or only some levels of the cost hierarchy. Inventory valuation for financial reporting requires *total* or only some manufacturing costs (all levels of the hierarchy) to be expressed on a per output-unit basis. In contrast, for cost management purposes, the cost hierarchy need not be unitized, as units of output is not the cost driver at each level in the hierarchy.

5-8 Four decisions for which ABC information is useful are:
(1)   pricing and product mix decisions,
(2)   cost reduction and process improvement decisions,
(3)   design decisions, and
(4)   planning and managing activities

5-10 "Tell-tale" signs that indicate when ABC systems are likely to provide the most benefits are:
1.   Significant amounts of indirect costs are allocated using only one or two cost pools.
2.   All or most indirect costs are identified as output-unit-level costs (i.e., few indirect costs are described as batch-level, product-sustaining, or facility-sustaining costs).
3.   Products make diverse demands on resources because of differences in volume, process steps, batch size, or complexity.
4.   Products that a company is well suited to make and sell show small profits, whereas products that a company is less suited to produce and sell show large profits.
5.   Complex products appear to be very profitable, and simple products appear to be losing money.
6.   Operations staff have significant disagreements with the accounting staff about the costs of manufacturing and marketing products and services.

5-12 No, ABC systems apply equally well to service companies such as banks, railroads, hospitals, and accounting firms, and to merchandising companies such as retailers and distributors.

5-14   Increasing the number of indirect-cost pools does NOT guarantee increased accuracy of product, service, or customer costs. If the existing cost pool is already homogeneous, increasing the number of cost pools will not increase accuracy. If the existing cost pool is not homogeneous, accuracy will increase only if the increased cost pools themselves increase in homogeneity vis-a-vis the single cost pool.

5-16   (30 min.)   Cost smoothing or peanut butter costing, cross-subsidization.

1.   Cost smoothing or peanut butter costing is a costing approach that uniformly assigns the cost of resources to customers when the individual customers use those resources in a nonuniform way. The reunion dinner averages the costs across all five people. These five people differ sizably in what they consume.

2.

Diner	Entree	Dessert	Drinks	Total
Armstrong	$27	$8	$24	$59
Gonzales	24	3	0	27
King	21	6	13	40
Poffo	31	6	12	49
Young	15	4	6	25
Average	$23.60	$5.40	$11.00	$40.00

The average-cost pricing will result in each person paying $40.

	Amount Over- or Undercosted
Accurately costed person	
• King, $40 – $40	$ 0
Undercosted people	
• Armstrong, $40 – $59	$(19)
• Poffo, $40 – $49	$(9)
Overcosted people	
• Gonzales, $40 – $27	$ 13
• Young, $40 – $25	$ 15

Yes, Young's complaint is justified. He is "overcharged" $15. He could point out likely negative behaviours with this approach to costing. These include:
   a.   It can lead some people to order the most expensive items because others will "subsidize" their extravagance.
   b.   It can lead to friction when those who dine economically are forced to subsidize those who dine extravagantly. At the limit, some people may decide not to attend the reunion dinners.

Likely benefits of this approach are:
   a.   it is simple, and
   b.   it (purportedly) promotes a group atmosphere at the dinner.

5-16 (cont'd)

3.   Each one of the costs in the data is directly traceable to an individual diner. This makes it straightforward to compute the individual cost per diner. Examples where this is not possible include:
- A plate of hors d'oeuvres is shared by two or more diners
- A loaf of garlic bread is shared by two or more diners
- A bottle of mineral water or wine is shared by two or more diners

Each of these items cannot be directly traced to only one diner.

Some possible behaviours if each person pays for his or her own bill are:
-    a.   Some people may reduce their ordering of more expensive items because they will not be subsidized by other diners.
-    b.   May encourage some potential diners to attend who otherwise would have stayed away.
-    c.   May encourage a person "trying to impress others with his or her success" to order the most expensive items.

5-18   (25 min.)   Cost hierarchy, ABC, distribution.

1.   Total distribution costs (given), $2,130,000

$$\frac{\text{Distribution cost}}{\text{per case under}} = \frac{\text{Total distribution costs}}{\text{Total cases of specialty and regular wine shipped}} = \frac{\$2,130,000}{200,000} = \$10.65 \text{ per case}$$

	Regular		Specialty	
		Per Case		Per Case
	Total	**(2) =**	**Total**	**(4) =**
	(1)	**(1) ÷ 120,000**	**(3)**	**(3) ÷ 80,000**
Distribution costs				
$10.65 × 120,000; $10.65 × 80,000	$1,278,000	$10.65	$852,000	$10.65

2a.   Promotional activity—distributor-level costs because these costs do not depend on the number of cases shipped or the number of batches in which the cases are shipped. An amount of $8,000 is incurred for each of Niagara's distributors.

Order-handling costs—batch-level costs because these costs are incurred each time a customer places an order regardless of the number of cases ordered. These costs total $300 per order.

Freight distribution costs—Unit-level costs because a cost of $8 is incurred on freight for each case shipped.

2b.

	Regular		Specialty	
	Total (1)	Per Case (2) = (1) ÷ 120,000	Total (3)	Per Case (4) = (3) ÷ 80,000
Distribution costs of freight				
$8 × 120,000 cases	$ 960,000	$8.00		
$8 × 80,000 cases			$ 640,000	$8.00
Ordering costs				
$300 × 10 orders/year × 10 distr.	30,000	0.25		
$300 × 20 orders/year × 30 distr.			180,000	2.25
Promotion costs				
$8,000 × 10 distributors	80,000	0.67		
$8,000 × 30 distributors			240,000	3.00
Total costs	$1,070,000	$8.92	$1,060,000	$13.25

3. The existing costing system uses cases shipped, a unit-level cost driver, as the only cost allocation base for distribution costs. As a result, the distribution cost per case is the same for specialty and regular wines ($10.65). In fact, specialty wines use distribution resources more intensively than regular wines: (a) Niagara spends $8,000 on promotional activity at each distributor independent of cases sold. Specialty wine distributors sell fewer cases a year than regular wine distributors. As a result the promotional cost per case of wine sold is higher for specialty wines than for regular wines. (b) Niagara's cost per order is $300 regardless of the number of cases sold in each order. Because specialty wine distributors order fewer cases per order, the ordering costs per case are higher for specialty wines than for regular wines.

The existing costing system undercosts distribution costs per case for specialty wines and overcosts distribution costs per case for regular wines.

Niagara's management can use the information from the ABC system to make better pricing and product mix decisions, to reduce costs by eliminating processes and activities that do not add value, to identify and evaluate new designs that reduce the activities demanded by various products, to reduce the costs of doing various activities, and to plan and manage activities.

5-20 (15 min.)   **Alternative allocation bases for a professional services firm.**

1.

Client	Direct Professional Time			Support Services		Amount Billed to Client
	Rate per Hour	Number of Hours	Total	Rate	Total	
(1)	(2)	(3)	(4) = (2) × (3)	(5)	(6) = (4) × (5)	(7) = (4) + (6)
WINNIPEG DOMINION						
Wolfson	$500	15	$7,500	30%	$2,250	$ 9,750
Brown	120	3	360	30	108	468
Anderson	80	22	1,760	30	528	2,288
						$12,506
TOKYO ENTERPRISES						
Wolfson	$500	2	$1,000	30%	$300	$1,300
Brown	120	8	960	30	288	1,248
Anderson	80	30	2,400	30	720	3,120
						$5,668

2.

Client	Direct Professional Time			Support Services		Amount Billed to Client
	Rate per Hour	Number of Hours	Total	Rate per Hour	Total	
(1)	(2)	(3)	(4) = (2) × (3)	(5)	(6) = (3) × (5)	(7) = (4)+(6)
WINNIPEG DOMINION						
Wolfson	$500	15	$7,500	$50	$ 750	$ 8,250
Brown	120	3	360	50	150	510
Anderson	80	22	1,760	50	1,100	2,860
						$11,620
TOKYO ENTERPRISES						
Wolfson	$500	2	$1,000	$50	$ 100	$1,100
Brown	120	8	960	50	400	1,360
Anderson	80	30	2,400	50	1,500	3,900
						$6,360

5-20 (cont'd)

	Requirement 1	Requirement 2
Winnipeg Dominion	$12,506	$11,620
Tokyo Enterprises	5,668	6,360
	$18,174	$17,980

Both clients use 40 hours of professional labour time. However, Winnipeg Dominion uses a higher proportion of Wolfson's time (15 hours), which is more costly. This attracts the highest support-services charge when allocated on the basis of direct professional labour costs.

3.   Assume that the Wolfson Group uses a cause-and-effect criterion when choosing the allocation base for support services. You could use several pieces of evidence to determine whether professional labour costs or hours is the driver of support-service costs:

a.   *Interviews with personnel.* For example, staff in the major cost categories in support services could be interviewed to determine whether Wolfson requires more support per hour than, say, Anderson. The professional labour costs allocation base implies that an hour of Wolfson's time requires 6.25 ($500 ÷ $80) times more support-service dollars than does an hour of Anderson's time.

b.   *Analysis of tasks undertaken for selected clients.* For example, if computer-related costs are a sizable part of support costs, you could determine if there was a systematic relationship between the percentage involvement of professionals with high billing rates on cases and the computer resources consumed for those cases.

5-22 (30 min.) **Department indirect-cost rates as activity rates (continuation of 5-21).**

1.

	2001 Variable MOH Costs	Total Driver Units	Rate
Design-CAD	$ 39,000	390	$100 per design-hour
Engineering	29,600	370	$ 80 per engineer-hour
Production	240,000	4,000	$ 60 per machine

2.

	United Motors	Holden Motors	Leland Vehicle
Design $100 × 110; 200; 80	$11,000	$ 20,000	$ 8,000
Engineering $80 × 70; 60; 240	5,600	4,800	19,200
Production $60 × 120; 2,800; 1,080	7,200	168,000	64,800
Total	$23,800	$192,800	$92,000

3.

	United Motors	Holden Motors	Leland Vehicle
a. Department rate (Exercise 5-22)	$23,800	$192,800	$92,000
b. Plantwide rate (Exercise 5-21)	9,258	216,020	83,322
Ratio of (a) ÷ (b)	2.57	0.89	1.10

The three contracts differ sizably in the way they use the resources of the three departments. The percentage of total driver units in each department is:

Department	United Motors	Holden Motors	Leland Vehicle
Design	28%	51%	21%
Engineering	19	16	65
Production	3	70	27

The United Motors contract uses only 3% of total machines-hours in 2001, yet uses 28% of CAD design-hours and 19% of engineering hours. The result is that the plantwide rate, based on machine-hours, will greatly underestimate the cost of resources used on the United Motors contract. Hence, the 157% increase in indirect costs assigned to the United Motors contract when department rates are used.

In contrast, the Holden Motors contract uses less of design (51%) and engineering (16%) than of machine-hours (70%). Hence, department rates will report lower indirect costs than does a plantwide rate.

5-24 (15–20 min.) **ABC, wholesale, customer profitability.**

	Chain			
	1	2	3	4
Gross sales	$50,000	$30,000	$100,000	$70,000
Sale returns	10,000	5,000	7,000	6,000
Net sales	40,000	25,000	93,000	64,000
Cost of goods sold (80%)	32,000	20,000	74,400	51,200
Gross margin	8,000	5,000	18,600	12,800
Customer-related costs:				
Regular orders				
$20 × 40; 150; 50; 70	800	3,000	1,000	1,400
Rush orders				
$100 × 10; 50; 10; 30	1,000	5,000	1,000	3,000
Returned items				
$10 × 100; 26; 60; 40	1,000	260	600	400
Catalogues and customer support	1,000	1,000	1,000	1,000
Customer related costs	3,800	9,260	3,600	5,800
Contribution (loss) margin	$ 4,200	$ (4,260)	$ 15,000	$ 7,000
Contribution (loss) margin as percentage of gross sales	8.4%	(14.2%)	15.0%	10.0%

The analysis indicates that customers' profitability (loss) contribution varies widely from (14.2%) to 15.0%. Immediate attention to Chain 2 is required which is currently showing a loss contribution. The chain has a disproportionate number of both regular orders and rush orders. Villeagas should work with the management of Chain 2 to find ways to reduce the number of orders, while maintaining or increasing the sales volume. If this is not possible, Villeagas should consider dropping Chain 2, if it can save the customer-related costs.

Chain 1 has a disproportionate number of the items returned as well as sale returns. The causes of these should be investigated so that the profitability contribution of Chain 1 could be improved.

5-26 (30 min.) **ABC, product costing at banks, cross-subsidization.**

1.

	Robinson	Skerrett	Farrel	Total
Revenues				
Spread revenue on annual basis (3% ×; $1,100, $800, $25,000)	$ 33	$ 24	$750.0	$ 807.0
Monthly fee charges ($20 ×; 0, 12, 0)	0	240	0.0	240.0
Total revenues	33	264	750.0	1,047.0
Costs				
Deposit/withdrawal with teller $2.50 × 40; 50; 5	100	125	12.5	237.5
Deposit/withdrawal with ATM $0.80 × 10; 20; 16	8	16	12.8	36.8
Deposit/withdrawal on prearranged basis: $0.50 × 0; 12; 60	0	6	30.0	36.0
Bank cheques written $8.00 × 9; 3; 2	72	24	16.0	112.0
Foreign currency drafts $12.00 × 4; 1; 6	48	12	72.0	132.0
Inquiries $1.50 × 10; 18; 9	15	27	13.5	55.5
Total costs	243	210	156.8	609.8
Operating income	$(210)	$ 54	$593.2	$ 437.2

The assumption that the Robinson and Farrel accounts exceed $1,000 every month and the Skerrett account is less than $1,000 each month means the monthly charges apply only to Skerrett.

One student with a banking background noted that in this solution 100% of the spread is attributed to the "borrowing side of the bank." He noted that often the spread is divided between the "borrowing side" and the "lending side" of the bank.

2.   Cross-subsidization across individual Premier Accounts occurs when profits made on some accounts are offset by losses on other accounts. The aggregate profitability on the three customers is $437.20. The Farrel account is highly profitable ($593.20), while the Robinson account is sizably unprofitable.

FIB should be very concerned about the cross-subsidization. Competition likely would "understand" that high-balance low-activity type accounts (such as Farrel) are highly profitable. Offering free services to these customers is not likely to retain these accounts if other banks offer higher interest rates. Competition likely will reduce the interest rate spread FIB can earn on the high-balance low-activity accounts they are able to retain.

5-26 (cont'd)

3.   Possible changes FIB could make are:
   a.   Offer higher interest rates on high-balance accounts to increase FIB's competitiveness in attracting and retaining these accounts.
   b.   Introduce charges for individual services. The ABC study reports the cost of each service. FIB has to decide if it wants to price each service at cost, below cost, or above cost. If it prices above cost, it may use advertising and other means to encourage additional use of those services by customers.

5-28 (20-30 min.)   **Activity-based job-costing system.**

1.   Solution Exhibit 5-28 presents costing overviews of the previous job costing system and the refined activity-based job-costing system.

SOLUTION EXHIBIT 5-28

Job-Costing Systems for Calgary Company

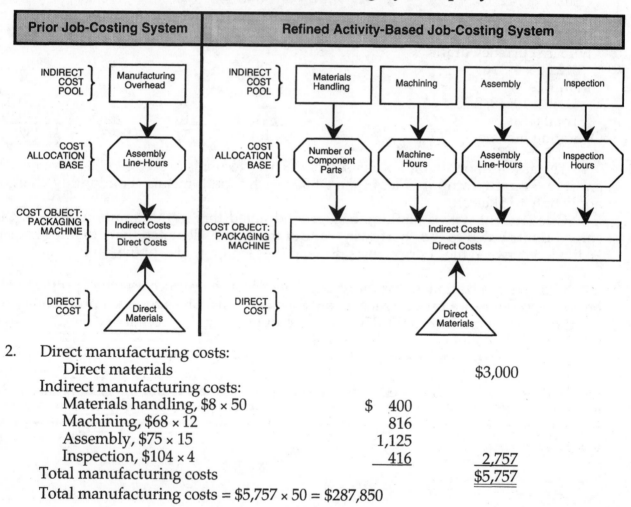

2.   Direct manufacturing costs:

Direct materials		$3,000
Indirect manufacturing costs:		
Materials handling, $8 × 50	$ 400	
Machining, $68 × 12	816	
Assembly, $75 × 15	1,125	
Inspection, $104 × 4	416	2,757
Total manufacturing costs		$5,757

Total manufacturing costs = $5,757 × 50 = $287,850

5-28 (cont'd)

3. A direct cost is a cost that is related to the particular cost object and that can be traced to it in an economically feasible way. Calgary may differ from its competitor in several ways.

    (a) Calgary uses a more automated production approach with the result that manufacturing labour provides support to the machines.

    (b) Calgary uses a less sophisticated information tracking system for manufacturing labour than its competitors.

Manufacturing labour costs are included in the individual indirect manufacturing (overhead) cost pools.

4. The refined activity-based costing system can provide information to:

    (a) Product designers—The indirect cost rates in each of the four indirect cost areas can guide decisions about how much (say) machine-hours to use versus assembly-line-hours when designing packaging machines.

    (b) Manufacturing personnel—Decisions about productivity and cost management can focus on ways to reduce the indirect cost rates (such as decisions on how to make more efficient use of machines).

    (c) Marketing personnel—The ABC approach can help guide pricing decisions and negotiations with potential customers on ways to manufacture a lower-cost packaging machine.

5-30 (15–20 min.) **Job costing with single direct-cost category, single indirect-cost pool, law firm.**

1.   Pricing decisions at Wigan Associates are heavily influenced by reported cost numbers. Suppose Wigan is bidding against Hull & Kingston for a client with a job similar to that of Widnes Coal. If the costing system overstates the costs of these jobs, Wigan may bid too high and fail to land the client. If the costing system understates the costs of these jobs, Wigan may bid low, land the client, and then lose money in handling the case.

2.   Panel A of Solution Exhibit 5-30/5-31/5-32 presents an overview of the single direct/single indirect (SD/SI) costing approach.

SOLUTION EXHIBIT 5-30/5-31/5-32
Alternative Job (Case)-Costing Approaches for Wigan Associates

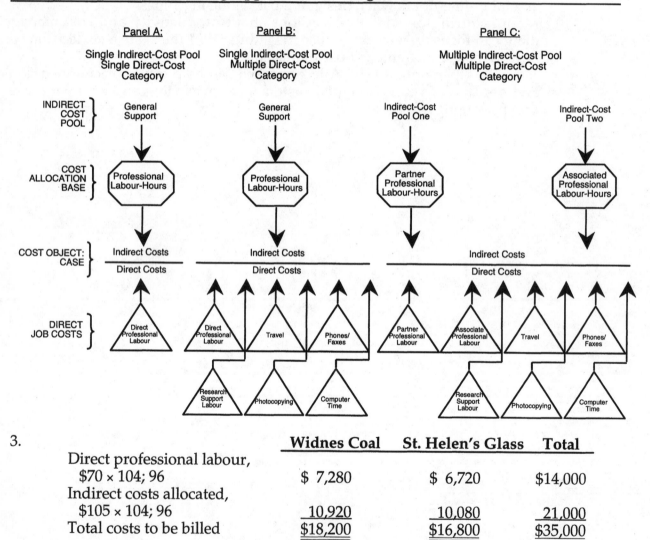

3.

	Widnes Coal	St. Helen's Glass	Total
Direct professional labour, $70 × 104; 96	$ 7,280	$ 6,720	$14,000
Indirect costs allocated, $105 × 104; 96	10,920	10,080	21,000
Total costs to be billed	$18,200	$16,800	$35,000

5-32 (30 min.) **Job costing with multiple direct-cost categories, multiple indirect-cost pools, law firm (continuation of 5-30 and 5-31).**

1. Panel C of the Solution Exhibit to 5/30/5-31/5-32 presents the costing overview for the multiple direct/multiple indirect (MD/MI) approach.

2.

	Widnes Coal	St. Helen's Glass	Total
Direct costs:			
Partner professional labour, $100 × 24; 56	$ 2,400	$ 5,600	$ 8,000
Manager professional labour, $50 × 80; 40	4,000	2,000	6,000
Research support labour	1,600	3,400	5,000
Computer time	500	1,300	1,800
Travel and allowances	600	4,400	5,000
Telephones/faxes	200	1,000	1,200
Photocopying	250	750	1,000
Total direct costs	$ 9,550	$18,450	$28,000
Indirect costs allocated:			
Indirect costs for partners, $57.50 × 24; 56	$ 1,380	$ 3,220	$ 4,600
Indirect costs for associates, $20 × 80; 40	1,600	800	2,400
Total indirect costs	2,980	4,020	7,000
Total costs to be billed	$12,530	$22,470	$35,000

	Widnes Coal	St. Helen's Glass	Total
Summary of data:			
SD/SI Approach			
Single direct cost/ Single indirect cost pool	$18,200	$16,800	$35,000
MD/MI Approach			
Multiple direct costs/ Multiple indirect cost pools	$12,530	$22,470	$35,000

The MD/MI approach has a higher percentage of direct costs to total costs than does the SD/SI approach:

	Direct Costs / Total Costs	Indirect Costs / Total Costs
SD/SI	40.0%	60.0%
MD/MI	80.0%	20.0%

The higher the percentage of costs directly traced to each case, the more accurate will be the product cost of each individual case.

The Widnes and St. Helen's cases differ in how they use "resource areas" of Wigan Associates:

	Widnes Coal	**St. Helen's Glass**
Partner professional labour	30.0%	70.0%
Associate professional labour	66.7	33.3
Research support labour	32.0	68.0
Computer time	27.8	72.2
Travel and allowances	12.0	88.0
Telephones/faxes	16.7	83.3
Photocopying	25.0	75.0

The Widnes Coal case makes relatively low use of the higher-cost partners but relatively higher use of the lower-cost associates than does St. Helen's Glass. The Widnes Coal case also makes relatively lower use of the support labour, computer time, travel, phones/faxes, and photocopying resource areas than does the St. Helen's Glass case.

The SD/SI approach imposes an averaging of the resources used in several (or all) of the seven "resource areas" recognized in MD/MI. The assumed use of resources in each of the seven "resource areas" by the SD/SI and MD/MI approaches are:

	SD/SI		**MD/MI**	
	Widnes	**St. Helen's**	**Widnes**	**St.Helen's**
Partners prof. labour	52.0%	48.0%	30.0%	70.0%
Associate prof. labour	52.0	48.0	66.7	33.3
Research support labour	52.0	48.0	32.0	68.0
Computer time	52.0	48.0	27.8	72.2
Travel and allowances	52.0	48.0	12.0	88.0
Telephones/faxes	52.0	48.0	16.7	83.3
Photocopying	52.0	48.0	25.0	75.0

5-32 (cont'd)

3. The specific areas where the MD/MI approach can provide better information for decisions at Wigan Associates include:

    a.   *Pricing and product (case) emphasis decisions.* In a bidding situation using SD/SI data, Wigan may win legal cases on which it will subsequently lose money. It may also not win legal cases on which it would make money with a lower-priced bid. MD/MI signals to senior managers those legal cases that are the most profitable; these signals can be used in decisions where Wigan should increase its business development efforts.

        From a strategic viewpoint, SD/SI exposes Wigan Associates to cherry-picking by competitors. Other law firms may focus exclusively on Widnes Coal-type cases and take sizable amounts of "profitable" business from Wigan Associates. MD/MI reduces the likelihood of Wigan Associates losing cases on which it would have made money.

    b.   *Client relationships.* MD/MI provides a better "road map" for clients to understand how costs are accumulated at Wigan Associates. Wigan can use this road map when meeting with clients to plan the work to be done on a case *before* it commences. Clients can negotiate ways to get a lower-cost case from Wigan, given the information in MD/MI—for example, (a) use a higher proportion of manager labour time and a lower proportion of partner time, and (b) use fax machines more and air travel less. If clients are informed in advance how costs will be accumulated, there is less likelihood of disputes about bills submitted to them *after* the work is done.

    c.   *Cost control.* The MD/MI approach better highlights the individual cost areas at Wigan Associates than does the SD/SI approach:

	MD/MI	SD/SI
Number of direct cost categories	7	1
Number of indirect cost categories	2	1
Total	9	2

MD/MI is more likely to promote better cost-control practices than SD/SI (as the nine cost categories in MD/MI may differ in terms of how to effectively manage costs).

5-34 (15 min.) Activity-based job costing.

1. An overview of the product-costing system is:

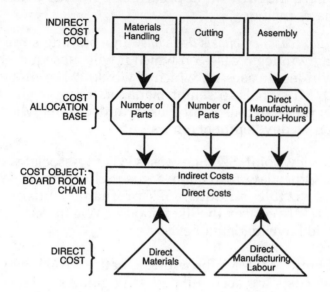

	Executive Chair	Chairperson Chair
Direct manufacturing costs:		
Direct materials	$ 600,000	$25,000
Direct manufacturing labour,		
$20 × 7,500; 500	150,000	10,000
Direct manufacturing costs	750,000	35,000
Indirect manufacturing costs:		
Materials handling,		
$0.25 × 100,000; 3,500	25,000	875
Cutting,		
$2.50 × 100,000; 3,500	250,000	8,750
Assembly,		
$25.00 × 7,500; 500	187,500	12,500
Indirect manufacturing costs	462,500	22,125
Total manufacturing costs	$1,212,500	$57,125

Unit Costs

Executive chair: $1,212,500 ÷ 5,000 = $242.50
Chairperson chair: $57,125 ÷ 100 = $571.25

2.

	Executive Chair	Chairperson Chair
Upstream costs	$ 60.00	$146.00
Manufacturing costs	242.50	571.25
Downstream costs	110.00	236.00
Total costs	$412.50	$953.25

5-36 (40 min.) **ABC, health care.**

1a.
$$\text{Medical supplies indirect cost rate} = \frac{\text{Medical supplies cost}}{\text{Number of physicians (or physician years)}} = \frac{\$300,000}{6} = \$50,000 \text{ per physician}$$

$$\text{General overhead rate} = \frac{\text{General overhead rate}}{\text{Total physician, psychologist, and nurse labour cost}} = \frac{\$1,275,000}{\$2,125,000} = 60\%$$

b.   The cost of each job (program) follows.

	Alcoholic Rehabilitation	Drug Rehabilitation	Children's Clinical	After-Care
Direct labour:				
Physicians at $100,000	—	$200,000	$ 400,000	—
Psychologist at $50,000	$300,000	200,000	—	$ 450,000
Nurse at $25,000	100,000	150,000	100,000	225,000
Total direct labour	400,000	550,000	500,000	675,000
Medical supplies:				
at $50,000 per physician year	—	100,000	200,000	—
General overhead:				
at 60% of direct labour	240,000	330,000	300,000	405,000
Total costs	$640,000	$980,000	$1,000,000	$1,080,000

The total cost of all programs is $3,700,000. The costs per patient-year for the alcoholic and drug programs are:

	Alcohol	Drug
Total costs	$640,000	$980,000
Divided by patient-years of service	40	50
Cost per patient-year	$16,000	$19,600

c.   Drug rehabilitation is 22.5% higher ($3,600 ÷ $16,000) than alcohol rehabilitation. Therefore, Clayton should apply additional funds to alcohol rehabilitation.

2a.   The activity-based approach would allocate costs to Alcohol and Drug Programs using the appropriate cost drivers and cost-driver rates.

$$\text{Medical supplies rate} = \frac{\text{Medical supplies costs}}{\text{Total number of patient-years}} = \frac{\$300,000}{200} = \$1,500/\text{patient-year}$$

$$\text{Rent and clinic maintenance rate} = \frac{\text{Rent and clinic mtce. costs}}{\text{Total amount of square feet of space}} = \frac{\$200,000}{40,000} = \$5 \text{ per square metre}$$

5-36 (cont'd)

$$\text{Admin. cost rate for patient charts, food, and laundry} = \frac{\text{Admin. costs to manage patient charts, food, laundry}}{\text{Total number of patient-years}} = \frac{\$800,000}{200} = \$4,000 \text{ per patient}$$

$$\text{Laboratory service rate} = \frac{\text{Laboratory services costs}}{\text{Total number of laboratory tests}} = \frac{\$275,000}{5,500} = \$50 \text{ per test}$$

These cost drivers are chosen as the ones that best match the descriptions of why the costs arise. Other answers are acceptable, provided clear explanations are given.

b.   Activity-based costs for each program and cost per patient-year of the alcohol and drug program follow:

	Alcohol	Drug	Children	After-Care
Direct labour				
Physicians at $100,000 × 0; 2; 4; 0	—	$200,000	$400,000	—
Psychologists at $50,000 × 6; 4; 0; 9	$300,000	200,000	—	$ 450,000
Nurses at $25,000 × 4; 6; 4; 9	100,000	150,000	100,000	225,000
Direct labour costs	400,000	550,000	500,000	675,000
Medical supplies[1] $1,500 × 40; 50; 50; 60	60,000	75,000	75,000	90,000
Rent and clinic maintenance[2] $5 × 9,000; 9,000; 10,000; 12,000	45,000	45,000	50,000	60,000
Administrative costs to manage patient charts, food, and laundry[3] $4,000 × 40; 50; 50; 60	160,000	200,000	200,000	240,000
Laboratory services[4] $50 × 400; 1,400; 3,000; 700	20,000	70,000	150,000	35,000
Total costs	$685,000	$940,000	$975,000	$1,100,000
Divided by number of patient-years	÷ 40	÷ 50		
Cost per patient-year	$ 17,125	$ 18,800		

[1]Allocated using patient-years
[2]Allocated using square metres of space
[3]Allocated using patient-years
[4]Allocated using number of laboratory tests

c.   The refining of the cost system (more direct tracing, more cost pools, and better cost drivers) results in the cost per drug patient per year being lower ($18,800) and the cost per alcohol patient per year being higher ($17,125). Using these numbers, the cost per drug patient per year would be only 9.8% ($1,675 ÷ $17,125) higher than alcohol rehabilitation. In these circumstances, the board's staff would have preferred to use the additional funds for drug rehabilitation (rather than alcohol rehabilitation as we concluded in requirement 1). The choice of cost system will have real effects on the allocation of Uppervale Health Centre's resources.

3.   The ABC system more accurately allocates greater costs to the alcohol rehabilitation program because it identifies better cost drivers. For example, the ABC system allocates $60,000 of medical supplies costs to alcohol rehabilitation, whereas the existing system allocates $0. The existing system allocates medical supplies costs based on physician labour-hours and physicians spent 0 hours in alcohol rehabilitation. Nevertheless, patients in the alcohol program required medical supplies. The ABC system allocates medical supplies costs based on patient-years, a more plausible cost driver. Similarly, the ABC system chooses cost drivers for the other overhead costs to have a better cause-and-effect relationship between the cost drivers and the costs. Of course, Clayton should continue to evaluate if better cost drivers can be found than the ones they have identified so far.

By implementing the ABC system, Clayton can gain a more detailed understanding of costs and cost drivers. This is valuable information from a cost management perspective. The system can yield insight into the efficiencies with which various activities are performed. Clayton can then examine if redundant activities can be eliminated or their efficiencies improved. For example, by tracking food and laundry costs per patient-day, Clayton can study trends and work toward improving the efficiency of these services.

4.   The concern with using costs per patient per year as the rule to allocate resources between drug and alcohol programs is that it emphasizes "input" to the exclusion of "outputs" or effectiveness of the programs. After all, Clayton's goal is to cure patients while controlling costs, not minimize costs per patient-year. The problem, of course, is measuring outputs in nonprofit organizations.

Unlike in many manufacturing companies, where the outputs are obvious because they are tangible and measurable, the outputs of nonprofit organizations are more difficult to measure. Examples are "cured" mental patients as distinguished from "processed" or "discharged" mental patients, "educated" as distinguished from "partially educated" students, and so on.

Also, an argument could be made to allocate funds where the need is more critical, drug or alcohol.

5-38 (30 min.) **Plantwide, department, and activity-cost rates.**

1. Budgeted manufacturing overhead rates:

    i. Plantwide rate:

    $$\frac{\$340,000}{20,000} = \$17.00 \text{ per direct labour-hour}$$

    ii. Departmental rates:

    Department 1: $\$240,000 \div 10,000 = \$24.00/\text{hour}$
    Department 2: $\$100,000 \div 10,000 = \$10.00/\text{hour}$

    Manufacturing overhead portion of ending inventories:

    i. Using plantwide overhead rate:
       800 units × 5 hours × $17.00 $68,000

    ii. Using department overhead rates:

    Product A: $200 \times [(4 \times \$24.00) + (1 \times \$10.00)] =$ $21,200
    Product B: $600 \times [(1 \times \$24.00) + (4 \times \$10.00)] =$ <u>38,400</u>
                                                                       $59,600

    The difference in inventory costs due to the different methods of allocating manufacturing overhead is $8,400 ($68,000 − $59,600).

2. *Product A*

	Plantwide Overhead Rate	Department Overhead Rates
Direct materials	$120.00	$120.00
Direct manufacturing labour	80.00	80.00
Manufacturing overhead:		
$17 × 5	85.00	—
($24 × 4) + ($10 × 1)	—	106.00
Total manufacturing costs	285.00	306.00
Markup		
($285 × 120%; $306 × 120%)	342.00	367.20
Selling price	$627.00	$673.20

5-38 (cont'd)

Product B

	Plantwide Overhead Rate	Department Overhead Rate
Direct materials	$150.00	$150.00
Direct manufacturing labour	80.00	80.00
Manufacturing overhead:		
$17 × 5	85.00	—
($24 × 1) + ($10 × 4)	—	64.00
Total manufacturing costs	315.00	294.00
Markup		
($315 × 120%; $294 × 120%)	378.00	352.80
Selling price	$693.00	$646.80

3. Sayther Company should use budgeted department manufacturing overhead rates because:

   a.   The two manufacturing departments differ sizably in their overhead cost structures, despite having the same budgeted direct manufacturing labour-hours. Department 1 has $240,000 budgeted overhead, and Department 2 has $100,000 budgeted overhead.

   b.   The two products use resources in the two manufacturing departments quite differently. The direct manufacturing labour-hours used in each department are:

Department	**Product A**	**Product B**
1	4	1
2	1	4

Differences a. and b. mean that more refined product costs will be calculated with budgeted department manufacturing overhead rates.

4.   Sayther should further subdivide the department cost pools into activity-cost pools if (a) significant costs are incurred on *different* activities within the department, (b) the different activities have different cost-allocation bases, and (c) different products use the different activities in different proportions.

5-40   (50 min.)   ABC, implementation, ethics.

1.   Applewood Electronics should not emphasize the Regal model and phase out the Monarch model. Under activity-based costing, the Regal model has an operating income percentage of less than 3%, while the Monarch model has an operating income percentage of nearly 43%.

Cost driver rates for the various activities identified in the activity-based costing (ABC) system are as follows:

Soldering	$ 942,000	÷	1,570,000	=	$0.60 per solder point
Shipments	860,000	÷	20,000	=	43.00 per shipment
Quality control	1,240,000	÷	77,500	=	16.00 per inspection
Purchase orders	950,400	÷	190,080	=	5.00 per order
Machine power	57,600	÷	192,000	=	0.30 per machine-hour
Machine setups	750,000	÷	30,000	=	25.00 per setup

5-40 (cont'd)

Applewood Electronics
Calculation of Costs of Each Model
under Activity-Based Costing

	Monarch	Regal
Direct costs		
Direct materials ($208 × 22,000; $584 × 4,000)	$ 4,576,000	$2,336,000
Direct manufacturing labour ($18 × 22,000; $42 × 4,000)	396,000	168,000
Machine costs ($144 × 22,000; $72 × 4,000)	3,168,000	288,000
Total direct costs	8,140,000	2,792,000
Indirect costs		
Soldering ($0.60 × 1,185,000; 385,000)	711,000	231,000
Shipments ($43 × 16,200; 3,800)	696,600	163,400
Quality control ($16 × 56,200; 21,300)	899,200	340,800
Purchase orders ($5 × 80,100; 109,980)	400,500	549,900
Machine power ($0.30 × 176,000; 16,000)	52,800	4,800
Machine setups ($25 × 16,000; 14,000)	400,000	350,000
Total indirect costs	3,160,100	1,639,900
Total costs	$11,300,100	$4,431,900

Profitability analysis

	Monarch	Regal	Total
Revenues	$19,800,000	$4,560,000	$24,360,000
Cost of goods sold	11,300,100	4,431,900	15,732,000
Gross margin	$ 8,499,900	$ 128,100	$ 8,628,000
Per-unit calculations:			
Units sold	22,000	4,000	
Selling price	$900.00	$1,140.00	
Cost of goods sold ($11,300,100 ÷ 22,000; $4,431,900 ÷ 4,000)	513.64	1,107.98	
Gross margin	$386.36	$ 32.02	
Gross margin percentage	42.9%	2.8%	

2. Applewood's existing costing system allocates all manufacturing overhead other than machine costs on the basis of machine-hours, an output unit-level cost driver. Consequently, the more machine-hours per unit that a product needs, the greater is the manufacturing overhead allocated to it. Because Monarch uses twice the number of machine-hours per unit compared with Regal, a large amount of manufacturing overhead is allocated to Monarch.

The ABC analysis recognizes several batch-level cost drivers such as purchase orders, shipments, and setups. Regal uses these resources much more intensively than Monarch. The ABC system recognizes Regal's use of these overhead resources. Consider, for example, purchase order costs. The existing system allocates these costs on the basis of machine-hours. As a result, each unit of Monarch is allocated twice the purchase order costs of each unit of Regal. The ABC system allocates $400,500 of purchase order costs to Monarch [equal to $18.20 ($400,500 ÷ 22,000) per unit] and $549,900 of purchase order costs to Regal [equal to $137.48 ($549,900 ÷ 4,000) per unit]. Each unit of Regal uses 7.55 ($137.48 ÷ $18.20) times the purchase order costs of each unit of Monarch.

Recognizing Regal's more intense use of manufacturing overhead results in Regal, showing a much lower profitability under the ABC system. By the same token, the ABC analysis shows that Monarch is quite profitable. The existing costing system overcosted Monarch, and so made it appear less profitable.

3. Duval's comments about ABC implementation are valid. When designing and implementing ABC systems, managers and management accountants need to trade off the costs of the system against its benefits. Adding more activities makes the system harder to understand and more costly to implement but would probably improve the accuracy of cost information, which, in turn, would help Applewood make better decisions. Similarly, using inspection-hours and setup-hours as allocation bases would also probably lead to more accurate cost information but would increase measurement costs.

4. Activity-based management (ABM) is the use of information from activity-based costing to make improvements in a firm. For example, a firm could revise product prices on the basis of revised cost information. For the long term, activity-based costing can assist management in making decisions regarding the viability of product lines, distribution channels, marketing strategies, etc. ABM highlights possible improvements, including reduction or elimination of non-value-added activities, selecting lower cost activities, sharing activities with other products, and eliminating waste. ABM is an integrated approach that focuses management's attention on activities with the ultimate aim of continuous improvement. As a whole-company philosophy, ABM focuses on strategic, as well as tactical and operational activities of the company.

5. Incorrect reporting of ABC costs with the goal of retaining both the Monarch and Regal product lines is unethical. In assessing the situation, the management accountant could consider the following:

Competence
Clear reports using relevant and reliable information should be prepared. Preparing reports on the basis of incorrect costs in order to retain product lines violates competence standards. It is unethical for Benzo to change the ABC system with the specific goal of reporting different product cost numbers that Duval favours.

5-40 (cont'd)

Integrity

The management accountant has a responsibility to avoid actual or apparent conflicts of interest and advise all appropriate parties of any potential conflict. Benzo may be tempted to change the product cost numbers to please Duval, the Division President. This action, however, would violate the responsibility for integrity.

Objectivity

The management accountant should require that information should be fairly and objectively communicated and that all relevant information should be disclosed. From a management accountant's standpoint, adjusting the product cost numbers to make both the Monarch and Regal lines look profitable would violate the standard of objectivity.

Benzo should indicate to Duval that the product cost calculations are, indeed, appropriate. If Duval still insists on modifying the product cost numbers, Benzo should raise the matter with one of Duval's superiors. If, after taking all these steps, there is continued pressure to modify product cost numbers, Benzo should consider resigning from the company, rather than engage in unethical behaviour.

CHAPTER 6
MASTER BUDGET AND RESPONSIBILITY ACCOUNTING

6-2   The budgeting cycle includes the following elements:
  a.   Planning the performance of the organization as a whole as well as its subunits. The entire management team agrees as to what is expected.
  b.   Providing a frame of reference, a set of specific expectations against which the actual results can be compared.
  c.   Investigating variations from the plans. If necessary, corrective action follows investigation.
  d.   Planning again, considering feedback and changed conditions.

6-4   Budgeted performance is better than past performance for judging managers. Why? Mainly because inefficiencies included in past results can be detected and eliminated in budgeting. Also, new opportunities in the future, which did not exist in the past, may be ignored if past performance is used.

6-6   A company that shares its own internal budget information with other companies can gain multiple benefits. One benefit is better coordination with suppliers, which can reduce the likelihood of supply shortages. Better coordination with customers can result in increased sales as demand by customers is less likely to exceed supply. Better coordination across the whole supply chain can also help a company reduce inventories and thus reduce the costs of holding inventories.

6-8   A *rolling budget* is a budget or plan that is always available for a specified future period by adding a month, quarter, or year in the future as the month, quarter or year just ended is dropped. For example, a 12-month rolling budget for the March 2000 to February 2001 period becomes a 12-month rolling budget for the April 2000 to March 2001 period the next month, and so on.

6-10   The revenue budget is typically the cornerstone for budgeting because production (and hence costs) and inventory levels generally depend on the forecasted level of demand and revenue.

6-12   Factors reducing the effectiveness of budgeting of companies include:
  1.   Lack of a well-defined strategy,
  2.   Lack of a clear linkage of strategy to operational plans,
  3.   Lack of individual accountability for results, and
  4.   Lack of meaningful performance measures.

6-14   Non-output-based cost drivers can be incorporated into budgeting by the use of activity-based budgeting (ABB). ABB focuses on the budgeted cost of activities necessary to produce and sell products and services. Non-output-based cost drivers, such as the number of part numbers, number of batches, and number of new products, can be used with ABB.

6-16   (15 min.)   **Production budget (in units), fill in the missing numbers.**

	Model 101	Model 201	Model 301
Budgeted sales	180^G	193^c	867^G
Add target ending FGI	14^a	6^G	33^G
Total requirements	194^G	199^G	900^e
Deduct beginning FGI	11^G	8^G	45^f
Units to be produced	183^b	191^d	855^G

^{a} 194 – 180 = 14 ^{d} 199 – 8 = 191   G = given
^{b} 194 – 11 = 183 ^{e} 867 + 33 = 900
^{c} 199 – 6 = 193 ^{f} 900 – 855 = 45

6-18   (5 min.)   **Direct materials budget.**

Direct materials to be used in production (bottles)	1,500,000
Add target ending direct materials inventory (bottles)	50,000
Total requirements (bottles)	1,550,000
Deduct beginning direct materials inventory (bottles)	20,000
Direct materials to be purchased (bottles)	1,530,000

6-20   (30 min.)   **Sales and production budget.**

1.

	Selling Price	Units Sold	Total Revenues
1-litre bottles	$0.25	$4,800,000^a$	$1,200,000
16-litre units	1.50	$1,200,000^b$	1,800,000
			$3,000,000

^{a} 400,000 × 12 months = 4,800,000
^{b} 100,000 × 12 months = 1,200,000

2.

Budgeted unit sales (1-litre bottles)	4,800,000
Add target ending finished goods inventory	600,000
Total requirements	5,400,000
Deduct beginning finished goods inventory	900,000
Units to be produced	4,500,000

3.

$$\text{Beginning inventory} = \text{Budgeted sales} + \text{Target ending inventory} - \text{Budgeted production}$$

= 1,200,000 + 200,000 – 1,300,000

= 100,000 16-litre units

6-22 (15-20 min.) **Revenue, production, and purchases budget.**

1. 800,000 motorcycles × 400,000 yen = 320,000,000,000 yen

2.
Budgeted sales (units)	800,000
Add target ending finished goods inventory	100,000
Total requirements	900,000
Deduct beginning finished goods inventory	120,000
Units to be produced	780,000

3.
Direct materials to be used in production, 780,000 × 2	1,560,000
Add target ending direct materials inventory	30,000
Total requirements	1,590,000
Deduct beginning direct materials inventory	20,000
Direct materials to be purchased	1,570,000
Cost per wheel in yen	16,000
Direct materials purchase cost in yen	25,120,000,000

Note the relatively small inventory of wheels. In Japan, suppliers tend to be located very close to the major manufacturer. Inventories are controlled by just-in-time and similar systems. Indeed, some direct materials inventories are almost nonexistent.

6-24 (20-30 min.) **Activity-based budgeting.**

1.

	Soft Drinks	Fresh Produce	Packaged Food	Total
Ordering				
$90 × 14; 24; 14	$1,260	$2,160	$1,260	$4,680
Delivery				
$82 × 12; 62; 19	984	5,084	1,558	7,626
Shelf-stocking				
$21 × 16; 172; 94	336	3,612	1,974	5,922
Customer-support				
$0.18 × 4,600; 34,200; 10,750	828	6,156	1,935	8,919
	$3,408	$17,012	$6,727	$27,147

2.   An ABB approach recognizes how different products require different mixes of support activities. The relative percentage of how each product area uses the cost driver in each activity area is:

Activity Area	Soft Drinks	Fresh Produce	Packaged Food	Total
Ordering	26.9	46.2	26.9	100.0%
Delivery	12.9	66.7	20.4	100.0
Shelf-stacking	5.7	61.0	33.3	100.0
Customer-support	9.3	69.0	21.7	100.0

By recognizing these differences, FS managers are better able to budget for different unit sales levels and different mix of individual product-line items sold. Using a single cost driver (such as COGS) assumes homogeneity across product lines which does not occur at FS.

Other benefits cited by managers include: (1) better identification of resource needs, (2) clearer linking of costs with staff responsibilities, and (3) identification of budgetary slack.

6-26 (20 min.)   **Budgeting and behaviour.**

1. (a) Gain additional insight into the strategy of an organization. Exhibit 6-1 shows arrows pointing both ways between strategy analysis and long-term planning and short-term planning. Detailed analysis for budgeting can sometimes highlight strategy assumptions (such as cost levels and demand levels) that are not likely to hold.
   (b) Anticipate resource demands in a timely way. Budgeting can highlight working capital shortages, cash shortages, personnel shortages, and so on. Early warning signals can enable a company to take action to avoid having small problems become large problems.

   (c) Improve the communication level in an organization. The budgeting process itself can assist in having diverse groups gain a better understanding of how other groups affect their performance. Sharing budgets across organizations in a supply chain can help a company better meet end-point customer demand. Communication with suppliers can reduce parts shortages.

2. Factors to consider when preparing sales forecasts include:
   (a) Any constraining variables on sales. For example, if demand outstrips available productive capacity or a key component is in short supply, the sales forecast should be based on the maximum units that could be produced.
   (b) Information from customers about their new product developments and advertising plans.
   (c) Feedback from customers about satisfaction with a company's products vis-à-vis satisfaction levels for the products of competitors.
   (d) Likely new product releases by competitors or new entrants into a market.

6-28 (30 min.)   **Appendix: Cash flow analysis**

1.   The cash that TabComp Inc. can expect to collect during April 2003 is calculated below:

April cash receipts:	
April cash sales ($400,000 × .25)	$100,000
April credit card sales ($400,000 × .30 × .96)	115,200
Collections on account:	
March ($480,000 × .45 × .70)	151,200
February ($500,000 × .45 × .28)	63,000
January (uncollectible—not relevant)	0
Total collections	$429,400

2.   (a) The projected number of the MZB-33 computer hardware units that TabComp Inc. will order on January 25, 2003, is calculated as follows.

	MZB-33 Units
March sales	110
Plus: Ending inventory[a]	27
Total needed	137
Less: Beginning inventory[b]	33
Projected purchases in units	104

[a] .30 × 90 unit sales in April

[b] .30 × 110 unit sales in March

(b) Purchase price =

$3,000 selling price per unit[c]	
× 60%	$ 1,800
× Projected unit purchases	104
Total MZB-33 purchases	$187,200

[c] Selling price = $2,025,000 ÷ 675 units

= $3,000 per unit

(c) In April 2003.

3.   Monthly cash budgets are prepared by companies such as TabComp Inc. in order to plan for their cash needs. This means identifying when both excess cash and cash shortages may occur. A company needs to know when cash shortages will occur so that prior arrangements can be made with lending institutions in order to have cash available for borrowing when the company needs it. At the same time, a company should be aware of when there is excess cash available for investment or for repaying loans.

6-30 (20 min.) **Continuous improvement, budgeting (continuation of 6-29).**

Areas where continuous improvement might be incorporated into the budgeting process:

(a)   Direct materials. An improvement in either usage or price could be budgeted. For example, the budgeted usage amounts could be related to the maximum improvement of 1 square foot for either desk:

- Executive: 16 square feet – 15 square feet minimum = 1 square foot
- Chairperson: 25 square feet – 24 square feet minimum = 1 square foot

Thus, a 1% reduction target per month could be:

- Executive: 15 square feet + (0.99 × 1) = 15.99
- Chairperson: 24 square feet + (0.99 × 1) = 24.99

Some students suggested the 1% be applied to the 16 and 25 square foot amounts. This is incorrect since, after several improvement cycles, the budgeted amount would be less than the minimum desk requirements.

(b)   Direct manufacturing labour. The budgeted usage of 3 hours/5 hours could be continuously revised on a monthly basis. Similarly, the manufacturing labour cost per hour of $30 could be continuously revised down. The former appears more feasible than the latter.

(c)   Variable manufacturing overhead. By budgeting more efficient use of the allocation base, a signal is given for continuous improvement. A second approach is to budget continuous improvement in the budgeted variable overhead cost per unit of the allocation base.

(d)   Fixed manufacturing overhead. The approach here is to budget for reductions in the year-to-year amounts of fixed overhead. If these costs are appropriately classified as fixed, then they are more difficult to adjust down on a monthly basis.

6-32 (30-40 min.) **Revenue and production budgets.**

This is a routine budgeting problem. The key to its solution is to compute the correct <u>quantities</u> of finished goods and direct materials. Use the following general formula:

$$\begin{pmatrix} \text{Budgeted} \\ \text{production} \\ \text{or purchases} \end{pmatrix} = \begin{pmatrix} \text{Target} \\ \text{ending} \\ \text{inventory} \end{pmatrix} + \begin{pmatrix} \text{Budgeted} \\ \text{sales or} \\ \text{materials used} \end{pmatrix} - \begin{pmatrix} \text{Beginning} \\ \text{inventory} \end{pmatrix}$$

1.

Scarborough Corporation
Revenue Budget
For 2001

	Units	Price	Total
Thingone	60,000	$165	$ 9,900,000
Thingtwo	40,000	250	10,000,000
Projected sales			$19,900,000

2.

Scarborough Corporation
Production Budget (in units)
For 2004

	Thingone	**Thingtwo**
Budgeted sales in units	60,000	40,000
Add target finished goods inventories, December 31, 2004	25,000	9,000
Total requirements	85,000	49,000
Deduct finished goods inventories, January 1, 2004	20,000	8,000
Units to be produced	65,000	41,000

3.

Scarborough Corporation
Direct Materials Purchases Budget (in quantities) for 2004

	Direct Materials		
	A	**B**	**C**
Direct materials to be used in production			
• Thingone (budgeted production of 65,000 units times 4 kg of A, 2 kg of B)	260,000	130,000	--
• Thingtwo (budgeted production of 41,000 units times 5 kg of A, 3 kg of B, 1 unit of C)	205,000	123,000	41,000
Total	465,000	253,000	41,000
Add target ending inventories, December 31, 2004	36,000	32,000	7,000
Total requirements in quantities	501,000	285,000	48,000
Deduct beginning inventories, January 1, 2004	32,000	29,000	6,000
Direct materials to be purchased (quantities)	469,000	256,000	42,000

6-32 (cont'd)

4.
Scarborough Corporation
Direct Materials Purchases Budget (in dollars) for 2004

	Budgeted Purchases (Quantities)	Expected Purchase Price per unit	Total
Direct material A	469,000	$12	$5,628,000
Direct material B	256,000	5	1,280,000
Direct material C	42,000	3	126,000
Budgeted purchases			$7,034,000

5.
Scarborough Corporation
Direct Manufacturing Labour Budget for 2004

	Budgeted Production (Units)	Direct Manufacturing Labour-Hours per Unit	Total Hours	Rate per Hour	Total
Thingone	65,000	2	130,000	$12	$1,560,000
Thingtwo	41,000	3	123,000	16	1,968,000
Total					$3,528,000

6.

Scarborough Corporation
Budgeted Finished Goods Inventory
At December 31, 2004

Thingone:

Direct materials costs:		
A, 4 kilograms at $12	$48	
B, 2 kilograms at $5	10	$ 58
Direct manufacturing labour costs,		
2 hours at $12		24
Manufacturing overhead costs at $20 per direct		
manufacturing labour-hour (2 hours)		40
Budgeted manufacturing costs per unit		$122

Finished goods inventory of Thingone	
$122 × 25,000 units	$3,050,000

Thingtwo:

Direct materials costs:		
A, 5 kilograms at $12	$60	
B, 3 kilograms at $5	15	
C, 1 each at $3	3	$ 78
Direct manufacturing labour costs,		
3 hours at $16		48
Manufacturing overhead costs at $20 per direct		
manufacturing labour-hour (3 hours)		60
Budgeted manufacturing costs per unit		$186

Finished goods inventory of Thingtwo	
$186 × 9,000 units	1,674,000
Budgeted finished goods inventory, December 31, 2004	$4,724,000

6-34 (60 min.) **Operating budget.**

1. **Schedule 1: Revenue Budget**
    for the Year Ended December 31, 2003

	Units	Selling Price	Total Revenues
Snowboards	1,000	$450	$450,000

2. **Schedule 2: Production Budget (in Units)**
    for the Year Ended December 31, 2003

	Snowboards
Budgeted unit sales (Schedule 1)	1,000
Add target ending finished goods inventory	200
Total requirements	1,200
Deduct beginning finished goods inventory	100
Units to be produced	1,100

3. **Schedule 3A: Direct Materials Usage Budget**
    for the Year Ended December 31, 2003

	Wood	Fiberglass	Total
Physical Budget			
To be used in production	5,500		
(Wood: 1,100 × 5.00 b.f.			
Fiberglass: 1,100 × 6.00 yards)		6,600	
	5,500	6,600	
Cost Budget			
Available from beginning inventory			
(Wood: 2,000 b.f. × $28.00	56,000		
Fiberglass: 1,000 yards × 4.80)		4,800	
To be used from purchases this period			
(Wood: (5,500 – 2,000) × $30.00	105,000		
Fiberglass: (6,600 – 1,000) × $5.00)		28,000	
Total cost of direct materials to be used	$161,000	$32,800	$193,800

Schedule 3B: Direct Materials Purchases Budget
For the Year Ended December 31, 2003

	Wood	Fiberglass	Total
Physical Budget			
Production usage (from Schedule 3A)	5,500	6,600	
Add target ending inventory	1,500	2,000	
Total requirements	7,000	8,600	
Deduct beginning inventory	2,000	1,000	
Purchases	5,000	7,600	
Cost Budget			
(Wood: 5,000 × $30.00	$150,000		
Fiberglass: 7,600 × $5.00)		$38,000	
	$150,000	$38,000	$188,000

6-34 (cont'd)

4. **Schedule 4: Direct Manufacturing Labour Budget**
for the Year Ended December 31, 2003

Labour Category	Cost Driver Units	DML Hours per Driver Unit	Total Hours	Wage Rate	Tot
Manufacturing Labour	1,100	5.00	5,500	$25.00	$137,

5. **Schedule 5: Manufacturing Overhead Budget**
for the Year Ended December 31, 2003

	At Budgeted Level of 5,500 Direct Manufacturing Labour-Hours
Variable manufacturing overhead costs ($7.00 × 5,500)	$ 38,500
Fixed manufacturing overhead costs	66,000
Total manufacturing overhead costs	$104,500

6. Budgeted manufacturing overhead rate: $\dfrac{\$104,500}{5,500}$ = $19.00 per hour

7. Budgeted manufacturing overhead cost per output unit: $\dfrac{\$104,500}{1,100}$ = $95.00 per output

8. **Schedule 6A: Computation of Unit Costs of Manufactured Finished Goods in 2003**

	Cost per Unit of Input[a]	Inputs[b]	Total
Direct materials			
Wood	$30.00	5.00	$150.00
Fiberglass	5.00	6.00	30.00
Direct manufacturing labour	25.00	5.00	125.00
Total manufacturing overhead			95.00
Total cost per unit			$400.00

[a]Cost is per board foot, yard, or hour.
[b]Inputs is the amount of input per board.

6-34 (cont'd)

9. **Schedule 6B: Ending Inventory Budget**
December 31, 2003

	Units	Cost per Unit	Total
Direct materials			
Wood	1,500	$ 30.00	$ 45,000
Fiberglass	2,000	5.00	10,000
Finished goods			
Snowboards	200	400.00	80,000
Total Ending Inventory			$135,000

10. **Schedule 7: Cost-of-Goods-Sold Budget**
for the Year Ended December 31, 2003

	From Schedule		Total
Beginning finished goods inventory January 1, 2003	Given		$ 37,480
Direct materials used	3A	$193,800	
Direct manufacturing labour	4	137,500	
Manufacturing overhead	5	104,500	
Cost of goods manufactured			435,800
Cost of goods available for sale			473,280
Deduct ending finished goods inventory, December 31, 2003	6B		80,000
Cost of goods sold			$393,280

11. **Budgeted Income Statement for Slopes**
for the Year Ended December 31, 2003

	From Schedule		Total
Revenues	Schedule 1		$450,000
Costs			
Cost of goods sold	Schedule 7		393,280
Gross margin			56,720
Operating costs			
Marketing costs ($250 × 30)		$ 7,500	
Other costs		30,000	37,500
Operating income			$ 19,220

6-36 (15 min.) **Responsibility of purchasing agent.**

The time lost in the plant should be charged to the purchasing department. Certainly, the plant manager could not be asked to underwrite a loss which is due to failure of delivery over which he had no supervision. Although the purchasing agent may feel that he has done everything he possibly could, he must realize that, in the whole organization, he is <u>the one</u> who is in the best position to evaluate the situation. He receives an assignment. He may accept it or reject it. But if he accepts, he must perform. If he fails, the damage is evaluated. Everybody makes mistakes. The important point is to avoid making too many mistakes and also to understand fully that the extensive control reflected in "responsibility accounting" is the necessary balance to the great freedom of action that individual executives are given.

<u>Discussions of this problem have again and again revealed a tendency among students (and among accountants and managers) to "fix the blame"—as if the variances arising from a responsibility accounting system should pinpoint misbehaviour and provide answers.</u> The point is that no accounting system or variances can provide answers. However, variances can lead to questions. In this case, in deciding where the penalty should be assigned, the student might inquire <u>who should be asked—not who should be blamed</u>.

Classroom discussions have also raised the following diverse points:

(a) Is the railway company liable?
(b) Costs of idle time are usually routinely charged to the production department. Should the information system be fine-tuned to reallocate such costs to the purchasing department?
(c) How will the purchasing managers behave in the future regarding willingness to take risks?

The text emphasizes the following: Beware of overemphasis on controllability. For example, a time-honoured theme of management is that responsibility should not be given without accompanying authority. Such a guide is a useful first step, but responsibility accounting is more far-reaching. The basic focus should be on <u>information</u> or <u>knowledge</u>, not on control. The key question is: "Who is the best informed?" Put another way, "Who is the person who can tell us the most about the specific item, regardless of ability to exert personal control?"

6-38   (20 min.) **Traditional budgeting and its critics.**

1.   Budgets can be a powerful means of coordination and communication in organizations. They help turn managers' perspectives forward. The extract is from the CEO of General Electric (John Welch).

        Exhibit 6-6 presents six criticisms of traditional budgeting. These criticisms echo some of the concerns raised by Welch. The proposals for change in Exhibit 6-6 indicate that the solution to problems with traditional budgeting is <u>not</u> to dispense with budgeting. This is "throwing the baby out with the bath water." Rather the solution is to revamp budgeting to incorporate stretch goals. Six months after the quoted interview with Welch, another General Electric executive noted how they "get more from people."

   a.   By definition, stretch goals are very difficult to meet. Don't punish people for not hitting them.
   b.   Don't set goals that stretch your employees crazily.
   c.   Understand that stretch targets can unexpectedly affect other parts of the organization.
   d.   Don't give tough stretch goals to those people already pushing themselves to the limit.
   e.   Share the wealth generated by reaching stretch goals.

Budgets are one mechanism by which some of these approaches can be implemented. For example, budgets highlight connections across parts of organizations.

2.   Dispensing with "the annual budget ritual" is not the same as dispensing with budgeting. The CEO should ask the marketing manager to identify those aspects of the annual budget that are ritualistic and to suggest alternatives. Marketing managers often like to have unlimited budgets for advertising and counter-moves against competitions. However, organizations are increasingly requiring marketing to accept the same budgeting discipline as other functional areas. This discipline is not the same as "an exercise in minimization." Rather it should focus on budgeting expenditures to enhance the economic value of the organization.

6-40 (40min.)   **Appendix: Cash budgeting for distributor.**

1.   The pro forma cash budget for Alpha-Tech for the second quarter of 2003 is presented below. Supporting calculations are presented on the next page.

Alpha-Tech Cash Budget
For the Second Quarter 2003

	April	May	June
Beginning balance	$ 500,000	$ 500,000	$1,230,000
Collections[1]			
February sales	4,000,000		
March sales	5,400,000	3,600,000	
April sales		6,900,000	4,600,000
May sales			7,500,000
Total receipts	9,400,000	10,500,000	12,100,000
Total cash available	9,900,000	11,000,000	13,330,000
Disbursements			
Accounts payable	4,155,000	4,735,000	5,285,000
Wages[2]	3,450,000	3,750,000	4,200,000
General & Administrative[3]	900,000	900,000	900,000
Property taxes			340,000
Income taxes[4]	1,280,000		
Total disbursements	9,785,000	9,385,000	10,725,000
Cash balance	115,000	1,615,000	2,605,000
Cash borrow	385,000		
Cash repaid		(385,000)	
Ending balance	$ 500,000	$1,230,000	$ 2,605,000

[1] 60% of sales in first month; 40% of sales in second month

[2] 30% of current month sales

[3] (Total less property taxes and amortization) ÷ 12

[4] 40% × $3,200,000

6-40 (cont'd)

Supporting Calculations

Accounts payable—parts received:

Cost of goods sold

Month	40% of revenues	Timing	February	March	April	May	June
February	$4,000,000	.30	$1,200,000				
March	3,600,000	.70	2,520,000				
March	3,600,000	.30		$1,080,000			
April	4,600,000	.70		3,220,000			
April	4,600,000	.30			$1,380,000		
May	5,000,000	.70			3,500,000		
May	5,000,000	.30				$1,500,000	
June	5,600,000	.70				3,920,000	
			$3,720,000	$4,300,000	$4,880,000	$5,420,000	

Payment

Month		Timing	February	March	April	May	June
February	$3,720,000	.25			$ 930,000		
March	4,300,000	.75			3,225,000		
March	4,300,000	.25				$1,075,000	
April	4,880,000	.75				3,660,000	
April	4,880,000	.25					$1,220,000
May	5,420,000	.75					4,065,000
			$ 0	$ 0	$4,155,000	$4,735,000	$5,285,000

2. Cash budgeting is important for Alpha-Tech because as sales grow so will expenditures for input factors. Since these expenditures generally precede cash receipts, the company must plan for possible financing to cover the gap between payments and receipts. The cash budget shows the probable cash position at certain points in time, allowing the company to plan for borrowing, as Alpha-Tech must do in April.

Cash budgeting also facilitates the control of excess cash. The company may be losing investment opportunities, if excess cash is left idle in a chequing account. The cash budget alerts management to periods when there will be excess cash available for investment, thus facilitating financial planning and cash control.

6-42 (30 min.) Activity-based budgeting.

a. Machining
Indirect materials [$0 + ($10/hour × 10,000 hours)]	$100,000
Indirect labour [$20,000 + ($15/hour × 10,000 hours)]	170,000
Utilities [$0 + ($5/hour × 10,000 hours)]	50,000
	$320,000

b. Setups and quality assurance
Indirect materials [$0 + $1,000/run × 40 runs]	40,000
Indirect labour [$0 + $1,200/run × 40 runs]	48,000
Inspection [$80,000 + ($2,000/run × 40 runs)]	160,000
	$248,000

c. Procurement
Indirect materials [$0 + ($4/order × 15,000 orders)]	$ 60,000
Indirect labour [$45,000 + $0]	45,000
	$105,000

d. Design
Engineering hours [$75,000 + ($50/hour × 100 hours)]	$ 80,000

e. Material handling
Indirect materials [$0 + ($2/sq. ft. × 100,000 sq. ft.)]	$200,000
Indirect labour ($30,000 + $0)	30,000
	$230,000

6-44 (15 min.) **Budgetary slack and ethics.**

The use of budgetary slack, particularly if it has a detrimental effect on the company, may be unethical. In assessing the situation, the management accountant should consider the following:

Competence
Clear reports using relevant and reliable information should be prepared. Reports prepared on the basis of incorrect revenue or cost projections would violate the management accountant's responsibility for competence. Ford's and Granger's performances would appear to look better than they actually are because their performances are being compared with understated and unreliable budgets.

Integrity
Any activity that subverts the legitimate goals of the company should be avoided. Incorrect reporting of revenue and cost budgets could be viewed as violating the responsibility for integrity. The management accountant should communicate unfavourable as well as favourable information. Atkins will probably regard Ford's and Granger's behaviour as unethical because it is attempting to project their results in a favourable light.

Objectivity
The management accountant should require that information be fairly and objectively communicated and that all relevant information be disclosed. From a management accountant's standpoint, Ford and Granger are clearly violating both these precepts. For the various reasons cited above, Atkins should take the position that the behaviour described by Ford and Granger is unethical.

CHAPTER 7
FLEXIBLE BUDGETS, VARIANCES, AND
MANAGEMENT CONTROL: I

7-2 Sources of information about budgeted amounts include (a) past amounts, and (b) detailed engineering studies.

7-4 The key difference is the output level used to set the budget. A *static budget* is based on the level of output planned at the *start of the budget period*. A *flexible budget* is developed using budgeted revenues or cost amounts based on the level of output actually achieved in the budget period. The actual level of output is not known until the *end of the budget period*.

7-6 The steps in developing a flexible budget are:

Step 1: Determine the budgeted selling price per unit, the budgeted variable costs per unit, and the budgeted fixed costs.

Step 2: Determine the actual quantity of the revenue driver.

Step 3: Determine the flexible budget for revenue based on the budgeted unit revenue and the actual quantity of the revenue driver.

Step 4: Determine the actual quantity of the cost driver(s).

Step 5: Determine the flexible budget for costs based on the budgeted unit variable costs and fixed costs and the actual quantity of the cost driver(s).

7-8 A manager should decompose the flexible-budget variance for direct materials into a price variance and an efficiency variance. The individual causes of these variances can then be investigated, recognizing possible interdependencies across these individual causes.

7-10 Direct materials price variances are often computed at the time of purchase while direct materials efficiency variances are often computed at the time of usage. Purchasing managers are typically responsible for price variances, while production managers are typically responsible for usage variances.

7-12 An individual business function, such as production, is interdependent with other business functions. Factors outside of production can explain why variances arise in the production area. For example.
  - poor design of products or processes can lead to a sizable number of defects, and
  - marketing personnel making promises for delivery times that require a large number of rush orders that create production-scheduling difficulties.

7-14 Variances can be calculated at the activity level as well as at the company level. For example, a price variance and an efficiency variance can be computed for an activity area.

7-16 (20-30 min.) **Flexible budget.**

	Actual Results (1)	Flexible-Budget Variances (2) = (1) – (3)	Flexible Budget (3)	Sales-Volume Variances (4) = (3) – (5)	Static Budget (5)
Units sold	2,800[G]		2,800		3,000[G]
Revenues	$313,600[a]	5,600 F	$308,000[b]	$22,000 U	$330,000[c]
Variable costs	229,600[d]	22,400 U	207,200[e]	14,800 F	222,000[f]
Contribution margin	84,000	16,800 U	100,800	7,200 U	108,000
Fixed costs	50,000[G]	4,000 F	54,000[G]	0	54,000[G]
Operating income	$ 34,000	$12,800 U	$ 46,800	$ 7,200 U	$ 54,000
		$12,800 U		$ 7,200 U	

Total flexible-budget variance Total sales-volume variance

$20,000 U

Total static-budget variance

[a] $112 × 2,800 = $313,600
[b] $110 × 2,800 = $308,000
[c] $110 × 3,000 = $330,000
[d] Given. Unit variable cost = $229,600 ÷ 2,800 = $82 per tire
[e] $74 × 2,800 = $207,200
[f] $74 × 3,000 = $222,000
[G] Given

2.   The key information items are:

	Actual	Budgeted
Units	2,800	3,000
Unit selling price	$ 112	$ 110
Unit variable cost	$ 82	$ 74
Fixed costs	$50,000	$54,000

The total static-budget variance in operating income is $20,000 U. There is both an unfavourable total flexible-budget variance ($12,800) and an unfavourable sales-volume variance ($7,200).

The unfavourable sales-volume variance arises solely because actual units manufactured and sold were 200 fewer than the budgeted 3,000 units. The unfavourable static-budget variance of $12,800 in operating income is due primarily to the $8 increase in unit variable costs. This increase in unit variable costs is only partially offset by the $2 increase in unit selling price and the $4,000 decrease in fixed costs.

7-18 (10 min.)   **Flexible budget.**

1.

Static-budget variance	=	Actual results	–	Static-budget amount
	=	$6,556,000	–	$3,150,000
	=	$3,406,000 F		

2.

Flexible-budget variance	=	Actual results	–	Flexible-budget amount
	=	$6,556,000	–	$6,930,000
	=	$ 374,000 U		

Sales-volume variance	=	Flexible-budget amount	–	Static-budget amount
	=	$6,930,000	–	$3,150,000
	=	$3,780,000 F		

3.

$374,000 U	$3,780,000 F
Total flexible-budget variance	Total sales-volume variance

$3,406,000 F

Total static-budget variance

The total flexible-budget variance is $374,000 unfavourable. This arises because for the actual output level: (a) selling prices were lower than budgeted, or (b) variable costs were higher than budgeted, or (c) fixed costs were higher than budgeted, or (d) some combination of (a), (b), and (c) existed.

7-20 (15 min.) Materials and manufacturing labour variances.

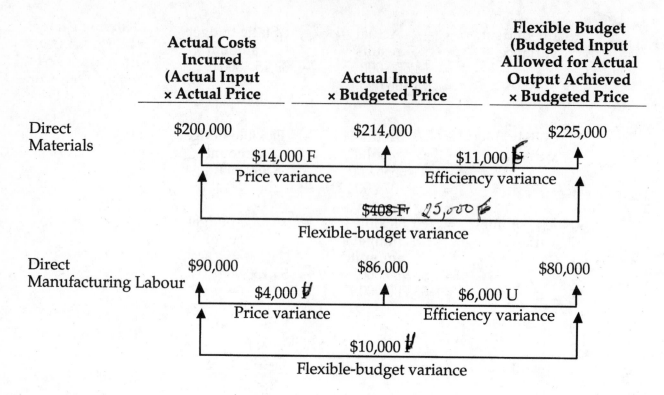

7-22 (30-40 min.) Comprehensive variance analysis.

1.

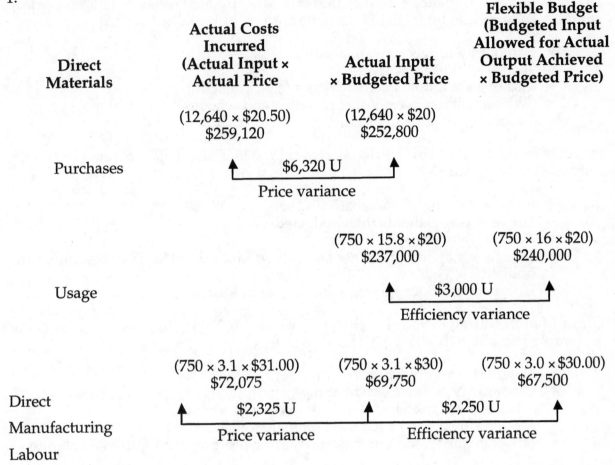

Direct Materials	Actual Costs Incurred (Actual Input × Actual Price	Actual Input × Budgeted Price	Flexible Budget (Budgeted Input Allowed for Actual Output Achieved × Budgeted Price)
	(12,640 × $20.50) $259,120	(12,640 × $20) $252,800	
Purchases	← $6,320 U → Price variance		
		(750 × 15.8 × $20) $237,000	(750 × 16 × $20) $240,000
Usage		← $3,000 U → Efficiency variance	
	(750 × 3.1 × $31.00) $72,075	(750 × 3.1 × $30) $69,750	(750 × 3.0 × $30.00) $67,500
Direct Manufacturing Labour	← $2,325 U → Price variance	← $2,250 U → Efficiency variance	

2.   **Direct Materials Price Variance** ($6,320 U, due to actual price of $20.50 exceeding budgeted price of $20.00)

- Standard wrongly (unrealistically) set
- Poor price negotiation
- Purchase of higher quality wood
- Materials price unexpectedly increased due to external shocks (e.g., a natural disaster in major forest areas)
- Purchased in smaller lot sizes than budgeted and did not get quantity discounts
- Change in supplier when lower-priced supplier went out of business

7-22 (cont'd)

Direct Materials Efficiency Variance ($3,000 F, due to actual usage of 15.8 square feet per desk, compared to budgeted 16.0 square feet)

- Standard wrongly (unrealistically) set
- Increased skills of workers
- Use of more automated machinery (e.g., laser cutting)
- Workers did more extensive planning and scheduling for materials usage
- Economies of scale in production

Direct Manufacturing Labour Price Variance ($2,325 U, due to actual rate of $31.00 compared to budgeted $30.00)

- Standard wrongly (unrealistically) set
- Use of higher skill mix than budgeted
- Poor negotiations with labour
- Overtime may have been necessary to produce the extra 50 decks more than budgeted
- Unexpected labour shortage due to external factors

Direct Manufacturing Labour Efficiency Variance ($2,250 U, due to actual time being 3.1 hours compared to budgeted 3.0 hours per desk)

- Standard wrongly (unrealistically) set
- Labour may be less efficient at higher output levels due to tiredness
- Scheduler assigned less skilled workers to desk production
- Machine breakdowns required more use of labour
- Lower quality wood purchased requiring more labour input to finish desks

7-24 (25-30 min.) **Flexible budget preparation and analysis.**

1. Variance Analysis for Bank Management Printers for September 2002
    Level 1 Analysis

	Actual Results (1)	Static-Budget Variances (2) = (1) – (3)	Static Budget (3)
Units sold	12,000	3,000 U	15,000
Revenue	$252,000[a]	$ 48,000 U	$300,000[c]
Variable costs	84,000[d]	36,000 F	120,000[f]
Contribution margin	168,000	12,000 U	180,000
Fixed costs	150,000	5,000 U	145,000
Operating income	$ 18,000	$ 17,000 U	$ 35,000

$17,000 U
Total static-budget variance

2. Level 2 Analysis

	Actual Results (1)	Flexible-Budget Variances (2) = (1) – (3)	Flexible Budget (3)	Sales-Volume Variances (4) = (3) – (5)	Static Budget (5)
Units sold	12,000	0	12,000	3,000 U	15,000
Revenue	$252,000[a]	$12,000 F	$240,000[b]	$60,000 U	$300,000[c]
Variable costs	84,000[d]	12,000 F	96,000[e]	24,000 F	120,000[f]
Contribution margin	168,000	24,000 F	144,000	36,000 U	180,000
Fixed costs	150,000	5,000 U	145,000	0	145,000
Operating income	$ 18,000	$19,000 F	$ (1,000)	$36,000 U	$ 35,000

$19,000 F $36,000 U
Total flexible-budget   Total sales-volume
variance   variance

$17,000 U
Total static-budget variance

[a] 12,000 × $21 = $252,000   [d] 12,000 × $7 = $ 84,000
[b] 12,000 × $20 = $240,000   [e] 12,000 × $8 = $ 96,000
[c] 15,000 × $20 = $300,000   [f] 15,000 × $8 = $120,000

3. Level 2 analysis provides a breakdown of the static-budget variance into a flexible-budget variance and a sales-volume variance. The primary reason for the static-budget variance being unfavourable ($17,000 U) is the reduction in unit volume from the budgeted 15,000 to an actual 12,000. One explanation for this reduction is the increase in selling price from a budgeted $20 to an actual $21. Operating management was able to reduce variable costs by $12,000 relative to the flexible budget. This reduction could be a sign of efficient management. Alternatively, it could be due to using lower-quality materials (which in turn adversely affected unit volume).

7-26 (45-50 min.) **Activity-based costing, flexible-budget variances for finance function activities.**

1. *Receivables*

Receivables is an output unit level activity. Its flexible-budget variance can be calculated as follows:

$$\text{Flexible-budget variance} = \text{Actual costs} - \text{Flexible-budget costs}$$

$$= (\$0.75 \times 948{,}000) - (\$0.639 \times 948{,}000)$$
$$= \$711{,}000 - \$605{,}772$$
$$= \$105{,}228 \text{ U}$$

Payables

Payables is a batch level activity.

	Static-budget Amounts	**Actual Amounts**
a. Number of deliveries	1,000,000	948,000
b. Batch size (units per batch)	5	4.468
c. Number of batches (a ÷ b)	200,000	212,175
d. Cost per batch	$2.90	$2.80
e. Total payables activity cost (c × d)	$580,000	$594,090

Step 1: The number of batches in which payables should have been processed = 948,000 actual units ÷ 5 budgeted units per batch = 189,600 batches

Step 2: The flexible-budget amount for payables
= 189,600 batches × $2.90 budgeted cost per batch
= $549,840

The flexible-budget variance can be computed as follows:

$$\text{Flexible-budget variance} = \text{Actual costs} - \text{Flexible-budget costs}$$

$$= (212{,}175 \times \$2.80) - (189{,}600 \times \$2.90)$$
$$= \$594{,}090 - \$549{,}840 = \$44{,}250 \text{ U}$$

Travel expenses

Travel expenses is a batch level activity.

	Static-Budget Amounts	**Actual Amounts**
a. Number of deliveries	1,000,000	948,000
b. Batch size (units per batch)	500	501.587
c. Number of batches (a ÷ b)	2,000	1,890
d. Cost per batch	$7.60	$7.40
e. Total travel expenses activity cost (c × d)	$15,200	$13,986

7-26 (cont'd)

Step 1: The number of batches in which the travel expense should have been processed
= 948,000 actual units ÷ 500 budgeted units per batch = 1,896 batches

Step 2: The flexible-budget amount for travel expenses
= 1,896 batches × $7.60 budgeted cost per batch
= $14,410

The flexible budget variance can be calculated as follows:

Flexible budget variance = Actual costs – Flexible-budget costs
= (1,890 × $7.40) – (1,896 × $7.60)
= $13,986 – $14,410 = $424 F

2. The flexible budget variances can be subdivided into price and efficiency variances.

$$\text{Price variance} = \left[\begin{array}{c} \text{Actual price} \\ \text{of input} \end{array} - \begin{array}{c} \text{Budgeted price} \\ \text{of input} \end{array} \right] \times \begin{array}{c} \text{Actual quantity} \\ \text{of input} \end{array}$$

$$\text{Efficiency variance} = \left[\begin{array}{c} \text{Actual quantity} \\ \text{of input used} \end{array} - \begin{array}{c} \text{Budgeted quantity of} \\ \text{input allowed for} \\ \text{actual output} \end{array} \right] \times \begin{array}{c} \text{Budgeted price} \\ \text{of input} \end{array}$$

Receivables

Price Variance	=	($0.750 – $0.639) × 948,000
	=	$105,228 U
Efficiency variance	=	(948,000 – 948,000) × $0.639
	=	$0

Payables

Price variance	=	($2.80 – $2.90) × 212,175
	=	$21,218 F
Efficiency variance	=	(212,175 – 189,600) × $2.90
	=	$65,468 U

Travel expenses

Price variance	=	($7.40 – $7.60) × 1,890
	=	$378 F
Efficiency variance	=	(1,890 – 1,896) × $7.60
	=	$46 F

7-28 (30 min.) **Flexible budget, direct materials and direct manufacturing labour variances.**

1.

	Actual Results (1)	Flexible-Budget Variances (2) = (1) − (3)	Flexible Budget (3)	Sales-Volume Variances (4) = (3) − (5)	Static Budget (5)
Units sold	6,000[a]—	0	6,000	1,000 F	5,000[a]
Direct materials	$ 594,000[f]	$ 6,000 F	$ 600,000[b]	$100,000 U	$ 500,000[c]
Direct manufacturing labour	950,000[a]	10,000 F	960,000[d]	160,000 U	800,000[e]
Fixed costs	1,005,000[a]	5,000 U	1,000,000[a]	0	1,000,000[a]
Total costs	$2,549,000	$11,000 F	$2,560,000	$260,000 U	$2,300,000

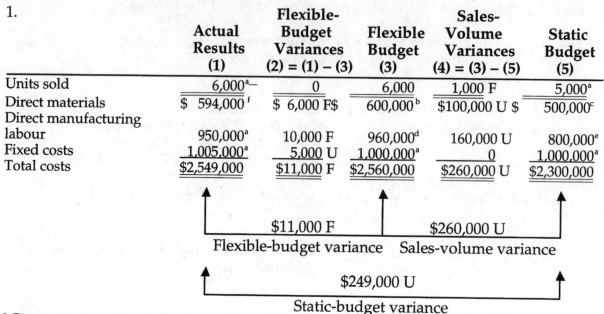

$11,000 F \qquad\qquad $260,000 U

Flexible-budget variance Sales-volume variance

$249,000 U

Static-budget variance

[a] Given
[b] $100 × 6,000 = $600,000
[c] $100 × 5,000 = $500,000
[d] $160 × 6,000 = $960,000
[e] $160 × 5,000 = $800,000
[f] $54,000 × $11/kilogram = $594,000

2.

	Actual Incurred (Actual Input Qty. × Actual Price)	Actual Input Qty. × Budgeted Price	Flexible Budget (Budgeted Input Qty. Allowed for Actual Output × Budgeted Price)
Direct materials	$594,000[a]	$540,000[b]	$600,000[c]

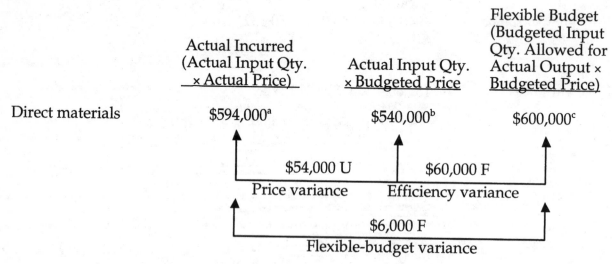

$54,000 U \qquad\qquad $60,000 F

Price variance Efficiency variance

$6,000 F

Flexible-budget variance

7-28 (cont'd)

Direct manufacturing labour $950,000^d $1,000,000^e $960,000^f

                        $50,000 F $40,000 U
                       Price variance   Efficiency variance

                                    $10,000 F
                           Flexible-budget variance

[a] 54,000 kilograms × \$11/kilogram = \$594,000
[b] 54,000 kilograms × \$10/kilogram = \$540,000
[c] 6,000 statues × 10 kilograms/statue × \$10/kilogram = 60,000 kilograms × \$10/kilogram
     = \$600,000
[d] 25,000 kilograms × \$38/kilogram = \$950,000
[e] 25,000 kilograms × \$40/kilogram = \$1,000,000
[f] 6,000 statues × 4 hours/statue × \$40/hour = 24,000 hours × \$40/hour = \$960,000

7-30   (20 min.)   **Continuous improvement (continuation of 7-29).**

1.   Standard quantity input amounts per output unit are:

Direct
Materials Direct
Manufacturing Labour January
February (Jan. × 0.997)
March (Feb. × 0.997) 10.0000
9.9700
9.9400 0.5000
0.4985
0.4970 2.   The answer to requirement 1 of Question 7-29 is identical except for the flexible-budget amount.

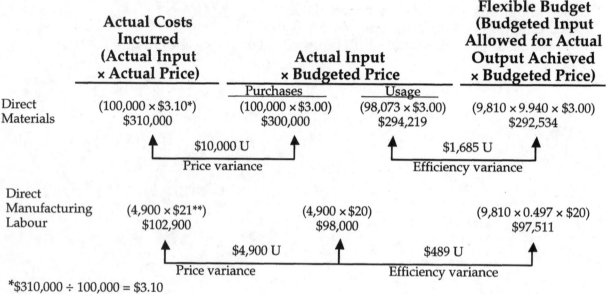

	Actual Costs Incurred (Actual Input × Actual Price)	**Actual Input × Budgeted Price**		**Flexible Budget (Budgeted Input Allowed for Actual Output Achieved × Budgeted Price)**
		Purchases	Usage	
Direct Materials	(100,000 × $3.10*) $310,000	(100,000 × $3.00) $300,000	(98,073 × $3.00) $294,219	(9,810 × 9.940 × $3.00) $292,534

$10,000 U → Price variance $1,685 U → Efficiency variance

Direct Manufacturing Labour	(4,900 × $21**) $102,900	(4,900 × $20) $98,000		(9,810 × 0.497 × $20) $97,511

$4,900 U → Price variance $489 U → Efficiency variance

*$310,000 ÷ 100,000 = $3.10
**$102,900 ÷ 4,900 = $21

Using continuous improvement standards sets a tougher benchmark. The efficiency variances for January (from Exercise 7-29) and March (from Exercise 7-30) are:

	January	March
Direct materials	$ 81 F	$1,685 U
Direct manufacturing labour	$100 F	$ 489 U

Note that the question assumes the continuous improvement applies only to quantity inputs. An alternative approach is to have continuous improvement apply to budgeted input cost per output unit ($30 for direct materials in January and $10 for direct manufacturing labour in January). This approach is more difficult to incorporate in a Level 2 variance analysis as Level 2 requires separate amounts for quantity inputs and the cost per input.

7-32 (15-25 min.) **Journal entries and T-accounts
(continuation of 7-31).**

The following journal entries relate to the measurement of variances when materials and manufacturing labour are used.

(a)	Work in Process Control	$400,000	
	Direct Materials Price Variance	7,400	
	Direct Materials Efficiency Variance		$ 30,000
	Materials Control		377,400
	To record direct materials used		

(b)	Work in Process Control	$200,000	
	Direct Manufacturing Labour Price Variance		$ 3,600
	Direct Manufacturing Labour Efficiency Variance		20,000
	Wages Payable Control		176,400
	To record liability and allocation of direct labour costs		

Materials Control		Direct Materials Price Variance		Direct Materials Efficiency Variance	
	(a) $377,400	(a) 7,400			(a) 30,000

Work in Process Control		Direct Manufacturing Labour Price Variance		Direct Manufacturing Labour Efficiency Variance	
(a) 400,000			(b) 3,600		(b) 20,000
(b) 200,000					

Wages Payable Control	
	(b) 176,400

The following journal entries pertain to the measurement of price variances when materials are purchased:

(c)	Materials Control	$600,000	
	Direct Materials Price Variance	12,000	
	Accounts Payable Control		$612,000
	To record direct materials purchased		

(d)	Work in Process Control	$400,000	
	Materials Control		$370,000
	Direct Materials Efficiency Variance		30,000
	To record direct materials used		

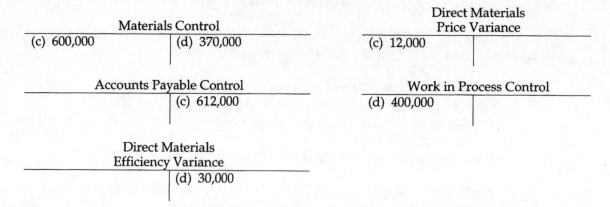

	Materials Control	
(c) 600,000	(d) 370,000	

	Accounts Payable Control
	(c) 612,000

	Direct Materials Efficiency Variance
	(d) 30,000

	Direct Materials Price Variance
(c) 12,000	

	Work in Process Control
(d) 400,000	

The difference between standard costing and normal costing for direct cost items is:

	Standard Costs	**Normal Costs**
Direct Costs	Standard price(s) × Standard input allowed for actual outputs achieved	Actual price(s) × Actual input

These journal entries differ from the <u>normal costing</u> entries because Work in Process Control is no longer carried at "actual" costs. Furthermore, Materials Control can also be carried at standard unit prices rather than actual unit prices. Finally, variances appear for direct materials and direct manufacturing labour under <u>standard costing</u> but not under <u>normal costing</u>.

7-34 (30 min.) **Flexible budget preparation, service sector.**

1. • Budgeted selling price (revenue per loan application)
   $1/2\% \times$ budgeted average loan amount $= 1/2\% \times \$200,000 = \$1,000$
   • Budgeted variable costs per output unit are:

Professional labour (6 × $40)	$240
Loan filing fees	100
Credit-worthiness checks	120
Courier mailings	50
Budgeted variable costs	$510

   • Budgeted fixed costs = $31,000 per month.

The static budget for the 90 loan applicant level (and the flexible budget for the 120 loan application level in Requirement 2) are:

	Requirement 1 90 Loan Applications	Requirement 2 120 Loan Applications
Budgeted revenue (90, 120 × $1,000)	$90,000	$120,000
Budgeted variable costs (90, 120 × $510)	45,900	61,200
Contribution margin	44,100	58,800
Fixed costs	31,000	31,000
Operating income	$13,100	$ 27,800

2. The actual results are:

Revenue (120 × 1/2% × $224,000)		$134,400
Variable costs:		
Professional labour (120 × 7.2 × $42)	$36,288	
Loan filing fees (120 × $100)	12,000	
Credit-worthiness checks (120 × $125)	15,000	
Courier mailings (120 × $54)	6,480	69,768
Contribution margin		64,632
Fixed costs		33,500
Operating income		$ 31,132

These actual results can be analyzed in a Level 2 variance analysis.

7-34 (cont'd)

<u>Level 2 Analysis</u>

	Actual Results (1)	Flexible-Budget Variances (2) = (1) – (3)	Flexible Budget (3)	Sales-Volume Variances (4) = (3) – (5)	Static Budget (5)
Units sold	120	0	120	30 F	90
Revenue	$134,400	$14,400 F	$120,000	$30,000 F	$90,000
Variable costs	69,768	8,568 U	61,200	15,300 U	45,900
Contribution margin	64,632	5,832 F	58,800	14,700 F	44,100
Fixed costs	33,500	2,500 U	31,000	0	31,000
Operating income	$ 31,132	$ 3,332 F	$ 27,800	$14,700 F	$13,100

$3,332 F $14,700 F

Total flexible-budget variance   Total sales-volume variance

$18,032 F

Total static-budget variance

Note that the $18,032 favourable static-budget variance is largely the result of an increase in loan applications from a budgeted 90 to an actual 120. In addition, the average size of a loan increased from a budgeted $200,000 to $224,000 which explains the flexible-budget variance of $14,400 F for revenues (0.5% × $24,000 × 120 = $14,400).

One possible explanation is a rapid decrease in interest rates leading to an increase in demand for loan refinancing.

7-36 (30-40 min.) **Direct materials variances, long-term agreement with supplier.**

1.

Month (1)	Total Actual Direct Materials Usage in Dollars (2)	Average Actual Direct Materials Purchase Price per Kilogram of Metal (3)	Total Actual Quantity of Direct Materials in Kilograms (4) = (2) ÷ (3)	Number of Machining Systems Produced (5)	Actual Direct Materials Input in Kilograms per Machining System (6) = (4) ÷ (5)
January	$242,400	$120	2,020	10	202
February	286,560	120	2,388	12	199
March	442,260	126	3,510	18	195
April	395,264	128	3,088	16	193
May	253,440	120	2,112	11	192

Materials Price Variance

Month (1)	Actual Costs Incurred: Actual Input × Actual Price (2)	Actual Input (3)	Budgeted Price per Unit of Input (4)	Actual Input × Budgeted Price (5) = (3) × (4)	Direct Materials Price Variance (6) = (2) − (5)
January	$242,400	2,020	$120	$242,400	$ 0
February	286,560	2,388	120	286,560	0
March	442,260	3,510	120	421,200	21,060 U
April	395,264	3,088	120	370,560	24,704 U
May	253,440	2,112	120	253,440	0

Materials Efficiency Variance

Month (1)	Actual Input × Budgeted Price (2)	Budgeted Input per Unit of Output (3)	Actual Output Achieved (4)	Budgeted Price per Unit of Input (5)	Flexible Budget (Budgeted Input Allowed for Actual Output Achieved × Budgeted Price) (6) = (3) × (4) × (5)	Direct Materials Efficiency Variance (7) = (2) − (6)
January	$242,400	198	10	$120	$237,600	$4,800 U
February	286,560	198	12	120	285,120	1,440 U
March	421,200	198	18	120	427,680	6,480 F
April	370,560	198	16	120	380,160	9,600 F
May	253,440	198	11	120	261,360	7,920 F

7-36 (cont'd)

2. The unfavourable materials price variances in March and April imply that Mazak paid more than $120 per kilogram above the 2,400 kilogram contract amount.

Month (1)	Total Actual Costs Incurred (2)	Contract Amount for 2,400 kg: 2,400 × $120 (3)	Cost for Purchases above 2,400 kg (4) = (2) − (3)	Quantity of Purchases above 2,400 kg (5)	Actual Price per Kilogram of Purchases above 2,400 kg (6) = (4) ÷ (5)
March	$442,260	$288,000	$154,260	1,110	$138.97
April	395,264	288,000	107,264	688	155.91

The percentage price increases for the additional purchases above 2,400 kilograms are:

	Actual Price	Standard Price	% Increase
March	$138.97	$120	15.8
April	155.91	120	29.9

With a long-term agreement that has a fixed purchase-price clause for a set minimum quantity, no price variance will arise when the purchase amount is below the minimum quantity (assuming the budgeted price per unit is the contract price per unit). A price variance will occur only when the purchased amount exceeds the set minimum quantity. A price variance signals that the purchased amount exceeds this set minimum quantity (2,400 kilograms per month).

It is likely that the supplier will charge a higher price (above $120) for purchases above the 2,400 base. If a lower price were charged, the purchaser might apply pressure to renegotiate the contract purchase price for the base amount. If the purchasing officer is able to negotiate only a small price increase for additional purchases above the base amount, the purchasing performance may well be "favourable" despite the materials price variance being labelled "unfavourable."

Mazak may see the advantage of a long-term contract in factors other than purchase price (for example, a higher quality of materials, a lower required level of inventories because of more frequent deliveries, and a guaranteed availability of materials). In general, the existence of a long-term agreement reduces the importance of materials price variances when evaluating the month-to-month performance of a purchasing officer.

7-38 (20-30 min.)   **Direct materials and manufacturing labour variances, solving unknowns.**

All given items are designated by an asterisk.

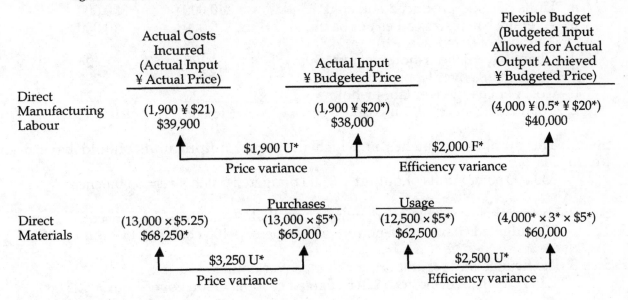

1.   4,000 × 0.5 = 2,000 hours
2.   1,900 hours [($40,000 − 2,000) ÷ $20 = 1,900 hours]
3. $21 [($38,000 + 1,900) ÷ 1,900 = $21]
4.   4,000 × 3 = 12,000 kilograms
5.   12,500 kilograms [($60,000 + 2,500) ÷ $5 = 12,500 kg]
6.   13,000 kilograms [($68,250 − 3,250) ÷ $5 = 13,000 kg]
7. $5.25 per kilogram [$68,250 ÷ 13,000 kg = $5.25]

7-40 (30 min.) **Activity-based costing, variance analysis.**

			Static-budget Amounts	Actual Amounts
1.	a.	Units of cakes produced and sold	240,000	330,000
	b.	Average batch size (cakes per batch)	6,000	10,000
	c.	Number of batches (a ÷ b) 40	33	
	d.	Changeover labour-hours per batch	20	24
	e.	Total changeover labour-hours (c × d)	800	792
	f.	Cost per changeover labour-hours	$20	$21
	g.	Total changeover labour cost (e × f)	$16,000	$16,632

Step 1: The number of batches in which the actual output units should have been produced:

  330,000 actual units of output ÷ 6,000 budgeted batch size = 55 batches

Step 2: The number of changeover labour-hours that should have been used:
  20 budgeted changeover-hours × 55 batches = 1,100 changeover-hours.

Step 3: The flexible-budget amount for changeover hours:
  1,100 changeover-hours × $20 budgeted cost per changeover-hour = $22,000.

Flexible-budget variance
$$= \text{Actual costs} - \text{Flexible-budget costs}$$
$$= (792 \times \$21) - (1{,}100 \times \$20)$$
$$= \$16{,}632 - \$22{,}000 = \$5{,}368 \text{ F}$$

2. Price variance $= \left[\begin{array}{c}\text{Actual price}\\ \text{of input}\end{array} - \begin{array}{c}\text{Budgeted price}\\ \text{of input}\end{array}\right] \times \begin{array}{c}\text{Actual quantity}\\ \text{of input}\end{array}$

  $= (\$21 - \$20) \times 792 = \$1 \times 792 = \$792 \text{ U}$

Efficiency variance $= \left[\begin{array}{c}\text{Actual quantity}\\ \text{of input used}\end{array} - \begin{array}{c}\text{Budgeted quantity}\\ \text{of input allowed}\\ \text{for actual output}\end{array}\right] \times \begin{array}{c}\text{Budgeted price}\\ \text{of input}\end{array}$

  $= (792 - 1{,}100) \times \$20 = 308 \times \$20 = \$6{,}160 \text{ F}$

The favourable flexible-budget variance of $5,368 is comprised of two offsetting amounts:

- Price variance of $792 U due to actual changeover labour cost of $21 per hour exceeding the $20 budgeted rate.
- Efficiency variance of $6,160 F due to the actual batch size of 10,000 being *sizably* above the budgeted batch size of 6,000. Efficiency variance is favourable because less batches were required to produce 330,000 cakes even though actual changeover labour-hours of 24 per batch were higher than the budgeted changeover-hours per batch of 20 hours.

7-40 (cont'd)

Explanations for the price variance of $792 U include:

- More highly trained workers hired to make changeovers.
- Change in labour market required unexpected increase in labour rates to retain workers.
- Budgeted amounts were set without adequate analysis.

Explanations for the efficiency variance of $6,160 F include:

- More highly trained workers were able to produce larger batch sizes.
- More automated machinery was acquired.
- Budgeted amounts were set without adequate analysis.

7-42 (30 min.) **Comprehensive variance analysis.**

1.(a)   Computing unit selling prices and unit costs of inputs:

Actual selling price $= \$3,555,000 \div 450,000$
$= \$7.90$

Budgeting selling price $= \$3,200,000 \div 400,000$
$= \$8.00$

Selling-price variance $= \left(\begin{array}{c}\text{Actual} \\ \text{selling price}\end{array} - \begin{array}{c}\text{Budgeted} \\ \text{selling price}\end{array}\right) \times \begin{array}{c}\text{Actual} \\ \text{units sold}\end{array}$

$= (\$7.90 - \$8.00) \times 450,000$
$= \$45,000 \text{ U}$

(b) to (e)

The actual and budgeted unit costs are:

	Actual	Budgeted
Direct materials		
Cookie mix	$0.02	$0.02
Milk chocolate	0.20	0.15
Almonds	0.50	0.50
Direct labour		
Mixing	14.40	14.40
Baking	18.00	18.00

The actual output achieved is 450,000 kilograms of chocolate nut supreme.

The direct cost price and efficiency variances are:

	Actual Costs Incurred (Actual Input × Actual Price) (1)	Price Variance (2) = (1) – (3)	Actual Input × Budgeted Prices (3)	Efficiency Variance (4) = (3) – (5)	Flex. Budget (Budgeted Input Allowed for Actual Output Achieved × Budgeted Price) (5)
Direct materials					
Cookie mix	$ 93,000	$ 0	$ 93,000[a]	$ 3,000 U	$ 90,000[h]
Milk chocolate	532,000	133,000 U	399,000[b]	61,500 U	337,500[i]
Almonds	240,000	0	240,000[c]	15,000 U	225,000[j]
	$865,000	$133,000 U	$732,000	$79,500 U	$652,500
Direct labour costs					
Mixing	$108,000	$ 0	$108,000[d]	$ 0	$108,000[k]
Baking	240,000	0	240,000[e]	30,000 F	270,000[l]
	$348,000	$ 0	$348,000	$30,000 F	$378,000

[a] $0.02 × 4,650,000 = $93,000
[b] $0.15 × 2,660,000 = $399,000
[c] $0.50 × 480,000 = $240,000
[d] $14.40 × (450,000 ÷ 60) = $108,000
[e] $18.00 × (800,000 ÷ 60) = $240,000

[h] $0.02 × 10 × 450,000 = $90,000
[i] $0.15 × 5 × 450,000 = $337,500
[j] $0.50 × 1 × 450,000 = $225,000
[k] $14.40 × (1/60) × 450,000 = $108,000
[l] $18.00 × (2/60) × 450,000 = $270,000

2. (a) Selling price variance. This may arise from a proactive decision to reduce price to expand market share or from a reaction to a price reduction by a competitor. It could also arise from unplanned price discounting by salespeople.

(b) Material price variance. The $0.05 increase in the price per ounce of milk chocolate could arise from uncontrollable market factors or from poor contract negotiations by Aunt Molly's.

(c) Material efficiency variance. For all three material inputs, usage is greater than budgeted. Possible reasons include lower quality inputs, use of lower quality workers, and the mixing and baking equipment not being maintained in a fully operational mode.

(d) Labour price variance. The zero variance is consistent with workers being on long-term contracts that are not renegotiated on a month-by-month basis.

(e) Labour efficiency variance. The favourable efficiency variance for baking could be due to workers eliminating non-valued-added steps in production.

7-44 (60 min.)   **Continuous improvement (continuation of 7-43).**

1. Monthly Standards

	Dec. 2001	Jan. 2002	Feb. 2002
Frames	3.00 grams	2.985 (3.00 × 0.995)	2.970075 (2.985 × 0.995)
Lenses	6.00 grams	5.97 (6.00 × 0.995)	5.94015 (5.97 × 0.995)

These are expressed in physical terms. Assuming a constant standard price ($2.20 for frames and $3.10 for lenses), we can express these in dollars:

	Dec. 2001	Jan. 2002	Feb. 2002
Frames	$6.60	$ 6.567	$ 6.534165
Lenses	18.60	18.507	18.414465

2. Pros: Puts in a culture of continuous improvement.
Can be flexible by allowing for different percentages to apply to different materials and to different stages in life cycle.

   Cons: Difficult to have 0.995 forever—you can't ever get down to zero material.
Far too incremental in perspective. A competitor may do a major redesign or use a new material that drops costs dramatically.

7-46 (30-40 min.) **Procurement costs, variance analysis, ethics.**

1.   Purchase price variances can be computed for each country.

$$\text{Purchase price variance} = \left(\begin{array}{c} \text{Actual price} \\ \text{of input} \end{array} - \begin{array}{c} \text{Budgeted price} \\ \text{of input} \end{array} \right) \times \begin{array}{c} \text{Actual quantity} \\ \text{of input} \end{array}$$

<u>Hergovia</u>

    =   ($13.30* – $12.00) × 250,000
    = $325,000 U

* $3,325,000 ÷ 250,000 = $13.30

On a per-unit basis, there is a $10.60 payment to the shoe manufacturer and a $2.70 payment for "other costs."

<u>Tanistan</u>

    =   ($11.65 – $12.00) × 900,000
    = $315,000 F

* $10,485,000 ÷ 900,000 = $11.65

On a per-unit basis, there is a $9.60 payment to the shoe manufacturer and a $2.05 payment for "other costs."

2.   The organization structure is:

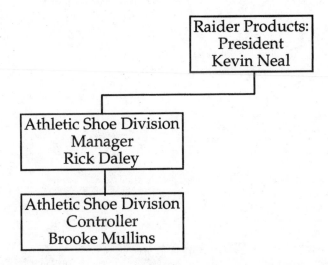

Daley and Mullins face many ethical issues:

(a)   Reliability of cost information to be presented to the board of directors. There are minimal or questionable receipts for $675,000 in Hergovia and $1,845,000 in Tanistan.

(b)   Potential existence of kickback payments in both Hergovia and Tanistan.

7-46 (cont'd)

(c)   Employment of young children (many of them under 15 years).

Should Daley and Mullins be forthright and present all their concerns on (a), (b) and (c)?

Both Daley and Mullins face the dilemma that any discussion of (a), (b) or (c) will raise questions about their own behaviour at the time the acquisitions were made. Board members may ask "when did they first know about (a), (b) and (c)?," and "if it is only recently, why did they not undertake examination of these issues at the time they supported the acquisitions?"

3.   Mullins has very high standards of ethical conduct to meet—see Exhibit 1-5 of the text. She should not make presentations to the Board based on information she has strong doubts about. If she decides to make the presentation, all her concerns and caveats should be presented.

She should require detailed documentation for all payments. No future payments should be made without adequate documentation.

Investigation of kickback allegations should be made, however difficult that may be. Mullins should be able to show she made a good-faith effort to ensure kickback payments are not an ongoing practice in Hergovia or Tanistan.

CHAPTER 8
FLEXIBLE BUDGETS, VARIANCES,
AND MANAGEMENT CONTROL: II

8-2   At the start of an accounting period, a larger percentage of fixed overhead costs are locked-in than is the case with variable overhead costs.

8-4   Steps in developing a budgeted variable-overhead cost rate are:
1.   Identify the costs to include in the variable-overhead cost pool(s),
2.   Select the cost allocation base(s), and
3.   Estimate the budgeted variable-overhead rates(s).

8-6   Reasons for a $25,000 favourable variable-overhead efficiency variance are:
- workers more skillful in using machines than budgeted
- production scheduler was able to schedule jobs better than budgeted, resulting in lower-than-budgeted machine-hours
- machines operated with fewer slowdowns than budgeted
- machine time standards set with padding built in by machine-workers.

8-8   Steps in developing a budgeted fixed-overhead rate are:
Step 1:   Choose the time period used to compute the budget,
Step 2:   Identify the costs in the fixed-overhead cost pool(s),
Step 3:   Estimate the budgeted quantity of the allocation base(s), and
Step 4:   Compute the budgeted fixed-overhead rate(s).

8-10   A 4-variance analysis relies on
(a)   a breakdown of overhead into its variable and fixed components, and
(b)   a breakdown into three components—spending, efficiency, and production volume.

A 3-variance analysis relies only on the breakdown of variances into the three components in (b).

A 2-variance analysis breaks down variances into only two components (flexible-budget and production-volume).

A 1-variance analysis reports only one variance where there is no breakdown of the (a) or (b) categories noted above.

8-12   Fixed manufacturing costs represent resources sacrificed in acquiring capacity that cannot be decreased if the resources needed are less than the resources acquired. A lump-sum amount of fixed costs will be unaffected by the degree of operating efficiency in a given budget period.

8-14   For planning and control purposes, fixed overhead costs are a lump sum amount that is not controlled on a per-unit basis. In contrast, for inventory costing purposes fixed overhead costs are allocated to products on a per-unit basis. See Exhibit 8-4 (page 289) in the text.

8-16 (20 min.) Variable manufacturing overhead, variance analysis.

1.

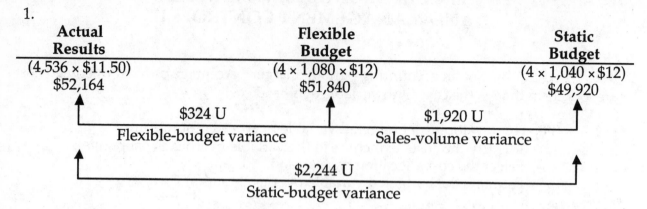

Actual Results		Flexible Budget		Static Budget
(4,536 × $11.50)		(4 × 1,080 × $12)		(4 × 1,040 × $12)
$52,164		$51,840		$49,920

$324 U — Flexible-budget variance

$1,920 U — Sales-volume variance

$2,244 U — Static-budget variance

2.   Esquire manufactured 40 suits more than the 1,040 budgeted. This accounts for the unfavourable sales-volume variance of $1,920 for variable manufacturing overhead.

The actual variable manufacturing overhead of $52,164 exceeds the flexible budget amount of $51,840 for 1,080 suits by $324—hence the flexible budget variance is $324 U.

NOT REQUIRED

Further insight into the flexible-budget variance of $324 U for variable MOH is provided by the spending and efficiency variances:

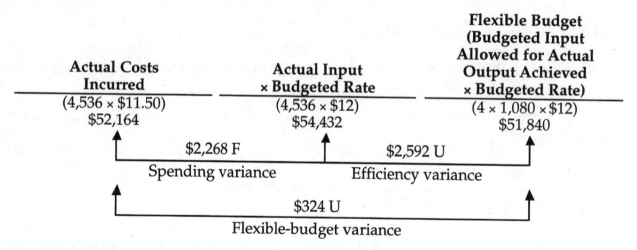

Actual Costs Incurred		Actual Input × Budgeted Rate		Flexible Budget (Budgeted Input Allowed for Actual Output Achieved × Budgeted Rate)
(4,536 × $11.50)		(4,536 × $12)		(4 × 1,080 × $12)
$52,164		$54,432		$51,840

$2,268 F — Spending variance

$2,592 U — Efficiency variance

$324 U — Flexible-budget variance

Esquire had a favourable spending variance of $2,268, (the actual variable overhead rate was $11.50 per direct manufacturing labour-hour versus the $12 budgeted). It had an unfavourable efficiency variance of $2,592 U (each suit averaged 4.2 labour-hours versus 4.00 budgeted).

8-18 (30 min.)   **Variable manufacturing overhead variance analysis.**

1. Denominator level =
    (3,200,000 × 0.02 hours) = 64,000 hours

2.

	Actual Results	Flexible Budget Amount
1. Output units (baguettes)	2,800,000	2,800,000
2. Direct labour-hours	50,400	56,000[a]
3. Labour-hours per output unit (2 ÷ 1)	0.018	0.020
4. Variable MOH costs	$680,400	$560,000
5. Variable MOH per labour-hour (4 ÷ 2)	$13.50	$10
6. Variable MOH per output unit (4 ÷ 1)	$0.243	$0.200

[a]2,800,000 × 0.020= 56,000 hours

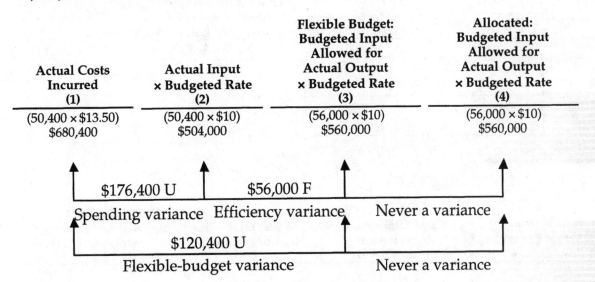

Actual Costs Incurred (1)	Actual Input × Budgeted Rate (2)	Flexible Budget: Budgeted Input Allowed for Actual Output × Budgeted Rate (3)	Allocated: Budgeted Input Allowed for Actual Output × Budgeted Rate (4)
(50,400 × $13.50) $680,400	(50,400 × $10) $504,000	(56,000 × $10) $560,000	(56,000 × $10) $560,000

$176,400 U	$56,000 F	
Spending variance	Efficiency variance	Never a variance
$120,400 U		
Flexible-budget variance		Never a variance

3. Spending variance of $176,400 U. It is unfavourable because variable manufacturing overhead was 35% higher than planned. A possible explanation could be an increase in energy rates relative to the rate per standard labour-hour assumed in the flexible budget.

Efficiency variance of $56,000 F. It is favourable because the actual number of direct manufacturing labour-hours required was lower than the number of hours budgeted. Labour was more efficient in producing the baguettes than management had anticipated in the budget. This could occur because of improved morale in the company, which could result from an increase in wages or an improvement in the compensation scheme.

Flexible-budget variance of $120,400 U. It is unfavourable because the favourable efficiency variance was not large enough to compensate for the large unfavourable spending variance.

8-20 (30-40 min.) Manufacturing overhead, variance analysis.

1. The summary analysis is:

	Spending Variance	Efficiency Variance	Production-Volume Variance
Variable Manufacturing Overhead	$40,700 F	$59,200 U	Never a variance
Fixed-Manufacturing Overhead	$23,420 U	Never a variance	$36,000 U

Variable Manufacturing Overhead

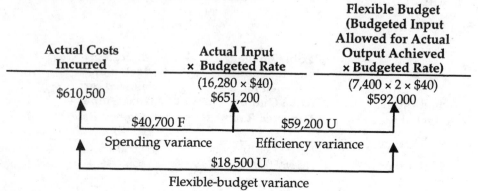

Fixed Manufacturing Overhead

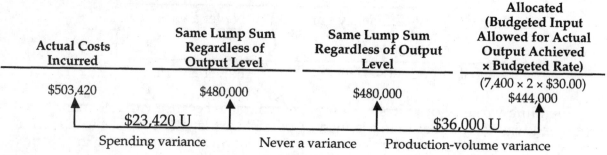

Summary information is:

	Actual	Flexible Budget	Static Budget
Output units	7,400	7,400	8,000
Allocation base (hours)	16,280	14,800[a]	16,000[b]
Allocation base per output unit	2.20	2.00	2.00
Variable MOH	$610,500	$592,000[c]	–
Variable MOH per hour	$37.50[d]	$40.00	–
Fixed MOH	$503,420	$480,000	$480,000
Fixed MOH per hour	$30.92[e]	–	$30.00[f]

[a] $7,400 \times 2.00 = 14,800$
[b] $8,000 \times 2.00 = 16,000$
[c] $7,400 \times 2 \times \$40 = \$592,000$
[d] $\$610,500 \div 16,280$ hours $= \$37.50$ per hour
[e] $\$503,420 \div 16,280$ hours $\simeq \$30.92$ per hour
[f] $\$480,000 \div 16,000$ hours $= \$30$ per hour

8-20 (cont'd)

2. Zyton produces 600 fewer CardioX units than were budgeted. The variable manufacturing-overhead-cost-efficiency variance of $59,200 U arises because more assembly time hours per output unit ($16,280 \div 7,400 = 2.2$ hours) were used than the budgeted 2.0 hours per unit. The variable manufacturing overhead cost spending variance of $40,700 F indicates one or more of the following probably occurred—(i) actual prices of individual items included in variable overhead differ from their budgeted prices, or (ii) actual usage of individual items included in variable overhead differs from their budgeted usage.

The fixed manufacturing overhead cost spending variance of $23,420 U means fixed overhead was above that budgeted. For example, it could be due to an unexpected increase in plant leasing costs. The unfavourable production-volume variance of $36,000 arises because actual output of 7,400 units is below the 8,000 units used in determining the $30.00 per assembly-hour budgeted rate.

3. Planning and control of *variable* manufacturing overhead costs has both a long-run and a short-run focus. It involves Zyton planning to undertake only value-added overhead activities (a long-run view) and then managing the cost drivers of those activities in the most efficient way (a short-run view). Planning and control of *fixed* manufacturing overhead costs at Zyton has primarily a long-run focus. It involves undertaking only value-added fixed-overhead activities for a budgeted level of output. Zyton makes most of the key decisions that determine the level of fixed-overhead costs at the start of the accounting period.

8-22 (20-25 min.)   **Spending and efficiency overhead variances, distribution.**

1.   Budgeted variable overhead rate   = $2 per hour of delivery time

$$\text{Budgeted fixed overhead rate} = \frac{\$120,000}{100,000 \times 0.25} = \frac{\$120,000}{25,000}$$

= $4.80 per hour of delivery time

A detailed comparison of actual and flexible budgeted amounts is:

	Actual	Flexible Budget	Static Budget
Output units (deliveries)	96,000	96,000	100,000
Allocation base (hours)	28,800	24,000a	25,000b
Allocation base per output unit	0.30c	0.25	0.25
Variable MOH	$60,000	$48,000d	–
Variable MOH per hour	$2.08e	$2.00	$2.00
Fixed MOH	$128,400	$120,000	$120,000
Fixed MOH per hour	$4.46f	—	$4.80g

a 96,000 × 0.25 = 24,000
b 100,000 × 0.25 = 25,000
c 28,800 ÷ 96,000 = 0.30
d 96,000 × 0.25 × $2.00 = $48,000
e $60,000 ÷ 28,800 = $2.08
f $128,400 ÷ 28,800 = $4.46
g $120,000 ÷ 25,000 = $4.80

The required variances are:

	Spending Variance	Efficiency Variance
Variable overhead	$2,400 U	9,600 U
Fixed overhead	$8,400 U	—

8-22 (cont'd)

These variances are computed as follows:

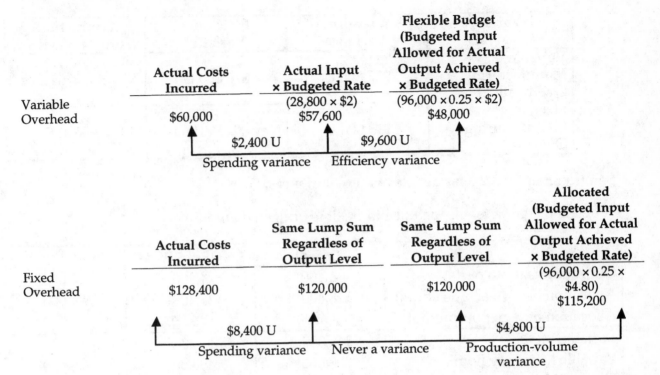

	Actual Costs Incurred	Actual Input × Budgeted Rate	Flexible Budget (Budgeted Input Allowed for Actual Output Achieved × Budgeted Rate)
Variable Overhead	$60,000	(28,800 × $2) $57,600	(96,000 × 0.25 × $2) $48,000

$2,400 U — Spending variance $9,600 U — Efficiency variance

	Actual Costs Incurred	Same Lump Sum Regardless of Output Level	Same Lump Sum Regardless of Output Level	Allocated (Budgeted Input Allowed for Actual Output Achieved × Budgeted Rate)
Fixed Overhead	$128,400	$120,000	$120,000	(96,000 × 0.25 × $4.80) $115,200

$8,400 U — Spending variance   Never a variance $4,800 U — Production-volume variance

The spending variances for variable and fixed overhead are both unfavourable. This means that PPS had increases in either or both the cost of individual items (such as gasoline and truck maintenance) or higher-than-budgeted usage of these individual items per unit of the allocation base (delivery time). The unfavourable efficiency variance for variable overhead results from less efficient use of the cost allocation base—each delivery takes 0.30 hours versus a budgeted 0.25 hours.

2. The single direct cost category is delivery driver payments. The major problem in managing these costs is to restrain the rate of increase in the rate paid to drivers per delivery. PPS faces the challenge of having a low-cost delivery infrastructure. For example, purchasing delivery trucks with low fuel consumption will help reduce variable overhead costs. Purchasing vehicles with low annual maintenance will help reduce fixed overhead costs. Variable overhead costs are controlled by both cost planning, well prior to their incurrence, and day-to-day decisions. In contrast, most fixed overhead cost items are controlled by planning decisions made prior to the start of the year.

8-24 (20-30 min.) **Straightforward four-variance overhead analysis.**

1. The budget for fixed manufacturing overhead is $4,000 \times 6 \times \$15 = \$360,000$.

4-Variance Analysis	Spending Variance	Efficiency Variance	Production-Volume Variance
Variable Manufacturing Overhead	$17,800 U	$16,000 U	Never a Variance
Fixed Manufacturing Overhead	$13,000 U	Never a Variance	$36,000 F

Solution Exhibit 8-24 has details of these variances.

A detailed comparison of actual and flexible budgeted amounts is:

	Actual	Flexible Budget	Static Budget
Output units (auto parts)	4,400	4,400	4,000
Allocation base (machine hours)	28,400	26,400[a]	24,000[b]
Allocation base per output unit	6.45[c]	6.00	6.00
Variable MOH	$245,000	$211,200[d]	–
Variable MOH per hour	$8.63[e]	$8.00	$8.00
Fixed MOH	$373,000	$360,000[f]	$360,000[f]
Fixed MOH per hour	$13.13[g]	–	$15.00[h]

[a] $4,400 \times 6.00 = 26,400$
[b] $4,000 \times 6.00 = 24,000$ hours
[c] $28,400 \div 4,400 = 6.45$
[d] $4,400 \times 6.00 \times \$8.00 = \$211,200$
[e] $\$245,000 \div 28,400 = \$8.63$
[f] $4,000 \times 6.00 \times \$15 = \$360,000$
[g] $\$373,000 \div 28,400 = \$13.13$
[h] $\$360,000 \div 24,000 = \$15.00$

8-24 (cont'd)

2. Variable Manufacturing Overhead Control $245,000
        Accounts Payable Control and other accounts $245,000

    Work in Process Control $211,200
        Variable Manufacturing Overhead Allocated $211,200

    Fixed Manufacturing Overhead Control $373,000
        Wages Payable Control, Accumulated Depreciation
            Control, etc. $373,000

    Work in Process Control $396,000
        Fixed Manufacturing Overhead Allocated $396,000

3.   The control of variable manufacturing overhead requires the identification of the cost drivers for such items as energy, supplies, and repairs. Control often entails monitoring nonfinancial measures that affect each cost item, one by one. Examples are kilowatts used, quantities of lubricants used, and repair parts and hours used. The most convincing way to discover why overhead performance did not agree with a budget is to investigate possible causes, line item by line item.

   Individual fixed manufacturing overhead items are not usually affected very much by day-to-day control. Instead, they are controlled periodically through planning decisions and budgeting procedures that may sometimes have horizons covering six months or a year (for example, management salaries) and sometimes covering many years (for example, long-term leases and depreciation on plant and equipment).

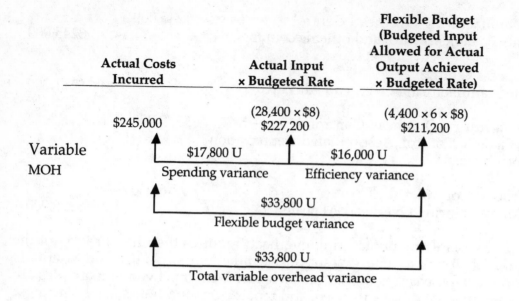

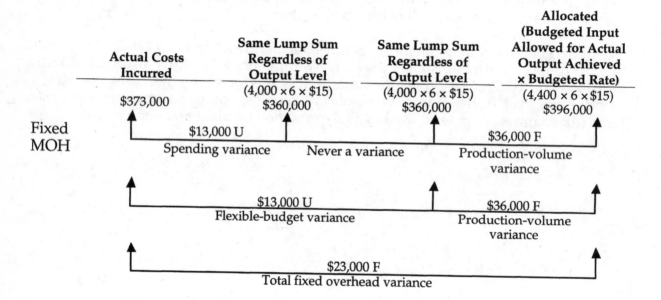

8-26 (35-50 min.) Total overhead, three-variance analysis.

1.   This problem has two major purposes: (a) to give experience with data allocated on a total overhead basis instead of on separate variable and fixed bases, and (b) to reinforce distinctions between actual hours of input, budgeted (standard) hours allowed for actual output, and denominator level.

An analysis of direct manufacturing labour will provide the data for actual hours of input and standard hours allowed. One approach is to plug the known figures (designated by asterisks) into the analytical framework and solve for the unknowns. The direct manufacturing labour efficiency variance can be computed by subtracting $9,640 from $14,440. The complete picture is:

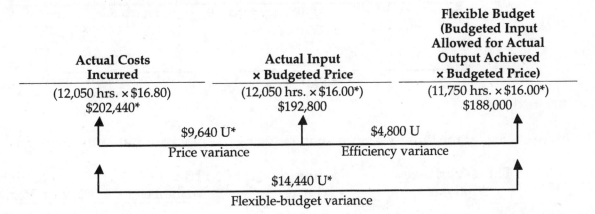

Actual Costs Incurred	Actual Input × Budgeted Price	Flexible Budget (Budgeted Input Allowed for Actual Output Achieved × Budgeted Price)
(12,050 hrs. × $16.80) $202,440*	(12,050 hrs. × $16.00*) $192,800	(11,750 hrs. × $16.00*) $188,000

$9,640 U* Price variance $4,800 U Efficiency variance

$14,440 U* Flexible-budget variance

Manufacturing Overhead

Variable overhead rate = $64,000* ÷ 8,000* hrs. = $8.00 per standard labour-hour

Budgeted fixed overhead costs = $197,600* − 10,000*($8.00) = $117,600

If total manufacturing overhead is allocated at 120% of direct standard manufacturing labour-hours, the single overhead rate must be 120% of $16.00, or $19.20 per hour. Therefore, the fixed overhead component of the rate must be $19.20 − $8.00, or $11.20 per direct standard manufacturing labour-hour.

Let D = denominator level in input units

$$\text{Budgeted fixed overhead rate per input unit} = \frac{\text{Budgeted fixed overhead costs}}{\text{Denominator level in input units}}$$

$$\$11.20 = \frac{\$117,600}{D}$$

$$D = 10,500 \text{ standard direct manufacturing labour-hours}$$

8-26 (cont'd)

A summary three-variance analysis for October follows:

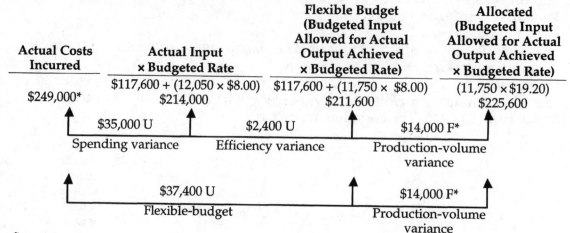

*Known figure

An overview of the three-variance analysis using the block format in the text is:

Three-Variance Analysis	Spending Variance	Efficiency Variance	Production-Volume Variance
Total Manufacturing Overhead	$35,000 U	$2,400 U	$14,000 F

2.   The control of variable manufacturing overhead requires the identification of the cost drivers for such items as energy, supplies, equipment, and maintenance. Control often entails monitoring nonfinancial measures that affect each cost item, one by one. Examples are kilowatts used, quantities of lubricants used, and equipment parts and hours used. The most convincing way to discover why overhead performance did not agree with a budget is to investigate possible causes, line item by line item.

Individual fixed manufacturing overhead items are not usually affected very much by day-to-day control. Instead, they are controlled periodically through planning decisions and budgeting that may sometimes have horizons covering six months or a year (for example, management salaries) and sometimes covering many years (for example, long-term leases and depreciation on plant and equipment).

8-28 (30 min.) **Overhead variances, missing information.**

1.

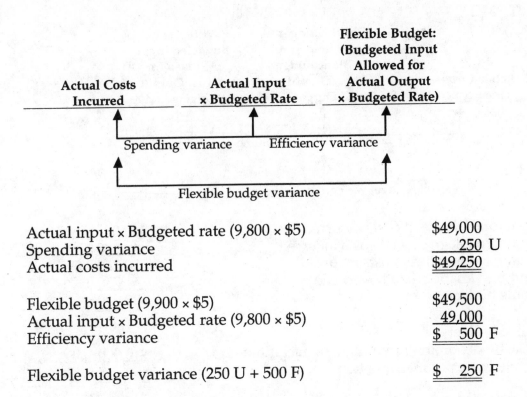

	Actual Costs Incurred	Actual Input × Budgeted Rate	Flexible Budget: (Budgeted Input Allowed for Actual Output × Budgeted Rate)

Spending variance   Efficiency variance

Flexible budget variance

Actual input × Budgeted rate (9,800 × $5)	$49,000
Spending variance	250 U
Actual costs incurred	$49,250
Flexible budget (9,900 × $5)	$49,500
Actual input × Budgeted rate (9,800 × $5)	49,000
Efficiency variance	$ 500 F
Flexible budget variance (250 U + 500 F)	$ 250 F

Variable overhead is overallocated in the amount of $250 (the same amount as favourable flexible-budget variance).

8-28 (cont'd)

2.

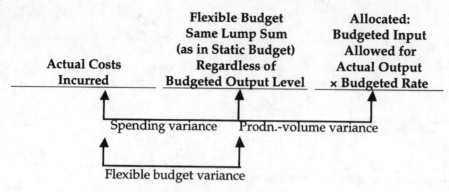

Actual Costs Incurred	Flexible Budget Same Lump Sum (as in Static Budget) Regardless of Budgeted Output Level	Allocated: Budgeted Input Allowed for Actual Output × Budgeted Rate

Spending variance   Prodn.-volume variance

Flexible budget variance

Actual total overhead costs incurred	$80,000
Actual variable overhead costs incurred	49,250
Actual fixed overhead costs incurred	$30,750
Spending variance (fixed overhead)	750 U
Flexible budget	$30,000
Flexible budget	$30,000
Divide by denominator volume in machine-hours	÷10,000
Budgeted rate per machine-hour	$ 3
Allocated ($3 × 9,900 machine-hours)	$29,700
Flexible budget	30,000
Production-volume variance	300 U
Flexible-budget variance = spending variance	$ 750 U
Underallocated amount ($300 U + $750 U)	$ 1,050

8-30 (15 min.) **Comprehensive review of Chapters 7 and 8, static budget.**

1.

	Actual Results (1)	Static-Budget Amounts (2)	Variances (3)
Revenues			
Circulation	$154,000	$140,000	$14,000 F
Advertising	394,600	360,000	34,600 F
	548,600	500,000	48,600 F
Costs			
Direct materials	224,640	180,000	44,640 U
Direct labour costs	50,112	45,000	5,112 U
Variable indirect costs	63,936	60,000	3,936 U
Fixed indirect costs	97,000	90,000	7,000 U
	435,688	375,000	60,688 U
Operating income	$112,912	$125,000	$12,088 U

2.   The *Monthly Herald* had an increase in total revenues of $48,600 above that budgeted. This arose from both a favourable circulation variance ($14,000 increase or 28,000 extra copies sold at $0.50 per copy) and a favourable advertising revenue variance of $34,600.

The actual costs are $60,688 above budget. The largest source of this increase is direct materials. The sources of this increase include (a) 20,000 extra copies printed, and (b) quality problems leading to many pages being unusable. The budgeted print pages for 320,000 copies of 50 pages each was 16,000,000 pages; an extra 1,280,000 pages were used above this budgeted amount.

8-32 (30-40 min.) **Graphs and overhead variances.**

1.

Variable Manufacturing Overhead

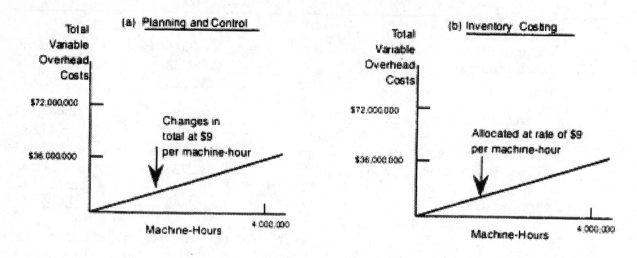

Fixed Manufacturing Overhead

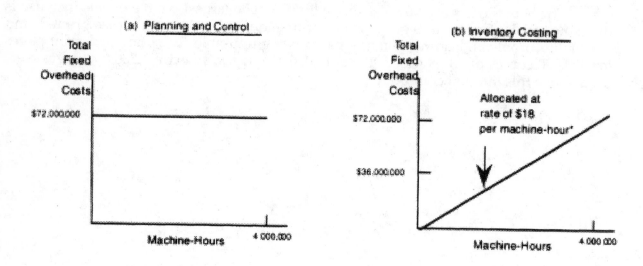

$$\text{*Budgeted fixed - manufacturing - overhead rate per hour} = \frac{\text{Budgeted fixed - manufacturing overhead}}{\text{Denominator level}}$$

$$= \frac{\$72,000,000}{4,000,000 \text{ hours}} = \$18 \text{ per machine - hour}$$

8-32 (cont'd)

2.

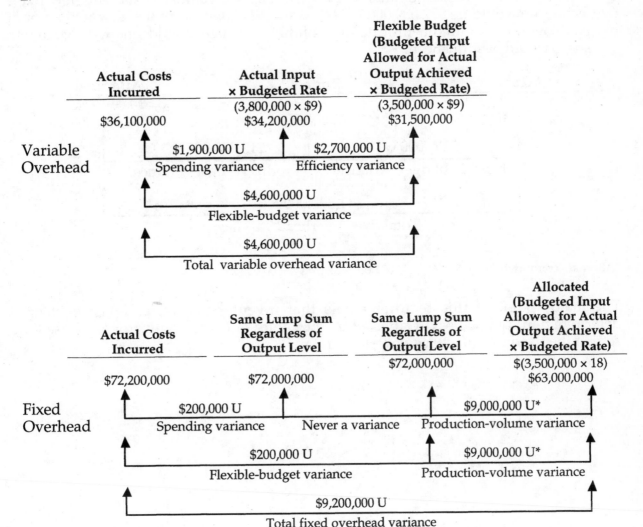

	Actual Costs Incurred	Actual Input × Budgeted Rate	Flexible Budget (Budgeted Input Allowed for Actual Output Achieved × Budgeted Rate)
		(3,800,000 × $9)	(3,500,000 × $9)
	$36,100,000	$34,200,000	$31,500,000
Variable Overhead		$1,900,000 U Spending variance	$2,700,000 U Efficiency variance
		$4,600,000 U Flexible-budget variance	
		$4,600,000 U Total variable overhead variance	

	Actual Costs Incurred	Same Lump Sum Regardless of Output Level	Same Lump Sum Regardless of Output Level	Allocated (Budgeted Input Allowed for Actual Output Achieved × Budgeted Rate)
			$72,000,000	$(3,500,000 × 18)
	$72,200,000	$72,000,000		$63,000,000
Fixed Overhead		$200,000 U Spending variance	Never a variance	$9,000,000 U* Production-volume variance
		$200,000 U Flexible-budget variance		$9,000,000 U* Production-volume variance
		$9,200,000 U Total fixed overhead variance		

*Alternative computation:
 4,000,000 denominator hours – 3,500,000 budgeted hours allowed = 500,000 hours
 500,000 × $18 = $9,000,000 U

3.   The underallocated manufacturing overheads were: variable, $4,600,000, and fixed, $9,200,000. The flexible-budget variance and underallocated overhead are always the same amount for variable overhead because the flexible-budget amount and the allocated amounts coincide. In contrast, the only time the budget and allocated amounts coincide for fixed overhead is when the budgeted input of the allocation base for the actual output level achieved exactly equals the denominator level.

8-32 (cont'd)

4. The choice of the denominator level will affect inventory costs. The new fixed overhead rate would be $72,000,000 ÷ 3,000,000 = $24.00. In turn, the allocated amount of fixed overhead and the production-volume variance would change. No other variances would be influenced:

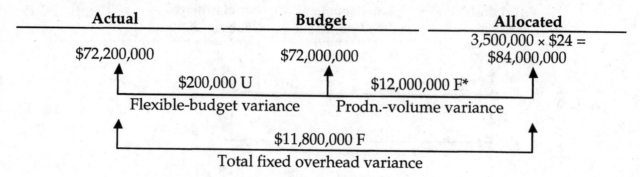

Actual	Budget	Allocated
		3,500,000 × $24 =
$72,200,000	$72,000,000	$84,000,000

$200,000 U $12,000,000 F*

Flexible-budget variance   Prodn.-volume variance

$11,800,000 F

Total fixed overhead variance

*Alternate computation: (3,000,000 – 3,500,000) × $24 = $12,000,000 F

The major point of this requirement is that inventory costs (and hence income determination) can be heavily affected by the choice of the denominator level used for setting the fixed manufacturing overhead rate.

8-34 (60 min.)   **Variance analysis for an activity area.**

The flexible budget is flexed on the number of technical-service hours, which has the budgeted relationship with output units of one hour of technical support for every 5,000 minutes of airtime sold (or every minute of airtime sold has a budgeted 0.0002 minutes of technical service). Key data items for August 31, 2002, are:

		Actual Results	Flexible Budget Amount	Static Budget Amount
1.	Output units (minutes)	7,350,000	7,350,000	6,850,000
2.	Technical service hours	1,500	1,470	1,370
3.	Technical service hours per minute	0.000204	0.0002	0.0002
4.	Variable technical service activity area costs	$31,500	$35,280	$32,880
5.	Variable technical service activity area costs per technical service hour (4/2)	$21.00	$24.00	$24.00
6.	Variable technical service activity area costs per minute (4/1)	$0.004286	$0.004800	$0.004800
7.	Fixed technical service activity area costs	$67,500	$69,870	$69,870
8.	Fixed technical service activity area costs per technical service hour (7/2)	$45.00	$47.53	$51.00
9.	Fixed technical service activity area costs per minute (7/1)	$0.0092	$0.0095	$0.0102

1.   Variable technical service activity area costs per technical service hour is calculated by dividing the total variable technical service activity area costs by the number of technical service hours.

Actual: $31,500/1,500 = $21.00
Budgeted: $32,880/1,370 = $24.00

The budgeted denominator of 1,370 is calculated as budgeted airtime sold (6,850,000) divided by 5,000.

2.   Allocated fixed technical service activity area overhead is calculated by multiplying the budgeted input allowed for actual output achieved (given as 1,470 technical service hours) by the budgeted rate for fixed overhead. The budgeted rate for fixed overhead is calculated by dividing the budgeted amount for fixed technical service activity area costs (given as $69,870) by the budgeted number of technical service hours (1,370):

$$\$69,870/1,370 = \$51.00$$

Allocated fixed technical service activity area overhead is therefore:

$$1,470 \times \$51.00 = \$74,970$$

3.   Variable overhead analysis:

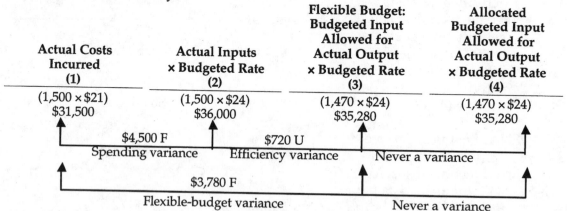

The favourable spending variance of $4,500 can be attributed to the lower variable costs incurred in the technical service activity area ($21 versus $24). The unfavourable efficiency variance ($720) is due to the larger number of technical service hours utilized compared with the number of hours that would have been allowed per plan for the actual number of minutes sold. Since the favourable spending variance is greater than the unfavourable efficiency variance, the flexible-budget variance, in the amount of $3,780, is favourable.

8-34 (cont'd)

4. Fixed overhead analysis:

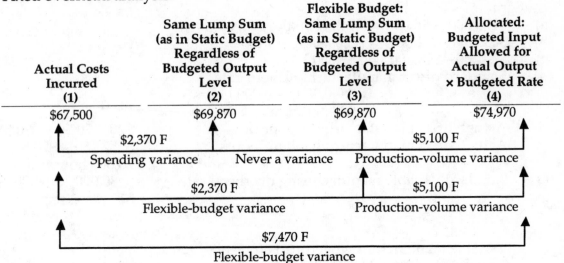

Actual Costs Incurred (1)	Same Lump Sum (as in Static Budget) Regardless of Budgeted Output Level (2)	Flexible Budget: Same Lump Sum (as in Static Budget) Regardless of Budgeted Output Level (3)	Allocated: Budgeted Input Allowed for Actual Output × Budgeted Rate (4)
$67,500	$69,870	$69,870	$74,970

$2,370 F
Spending variance

Never a variance

$5,100 F
Production-volume variance

$2,370 F
Flexible-budget variance

$5,100 F
Production-volume variance

$7,470 F
Flexible-budget variance

CellOne management overalloced fixed overhead by $7,470.

8-36 (30-40 min.) **Working backward from given variances.**

1.   Solution Exhibit 8-36 outlines the Chapter 7 and 8 framework underlying this solution:
(a) $176,000 ÷ $1.10 = 160,000 kilograms
(b) $69,000 ÷ $11.50 = 6,000 kilograms
(c) $10,350 – $18,000 = $7,650 F
(d)   Standard direct manufacturing labour rate
                              = $800,000 ÷ 40,000 hours
                              = $20 per hour

Actual direct manufacturing labour rate	=	$20 + $0.50 = $20.50
Actual direct manufacturing labour hours	=	$552,750 ÷ $20.50
	=	25,500 hours

(e)   Standard variable manufacturing overhead rate = $480,000 ÷ 40,000
                              = $12 per direct manufacturing labour-hour

Variable manufacturing overhead efficiency variance of $18,000 ÷ $12	=	1,500 excess hours
Actual hours – Excess hours	=	Standard hours allowed
25,500 – 1,500	=	24,000 hours

(f)   Budgeted fixed manufacturing overhead rate = $640,000 ÷ 40,000 hours
                              = $16 per direct manufacturing labour-hour

Fixed manufacturing overhead allocated	=	$16 × 24,000 hours
	=	$384,000
Production-volume variance	=	$640,000 – $384,000
	=	$256,000 U

2.   The control of variable manufacturing overhead requires the identification of the cost drivers for such items as energy, supplies, and repairs. Control often entails monitoring nonfinancial measures that affect each cost item, one by one. Examples are kilowatts used, quantities of lubricants used, and repair parts and hours used. The most convincing way to discover why overhead performance did not agree with a budget is to investigate possible causes, line item by line item.

       Individual fixed overhead items are not usually affected very much by day-to-day control. Instead, they are controlled periodically through planning decisions and budgeting procedures that may sometimes have planning horizons covering six months or a year (for example, management salaries) and sometimes covering many years (for example, long-term leases and depreciation on plant and equipment).

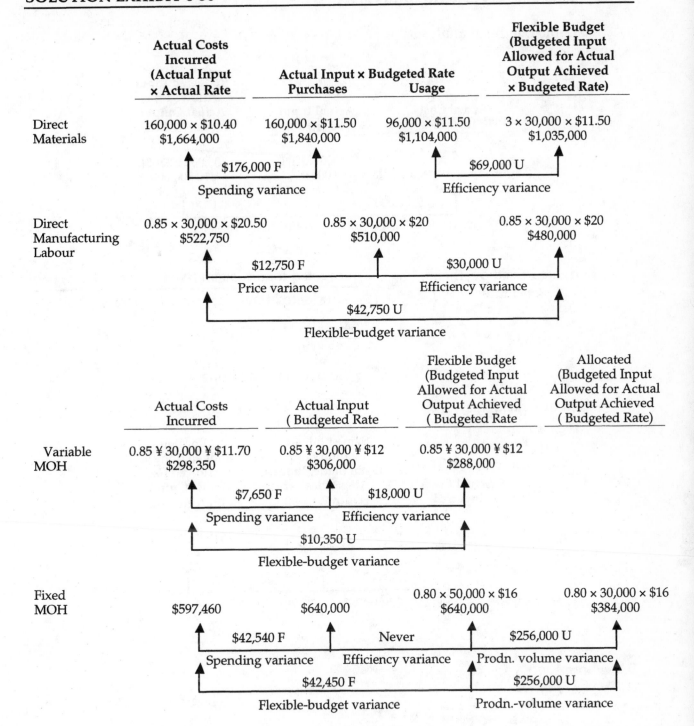

8-38 (30 min.) Overhead analysis.

1. Variable overhead analysis.

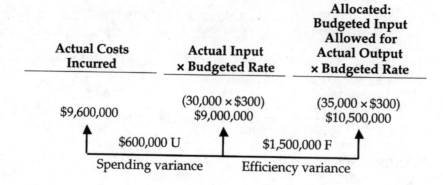

2.

$$\text{Budgeted fixed overhead cost rate} = \frac{\text{Budgeted total costs in fixed overhead cost pool}}{\text{Budgeted total quantity of machine - hours}}$$

$$= \frac{\$4,950,000}{33,000}$$

$$= \$150 \text{ per machine-hour}$$

Fixed overhead analysis:

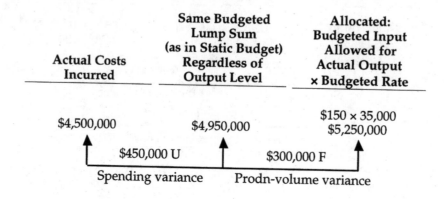

8-40 (40 min.) **Activity-based costing, variance analysis.**

1.

		Static-Budget Amounts	Actual Amounts
a.	Units of SFA produced and sold	21,000	22,000
b.	Batch size	500	550
c.	Number of batches (a ÷ b)	42	40
d.	Testing-hours per batch	5.5	5.4
e.	Total testing-hours (c × d)	231	216
f.	Variable overhead cost per testing-hour	$40	$42
g.	Variable testing overhead costs (e × f)	$9,240	$9,072
h.	Total fixed testing overhead costs	$28,875	$27,216
i.	Fixed overhead cost per testing hour (h ÷ e)	$125	$126

The flexible budget is based on the budgeted number of testing-hours for the actual output achieved, 22,000 units ÷ 500 units per batch = 44 batches.

Computation of variable testing overhead cost variances follows:

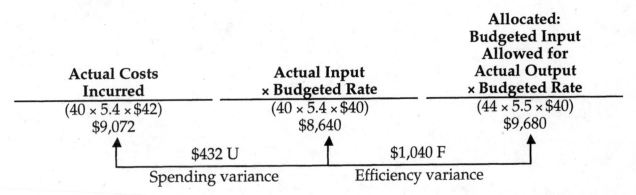

The unfavourable spending variance is due to the actual variable overhead cost per testing-hour increasing from the budgeted $40 per hour to the actual rate of $42 per hour. The favourable efficiency variance is due to the actual output of 22,000 units (1) requiring fewer batches, 40, than the budgeted amount of 42 and (2) each batch taking less time, 5.4 hours, than the budgeted time of 5.5 hours.

8-40 (cont'd)

2.   Computation of the fixed testing overhead cost variances follows:

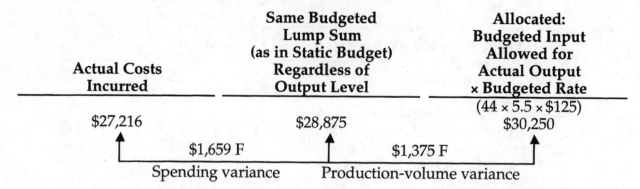

Actual Costs Incurred		Same Budgeted Lump Sum (as in Static Budget) Regardless of Output Level		Allocated: Budgeted Input Allowed for Actual Output × Budgeted Rate
				(44 × 5.5 × $125)
$27,216		$28,875		$30,250
	$1,659 F		$1,375 F	
	Spending variance		Production-volume variance	

The fixed testing overhead cost spending variance is $1,659 F because the amount of actual costs was lower than the budgeted amount of $28,875. The production-volume variance is $1,375 F because the actual number of SFA produced and sold required less costs than budgeted.

8-42 (60 min.) **Journal entries (continuation of 8-41).**

Key information underlying the computation of variances is:

		Actual Results	Flexible Budget Amount	Static-Budget Amount
1.	Output units (panels)	19,200	19,200	17,760
2.	Machine-hours	36,480	38,400	35,520
3.	Machine-hours per panel	1.90	2.00	2.00
4.	Variable MOH costs	$1,532,160	$1,536,000	$1,420,800
5.	Variable MOH costs per machine-hour (4/2)	$42.00	$40.00	$40.00
6.	Variable MOH costs per unit (4/1)	$79.80	$80.00	$80.00
7.	Fixed MOH costs	$7,004,160	$6,961,920	$6,961,920
8.	Fixed MOH costs per machine-hour (7/2)	$192.00	$181.30	$196.00
9.	Fixed MOH costs per unit (7/1)	$364.80	$362.60	$392.00

Solution Exhibit 8-42 has the computation of the variances.

8-42 (cont'd)

SOLUTION EXHIBIT 8-42

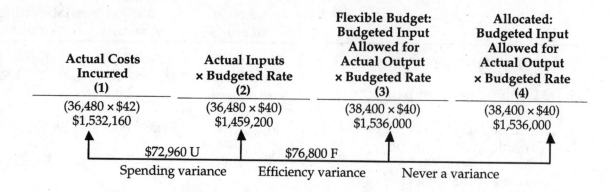

Actual Costs Incurred (1)	Actual Inputs × Budgeted Rate (2)	Flexible Budget: Budgeted Input Allowed for Actual Output × Budgeted Rate (3)	Allocated: Budgeted Input Allowed for Actual Output × Budgeted Rate (4)
(36,480 × $42) $1,532,160	(36,480 × $40) $1,459,200	(38,400 × $40) $1,536,000	(38,400 × $40) $1,536,000

$72,960 U ← Spending variance → | $76,800 F ← Efficiency variance → | ← Never a variance →

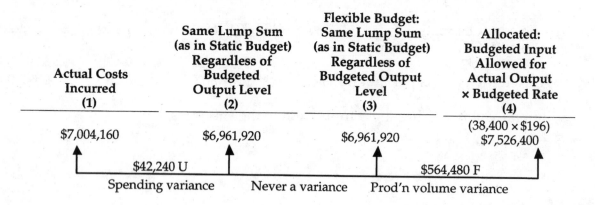

Actual Costs Incurred (1)	Same Lump Sum (as in Static Budget) Regardless of Budgeted Output Level (2)	Flexible Budget: Same Lump Sum (as in Static Budget) Regardless of Budgeted Output Level (3)	Allocated: Budgeted Input Allowed for Actual Output × Budgeted Rate (4)
$7,004,160	$6,961,920	$6,961,920	(38,400 × $196) $7,526,400

$42,240 U ← Spending variance → | ← Never a variance → | $564,480 F ← Prod'n volume variance →

8-42 (cont'd)

1. **Journal entries for variable MOH, year ended December 31, 2002:**

Variable MOH Control	1,532,160	
Accounts Payable Control and Other Accounts		1,532,160
Work-in-Process Control	1,536,000	
Variable MOH Allocated		1,536,000
Variable MOH Allocated	1,536,000	
Variable MOH Spending Variance	72,960	
Variable MOH Control		1,532,160
Variable MOH Efficiency Variance		76,800

Journal Entries for fixed MOH, year ended December 31, 2002:

Fixed MOH Control	7,004,160	
Wages Payable, Accumulated Depreciation, etc.		7,004,160
Work-in-Process Control	7,526,400	
Fixed MOH Allocated		7,526,400
Fixed MOH Allocated	7,526,400	
Fixed MOH Spending Variance	42,240	
Fixed MOH Control		7,044,160
Fixed MOH Production-Volume Variance		564,480

2. **Adjustment of COGS**

Cost of Goods Sold		526,080
Variable MOH Efficiency Variance	76,800	
Fixed MOH Production-Volume Variance	564,480	
Variable MOH Spending Variance		72,960
Fixed MOH Spending Variance		42,240

8-44 (20-30 min.) **Variance analysis for ABC.**

1.   ABC Variance Analysis—Calculation of Key Information

	Actual Results	Flexible Budget Amount	Static Budget Amount
1. Output units (test)	265	265	250
2. Launching hours	5,300	5,300	5,500
3. Launching hours per test (2/1)	20	20	22
4. Variable launch activity area costs	$371,000,000	$360,400,000	$374,000,000
5. Variable launch activity area costs per testing hour (4/2)	$70,000	$68,000	$68,000
6. Variable launch activity area costs per test (4/1)	$1,400,000	$1,360,000	$1,496,000
7. Fixed launch activity area costs	$1,643,000,000	$1,694,000,000	$1,694,000,000
8. Fixed launch activity area costs per testing hour (7/2)	$310,000	$319,623	$308,000
9. Fixed launch activity area costs per test (7/1)	$6,200,000	$6,392,453	$6,776,000

2,3.   Starport engaged in 15 (265 – 250) more launches than planned. Each launch took 2 (20 – 22) hours less than budgeted. The cost of each launch hour was $2,000 ($70,000 – $60,000) more than budgeted, and each launch was $40,000 ($1,400,000 – $1,360,000) more than budgeted. The fixed costs incurred totalled $51,000,000 ($1,643,000,000 – $1,694,000,000) less than budget.

CHAPTER 9
INCOME EFFECTS OF ALTERNATIVE INVENTORY COSTING METHODS

9-2 The term **direct costing** is a misnomer for variable costing for two reasons:
   a. Variable costing does not include all direct costs as inventoriable costs. Only variable direct manufacturing costs are included. Any fixed direct manufacturing costs and any direct nonmanufacturing costs (either variable or fixed) are excluded from inventoriable costs.
   b. Variable costing includes as inventoriable costs not only direct manufacturing costs but also some indirect costs (variable indirect manufacturing costs).

9-4 The main issue between variable costing and absorption costing is the proper timing of the release of fixed manufacturing costs as costs of the period:
   a. at the time of incurrence, or
   b. at the time the finished units to which the fixed overhead relates are sold.
Variable costing uses (a) and absorption costing uses (b).

9-6 Variable costing does not view fixed costs as unimportant or irrelevant, but it maintains that the distinction between behaviours of different costs is crucial for certain decisions. The planning and management of fixed costs is critical, irrespective of what inventory costing method is used.

9-8 The factors that affect the breakeven point under variable costing are:

   1. Fixed costs
   2. Unit contribution margin
   3. Sales level in units

9-10 Examples of dysfunctional decisions managers may make to increase reported operating income are:
   a. Plant managers may switch production to those orders that absorb the highest amount of manufacturing overhead, irrespective of the demand by customers.
   b. Plant managers may accept a particular order to increase production even though another plant in the same company is better suited to handle that order.
   c. Plant managers may defer maintenance beyond the current period to free-up more time for production.

9-12 The *downward demand spiral* is the continuing reduction in demand for its product that occurs when the prices of competitors' products are not met and (as demand drops further), higher and higher unit costs result in more and more reluctance to meet competitors' prices. Pricing decisions need to consider competitors and customers as well as costs.

9-14 The *theoretical capacity* and *practical capacity* denominator-level concepts emphasize what a plant can supply. The *normal utilization* and *master-budget utilization* concepts emphasize what customers demand in products produced by a plant.

9-16 (30 min.) **Variable and absorption costing, explaining operating income differences.**

1. Key inputs for income statement computations are:

	April	May
Beginning inventory	0	150
Production	500	400
Goods available for sale	500	550
Units sold	350	520
Ending inventory	150	30

The unit fixed and total manufacturing costs per unit under absorption costing are:

		April	May
(a)	Fixed manufacturing costs	$2,000,000	$2,000,000
(b)	Units produced	500	400
(c)=(a)÷(b)	Unit fixed manufacturing costs	$4,000	$5,000
(d)	Unit variable manufacturing costs	$10,000	$10,000
(e)=(c)+(d)	Unit total manufacturing costs	$14,000	$15,000

9-16 (cont'd)

(a) Variable costing

	April 2002		May 2002	
Revenues[a]		$8,400,000		$12,480,000
Variable costs				
Beginning inventory	$ 0		$1,500,000	
Variable cost of goods manufactured[b]	5,000,000		4,000,000	
Cost of goods available for sale	5,000,000		5,500,000	
Ending inventory[c]	1,500,000		300,000	
Variable manufacturing cost of goods sold	3,500,000		5,200,000	
Variable marketing costs	1,050,000		1,560,000	
Total variable costs[d]		4,550,000		6,760,000
Contribution margin		3,850,000		5,720,000
Fixed costs				
Fixed manufacturing costs	2,000,000		2,000,000	
Fixed marketing costs	600,000		600,000	
Total fixed costs		2,600,000		2,600,000
Operating income		$1,250,000		$3,120,000

a $24,000 × 350; 520
b $10,000 × 500; 400
c $10,000 × 150; 30
d $3,000 × 350; 520

9-16 (cont'd)

(b) Absorption costing

	April 2002		May 2002	
Revenues[a]		$8,400,000		$12,480,000
Cost of goods sold				
Beginning inventory	0		$2,100,000	
Variable manufacturing costs[b]	$5,000,000		4,000,000	
Fixed manufacturing costs[c]	2,000,000		2,000,000	
Cost of goods available for sale	7,000,000		8,100,000	
Ending inventory[d]	2,100,000		450,000	
Cost of goods sold		4,900,000		7,650,000
Gross margin		3,500,000		4,830,000
Marketing costs				
Variable marketing costs[e]	1,050,000		1,560,000	
Fixed marketing costs	600,000		600,000	
Total marketing costs		1,650,000		2,160,000
Operating income		$1,850,000		$ 2,670,000

a $24,000 × 350; 520
b $10,000 × 500; 400
c ($4,000 × 500); ($5,000 × 400)
d ($14,000 × 150; $15,000 × 30)
e ($3,000 × 350; $3,000 × 520)

2. $\left(\begin{array}{c}\text{Absorption-costing}\\\text{operating income}\end{array}\right) - \left(\begin{array}{c}\text{Variable-costing}\\\text{operating income}\end{array}\right) = \left(\begin{array}{c}\text{Fixed manufacturing}\\\text{costs in}\\\text{ending inventory}\end{array}\right) - \left(\begin{array}{c}\text{Fixed manufacturing}\\\text{costs in}\\\text{beginning inventory}\end{array}\right)$

April:

$$\begin{aligned} \$1,850,000 - \$1,250,000 &= (\$4,000 \times 150) - (\$0) \\ \$600,000 &= \$600,000 \end{aligned}$$

May:

$$\begin{aligned} \$2,670,000 - \$3,120,000 &= (\$5,000 \times 30) - (\$4,000 \times 150) \\ -\$450,000 &= \$150,000 - \$600,000 \\ -\$450,000 &= -\$450,000 \end{aligned}$$

The difference between absorption and variable costing is due solely to moving fixed manufacturing costs into inventories as inventories increase (as in April) and out of inventories as they decrease (as in May).

9-18 (40 min.) Variable and absorption costing, explaining operating income differences.

1. Key inputs for income statement computations are:

	January	February	March
Beginning inventory	0	300	300
Production	1,000	800	1,250
Goods available for sale	1,000	1,100	1,550
Units sold	700	800	1,500
Ending inventory	300	300	50

The unit fixed and total manufacturing costs per unit under absorption costing are:

		January	February	March
(a)	Fixed manufacturing costs	$400,000	$400,000	$400,000
(b)	Units produced	1,000	800	1,250
(c)=(a)÷(b)	Unit fixed manufacturing costs	$ 400	$ 500	$ 320
(d)	Unit variable manufacturing costs	$ 900	$ 900	$ 900
(e)=(c)+(d)	Unit total manufacturing costs	$ 1,300	$ 1,400	$ 1,220

9-18 (cont'd)

(a) Variable Costing

	January 2002	February 2002	March 2002
Revenues[a]	$1,750,000	$2,000,000	$3,750,000
Variable costs			
Beginning inventory[b]	$ 0	$270,000	$ 270,000
Variable cost of goods manufactured[c]	900,000	720,000	1,125,000
Cost of goods available for sale	900,000	990,000	1,395,000
Ending inventory[d]	270,000	270,000	45,000
Variable manufacturing cost of goods sold	630,000	720,000	1,350,000
Variable marketing costs[e]	420,000	480,000	900,000
Total variable costs	1,050,000	1,200,000	2,250,000
Contribution margin	700,000	800,000	1,500,000
Fixed costs			
Fixed manufacturing costs	400,000	400,000	400,000
Fixed marketing costs	140,000	140,000	140,000
Total fixed costs	540,000	540,000	540,000
Operating income	$ 160,000	$ 260,000	$ 960,000

a $2,500 × 700; 800; 1,500

b 0; $900 × 300; 300

c $900 × 1,000; 800; 1,250

d $900 × 300; 300; 50

e $600 × 700; 800; 1,500

9-6

9-18 (cont'd)

(b) Absorption Costing

	January 2002		February 2002		March 2002	
Revenues[a]		$1,750,000		$2,000,000		$3,750,000
Cost of goods sold						
Beginning inventory[b]	$ 0		$390,000		420,000	
Variable manufacturing costs[c]	900,000		720,000		1,125,000	
Fixed manufacturing costs[d]	400,000		400,000		400,000	
Cost of goods available for sale	1,300,000		1,510,000		1,945,000	
Ending inventory[e]	390,000		420,000		61,000	
Cost of goods sold		910,000		1,090,000		1,884,000
Gross margin		840,000		910,000		1,866,000
Marketing costs						
Variable marketing costs[f]	420,000		480,000		900,000	
Fixed marketing costs	140,000		140,000		140,000	
Total marketing costs		560,000		620,000		1,040,000
Operating income		$280,000		$ 290,000		$ 826,000

a $2,500 × 700; 800; 1,500
b (0; $1,300 × 300; $1,400 × 300)
c $900 × 1,000, 800, 1,250
d ($400 × 1,000); ($500 × 800); ($320 × 1,250)
e ($1,300 × 300); ($1,400 × 300); ($1,220 × 50)
f $600 × 700; 800; 1,500

9-18 (cont'd)

2. $\begin{pmatrix} \text{Absorption-costing} \\ \text{operating income} \end{pmatrix} - \begin{pmatrix} \text{Variable-costing} \\ \text{operating income} \end{pmatrix} = \begin{pmatrix} \text{Fixed manufacturing} \\ \text{costs in} \\ \text{ending inventory} \end{pmatrix} - \begin{pmatrix} \text{Fixed manufacturing} \\ \text{costs in} \\ \text{beginning inventory} \end{pmatrix}$

January: $\$280,000 - \$160,000 = \$120,000 - \$0$
             $\$120,000 = \$120,000$

February: $\$290,000 - \$260,000 = \$150,000 - \$120,000$
             $\$30,000 = \$30,000$

March: $\$826,000 - \$960,000 = \$16,000 - \$150,000$
             $-\$134,000 = -\$134,000$

The difference between absorption and variable costing is due solely to moving fixed manufacturing costs into inventories as inventories increase (as in January) and out of inventories as they decrease (as in March).

9-20 (10 min.) **Absorption and variable costing.**

The answers are 1(a), $440,000, and 2(c), $200,000. Computations follow:

1. **Absorption Costing:**

Revenues[a]		$4,800,000
Cost of goods sold:		
Variable manufacturing costs[b]	$2,400,000	
Fixed manufacturing costs[c]	360,000	2,760,000
Gross margin		2,040,000
Marketing and administrative costs:		
Variable marketing and administrative[d]	1,200,000	
Fixed marketing and administrative	400,000	1,600,000
Operating income		$ 440,000

[a]$40 × 120,000
[b]$20 × 120,000
[c]Fixed manufacturing rate $\quad = \quad$ $600,000 ÷ 200,000
$\qquad\qquad\qquad\qquad\qquad\;\; = \quad$ $3 per output unit

$3 × 120,000
[d]$10 × 120,000

2. **Variable Costing:**

Revenues[a]		$4,800,000
Variable costs:		
Variable manufacturing costs of goods sold[b]	$2,400,000	
Variable marketing and administrative costs[c]	1,200,000	3,600,000
Contribution margin		1,200,000
Fixed costs:		
Fixed manufacturing costs	600,000	
Fixed marketing and administrative costs	400,000	1,000,000
Operating income		$ 200,000

[a]$40 × 120,000
[b]$20 × 120,000
[c]$10 × 120,000

9-22 (30-40 min.) **Income statements.**

1.

The Mass Company
Income Statements for the Year 2003
(in thousands)

(a) **Variable Costing:**

Revenues (25,000 × $40)		$1,000
Variable costs:		
Beginning inventory (1,000 × $24)	$ 24	
Variable cost of goods manufactured (29,000 × $24)	696	
Cost of goods available for sale	720	
Ending inventory (5,000 × $24)	120	
Variable manufacturing cost of goods sold	600	
Variable marketing and administrative costs		
(25,000 × $1.20)	30	
Variable costs		630
Contribution margin		370
Fixed costs:		
Fixed manufacturing overhead costs	120	
Fixed marketing and admin. costs	190	
Fixed costs		310
Operating income		$ 60

(b) **Absorption Costing:**

Revenues (25,000 × $40)		$1,000
Cost of goods sold:		
Beginning inventory (1,000 × $28)	$ 28	
Variable manufacturing costs (29,000 × $24)	696	
Fixed manufacturing costs (given)	120	
Cost of goods available for sale	844	
Ending inventory (5,000 × $28)	140	
Cost of goods sold		704
Gross margin		296
Marketing and administrative costs:		
Variable marketing and admin. costs (25,000 × $1.20)	30	
Fixed marketing and admin. costs	190	
Marketing and admin. costs		220
Operating income		$ 76

9-22 (cont'd)

2.
$$\begin{pmatrix} \text{Absorption} \\ \text{costing} \\ \text{operating} \\ \text{income} \end{pmatrix} - \begin{pmatrix} \text{Variable} \\ \text{costing} \\ \text{operating} \\ \text{income} \end{pmatrix} = \begin{pmatrix} \text{Fixed} \\ \text{manuf. costs} \\ \text{in ending} \\ \text{inventory} \end{pmatrix} - \begin{pmatrix} \text{Fixed} \\ \text{manuf. costs} \\ \text{in beginning} \\ \text{inventory} \end{pmatrix}$$

$$
\begin{aligned}
\$76{,}000 - \$60{,}000 &= [(5{,}000 \times \$4) - (1{,}000 \times \$4)] \\
&= \$20{,}000 - \$4{,}000 \\
&= \$16{,}000
\end{aligned}
$$

The operating income figures differ because the amount of fixed manufacturing costs in the ending inventory differs from that in beginning inventory.

3. Advantages:

(a) The fixed costs are reported as period costs (and not allocated to inventory), thus increasing the likelihood of better control of these costs.
(b) Operating income is directly influenced by changes in unit sales (and not influenced by build-up of inventory).
(c) The impact of fixed costs on operating income is emphasized.
(d) The income statements are in the same form as used for cost-volume-profit analysis.
(e) Product line, territory, etc., contribution margins are emphasized and more readily ascertainable.

Disadvantages:
(a) Total costs may be overlooked when considering operating problems.
(b) Distinction between fixed and variable costs is arbitrary for many costs.
(c) Emphasis on variable costs may cause some managers to ignore fixed costs.
(d) A new variable-costing system may be too costly to install unless top managers think that operating decisions will be improved collectively.

9-24 (10-20 min.) **Breakeven under absorption costing (continuation of 9-23).**

1.   The unit contribution margin is $5 − $3 − $1 = $1. Total fixed costs ($540,000) divided by the unit contribution margin ($1.00) equals 540,000 units. Therefore, under variable costing, 540,000 units must be <u>sold</u> to break even.

2.   If there are no changes in inventory levels, the breakeven point can be the same, 540,000 units, under both variable costing and absorption costing. However, as the preceding problem demonstrates, under absorption costing the breakeven point is not unique; operating income is a function of both sales and production. Some fixed overhead is "held back" when inventories rise (10,000 units × $0.70 = $7,000), so operating income is positive even though sales are at the breakeven level as commonly conceived.

$$\text{Breakeven sales in units} = \frac{\left(\begin{array}{c}\text{Total fixed}\\\text{costs}\end{array}\right) + \left[\left(\begin{array}{c}\text{Fixed manuf.}\\\text{overhead}\\\text{rate}\end{array}\right) \times \left(\begin{array}{c}\text{Breakeven}\\\text{sales in}\\\text{units}\end{array} - \begin{array}{c}\text{Units}\\\text{produced}\end{array}\right)\right]}{\text{Unit contribution margin}}$$

Let N   =   Breakeven sales in units

$$N = \frac{\$540,000 + \$0.70(N - 550,000)}{\$1.00}$$

$$N = \frac{\$540,000 + \$0.70N - \$385,000}{\$1.00}$$

$$\$0.30N = \$155,000$$

$$N = 516,667 \text{ units (rounded)}$$

Therefore, under absorption costing when 550,000 units are produced, 516,667 units must be sold for the income statement to report zero operating income.

Proof of 2002 breakeven point:

Gross margin, 516,667 units × ($5.00 − $3.70)		$671,667
Output level MOH variance, as before	$ 35,000	
Marketing and administrative costs:		
Variable, 516,667 units × $1.00	516,667	
Fixed	120,000	671,667
Operating income		$ 0

9-24 (cont'd)

3.   If no units are sold, variable costing will show an operating loss equal to the fixed manufacturing costs, $420,000 in this instance. In contrast, the company would break even under absorption costing, although nothing was sold to customers. This is an extreme example of what has been called "selling fixed manufacturing overhead to inventory."

A final note: We find it helpful to place the following comparisons on the board, keyed to the three parts of this problem:

    1. Breakeven = f (sales)
    2. Breakeven = f (sales and production)
    3. Breakeven = f (0 units sold and 540,000 units produced), an extreme case

9-26 (40 min) Absorption vs. variable costing.

1. The number of Mimic™ pills sold in 2002 is:
    $44,800 \times 365 \times 3 = 49,056,000$ pills

Ending inventory on December 31, 2002, is 5,694,000 pills:

Unit data	
Beginning inventory	0
Production	54,750,000
Sales	49,056,000
Ending inventory	5,694,000

Variable cost data	
Manufacturing costs per pill produced	
Direct materials	$0.05
Direct manufacturing labour	0.04
Manufacturing overhead	0.11
Total variable manufacturing costs	$0.20

Fixed cost data	
Manufacturing costs	$ 7,358,400
R&D	4,905,600
SG&A	19,622,400

Wholesale selling price per pill	$1.20
Fixed manufacturing costs allocation rate per pill (7,358,400 ÷ 54,750,000)	$0.15 (Given)

2. Variable costing:

Revenues: $1.20 × 49,056,000		$58,867,200
Variable costs		
Beginning inventory	$ 0	
Variable manuf. cost: $0.20 × 54,750,000	10,950,000	
Cost of goods available for sale	10,950,000	
Deduct ending inventory: $0.20 × 5,694,000	1,138,800	
Variable cost of goods sold	9,811,200	
Variable marketing costs: $0.07 × 49,056,000	3,433,920	
Adjust for variable-cost variance	0	
Total variable costs		13,245,120
Contribution margin		45,622,080
Fixed costs		
Fixed manufacturing costs	7,358,400	
Fixed R&D	4,905,600	
Fixed marketing	19,622,400	
Total fixed costs		31,886,400
Operating income		$13,735,680

9–26 (cont'd.)

Absorption costing:

Revenues: $1.20 × 49,056,000		$58,867,200
Costs of goods sold		
Beginning inventory	$ 0	
Variable manuf. cost: $0.20 × 54,750,000	10,950,000	
Fixed manuf. costs: $0.15 × 54,750,000	8,212,500	
Cost of goods available for sale	19,162,500	
Deduct ending inventory: $0.35 × 5,694,000	(1,992,900)	
Adjust for manuf. variances [a]	(854,100)	
Cost of goods sold		16,315,500
Gross margin		42,551,700
Operating costs		
Variable marketing costs: $0.07 × 49,056,000	3,433,920	
Fixed R&D	4,905,600	
Fixed marketing	19,622,400	
Adjustment for operating cost variances	0	
Total operating costs		27,961,920
Operating income		$14,589,780

[a] Production - volume variance = (0.15 × 54,750,000 units) – $7,358,4000 = $854,100F

3. The difference of $854,100 is due to:

$$= \left(\begin{array}{c} \text{Fixed manufacturing} \\ \text{costs in ending inventory} \\ \text{under absorption costing} \end{array} \right) - \left(\begin{array}{c} \text{Fixed manufacturing} \\ \text{costs in beginning inventory} \\ \text{under absorption costing} \end{array} \right)$$

$$= (\$0.15 \times 5,694,000) - \$0$$

$$= \mathbf{\$854,100}$$

9-28 (10 min.) **Capacity management, denominator-level capacity concepts.**

1. d
2. c, d
3. d
4. a
5. c
6. a, b
7. a
8. b
9. c, d
10. b
11. a, b

9-30 (25-30 min.) **Alternative denominator-level concepts.**

1.

Denominator-Level Concept	Budgeted Fixed Manufacturing Overhead per Period	Budgeted Denominator Level	Budgeted Fixed Manufacturing Overhead Cost Rate
Theoretical capacity	$42,000,000	5,256,000	$ 7.99
Practical capacity	42,000,000	3,500,000	12.00
Normal utilization	42,000,000	2,800,000	15.00
Master-budget utilization			
(a) Jan.-June 2000	21,000,000	1,120,000	18.75
(b) July-Dec. 2000	21,000,000	1,680,000	12.50

The differences arise for several reasons:

a. The theoretical and practical capacity concepts emphasize supply factors, while normal utilization and master-budget utilization emphasize demand factors.

b. The two separate six-month rates for the master-budget utilization concept differ because of seasonal differences in budgeted production.

2. Theoretical capacity—based on the production of output at maximum efficiency for 100% of the time.

Practical capacity—reduces theoretical capacity for unavoidable operating interruptions such as scheduled maintenance time, shutdowns for holidays and other days, and so on.

9-30 (cont'd)

For each of the three determinants of capacity in Lucky Lager's plant, practical capacity is less than theoretical capacity:

	Barrels per Hour	Working Hours per Day	Working Days per Year	Capacity
Theoretical capacity	600	× 24	× 365	= 5,256,000
Practical capacity	500	× 20	× 350	= 3,500,000

3. The smaller the denominator, the higher will be the amount of overhead costs capitalized for inventory units. Thus, if the plant manager wishes to be able to "adjust" plant operating income by building inventory, master-budget utilization or possibly normal utilization would be preferred.

9-32 (60 min.)Standard absorption, variable and throughput costing.

1.

$$\text{Unit fixed manufacturing overhead cost} = \frac{\$10,000}{2,000}$$

$$= \$5 \text{ per unit produced}$$

Unit manufacturing costs

(a) Absorption costing

	2002	2003
Variable direct manuf. costs per unit	$40.00	$40.00
Variable indirect manuf. costs per unit	15.00	15.00
Fixed manuf. costs per unit	5.00	5.00
Total manuf. cost per unit	$60.00	$60.00

b) Variable costing

	2002	2003
Variable direct manuf. costs per unit	$40.00	$40.00
Variable indirect manuf. costs per unit	15.00	15.00
Total variable manuf. cost per unit	$55.00	$55.00

c) Throughput costing

	2002	2003
Variable direct materials per unit	$23.00	23.00

Unit data for 2002 and 2003 are:

	2002	2003
Beginning inventory	900	1,400
Production	2,000	400
Goods available for sale	2,900	1,800
Sales	1,500	1,700
Ending inventory	1,400	100

9-32 (cont'd)

(a) <u>Absorption costing</u>

	2002	**2003**
Revenues[a]	<u>$150,000</u>	<u>$170,000</u>
Cost of goods sold		
Beginning inventory[b]	54,000	84,000
Variable manuf. costs[c]	110,000	22,000
Fixed manuf. costs[d]	<u>10,000</u>	<u>2,000</u>
Cost of goods available for sale	174,000	108,000
Ending inventory[e]	<u>84,000</u>	<u>6,000</u>
Cost of goods sold (at std. cost)	90,000	102,000
Adjustment for variances-variable	1,000 U	1,000 U
Adjustment for variances-fixed[f]	<u>0</u>	<u>8,000</u> U
Total cost of goods sold	<u>91,000</u>	<u>111,000</u>
Gross margin	59,000	59,000
Variable marketing costs[g]	1,500	1,700
Fixed marketing costs	<u>3,000</u>	<u>3,000</u>
Total marketing costs	<u>4,500</u>	<u>4,700</u>
Operating income	<u>$ 54,500</u>	<u>$ 54,300</u>

a $100 × 1,500; $100 × 1,700
b $60 × 900; $60 × 1,400
c $55 × 2,000; $55 × 400
d $5 × 2,000; $5 × 400
e $60 × 1,400; $60 × 100
f   Production-volume variance = (2,000 − 400) × $5
g $1 × 1,500; $1 × 1,700

9-32 (cont'd)

(b) Variable costing

	2002	2003
Revenues[a]	$150,000	$170,000
Variable costs		
Beginning inventory[b]	49,500	77,000
Variable cost of goods manufactured[c]	110,000	22,000
Cost of goods available for sale	159,500	99,000
Ending inventory[d]	77,000	5,500
Variable manuf. COGSs	82,500	93,500
Variable marketing costs[e]	1,500	1,700
Variable costs (at standard costs)	84,000	95,200
Adjustment for variances	1,000 U	1,000 U
Total variable costs	85,000	96,200
Contribution margin	65,000	73,800
Fixed costs		
Fixed manufacturing overhead costs	10,000	10,000
Fixed marketing costs	3,000	3,000
Fixed costs (at standard costs)	13,000	13,000
Adjustment for variances	0	0
Total fixed costs	13,000	13,000
Operating income	$ 52,000	$ 60,800

[a]$100 × 1,500; $100 × 1,700
[b]$55 × 900; $55 × 1,400
[c]$55 × 2,000; $55 × 400
[d]$55 × 1,400; $55 × 100
[e]$1 × 1,500; $1 × 1,700

9-32 (cont'd)

(c) Throughput costing

	2002	2003
Revenues[a]	$150,000	$170,000
Variable direct materials costs		
Beginning inventory[b]	20,700	32,200
Direct materials in goods manuf.[c]	46,000	9,200
Cost of goods available for sale	66,700	41,400
Ending inventory[d]	32,200	2,300
Direct materials costs (at std.)	34,500	39,100
Adjustment for direct materials variances	0	0
Total variable direct materials costs	34,500	39,100
Throughput contribution	115,500	130,900
Other costs		
Manufacturing	74,000[e]	22,800[f]
Marketing	4,500[g]	4,700[h]
Adjustment for variances	1,000 U	1,000 U
Total other costs	79,500	28,500
Operating income	$ 36,000	$102,400

[a] $100 × 1,500; $100 × 1,700
[b] $23 × 900; $23 × 1,400
[c] $23 × 2,000; $23 × 400
[d] $23 × 1,400; $23 × 100

[e] [($17+$15) × 2,000] + $10,000 = $74,000
[f] [($17+$15) × 400] + $10,000 = $22,800
[g] [($1 × 1,500) +$ 3,000] = $4,500
[h] [($1 × 1,700) + $3,000] = $4,700

2. Absorption costing makes operating income a function of both sales levels and production levels. This can create an incentive for managers to manipulate production levels to increase their operating income in a period when this is not in Byrd Company's best interest. It is not always the case that managers will manipulate production to increase inventory levels. They would also consider differences across periods in the fixed manufacturing overhead rates.

Variable costing highlights the effect of changes in units sold on operating income. It thus reduces the incentives for showing production variations to "manage" operating income for manager performance evaluation purposes.

3. Pros of Throughput Costing

(a) Extreme form of variable costing. There is even less incentive to build for inventory than under variable costing. Indeed, managers who produce but do not sell the output in the same period, will see operating income decline because of variable costs other than direct materials being expensed to that period. Hence there is a disincentive for inventory buildup.

(b) Very simple to operate.

9-32 (cont'd)

(c)   Avoids disputes between absorption costing and variable costing over, say, whether a manufacturing cost item is variable indirect or fixed indirect. Throughput costing reduces incentives of managers to play games with respect to cost classifications.

Cons of Throughput Costing

(a)   Procuring for inventory is not universally a negative. In industries where there is high uncertainty about demand and huge economies of scale in production, having some inventory may be economically appropriate. Throughput costing does not reinforce the economics of such situations.

(b)   Can lead to large swings over time in operating income that managers may not feel represents their underlying performance.

(c)   Some managers have maintained that when inventory is reported at only direct materials costs there is an incentive to reduce selling prices at the end of the year to get large increases in reported operating income for that period. This may not be in the company's best interest. This effect is marked for industries with a low direct materials cost to total manufacturing cost ratio.

(d)   Can create need to run "dual" systems because of throughput costing's being unacceptable for financial reporting or taxation.

9-34 (30 min.) The Semi-Fixed Company.

1. a. Variable-Costing Income Statements (in thousands):

		2001	2002	Together
Revenues		$300	$300	$600
Variable cost of sales		70	70	140
Contribution margin		230	230	460
Fixed manufacturing costs	$140			
Fixed marketing and admin. costs	40	180	180	360
Operating income		$ 50	$ 50	$100

b. Absorption-Costing Income Statements (in thousands):

	Alternative 1			Alternative 2		
	2001	2002	Together	2001	2002	Together
Revenues	$300	$300	$600	$300	$300	$600
Beginning inventory	–	140	–	–	210	–
Manufacturing costs	280	–	280	420	–	420
Available for sales	280	140	280	420	210	420
Ending inventory	140	–	–	210	–	–
Cost of goods sold	140	140	280	210	210	420
Underallocated overhead	–	140	140	–	140	–
Overallocated overhead	–	–	–	(140)	–	–
Marketing & administrative costs	40	40	80	40	40	80
Total costs	180	320	500	110	390	500
Operating income (loss)	$120	$ (20)	$100	$190	$ (90)	$100

Alternative 1: Rate for fixed manufacturing overhead allocation based on 20,000 units: $140,000 ÷ 20,000 = $7.00 per tonne.

Alternative 2: Rate for fixed manufacturing overhead allocation based on 10,000 units: $140,000 ÷ 10,000 = $14.00 per tonne.

9-22

2. The Semi-Fixed Company has a positive operating income because some of its costs were variable. They could be avoided when the plant shut down for the second year. Variable costs can be "stored" as measures of assets, while fixed costs cannot. When the Semi-Fixed Co. paid $70,000 for direct materials, direct manufacturing labour, and variable manufacturing overhead to produce 10,000 additional tonnes of fertilizer during the first year for sale in the second year, it saved that amount of cost in the second year.

3.

	Variable Costing	Absorption Costing	
		20,000 Unit Base*	10,000 Unit Base
Inventory, end of 2001	$70,000	$140,000	$210,000
Inventory, end of 2002	0	0	0

*Fixed manufacturing overhead rate is $7.00 when denominator level is 20,000 units and is $14.00 when denominator level is 10,000 units.

4. Reported operating income is affected by both production and sales under absorption costing. Hence, most managers would prefer absorption costing because their performance in any given reporting period, at least in the short run, is influenced by how much production is scheduled near the end of a reporting period.

9-36 (20-30 min.) **Inventory costing and management planning.**

Note that under variable costing the production schedule will not affect the bonus because all fixed manufacturing overhead is an expense in any event. Therefore, the production decision can be influenced by marketing needs, and unaffected by how costs are being charged to inventory or income.

1.   Under absorption costing, the greater the production, the greater the operating income. The division manager would want to maximize production, given the constraints of storage space and practical capacity.

Target ending inventory	200
December expected sales	70
Total needs	270
November 30 inventory	150
Production to be scheduled	120 units

2.   Operating income would be lower under variable costing because inventories are increasing. Specifically, inventory increased by 110 (150 + 80 – 70 – 50) units at a fixed manufacturing overhead rate of $600; so standard absorption-costing operating income would be $66,000 higher than under variable costing.

3.   The division manager should set the minimum production schedule of 40 units, because the outlook for ending inventory is far in excess of reasonable sales demands.

4.   40 units. This amount of production will maximize the unfavourable output level variance and will minimize income taxes for 2002. In other words, the deductions that are taken now rather than later are extremely valuable because their impact on tax savings is greater now than in 2003.

5.   If 70 units fewer are scheduled in 2002, 70 units more must be scheduled in 2003. Therefore, operating income will be lower in 2002 and higher in 2003 by $42,000.

Impact on operating income:	
Schedule 50 units	
Production-volume variance,	
(100 – 50) units × $600	$30,000 U
Schedule 120 units	
Production-volume variance,	
(100 – 120) units × $600	12,000 F
Impact on operating income	$42,000 lower

The 2003 income must be higher because the total production level will be 70 units higher, resulting in a favourable effect on the output level variance of 70 units × $600 = $42,000.

9-38 (20-35 min.) **Effects of denominator-level concept choice.**

1.   Normal utilization. Givens are denoted by *.

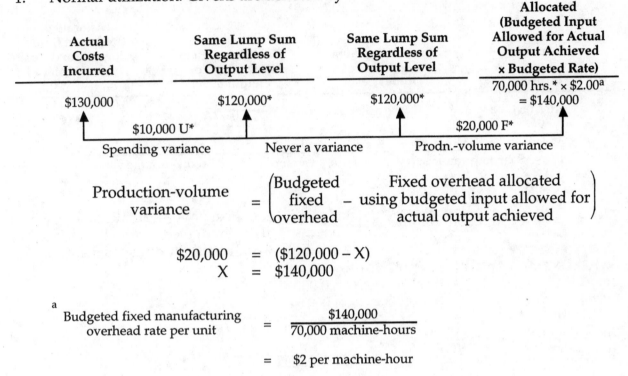

Actual Costs Incurred	Same Lump Sum Regardless of Output Level	Same Lump Sum Regardless of Output Level	Allocated (Budgeted Input Allowed for Actual Output Achieved × Budgeted Rate)
$130,000	$120,000*	$120,000*	70,000 hrs.* × $2.00[a] = $140,000

$10,000 U* ——— Spending variance

Never a variance

$20,000 F* ——— Prodn.-volume variance

$$\text{Production-volume variance} = \left(\begin{array}{c} \text{Budgeted} \\ \text{fixed} \\ \text{overhead} \end{array} - \begin{array}{c} \text{Fixed overhead allocated} \\ \text{using budgeted input allowed for} \\ \text{actual output achieved} \end{array} \right)$$

$$\$20,000 = (\$120,000 - X)$$
$$X = \$140,000$$

[a]
$$\text{Budgeted fixed manufacturing overhead rate per unit} = \frac{\$140,000}{70,000 \text{ machine-hours}}$$

$$= \$2 \text{ per machine-hour}$$

$$\text{Denominator level} = \frac{\$120,000}{\$2}$$

$$= 60,000 \text{ machine-hours}$$

9-38 (cont'd)

2. Practical capacity. Givens denoted*

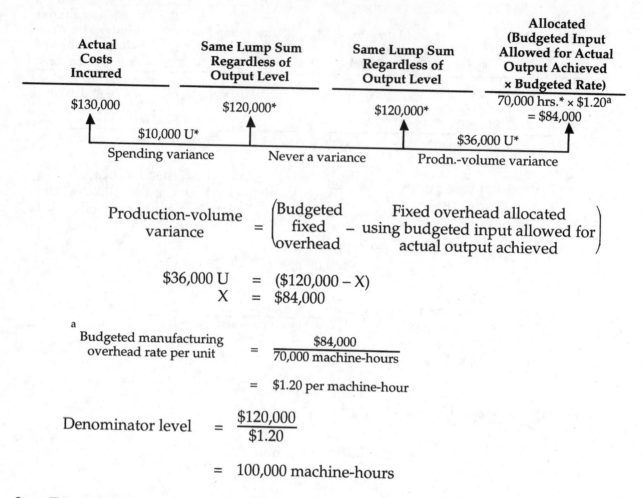

Actual Costs Incurred	Same Lump Sum Regardless of Output Level	Same Lump Sum Regardless of Output Level	Allocated (Budgeted Input Allowed for Actual Output Achieved × Budgeted Rate)
$130,000	$120,000*	$120,000*	70,000 hrs.* × $1.20[a] = $84,000

$10,000 U* ← Spending variance

Never a variance

$36,000 U* ← Prodn.-volume variance

$$\text{Production-volume variance} = \left(\begin{array}{c} \text{Budgeted} \\ \text{fixed} \\ \text{overhead} \end{array} - \begin{array}{c} \text{Fixed overhead allocated} \\ \text{using budgeted input allowed for} \\ \text{actual output achieved} \end{array} \right)$$

$$\$36,000\ U = (\$120,000 - X)$$
$$X = \$84,000$$

[a]
$$\text{Budgeted manufacturing overhead rate per unit} = \frac{\$84,000}{70,000 \text{ machine-hours}}$$

$$= \$1.20 \text{ per machine-hour}$$

$$\text{Denominator level} = \frac{\$120,000}{\$1.20}$$

$$= 100,000 \text{ machine-hours}$$

3. To maximize operating income, the executive vice-president would favour using normal utilization rather than practical capacity. Why? Because normal utilization is a smaller base than practical capacity, resulting in any year-end inventory having a higher unit cost. Thus, less fixed manufacturing overhead would become a 2002 expense if normal utilization were used as the denominator level.

9-40 (20 min.) **Cost allocation, downward demand spiral.**

1.

$$\text{Budgeted fixed costs per meal} = \frac{\text{Budgeted fixed costs}}{\text{Budgeted denominator level}}$$

$$= \frac{\$4,380,000}{\$1.50}$$

$$= 2,920,000 \text{ meals}$$

WHM is using budgeted usage as its denominator level for calculating the budgeted fixed costs per meal in 2002.

2. Alternative denominator levels include:

a.   Capacity available. The data in the problem note that the facility can serve 3,650,000 meals a year. With this denominator level, there will be budgeted unused capacity, which could be recorded as a separate line in the cost report for the Santa Monica facility.

b.   Budgeted usage of capacity. With the 2002 budgeted usage of 2,920,000 meals, the fixed costs charge is $1.50 per meal. The marketplace is signaling that WHM's own central food-catering facility is not providing value for the costs charged. If Jenkins decides to raise prices to recover fixed costs from a declining demand base, he will likely encounter the downward demand spiral:

Budgeted Denominator (1)	Variable Cost per Meal (2)	Fixed Cost per Meal $4,380,000 ÷ (1) (3)	Total Cost per Meal (4)
3,650,000	$3.80	$1.20	$5.00
2,920,000	3.80	1.50	5.30
2,550,000	3.80	1.72	5.52
2,000,000	3.80	2.19	5.99

Jenkins might adopt a contribution margin approach, which means viewing the $3.80 variable cost as the only per-unit cost and the $4,380,000 as a fixed cost. Alternatively, Jenkins could use practical capacity to cost the meals and work to reduce costs of unused capacity.

9-40 (cont'd)

3. Three factors managers should consider in pricing decisions:
   a. Customers. Jenkins is facing customers who are dissatisfied with both the cost and the quality of the meal service. Three of the 10 hospitals have already elected to use an outside canteen service.
   b. Competitors. For the three hospitals terminating use of the Santa Monica facility, at least one competitor is more cost-effective. The seven remaining hospitals likely will be very interested in how this competitor performs at the three hospitals.
   c. Costs. Jenkins should consider ways to reduce both the variable costs per meal and the fixed costs.

9-42 (15 min.) ABC and capacity usage.

1.

Activity	Rate per Unit of Cost Driver
Power	$200,000 activity costs ÷ 50,000 kilowatt hours = $4 per kilowatt hour
Quality inspection	$300,000 activity costs ÷ 10,000 inspections = $30 per inspection

Cost allocation:

Power

Tulsa (10,000 kilowatt hours × $4)	$ 40,000
Okla (35,000 kilowatt hours × $4)	140,000
Total power costs allocation	$180,000

Quality inspection

Tulsa (5,000 inspections × $30)	$150,000
Okla (4,000 inspections × $30)	120,000
Total quality inspection costs allocation	$270,000

2. Cost of unused capacity:

Power ($200,000 – $180,000)	$ 20,000
Quality inspection ($300,000 – $270,000)	30,000
Total cost of unused capacity	$ 50,000

9-44 (20 min.) Downward demand spiral.

1.

Budgeted variable manufacturing costs per unit	$200
Allocated fixed manufacturing overhead costs per unit	100[a]
Budgeted total manufacturing costs per unit	300
Markup (100% × $300)	300
Budgeted selling price	$600

[a] $1,000,000 ÷ 10,000 units = $100 per unit

2.

Budgeted variable manufacturing costs per unit	$200
Allocated fixed manufacturing overhead costs per unit	125[b]
Budgeted total manufacturing costs per unit	325
Markup (100% × $325)	325
Revised budgeted selling price	$650

[b] $1,000,000 ÷ 8,000 units = $125 per unit

3.   Considering that the market is highly competitive, raising the selling price, in an attempt to recover fixed manufacturing overhead costs, will make Pismo Company less competitive. Pismo's higher selling price would likely make it lose its customers to the competitors. This is the classic syndrome of the start of a downward demand spiral. Pismo Company should use its practical capacity to allocate fixed manufacturing overhead costs. If an upturn is expected, Pismo should keep its excess capacity. Otherwise, it should either lease or get rid of the excess capacity in order to bring down its fixed manufacturing overhead costs to the demand level.

9-46 (30 min.)   **Variable and absorption costing and breakeven points.**

1. Production   = Sales + Ending Inventory – Beginning Inventory
                = 242,400 + 24,800 – 32,600
                = 234,600

2. Breakeven point in cases:

   a. Variable Costing:

   $$QT = \frac{\text{Total Fixed Costs} + \text{Target Operating Income}}{\text{Contribution Margin per Unit}}$$

   $$QT = \frac{(\$3,753,600 + \$6,568,800) + \$0}{\$94 - (\$16 + \$10 + \$6 + \$14 + \$2)}$$

   $$QT = \frac{\$10,322,400}{\$46}$$

   $$QT = 224,400 \text{ cases}$$

   b. Absorption costing:

   $$QT = \frac{\begin{array}{c}\text{Total Fixed} \\ \text{Cost}\end{array} + \begin{array}{c}\text{Target} \\ \text{IO}\end{array} + \left[\begin{array}{c}\text{Fixed Manuf.} \\ \text{Cost Rate}\end{array} \times \left(\begin{array}{c}\text{Breakeven} \\ \text{Sales in Units}\end{array} - \begin{array}{c}\text{Units} \\ \text{Produced}\end{array}\right)\right]}{\text{Contribution Margin per Unit}}$$

   $$QT = \frac{\$10,322,400 + \left[\$16\,(QT - 234,600)\right]}{\$46}$$

   $$QT = \frac{\$10,322,400 + 16\,QT - 3,753,600}{\$46}$$

   $$QT = \frac{\$6,568,800 + 16\,QT}{\$46}$$

   $$46\,QT - 16\,QT = \$6,568,800$$

   $$30\,QT = \$6,568,800$$

   $$QT = 218,960 \text{ cases}$$

9-46 (cont'd)

3. If grape prices increase by 25%, the cost of grapes per case will increase from $16 in 2000 to $20 in 2003. This will decrease the unit contribution margin from $46 in 2002 to $42 in 2003.

    a. Variable Costing:

$$QT = \frac{\$10,322,400}{\$42}$$

$$= 245,772 \text{ cases}$$

    b. Absorption Costing:

$$QT = \frac{\$6,568,800 + \$16\ QT}{\$42}$$

$$\$42\ QT = \$6,568,800 + \$16\ QT$$

$$\$26\ QT = \$6,568,800$$

$$QT = 252,647 \text{ cases}$$

9-48 (20 min.) **Absorption costing, management ethics (continuation of 9-47).**

1.   Behaviours that might suggest problems for IEC with the existing bonus plan and accounting system include:

   a.   Plant managers switching production orders at year-end to those orders that absorb the highest amount of manufacturing overhead, irrespective of the demand by customers of IEC.
   b.   Plant managers at one division of IEC accepting orders that they know another plant of IEC is better suited to handle.
   c.   Plant managers deferring maintenance beyond the normal maintenance period.

2.   Possible changes include:

   a.   Change the incentive scheme so that there are not the major discontinuities at 15% and 10%.
   b.   Change the operating income measure to variable costing rather than absorption costing.
   c.   Add other performance measures (such as inventory turnover) that explicitly penalize "building for inventory."
   d.   Emphasize the importance of managers considering IEC total benefits and costs of their decisions. This could be done via persuasion or by an incentive system based on IEC operating income rather than 100% of each division's operating income.

9-48 (cont'd)

2. Amounts in thousands.

	Absorption Costing		
	January	February	March
Revenues	$32,000	$46,400	$51,200
Cost of goods sold			
Beginning inventory	0	14,760	8,610
Variable manufacturing costs	31,360	23,520	37,240
Fixed manufacturing costs	8,000	6,000	9,500
Cost of goods available for sale	39,360	44,280	55,350
Ending inventory	14,760	8,610	15,990
Cost of goods sold (at standard cost)	24,600	35,670	39,360
Adjustment for variances	500 F	1,500 U	2,000 F
Total cost of goods sold	24,100	37,170	37,360
Gross margin	7,900	9,230	13,840
Marketing costs	0	0	0
Operating income	$ 7,900	$ 9,230	$13,840
Inventory Details (Units)			
Beginning inventory	0	1,200	700
Production	3,200	2,400	3,800
Goods available for sale	3,200	3,600	4,500
Sales	2,000	2,900	3,200
Ending inventory	1,200	700	1,300
Inventory Details ($12,300 per unit)			
Beginning inventory ($12,300 per unit)	$ 0	$14,760	$ 8,160
Ending inventory ($1,000s)	$14,760	$ 8,610	$15,990

Computation of Bonus	January	February	March
Operating income	$7,900,000	$9,230,000	$13,840,000
× 0.5%	$ 39,500	$46,150	$ 69,200

9-48 (cont'd)

3. Amounts in thousands

	Variable Costing		
	January	February	March
Revenues	$32,000	$46,400	$51,200
Variable Costs			
Beginning inventory	0	11,760	6,860
Variable cost of goods manufactured	31,360	23,520	37,240
Cost of goods available for sale	31,360	35,280	44,100
Ending inventory	11,760	6,860	12,740
Variable manuf. COGS	19,600	28,420	31,360
Variable marketing costs	0	0	0
Variable costs (at standard cost)	19,600	28,420	31,360
Adjustment for variances	0	0	0
Total variable costs	19,600	28,420	31,360
Contribution margin	12,400	17,980	19,840
Fixed costs			
Fixed manuf. overhead costs	7,500	7,500	7,500
Fixed marketing costs	0	0	0
Fixed costs (at standard cost)	7,500	7,500	7,500
Adjustment for variances	0	0	0
Total fixed costs	7,500	7,500	7,500
Operating income	$ 4,900	$10,480	$12,340
Inventory details ($9,800 per unit)			
Beginning inventory (units)	0	1,200	700
Ending inventory (units)	1,200	700	1,300
Beginning inventory $000s	$0	$11,760	$ 6,860
Ending inventory ($000s)	$11,760	$ 6,860	$12,740

Computation of Bonus	January	February	March
Operating income	$4,900,000	$10,480,000	$12,340,000
× 0.5%	$ 24,500	$52,400	$ 61,700

4.

	January	February	March	Total
Absorption Costing Bonus	$39,500	$46,150	$69,200	$154,850
Variable-Costing Bonus	24,500	52,400	61,700	138,600
Difference	$15,000	$ (6,250)	$ 7,500	$16,250

The difference between absorption and variable costing arises because of differences in production and sales:

	January	February	March	Total
Production	3,200	2,400	3,800	9,400
Sales	2,000	2,900	3,200	8,100
Δ in Inventory	1,200	(500)	600	1,300

9-48 (cont'd)

By building for inventory, Hart can capitalize $2,500 of fixed manufacturing overhead costs per unit. This will provide a bonus payment of $12.50 per unit, as operating income under absorption costing will exceed that under variable costing when production is greater than sales. Over the three-month period, the inventory buildup is 1,300 units giving a difference of $16,250 in bonus payments.

5. Amounts in thousands

	Throughput Costing		
	January	February	March
Revenues	$32,000	$46,400	$51,200
Variable direct materials costs			
Beginning inventory	0	7,200	4,200
Direct materials in goods manufactured	19,200	14,400	22,800
Cost of goods available for sale	19,200	21,600	27,000
Ending inventory	7,200	4,200	7,800
Total variable direct materials costs	12,000	17,400	19,200
Throughput contribution	20,000	29,000	32,000
Other costs			
Manufacturing[a]	19,660	16,620	21,940
Marketing	0	0	0
Total other costs	19,660	16,620	21,940
Operating income	$ 340	$12,380	$10,060

[a] ($3,800 × 3,200) + $7,500,000
   ($3,800 × 2,400) + $7,500,000
   ($3,800 × 3,800) + $7,500,000

Computation of Bonus	January	February	March
Operating income	$340,000	$12,380,000	$10,060,000
× 0.5%	$ 1,700	$ 61,900	$ 50,300

A summary of the bonuses paid is:

	January	February	March	Total
Absorption Costing	$39,500	$46,150	$69,200	$154,850
Variable Costing	24,500	52,400	61,700	138,600
Throughput Costing	1,700	61,900	50,300	113,900

6. Alternative approaches include:
  (a) Use an alternative income computation approach to absorption costing, e.g.,
    (i) Variable costing
    (ii) Throughput costing
  (b) Use a financial charge for inventory buildup to reduce dysfunctional aspects of absorption costing—e.g., opportunity costs of funds tied up in inventory.
  (c) Adopt non-financial performance targets—e.g., attaining but not exceeding inventory levels.
  (d) Change the compensation package to have a longer-term focus, using either an external variable (e.g., stock options) or an internal variable (e.g., five-year average income).

CHAPTER 10
DETERMINING HOW COSTS BEHAVE

10-2   Three alternative linear cost functions are:
1.   Variable cost function—a cost function in which total costs change in proportion to the cost driver in the relevant range.
2.   Fixed cost function—a cost function in which total costs do not change with changes in the cost driver in the relevant range.
3.   Mixed cost function—a cost function that has both variable and fixed elements. Total costs change but not in proportion to the changes in the cost driver in the relevant range.

10-4   No. High correlation merely indicates that the two variables move together in the data examined. It is essential to consider also economic plausibility before making inferences about cause and effect. Without any economic plausibility for a relationship, it is less likely that a high level of correlation observed in one set of data will be similarly found in other sets of data.

10-6   The conference method develops cost estimates on the basis of analysis and opinions gathered from various departments of an organization (purchasing, process engineering, manufacturing, employee relations, etc.). Advantages of the conference method include:
1.   The speed with which cost estimates can be developed.
2.   The pooling of knowledge from experts across functional areas.
3.   The improved credibility of the cost function to all personnel.

10-8   The six steps are:
1.   Choose the dependent variable (the variable to be predicted, which is some type of cost).
2.   Identify the cost driver(s) (independent variables).
3.   Collect data on the dependent variable and the cost driver(s).
4.   Plot the data.
5.   Estimate the cost function.
6.   Evaluate the estimated cost function.

Step 3 typically is the most difficult for a cost analyst.

10-10   Criteria important when choosing among alternative cost functions are:
1.   Economic plausibility.
2.   Goodness of fit.
3.   Slope of the regression line.

10-12 Frequently encountered problems when collecting cost data on variables included in a cost function are:
1. The time period used to measure the dependent variable is not properly matched with the period used to measure the cost driver(s).
2. Fixed costs are allocated as if they are variable.
3. Data either are not available for all observations or are not uniformly reliable.
4. Extreme values of observations occur.
5. A homogeneous relationship between the individual cost items in the dependent variable and the cost driver(s) does not exist.
6. The relationship between cost and the cost driver is not stationary.
7. Inflation has occurred in a dependent variable, a cost driver, or both.

10-14 No. A cost driver is any factor whose change causes a change in the total cost of a related cost object. A cause-and-effect relationship underlies selection of a cost driver. Some users of regression analysis include numerous independent variables in a regression model in an attempt to maximize goodness of fit, irrespective of the economic plausibility of the independent variables included. Some of the independent variables included may not be cost drivers.

10-16 (10 min.) **Estimating a cost function.**

1. Slope coefficient $= \dfrac{\text{Difference in costs}}{\text{Difference in machine-hours}}$

$$= \frac{\$3,900 - \$3,000}{7,000 - 4,000}$$

$$= \frac{\$900}{3,000} = \$0.30 \text{ per machine-hour}$$

Constant = Total cost – (Slope coefficient × Quantity of cost driver)
= $3,900 – ($0.30 × 7,000) = $1,800
= $3,000 – ($0.30 × 4,000) = $1,800

The cost function based on the two observations is:

Maintenance costs = $1,800 + $0.30 (machine-hours)

2. The cost function in requirement 1 is an estimate of how costs behave within the relevant range, not at cost levels outside the relevant range. If there are no months with zero machine-hours represented in the maintenance account, data in that account cannot be used to estimate the fixed costs at the zero machine-hours level. Rather, the constant component of the cost function provides the best available starting point for a straight line that approximates how a cost behaves within the relevant range.

10-18 (20 min.) **Various cost-behaviour patterns.**

1. K
2. B
3. G
4. J Note that A is incorrect because, although the cost per kilogram eventually equals a constant at $9.20, the total dollars of cost increases linearly from that point onward.
5. I The total costs will be the same regardless of the volume level.
6. L
7. F This is a classic step-function cost.
8. K
9. C

10-20 (20 min.) **Account analysis method.**

1.
Variable costs:
Car wash labour	$240,000
Soap, cloth, and supplies	32,000
Water	28,000
Power to move conveyor belt	72,000
Total variable costs	$372,000

Fixed costs:
Depreciation	$ 64,000
Supervision	30,000
Cashier	16,000
Total fixed costs	$110,000

2. Variable costs per car = $\dfrac{\$372,000}{80,000}$ = $4.65 per car

Total costs estimated for 90,000 cars = $110,000 + ($4.65 × 90,000) = $528,500

3. Average cost in 2002 = $\dfrac{\$372,000 + \$110,000}{80,000} = \dfrac{\$482,000}{80,000}$ = $6.025

Average cost in 2003 = $\dfrac{\$528,500}{90,000}$ = $5.87

Some students may assume that power costs of running the continuously moving conveyor belt is a fixed cost. In this case the variable costs in 2002 will be $300,000 and the fixed costs $182,000.

The variable costs per car in 2002 = $300,000 ÷ 80,000 cars = $3.75 per car

Total costs for 90,000 cars in 2003 = $182,000 + ($3.75 × 90,000) = $519,500

The average cost of washing a car in 2003 = $519,500 ÷ 90,000 = $5.77.

10-22 (20 min.) Estimating a cost function, high-low method.

1.　　See Solution Exhibit 10-22. There is a positive relationship between the number of service reports (a cost driver) and the customer service department costs. This relationship is economically plausible.

2.

	Number Of Service Reports	Customer Service Department Costs
Highest observation of cost driver	436	$21,890
Lowest observation of cost driver	122	12,941
Difference	314	$ 8,949

Customer service department costs = $a + b$ (number of service reports)

$$\text{Slope coefficient } (b) = \frac{\$8,949}{314} = \$28.50 \text{ per service report}$$

$$\text{Constant } (a) = \$21,890 - \$28.50\,(436) = \$9,464$$
$$= \$12,941 - \$28.50\,(122) = \$9,464$$

Customer service
department costs　　= $9,464 + $28.50 (number of service reports)

3.　　Other possible cost drivers of customer service department costs are:
   (a)　Number of products replaced with a new product (and the dollar value of the new products charged to the customer service department).
   (b)　Number of products repaired and the time and cost of repairs.

10-22 (cont'd)

Plot of Number of Service Reports Versus
Customer Service Costs for Capitol Products

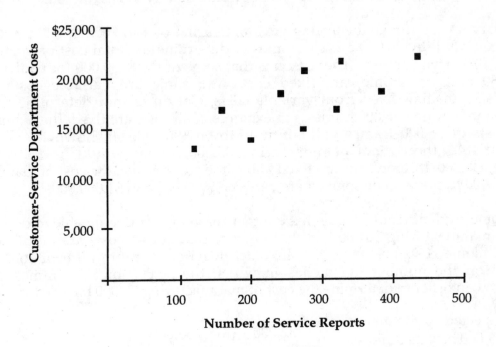

10-24 (20 min.) **Cost-volume-profit and regression analysis.**

1a. Average cost of manufacturing $= \dfrac{\text{Total manufacturing costs}}{\text{Number of bicycle frames}}$

$\qquad\qquad\qquad\qquad\qquad\qquad = \dfrac{\$900,000}{30,000} = \$30 \text{ per frame}$

This cost is greater than the $28.50 per frame that Ryan has quoted.

1b. Garvin cannot take the average manufacturing cost in 2002 of $30 per frame and multiply it by 36,000 bicycle frames to determine the total cost of manufacturing 36,000 bicycle frames. The reason is that some of the $900,000 (or equivalently the $30 cost per frame) are fixed costs and some are variable costs. Without distinguishing fixed from variable costs, Garvin cannot determine the cost of manufacturing 36,000 frames. For example, if all costs are fixed, the manufacturing costs of 36,000 frames will continue to be $900,000. If, however, all costs are variable, the cost of manufacturing 36,000 frames would be $30 × 36,000 = $1,080,000. If some costs are fixed and some are variable, the cost of manufacturing 36,000 frames will be somewhere between $900,000 and $1,080,000.

Some students could argue that another reason for not being able to determine the cost of manufacturing 36,000 bicycle frames is that not all costs are output unit-level costs. If some costs are, for example, batch-level costs, more information would be needed on the number of batches in which the 36,000 bicycle frames would be produced, in order to determine the cost of manufacturing 36,000 bicycle frames.

2. Expected cost to make
    36,000 bicycle frames $\quad = \$432,000 + (\$15 \times 36,000)$

$\qquad\qquad\qquad\qquad\qquad = \$432,000 + \$540,000 = \$972,000$

Purchasing bicycle frames from Ryan will cost $28.50 × 36,000 = $1,026,000. Hence it will cost Garvin $1,026,000 − $972,000 = $54,000 more to purchase the frames from Garvin rather than manufacture them in-house.

3. Garvin would need to consider several factors before being confident that the equation in requirement 2 accurately predicts the cost of manufacturing bicycle frames.
   a. Is the relationship between total manufacturing costs and quantity of bicycle frames economically plausible? For example, is the quantity of bicycles made the only cost driver or are there other cost-drivers (for example, batch-level costs of setups, production-orders, or material handling) that affect manufacturing costs?
   b. How good is the goodness of fit? That is, how well does the estimated line fit the data?
   c. Is the relationship between the number of bicycle frames produced and total manufacturing costs linear?
   d. Does the slope of the regression line indicate that a strong relationship exists between manufacturing costs and the number of bicycle frames produced?

10-24 (cont'd)

e. Are there any data problems such as, for example, errors in measuring costs, trends in prices of materials, labour or overheads that might affect variable or fixed costs over time, extreme values of observations, or a nonstationary relationship over time between total manufacturing costs and the quantity of bicycles produced?

10-26 (30–40 min.) **Regression analysis, activity-based costing, choosing cost drivers.**

1a. Solution Exhibit 10-26A presents the plots and regression line of number of packaged units moved on distribution costs.

SOLUTION EXHIBIT 10-26A
Plots and Regression Line of Number of Packaged Units Moved on Distribution Costs

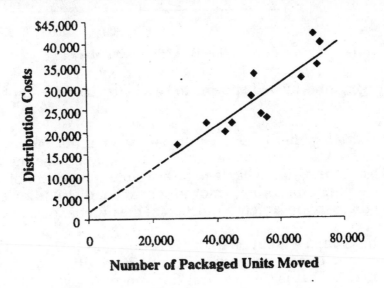

1b. Solution Exhibit 10-26B presents the plots and regression line of number of shipments made on distribution costs.

10-26 (cont'd)

SOLUTION EXHIBIT 10-26B
Plots and Regression Line of Number of Shipments Made on Distribution Costs

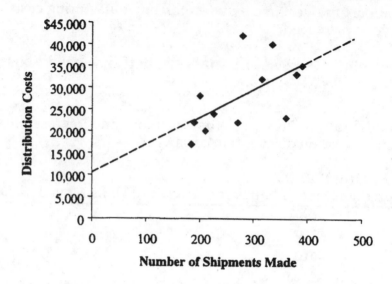

Number of packaged units moved appears to be a better cost driver of distribution costs for the following reasons:

(i) *Economic plausibility.* Both number of packaged units moved and number of shipments are economically plausible cost drivers. Because the product is heavy, however, costs of freight are likely to be a sizable component of distribution costs. Thus, number of packaged units moved will affect distribution costs significantly because freight costs are largely a function of the number of units transported.

(ii) *Goodness of fit.* Compare Solution Exhibits 10-26A and 10-26B. Number of packaged units moved has a better goodness of fit with distribution costs than do number of shipments made. That is, the vertical differences between actual and predicted number of shipments made are smaller for the number of packaged units moved regression than for the number of shipments made regression.

(iii) *Slope of regression line.* Again, compare Solution Exhibits 10-26A and 10-26B. The number of packaged units moved regression line has a relatively steep slope indicating a strong relationship between number of packaged units moved and distribution costs. On average, distribution costs increase with the number of packaged units moved. The number of shipments made regression line is flatter and has a wider scatter of observations about the line, indicating a weak relationship between number of shipments made and distribution costs. On average, the number of shipments made has a smaller effect on distribution costs.

2. Using the preferred cost function,
Distribution costs = $1,349 + ($0.496 × Number of packaged units moved),
Flaherty would budget distribution costs of
$1,349 + ($0.496 × 40,000) = $1,349 + 19,840 = $21,189

10-26 (cont'd)

3.   Using the "other" cost function
        Distribution costs = $10,417 + ($63.77 × Number of shipments made),
Flaherty would budget distribution costs of
        $10,417 + ($63.77 × 220) = $10,417 + $14,029 = $24,446

The actual costs are likely to be lower than the prediction of $24,446 made using the number of shipments as the cost driver. The reason is that budgeted distribution costs are likely to be closer to the $21,189 predicted by the regression equation with number of packaged units moved as the cost driver. This regression equation provides a better explanation of the factors that affect distribution costs.

Choosing the "wrong" cost driver and estimating the incorrect cost function can have repercussions for pricing, cost management, and cost control. To the extent that Flaherty uses predicted costs of $24,446 for making pricing decisions, she may overprice the 40,000 packages she expects to move and could potentially lose business.

To see the problems in cost management, suppose Waterloo Corporation moves 40,000 units in 220 shipments in the next month while incurring actual costs of $23,500. Compared with the budget of $24,446, management would consider this a good performance and seek ways to replicate it. In fact, on the basis of the preferred cost driver, the number of packaged units moved, actual distribution costs of $23,500 are higher than what they should be ($21,189)—a performance that management should seek to correct and improve rather than replicate.

10-28 (20 min.) **Learning curve, incremental unit-time learning curve**

1.   The direct manufacturing labour-hours (DMLH) required to produce the first 2, 3, and 4 units given the assumption of an incremental unit-time learning curve of 90% is as follows:

Cumulative Number of Units (1)	Individual Unit Time for Xth Unit (2)	Cumulative Total Time (3)
1	3,000	3,000
2	2,700 (3,000 × 0.90)	5,700
3	2,539	8,239
4	2,430 (2,700 × 0.90)	10,669

Values in column 2 are calculated using the formula $y = pX^q$

where p = 3,000, X = 2, 3, or 4 and q = –0.1520, which gives

when X = 2, $y = 3,000 \times 2^{-0.1520} = 2,700$
when X = 3, $y = 3,000 \times 3^{-0.1520} = 2,539$
when X = 4, $y = 3,000 \times 4^{-0.1520} = 2,430$

	Variable costs of producing		
	2 units	3 units	4 units
Direct materials $80,000 × 2; 3; 4	$160,000	$240,000	$ 320,000
Direct manufacturing labour $25 × 5,700; 8,239; 10,669	142,500	205,975	266,725
Variable manufacturing overhead $15 × 5,700; 8,239; 10,669	85,500	123,585	160,035
Total variable costs	$388,000	$569,560	$746,760

2.

	Variable costs of producing	
	2 units	4 units
Incremental unit-time learning curve (from requirement 1)	$388,000	$746,760
Cumulative average-time learning curve (from Exercise 10-27)	376,000	708,800
Difference	$ 12,000	$ 37,960

10-28 (cont'd)

Total variable costs for manufacturing 2 and 4 units are lower under the cumulative average-time learning curve relative to the incremental unit-time learning curve. Direct manufacturing labour-hours required to make additional units declines more slowly in the incremental unit-time learning curve relative to the cumulative average-time learning curve assuming the same 90% factor is used for both curves. The reason is that, in the incremental unit-time learning curve, as the number of units doubles, only the last unit produced has a cost of 90% of the initial cost. In the cumulative average-time model, doubling the number of units causes the average cost of *all* the additional units produced (not just the last unit) to be 90% of the initial cost.

10-30 (30–40 min.) **High-low versus regression method.**

1. Solution Exhibit 10-30 presents the plots of advertising costs on revenues.

SOLUTION EXHIBIT 10-30
Plot and Regression Line of Advertising Costs on Revenues

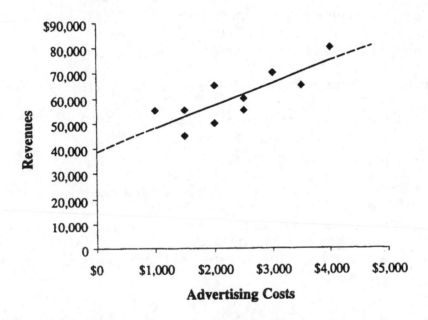

2. Solution Exhibit 10-30 also shows the regression line of advertising costs on revenues. We evaluate the estimated regression equation using the criteria of economic plausibility, goodness of fit, and slope of the regression line.

Economic plausibility. Advertising costs appears to be a plausible cost driver of revenues. Restaurants frequently use newspaper advertising to promote their restaurants and increase their patronage.

Goodness of fit. The vertical differences between actual and predicted revenues appears to be reasonably small. This indicates that advertising costs are related to restaurant revenues.

10-11

10-30 (cont'd)

Slope of regression line. The slope of the regression line appears to be relatively steep. This indicates that, on average, restaurant revenues increase with newspaper advertising.

3.   The high-low method would estimate the cost function as follows:

	Advertising Costs	Revenues
Highest observation of cost driver	$4,000	$80,000
Lowest observation of cost driver	1,000	55,000
Difference	$3,000	$25,000

$$\text{Revenues} = a + (b \times \text{advertising costs})$$

$$\text{Slope coefficient } (b) = \frac{\$25,000}{\$3,000} = 8.333$$

$$\text{Constant } (a) = \$80,000 - (\$4,000 \times 8.333)$$
$$= \$80,000 - 33,332 = \$46,668$$
$$or \quad \text{Constant } (a) = \$55,000 - (\$1,000 \times 8.333)$$
$$= \$55,000 - 8,333 = \$46,667$$

Revenues = $46,667 + (8.333 × Advertising costs)

4.   The increase in revenues for each $1,000 spent on advertising within the relevant range is
    a.   Using the regression equation, 8.723 × $1,000 = $8,723
    b.   Using the high-low equation, 8.333 × $1,000 = $8,333

5.   The high-low equation does fairly well in estimating the relationship between advertising costs and revenues. However, Martinez and Brown should use the regression equation. The reason is that the regression equation uses information from all observations, whereas the high-low method relies only on the observations that have the highest and lowest values of the cost driver. These observations are generally not representative of all the data.

10-32 (30-40 min.) **Cost estimation, cumulative average-time learning curve.**

1. Cost to Produce the Second through the Eighth Troop Deployment Boats:

Direct materials, 7 × $100,000	$ 700,000
Direct manufacturing labour, 39,130* × $30	1,173,900
Variable manufacturing overhead, 39,130 × $20	782,600
Other manufacturing overhead, 25% of $1,173,900	293,475
Total costs	$2,949,975

*The direct manufacturing labour-hours to produce the second to eighth boats can be calculated in several ways, given the assumption of a cumulative average-time learning curve of 85%:

(a)   Use of Table Format:

Cumulative Number of Units	Cumulative Average-Time per Unit	Cumulative Total Time
1	10,000.00	10,000
2	8,500.00 (10,000 × 0.85)	17,000
4	7,225.00 (8,500 × 0.85)	28,900
8	6,141.25 (7,225 × 0.85)	49,130

The direct labour-hours required to produce the second through the eight boats is 49,130 – 10,000 = 39,130 hours.

(b)   Use of Formula:

$$y = pX^q$$

where $p = 10,000$, $X = 8$, and $q = -.2345$.

$$y = 10,000 \times 8^{-.2345} = 6,141 \text{ hours (rounded)}$$

The total direct labour-hours for 8 units is $6,141 \times 8 = 49,128$ hours

The direct labour-hours required to produce the second through the eighth boats is $49,128 - 10,000 = 39,128$ hours. (By taking the q factor to 6 decimal digits, an estimate of 49,130 hours would result.)

<u>Note</u>:   Some students will debate the exclusion of the tooling cost. The question specifies that the tooling cost was assigned to the first boat. Although Nautilus may well seek to ensure that its total revenue covers the $725,000 cost of the first boat, the concern in this question is only with the cost of producing seven more PT109s.

2.   Cost to Produce the Second through the Eighth Boats Assuming Linear Function for Direct Labour-Hours and Units Produced:

Direct materials, 7 × $100,000	$ 700,000
Direct manufacturing labour, 7 × 10,000 hours × $30	2,100,000
Variable manufacturing overhead, 7 × 10,000 hours × $20	1,400,000
Other manufacturing overhead, 25% of $2,100,000	525,000
Total costs	$4,725,000

The difference in predicted costs is:

• Predicted cost in requirement 2 (based on linear cost function)	$4,725,000
• Predicted cost in requirement 1 (based on an 85% learning curve)	2,949,975
Difference	$1,775,025

10-34 (30 min.) **Appendix: Promotion of a new product, simple and multiple regression analysis.**

1. The t-values (value of the coefficient ÷ standard error of the coefficient) of the coefficients in each of the regressions follow. A t-value greater than 2 indicates that the coefficient is significantly different from zero.

Regression 1: t-value of coefficient of X_1 = $3.98 ÷ $1.73 = 2.30, indicating that there is a relation between dollars incurred on discount coupons and estimated sales.

Regression 2: t-value of coefficient of X_2 = $4.23 ÷ $1.86 = 2.27, indicating that there is a relation between dollars spent on TV advertising and estimated sales.

Regression 3: t-value of coefficient of X_1 = $0.87 ÷ $0.79 = 1.11, indicating that there is no relation between dollars incurred on discount coupons and estimated sales given direct materials costs; t-value of coefficient of X_2 = $0.91 ÷ $0.99 = 0.92, indicating that there is no relation between dollars spent on TV advertising and estimated sales given dollars incurred on discount coupons.

2. The t-value indicates that the coefficients in the simple regressions are statistically significant, but that the coefficients of the same variables are insignificant in a multiple regression. The likely reason is multicollinearity. Because the two independent variables are correlated, the standard errors of the coefficients increase and make the variables appear insignificant and difficult to interpret.

3. Omitting a correlated variable (as the first two regressions do) causes the estimated coefficient of the independent variable to be biased away from its true value. Including both variables induces multicollinearity, which makes interpreting the significance of the coefficients difficult. To make predictions about estimated sales, it is probably best to use both dollars incurred on discount coupons and dollars spent on TV advertising despite the multicollinearity problems.

To understand the separate effects of dollars incurred on discount coupons and dollars spent on TV advertising on estimated sales, Rivk would need to find months of data where either dollars incurred on discount coupons and dollars spent on TV advertising were high, but not both. Such new data will not suffer from the problems of multicollinearity and will allow Rivk to estimate the relationship between each cost driver and estimated sales.

10-36 (30 min.)   **Appendix: Evaluating multiple regression models, not for profit (continuation of 10-35).**

1.   It is economically plausible that the correct form of the model of overhead costs includes both number of academic programs and number of enrolled students as cost drivers. The findings in Problem 10-35 indicate that each of the independent variables affects overhead costs. (Each regression has a significant r^2 and t-value on the independent variable.) Hanks could choose to divide overhead costs into two cost pools, (i) those overhead costs that are more closely related to number of academic programs and (ii) those overhead costs more closely related to number of enrolled students, and rerun the simple regression analysis on each overhead cost pool. Alternatively, Hanks could run a multiple regression analysis with total overhead costs as the dependent variable and the number of academic programs and number of enrolled students as the two independent variables.

2.   Solution Exhibit 10-36A evaluates the multiple regression model using the format of Exhibit 10-21. Hanks should use the multiple regression model rather than the two simple regression models of Problem 10-35. The multiple regression model appears economically plausible and the regression model performs very well when estimating overhead costs. It has an excellent goodness of fit, significant t-values on both independent variables, and meets all the specification assumptions for ordinary least squares regression.

      There is some correlation between the two independent variables, but multi-collinearity does not appear to be a problem here. The significance of both independent variables (despite some correlation between them) suggests that each variable is a driver of overhead cost. Of course, as the chapter describes, even if the independent variables exhibited multicollinearity, Hanks should still prefer to use the multiple regression model over the simple regression models of Problem 10-35. Omitting any one of the variables will cause the estimated coefficient of the independent variable included in the model to be biased away from its true value.

3.   Possible uses for the multiple regression results include:

a.   Planning and budgeting at Eastern University. The regression analysis indicates the variables (number of academic programs and number of enrolled students) that help predict changes in overhead costs.

b.   Cost control and performance evaluation. Hanks could compare actual performance with budgeted or expected numbers and seek ways to improve the efficiency of the university operations, and evaluate the performance of managers responsible for controlling overhead costs.

c.   Cost management. If cost pressures increase, the University could save costs by closing down academic programs that have few students enrolled.

SOLUTION EXHIBIT 10-36A
Evaluation of Cost Function for Overhead Costs Estimated with Multiple Regression for Eastern University

Criterion	Number of Academic Programs and Number of Enrolled Students as Independent Variables
1. Economic Plausibility	A positive relationship between overhead costs and number of academic programs and number of enrolled students is economically plausible at Eastern University.
2. Goodness of Fit	$r^2 = 0.81$ Excellent goodness of fit
3. Significance of Independent Variable(s)	t-values of 3.46 on number of academic programs and 2.03 on number of enrolled students are both significant.
4. Specification Analysis of Estimation Assumptions	The assumptions of linearity, constant variance, and normality of residuals hold, but inferences drawn from only 12 observations are not reliable; the Durbin Watson statistic = 1.84 indicates that independence of residuals holds.

10-38 (30-40 min.) **Appendix: Purchasing department cost drivers, multiple regression analysis (continuation of 10-37).**

The problem reports the exact t-values from the computer runs of the data. Because the coefficients and standard errors given in the problem are rounded to three decimal places, dividing the coefficient by the standard error may yield slightly different t-values.

(a)   Regression 4 is a well-specified regression model:

<u>Economic plausibility:</u> Both independent variables are plausible and are supported by the findings of the Couture Fabrics study.

<u>Goodness of fit:</u> The r^2 of 0.63 indicates an excellent goodness of fit.

<u>Significance of independent variables:</u> The t-value on # of POs is 2.14, while the t-value on # of Ss is 2.00. These t-values are either significant or border on significance.

<u>Specification analysis:</u> Results are available to examine the independence of residuals assumption. The Durbin-Watson statistic of 1.90 indicates that the assumption of independence is not rejected.

Regression 4 is consistent with the findings in Problem 10-37 that both the number of purchase orders and the number of suppliers are drivers of purchasing department costs. Regressions 2, 3, and 4 all satisfy the four criteria outlined in the text. Regression 4 has the best goodness of fit (0.63 for Regression 4 compared with 0.42 and 0.39 for Regressions 2 and 3, respectively). Most importantly, it is economically plausible that both the number of purchase orders and the number of suppliers drive purchasing department costs. We would recommend that Lee use Regression 4 over Regressions 2 and 3.

2.   Regression 5 adds an additional independent variable (MP$) to the two independent variables in Regression 4. This additional variable (MP$) has a t-value of –0.07, implying that its slope coefficient is insignificantly different from zero. The r^2 in Regression 5 (0.63) is the same as that in Regression 4 (0.63), implying that the addition of this third independent variable adds close to zero explanatory power. In summary, Regression 5 adds very little to Regression 4. We would recommend that Lee use Regression 4 over Regression 5.

3.   Budgeted purchasing department costs for the Saskatoon store next year are:

$485,384 + ($123.22 × 3,900) + ($2,952 × 110) = $1,290,662

10-38 (cont'd)

4. Multicollinearity is a frequently encountered problem in cost accounting; it does not arise in simple regression because there is only one independent variable in a simple regression. One consequence of multicollinearity is an increase in the standard errors of the coefficients of the individual variables. This frequently shows up in reduced t-values in the multiple regression relative to the t-values in the simple regression:

Variables	t-value in Multiple Regression	t-value from Simple Regressions in Problem 10-37
Regression 4:		
# of POs	2.14	2.43
# of Ss	2.00	2.28
Regression 5:		
# of POs	1.95	2.43
# of Ss	1.84	2.28
MP$	−0.07	0.84

The declines in the t-values in the multiple regressions are consistent with some (but not very high) collinearity among the independent variables. Pairwise correlations between the independent variables are:

	Correlation
# of POs / # of Ss	0.29
# of POs / MP $	0.27
# of Ss / MP$	0.34

5. Decisions in which the regression results in Problems 10-37 and 10-38 could be used are:

Cost management decisions: Fashion Flair could restructure relationships with the suppliers so that fewer separate purchase orders are made. Alternatively, it may aggressively reduce the number of existing suppliers.

Purchasing policy decisions: Fashion Flair could set up an internal charge system for individual retail departments within each store. Separate charges to each department could be made for each purchase order and each new supplier added to the existing ones. These internal changes would signal to each department ways in which their own decisions affect the total costs of Fashion Flair.

Accounting system design decisions: Fashion Flair may want to discontinue allocating purchasing department costs on the basis of the dollar value of merchandise purchased. Allocation bases better capturing cause-and-effect relations at Fashion Flair are the number of purchase orders and the number of suppliers.

10-40 (20 min.) **Data analysis and ethics.**

1(a)		
	Average annual labour costs over the last ten years	$1,200,000
	Expected annual labour costs if robots introduced	550,000
	Expected annual savings	$ 650,000

1(b)		
	Average annual labour costs over the last three years	$ 800,000
	Expected annual labour costs if robots introduced	550,000
	Expected annual savings	$ 250,000

Yes, it makes a difference in terms of justifying the robot investment. Using a 10-year average, the expected annual savings exceed the desired amount of $400,000 per year. Using average annual labour costs over the last three years, expected annual savings in labour costs falls short of the $400,000 target needed to justify the robot investment.

2. One explanation for average labour costs over the most recent three-year period being less than the average labour costs over the past ten years is learning curve effects. Learning-by-doing has caused workers to become more efficient. Alternatively, Comdex may have changed the VCR design to simplify manufacturing and reduce costs. Comdex may also have introduced new equipment that reduced labour costs.

3. The behaviour of both Helen Gibbs and Joan Hansen to overestimate deliberately the savings in labour costs to justify investments in robots is unethical. In assessing the situation, and considering the "Code of Professional Ethics" described in Exhibit 1-5, the issues that Joan Hansen, the management accountant, should consider are listed below.

(a) Clear reports using relevant and reliable information should be prepared. Reports prepared on the basis of overestimating savings in direct and indirect manufacturing labour (by considering older costs that are much higher than current costs) violate the management accountant's responsibility for competence. It is unethical for Gibbs to suggest that Hansen overestimate the cost savings that were computed for the robot investment and for Hansen to change the numbers to justify the investment in robots.

(b) Management accountants should communicate favourable as well as unfavourable information. In this regard, both Gibbs's and Hansen's behaviour of inflating manufacturing labour cost savings to justify the investment in robots could be viewed as unethical.

10-40 (cont'd)

(c)   Management accountants should communicate information fairly and objectively and all relevant information should be disclosed. From a management accountant's standpoint, overestimating manufacturing labour cost savings to justify the robot investment violates objectivity. For the various reasons cited above, we should take the position that the behaviour of Gibbs and Hansen is unethical.

4.   Hansen should indicate to Gibbs that the savings in manufacturing labour costs alone are not large enough to justify the robot investment. She should also indicate to Gibbs her concern about inflating cost savings to justify the robot investment, quite independent of how important she thinks it is for the company to invest in the robots. She may wish to point out that part of the problem is the excessive focus on cost savings alone to justify the robot investment. An important benefit of the robot investment is the ability to generate higher revenues by producing superior products. If Gibbs still insists on inflating costs to justify the investment, Hansen should raise the matter with Gibbs's superior. If, after taking all these steps, there is continued pressure to overstate cost savings, Hansen should consider resigning from the company, rather than engage in unethical behaviour.

CHAPTER 11
DECISION MAKING AND
RELEVANT INFORMATION

11-2 *Relevant costs* are those expected future costs that differ among alternative courses of action. Historical costs are irrelevant because they are past costs and therefore cannot differ among alternative future courses of action.

11-4 *Quantitative factors* are outcomes that are measured in numerical terms. Some quantitative factors are financial—that is, they can be easily expressed in financial terms. Direct materials is an example of a quantitative financial factor. *Qualitative factors* are factors that are not measured in numerical terms. An example is employee morale.

11-6 No. Some variable costs may not differ among the alternatives under consideration and hence will be irrelevant. Some fixed costs may differ among the alternatives and hence will be relevant.

11-8 *Opportunity cost* is the contribution to income that is forgone (rejected) by not using a limited resource in its next-best alternative use.

11-10 No. Managers should aim to get the highest contribution margin per unit of the constraining (that is, scarce, limiting, or critical) factor. The constraining factor is what restricts or limits the production or sale of a given product (for example, availability of machine-hours).

11-12 Cost written off as amortization is irrelevant when it pertains to a past cost. But the purchase cost of new equipment to be acquired in the future that will then be written off as depreciation is often relevant.

11-14 The three steps in solving a linear programming problem are:
(a)   Determine the objective.
(b)   Specify the constraints.
(c)   Compute the optimal solution.

11-16 (20 min.) Disposal of assets.

1.   This is an unfortunate situation, yet the $80,000 costs are irrelevant regarding the decision to remachine or scrap. The only relevant factors are the future revenues and future costs. By ignoring the accumulated costs and deciding on the basis of expected future costs, operating income will be maximized (or losses minimized). The difference in favour of remachining is $3,000:

	(a) Remachine	(b) Scrap
Future revenues	$35,000	$2,000
Deduct future costs	30,000	—
Operating income	$ 5,000	$2,000

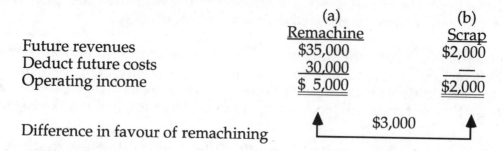

Difference in favour of remachining $3,000

2.   This too is an unfortunate situation. But the $100,000 original cost is irrelevant to this decision. The difference in favour of rebuilding is $7,000:

	(a) Replace	(b) Rebuild
New truck	$102,000	–
Deduct current disposal price of existing truck	10,000	–
Rebuild existing truck	–	$85,000
	$ 92,000	$85,000

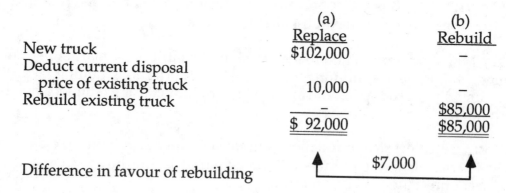

Difference in favour of rebuilding $7,000

Note here that the current disposal price of $10,000 is relevant, but the original cost (or book value, if the truck were not brand new) is irrelevant.

11-18 (15 min.) **Multiple choice.**

1. (b)
Special order price per unit	$6.00
Variable manufacturing costs per unit	4.50
Contribution margin per unit	$1.50

$$\text{Effect on operating income} = \$1.50 \times 20{,}000 \text{ units}$$
$$= \$30{,}000 \text{ increase}$$

2. (b) Costs of purchases, 20,000 units × $60 $1,200,000

     Total relevant costs of making:

Variable manufacturing costs, $64 – $16	$48	
Fixed costs eliminated	9	
Costs saved by not making	$57	
Multiply by 20,000 units, so total costs saved are $57 × 20,000		1,140,000
Extra costs of purchasing outside		60,000
Minimum savings necessary for Part No. 575		25,000
Necessary relevant costs that would have to be saved in manufacturing Part No. 575		$ 85,000

11-20 (30 min.)   **Make versus buy, activity-based costing.**

1.   The expected manufacturing cost per unit of CMCBs in 2003 is as follows:

	Total Manufacturing Costs of CMCB (1)	Manufacturing Cost per Unit (2) = (1) ÷ 10,000
Direct materials $170 ¥ 10,000	$1,700,000	$170
Direct manufacturing labour $45 ¥ 10,000	450,000	45
Variable batch manufacturing costs $1,500 ¥ 80	120,000	12
Fixed manufacturing costs		
Avoidable fixed manufacturing costs	320,000	32
Unavoidable fixed manufacturing costs	800,000	80
Total manufacturing costs	$3,390,000	$339

2.   The following table identifies the incremental costs in 2003 if Svenson (a) made CMCBs and (b) purchased CMCBs from Minton.

	Total Incremental Costs		Per-Unit Incremental Costs	
Incremental Items	**Make**	**Buy**	**Make**	**Buy**
Cost of purchasing CMCBs from Minton		$ 3,000,000		$300
Direct materials	$1,700,000		$170	
Direct manufacturing labour	450,000		45	
Variable batch manufacturing costs	120,000		12	
Avoidable fixed manufacturing costs	320,000	–	32	
Total incremental costs	$2,590,000	$3,000,000	$259	$300
Difference in favour of making	↑_____$410,000____↑		↑____$41____↑	

Note that the opportunity cost of using capacity to make CMCBs is zero since Svenson would keep this capacity idle if it purchases CMCBs from Minton.

Svenson should continue to manufacture the CMCBs internally, since the incremental costs to manufacture are $259 per unit compared with the $300 per unit that Minton has quoted. Note that the unavoidable fixed manufacturing costs of $800,000 ($80 per unit) will continue to be incurred whether Svenson makes or buys CMCBs. These are not incremental costs under either the make or the buy alternative and are hence irrelevant.

3.   Svenson should continue to make CMCBs. The simplest way to solve this problem is to recognize that Svenson would prefer to keep any excess capacity idle rather than use it to make CB3s. Why? Because expected incremental future revenues from CB3s ($2,000,000) are less than expected incremental future costs ($2,150,000). If Svenson keeps its capacity idle, we know from requirement 2 that it should make CMCBs rather than buy them.

11-20 (cont'd)

An important point to note is that, because Svenson forgoes no contribution by not being able to make and sell CB3s, the opportunity cost of using its facilities to make CMCBs is zero. It is therefore not forgoing any profits by using the capacity to manufacture CMCBs. If it does not manufacture CMCBs, rather than lose money on CB3s, Svenson will keep the capacity idle.

A longer and more detailed approach is to use the total alternatives or opportunity cost analyses shown in the chapter.

TOTAL-ALTERNATIVES APPROACH TO MAKE-OR-BUY DECISIONS

	Choices for Svenson		
Relevant Items	Make CMCBs and Do Not Make CB3s	Buy CMCBs and Do Not Make CB3s	Buy CMCBs and Make CB3s
Total incremental costs of making/buying CMCBs (from requirement 2)	$2,590,000	$3,000,000	$3,000,000
Excess of future costs over future revenues from CB3s	0	0	150,000
Total relevant costs	$2,590,000	$3,000,000	$3,150,000

Svenson will minimize manufacturing costs by making CMCBs.

OPPORTUNITY COST APPROACH TO MAKE-OR-BUY DECISIONS

	Choices for Svenson	
Relevant Items	Make CMCB	Buy CMCB
Total incremental costs of making/buying CMCBs (from requirement 2)	$2,590,000	$3,000,000
Opportunity cost: profit contribution forgone because capacity cannot be used to make CB3s	0*	0
Total relevant costs	$2,590,000	$3,000,000

Difference in favour of making CMCBs $410,000

* Opportunity cost is 0 because Svenson does not give up anything by manufacturing CMCBs. Had it not manufactured CMCBs, it would be best off leaving the capacity idle (rather than manufacturing and selling CB3s).

11-22 (10 min.) **Inventory decision, opportunity cost.**

1.
Unit cost, orders of 20,000	$8.00
Unit cost, order of 240,000 (0.95 × $8.00)	$7.60

Alternatives under consideration:
(a) Buy 240,000 units at start of year.
(b) Buy 20,000 units at start of each month.

Average investment in inventory:
(a) (240,000 × $7.60) ÷ 2	$912,000
(b) (20,000 × $8.00) ÷ 2	80,000
Difference in average investment	$832,000

Opportunity cost of interest forgone from 240,000-unit purchase at start of year
= $832,000 × 0.08 = $66,560

2. No. The $66,560 is an opportunity cost rather than an incremental or outlay cost. No actual transaction records the $66,560 as an entry in the accounting system.

3. The following table presents the two alternatives:

	Alternative A: Purchase 240,000 spark plugs at beginning of year (1)	Alternative B: Purchase 20,000 spark plugs at beginning of each month (2)	Difference (3)=(1)–(2)
Annual purchase (incremental) costs (240,000 × $7.60; 240,000 × $8)	$1,824,000	$1,920,000	$(96,000)
Annual interest income that could be earned if investment in inventory were invested (opportunity cost) (8% × $912,000; 8% × $80,000)	72,960	6,400	66,560
Relevant costs	$1,896,960	$1,926,400	$(29,440)

Column (3) indicates that purchasing 240,000 spark plugs at the beginning of the year is preferred relative to purchasing 20,000 spark plugs at the beginning of each month because the lower purchase cost exceeds the opportunity cost of holding larger inventory. If other incremental benefits of holding lower inventory such as lower insurance, materials handling, storage, obsolescence, and breakage costs were considered, the costs under Alternative A would have been higher, and Alternative B might have been preferred.

11-24 (10 min.) Selection of most profitable product.

Only Model 14 should be produced. The key to this problem is the relationship of manufacturing overhead to product. Note that it takes twice as long to produce Model 9; machine-hours for Model 9 are twice that for Model 14. Management should choose the product mix that maximizes operating income for a given production capacity (the scarce resource in this situation). In this case, Model 14 will yield a $19.00 contribution to fixed costs per unit of machine time, and Model 9 will yield $18.00:

	Model 9	Model 14
Selling price per unit	$100.00	$70.00
Variable costs per unit	82.00	60.50
Contribution margin per unit	$ 18.00	$ 9.50
Relative use of machine-hours per unit of product	× 1	× 2
Contribution margin per unit of machine time	$ 18.00	$19.00

11-26 (20-25 min.) Customer profitability, choosing customers.

1.   Broadway should not drop the Kelly Corporation business as the following analysis shows.

Loss in revenues from dropping Kelly	$(80,000)
Savings in costs:	
Variable costs	48,000
Fixed costs 20% × $100,000	20,000
Total savings in costs	68,000
Effect on operating income	$(12,000)

Broadway Printers would be worse off by $12,000 if it drops the Kelly Corporation business.

2.   If Broadway accepts the additional business from Kelly, it would take an additional 500 hours of machine time. If Broadway accepts all of Kelly's and Taylor's business for February, it would require 2,500 hours of machine time (1,500 hours for Taylor and 1,000 hours for Kelly). Broadway only has 2,000 hours of machine capacity. It must therefore choose how much of the Taylor and Kelly business to accept. If Broadway accepts any additional business from Kelly, it must forgo some of Taylor's business.

To maximize operating income, Broadway should maximize contribution margin per unit of the constrained resource. (Fixed costs will remain unchanged at $100,000, whatever business Broadway chooses to accept in February, and is therefore irrelevant.) The contribution margin per unit of the constrained resource for each customer in January is:

	Taylor Corporation	Kelly Corporation
Revenues	$120,000	$80,000
Variable costs	42,000	48,000
Contribution margin	$ 78,000	$32,000

Contribution margin per machine-hour $\frac{\$78,000}{1,500} = \$52$ $\frac{\$32,000}{500} = \$64$

Since the $80,000 of additional Kelly business in February is identical to jobs done in January, it will also have a contribution margin of $64 per machine-hour, which is greater than the contribution margin of $52 per machine-hour from Taylor. To maximize operating income, Broadway should first allocate all the capacity needed to take the Kelly Corporation business (1,000 machine-hours) and then allocate the remaining 1,000 (2,000 – 1,000) machine-hours to Taylor. Broadway's operating income in February would then be $16,000 as shown below, greater than the $10,000 operating income in January.

	Taylor Corporation	Kelly Corporation	Total
Contribution margin per machine-hour	$ 52	$ 64	
Machine hours to be worked	1,000	1,000	
Contribution margin	$52,000	$64,000	$116,000
Fixed costs			100,000
Operating income			$ 16,000

Alternatively, we could present Broadway's operating income by taking 2/3rds (1,000 ÷ 1,500 machine-hours) of Taylor's January revenues and variable costs, and doubling (1,000 ÷ 500 machine-hours) Kelly's January revenues and variable costs.

	Taylor Corporation	Kelly Corporation	Total
Revenues	$80,000	$160,000	$240,000
Variable costs	28,000	96,000	124,000
Contribution margin	52,000	64,000	116,000
Fixed costs			100,000
Operating income			$ 16,000

The problem indicated that Broadway could choose to accept as much of the Taylor and Kelly business for February as it wants. However, some students may raise the question that Broadway should think more strategically before deciding what to do. For example, how would Taylor react to Broadway's inability to satisfy its needs? Will Kelly continue to give Broadway $160,000 of business each month or is the additional $80,000 of business in February a special order? For example, if Kelly's additional work in February is only a special order and Broadway wants to maintain a long-term relationship with Taylor, it may in fact prefer to turn down the additional Kelly business. It may feel that the additional $6,000 in operating income in February is not worth jeopardizing Taylor's long-term relationship. Other students may raise the possibility of Broadway accepting all the Taylor and Kelly business for February if it can subcontract some of it to another reliable, high-quality printer.

11-28 (30 min.) Equipment upgrade versus replacement.

1. Solution Exhibit 11-28 presents a cost comparison of the upgrade and replacement alternatives for the three years taken together. It indicates that Pacifica Corporation should replace the production line because it is better off by $180,000 by replacing rather than upgrading.

2(a) Suppose the capital expenditure to replace the production line is $X. Using data from Solution Exhibit 11-28, the cost of replacing the production line is equal to $1,620,000 – $90,000 + $X. Using data from Solution Exhibit 11-28, the cost of upgrading the production line is equal to $2,160,000 + $300,000 = $2,460,000. We want to find $X such that

$$\$1,620,000 - \$90,000 + \$X = \$2,460,000$$

that is,
$$\$1,530,000 + \$X = \$2,460,000$$

that is,
$$\$X = \$2,460,000 - \$1,530,000$$

or
$$\$X = \$\ 930,000$$

Pacifica would prefer replacing rather than upgrading the existing line if the replacement cost of the new line does not exceed $930,000.

2(b) Suppose the units produced and sold each year equals y. Using data from Solution Exhibit 11-28, the cost of replacing the production line is $9y$ – $90,000 + $750,000, while the cost of upgrading is $12y$ + $300,000. We solve for the y at which the two costs are the same:

$$\$9y - \$90,000 + \$750,000 = \$12y + \$300,000$$
$$\$9y + \$660,000 = \$12y + \$300,000$$
$$\$3y = \$360,000$$
$$y = 120,000 \text{ units}$$

For expected production and sales of less than 120,000 units over 3 years (40,000 units per year), the upgrade alternative is cheaper. When production and sales are low the higher operating costs of upgrading are more than offset by the significant savings in capital costs when upgrading relative to replacing. For expected production and sales exceeding 120,000 units over 3 years, the replace alternative is cheaper. For high output the benefits of the lower operating costs of replacing relative to upgrading exceed the higher capital costs.

11-28 (cont'd)

SOLUTION EXHIBIT 11-28
Comparing Upgrade and Replace Alternatives

	Three Years Together		
	Upgrade (1)	Replace (2)	Difference (3) = (1) − (2)
Cash-operating costs $12; $9 × 180,000	$2,160,000	$1,620,000	$ 540,000
Current disposal price		(90,000)	90,000
One-time capital costs, written off periodically as depreciation	300,000	750,000	(450,000)
Total relevant costs	$2,460,000	$2,280,000	$ 180,000

Note that sales and book value of the existing machine are the same under both alternatives and hence irrelevant.

3.   Operating income for the first year under the upgrade and replace alternatives are as follows:

	Upgrade	Replace
Sales $25 × 60,000	$1,500,000	$1,500,000
Cash-operating costs $12; $9 × 60,000	720,000	540,000
Depreciation	220,000[a]	250,000[b]
Loss on disposal of old production line	—	270,000[c]
Total costs	940,000	1,060,000
Operating income	$ 560,000	$ 440,000

[a] $360,000 + $300,000 ÷ 3 = $220,000   [b] $750,000 ÷ 3 = $250,000
[c] Book value − current disposal price = $360,000 − $90,000 = $270,000

First-year operating income is higher by $120,000 under the upgrade alternative. If first year's operating income is an important component of Azinger's bonus, he would prefer the upgrade over the replace alternative even though the decision model in requirement 1 prefers the replace to the upgrade alternative. This exercise illustrates the conflict between the decision model and the performance-evaluation model (requirement 3).

11-30 (15 min.)   **Make or buy (continuation of 11-29).**

The maximum price Class Company should be willing to pay is $3.9417 per unit.

Expected unit production and sales of the new product must be half of the old product ($1/2 \times 240,000 = 120,000$) because the fixed manufacturing overhead rate for the new product is twice that of the fixed manufacturing overhead rate for the old product.

	Present	Proposed Make New Product	Proposed Old Product	Total
Sales	$1,440,000	$1,080,000	$1,440,000	$2,520,000
Variable (or purchase) costs:				
Manufacturing	720,000	600,000	946,000*	1,546,000
Marketing and other	360,000	240,000	288,000	528,000
Total variable costs	1,080,000	840,000	1,234,000	2,074,000
Contribution margin	360,000	240,000	206,000	446,000
Fixed costs:				
Manufacturing	120,000	120,000	–	120,000
Marketing and other	216,000	60,000	216,000	276,000
Total fixed costs	336,000	180,000	216,000	396,000
Operating Income	$ 24,000	$ 60,000	$ –10,000	$ 50,000

*This is an example of opportunity costs, whereby subcontracting at a price well above the $3.50 current manufacturing (absorption) cost is still desirable because the old product will be displaced in manufacturing by a new product that is more profitable.

Because the new product promises an operating income of $60,000 (ignoring the irrelevant problems of how fixed marketing costs may be newly reallocated between products), the old product can sustain up to a $10,000 loss and still help accomplish management's overall objectives. Maximum costs that can be incurred on the old product are $1,440,000 plus the $10,000 loss, or $1,450,000. Maximum purchase cost: $1,450,000 − ($288,000 + $216,000) = $946,000. Maximum purchase cost per unit: $946,000 ÷ 240,000 units = $3.9417 per unit.

11-30 (cont'd)

Alternative Computation

Operating income is $9.00 – $8.50 = $0.50 per unit for 120,000 new units	$60,000	
Target operating income	50,000	
Maximum loss allowed on old product	$10,000	
Maximum loss per unit allowed on old product, $10,000 ÷ 240,000 =		$0.0417
Sales price of old product		$6.0000
Allowance for loss		0.0417
Total costs allowed per unit		6.0417
Continuing costs for old product other than purchase cost:		
Fixed manufacturing costs—all transferred to new product	$ –	
Variable marketing costs	1.20	
Fixed marketing costs	0.90	2.1000
Maximum purchase cost per unit		$3.9417

11-32 (30-40 min.) **Product mix, relevant costs.**

	R3	HP6
Selling price	$100	$150
Variable manufacturing costs per unit	60	100
Variable marketing costs per unit	15	35
Total variable costs per unit	75	135
Contribution margin per unit	$ 25	$ 15

	R3	HP6
Contribution margin per hour of the constrained resource (the regular machine)	$\dfrac{\$25}{1} = \$25$	$\dfrac{\$15}{0.5} = \$30$

	R3	HP6
Total contribution margin from selling Only R3 or only HP6 R3: $25 × 50,000; HP6: $30 × 50,000	$1,250,000	$1,500,000
Less: Lease costs of high-precision machine to produce and sell HP6	-	300,000
Net relevant benefit	$1,250,000	$1,200,000

Even though HP6 has the higher contribution margin per unit of the constrained resource, the fact that Pendleton must incur additional costs of $300,000 to achieve this higher contribution margin means that Pendleton is better off using its entire 50,000-hour capacity on the regular machine to produce and sell 50,000 units (50,000 hours ÷ 1 hour per unit) of R3. The additional contribution from selling HP6 rather than R3 is $250,000 ($1,500,000 – $1,250,000), which is not enough to cover the additional costs of leasing the high-precision machine. Note that, because all other overhead costs are fixed and cannot be changed, they are irrelevant for the decision.

11-32 (cont'd)

2. If capacity of the regular machines is increased by 15,000 machine-hours to 65,000 machine-hours (50,000 originally + 15,000 new), the net relevant benefit from producing R3 and HP6 is as follows:

	R3	HP6
Total contribution margin from selling only R3 or only HP6 R3: $25 × 65,000; HP6: $30 × 65,000	$1,625,000	$1,950,000
Less: Lease costs of high-precision machine that would be incurred if HP6 is produced and sold	—	300,000
Less: Cost of increasing capacity by 15,000 hours on regular machine	150,000	150,000
Net relevant benefit	$1,475,000	$1,500,000

Investing in the additional capacity increases Pendleton's operating income by $250,000 ($1,500,000 calculated in requirement 2 *minus* $1,250,000 calculated in requirement 1), so Pendleton should add 15,000 hours to the regular machine. With the extra capacity available to it, Pendleton should use its entire capacity to produce HP6. Using all 65,000 hours of capacity to produce HP6 rather than to produce R3 generates additional contribution margin of $325,000 ($1,950,000 – $1,625,000) which is more than the additional cost of $300,000 to lease the high-precision machine. Pendleton should therefore produce and sell 130,000 units of HP6 (65,000 hours ÷ 0.5 hours per unit of HP6) and zero units of R3.

3.

	R3	HP6	S3
Selling price per unit	$100	$150	$120
Variable manufacturing costs per unit	60	100	70
Variable marketing costs per unit	15	35	15
Total variable costs per unit	75	135	85
Contribution margin per unit	$ 25	$ 15	$ 35
Contribution margin per hour of the constrained resource (the regular machine)	$\frac{\$25}{1} = \$25$	$\frac{\$15}{0.5} = \$30$	$\frac{\$35}{1} = \$35$

The first step is to compare the operating profits that Pendleton could earn if it accepted the Carter Corporation offer for 20,000 units with the operating profits Pendleton is currently earning. S3 has the highest contribution margin per hour on the regular machine and requires no additional investment such as leasing a high-precision machine. To produce the 20,000 units of S3 requested by Carter Corporation, Pendleton would require 20,000 hours on the regular machine, resulting in a contribution margin of $35 × 20,000 = $700,000.

11-32 (cont'd)

Pendleton now has 45,000 hours available on the regular machine to produce R3 or HP6.

	R3	HP6
Total contribution margin from selling only R3 or only HP6		
R3: $25 × 45,000; HP6: $30 × 45,000	$1,125,000	$1,350,000
Less: Lease costs of high-precision machine to produce and sell HP 6	–	300,000
Net relevant benefit	$1,125,000	$1,050,000

Pendleton should use all the 45,000 hours of available capacity to produce 45,000 units of R3. Thus, the product mix that maximizes operating income is 20,000 units of S3, 45,000 units of R3, and zero units of HP6. This optimal mix results in a contribution margin of $1,825,000 ($700,000 from S3 and $1,125,000 from R3). Relative to requirement 2, operating income increases by $325,000 ($1,825,000 minus $1,500,000 calculated in requirement 2). Hence, Pendleton should accept the Carter Corporation business and supply 20,000 units of S3.

11-34 (20 min.) Opportunity cost.

1.   The opportunity cost to Wolverine of producing the 2,000 units of Orangebo is the contribution margin lost on the 2,000 units of Rosebo that would have to be forgone, as computed below:

Revenue per unit		$20
Variable costs per unit:		
Direct materials	$2	
Direct manufacturing labour	3	
Variable manufacturing overhead	2	
Variable nonmanufacturing costs	4	11
Contribution margin per unit		$ 9
Contribution margin for 2,000 units		$ 18,000

The opportunity cost is $18,000. Opportunity cost is the maximum contribution to operating income that is forgone (rejected) by not using a limited resource in its next-best alternative use.

11-34 (cont'd)

2. Contribution margin from manufacturing 2,000 units of Orangebo and purchasing 2,000 units of Rosebo from Buckeye is $16,000 as follows:

	Manufacture Orangebo	Purchase Rosebo	Total
Revenue per unit	$15	$20	
Variable costs per unit:			
Purchase costs	–	14	
Direct materials	2		
Direct manufacturing labour	3		
Variable manufacturing overhead	2		
Variable nonmanufacturing overhead	2	4	
Variable costs per unit	9	18	
Contribution margin per unit	$ 6	$ 2	
Contribution margin from selling 2,000 units of Orangebo and 2,000 units of Rosebo	$12,000	$4,000	$16,000

As calculated in requirement 1, Wolverine's contribution margin from continuing to manufacture 2,000 units of Rosebo is $18,000. Accepting the Windsor Company order and the Buckeye offer will cost Wolverine $2,000 ($16,000 – $18,000). Hence Wolverine should refuse the Windsor Company order and Buckeye Corporation's offer.

3. The minimum price would be $9, the sum of the incremental costs as computed in requirement 2. This follows because if Wolverine has surplus capacity, the opportunity cost = $0. For the short-run decision of whether to accept Orangebo's offer, fixed costs of Wolverine are irrelevant. Only the incremental costs need to be covered for it to be worthwhile for Wolverine to accept the Orangebo offer.

11-36 (30-40 min.) **Considering three alternatives.**

1. The 5% surcharge is irrelevant.

	Sell to Kaytell as Special Order	Convert to Standard Model	Sell as Special Order as Is
Selling price	$68,400	$62,500	$52,000
Deduct cash discount	–	1,250	–
Net selling price	68,400	61,250	52,000
Additional manufacturing costs:			
Direct materials	6,200	2,850	–
Direct manufacturing labour	4,200	3,300	–
Variable manufacturing overhead	2,100	1,650	–
Total additional manufacturing costs	12,500	7,800	–
Commissions	2,052	1,225	1,560
Total costs	14,552	9,025	1,560
Contribution to operating income	$53,848	$52,225	$50,440

2.

Kaytell contribution	$53,848
Next-best alternative:	
Standard model contribution	52,225
Change in contribution to operating income	$ 1,623

$$\text{Change in net sales price} = \frac{\text{Change in contribution}}{1 - \text{Commission \%}}$$

$$= \frac{\$1,623}{1 - .03} = \frac{\$1,623}{0.97}$$

$$= \$1,673 \text{ (rounded)}$$

Original Kaytell price	$68,400
Reduction in contribution permissible before Auer switches to the next-best alternative	1,673
Minimum price Auer should accept from Kaytell and be indifferent between standard model and Kaytell offer.	$66,727

11-17

11-36 (cont'd)

3. Fixed manufacturing overhead should have no influence on the selling price quoted by Auer Company for (one-time-only) special orders:

   (a) Auer Company should accept special orders whenever the company is operating substantially below capacity, including below the breakeven point, if incremental revenue from an order exceeds incremental cost. Normally, this approach would mean that the order should be accepted as long as the selling price of the order exceeds the variable manufacturing costs. The special order will result in a positive contribution toward fixed costs. The fixed manufacturing overhead is not considered in the pricing because it will be incurred whether the order is accepted or not.

   (b) If Auer Company is operating above its breakeven point and if a special order will allow the company to utilize unused capacity efficiently, the special order should be accepted as long as incremental revenue exceeds incremental cost, or, in most cases, the selling price exceeds the variable manufacturing costs. If the selling price exceeds the variable manufacturing costs, the order will yield a positive contribution toward the company's fixed costs. Fixed manufacturing overhead is not considered because it will be incurred whether the order is accepted or not. The only time the fixed manufacturing overhead would be relevant would be if Auer were near capacity and additional fixed costs would have to be incurred to complete the order. If this situation occurred, Auer's incremental costs would be higher, and they would have to be covered by the selling price.

11-38 (30-40 min.) **Make or buy, unknown level of volume.**

1. Let X = 1 starter assembly. The variable costs required to manufacture 150,000X are:

Direct materials	$200,000
Direct manufacturing labour	150,000
Variable manufacturing overhead	100,000
Total variable costs	$450,000

The total variable costs per unit is $450,000 ÷ 150,000 = $3.00 per unit.

The data can be presented in both "all data" and "relevant data" formats:

	All Data		Relevant Data	
	Alternative 1: Make	Alternative 2: Buy	Alternative 1: Make	Alternative 2: Buy
Variable manufacturing costs	$ 3X	–	$ 3X	–
Fixed general manufacturing overhead	150,000	$150,000	–	–
Fixed overhead—avoidable	100,000	–	100,000	–
Division 2 manager's salary	40,000	50,000	40,000	$50,000
Division 3 manager's salary	50,000	–	50,000	–
Purchase cost—if bought from Tidnish Electronics	–	4X	–	4X
Total	$340,000 + $ 3X	$200,000 + $ 4X	$190,000 + $ 3X	$50,000 + $ 4X

11-38 (cont'd)

The number of units at which the costs of make and buy are equivalent is:

All data analysis:

$$\$340{,}000 + \$3X = \$200{,}000 + \$4X$$
$$X = 140{,}000$$

or

Relevant data analysis:

$$\$190{,}000 + \$3X = \$50{,}000 + \$4X$$
$$X = 140{,}000$$

Assuming cost minimization is the objective, then:
- If production is expected to be less than 140,000 units, it is preferable to buy units from Tidnish.
- If production is expected to exceed 140,000 units, it is preferable to manufacture internally (make) the units.
- If production is expected to be 140,000 units, this is the indifference point between buying units from Tidnish and internally manufacturing (making) the units.

2.   The information on the storage cost, which is avoidable if self-manufacture is discontinued, is relevant; these storage charges represent current outlays that are avoidable if self-manufacture is discontinued. Assume these $50,000 charges are represented as an opportunity cost of the make alternative. The costs of internal manufacture that incorporate this $50,000 opportunity cost is:

All data analysis: $390,000 + $3X

Relevant data analysis: $240,000 + $3X

The number of units at which the costs of make and buy are equivalent are:

All data analysis:

$$\$390{,}000 + \$3X = \$200{,}000 + \$4X$$
$$X = 190{,}000$$

Relevant data analysis:

$$\$240{,}000 + \$3X = \$50{,}000 + \$4X$$
$$X = 190{,}000$$

If production is expected to be less than 190,000, it is preferable to buy units from Tidnish. If production is expected to exceed 190,000, it is preferable to manufacture the units internally.

11-40 (30-40 min.)   **Relevant cost of materials.**

1.   Hernandez Corporation has already purchased the 10,000 kilograms of the special cement that it needs, so it will incur no incremental costs. Alternatively stated, the costs of materials are past (sunk) costs.

If Hernandez obtained Contract No. 2 a month from now, it would cost $21,000 in substitute material (10,000 kilograms x $2.10 per kilogram). There is, therefore, a cost (lost benefit) of $21,000 by using the special cement on Contract No. 1 now. Alternatively, Hernandez could sell the special cement immediately for $16,000. The opportunity cost that Hernandez should use is the benefit it would get in the next-best alternative should it not use the cement in Contract No. 1. The greater of these two benefits is using the cement in Contract No. 2. The opportunity cost is $21,000. The relevant cost that Gomez should use when bidding on Contract No. 1 is:

Incremental cost	$ 0
Plus opportunity cost	21,000
Relevant cost	$21,000

2.   As in Question 1, the incremental costs of acquiring the special cement for use on Contract No. 1 are zero because Hernandez has already purchased the material. If Hernandez does not land Contract No. 2, the opportunity cost of using the special cement for Contract No. 1 is $15,000 (10,000 kilograms × $1.50 per kilogram), the amount Hernandez would get if it sold the special cement one month from now.

Gomez assesses a probability of 0.7 that the special cement will be used on Contract No. 2 and a probability of 0.3 that the special cement will be sold.

The expected benefit of holding the special cement and not using it on Contract No. 1 is

$$= \quad (0.7 \times \$21{,}000^*) + (0.3 \times \$15{,}000^{**})$$
$$= \quad \$14{,}700 + \$4{,}500 \ = \ \$19{,}200$$

* relevant cost if special cement is used in Contract No. 2 (see requirement 1)
** relevant cost if special cement is sold one month from now

Alternatively, the special cement can be sold right away and fetch $16,000. The opportunity cost is the greater of these two benefits and hence equals $19,200. When bidding on the Contract, Gomez should use:

Incremental cost	$ 0
Plus opportunity cost	19,200
Relevant cost	$19,200

3.   In this case, the benefit of selling the cement now is $23,000, while the benefit of using the cement in Contract No. 2 is $21,000. The opportunity cost of using the cement in Contract No. 1 is the greater of these two numbers, $23,000.

Incremental cost	$ 0
Plus opportunity cost	23,000
Relevant cost	$23,000

11-42 (30 min.) **Appendix: Optimal production plan, computer manufacturer.**

1. Let X = Units of printers
    and Y = Units of desktop computers

    Objective: Maximize total contribution margin of $200X + $100Y
    Constraints:

For production line 1:	6X	+ 4Y	24
For production line 2:	10X		20
Sales of X and Y:	X	– Y	0
Negative production impossible:	X		0
		Y	0

2. Solution Exhibit 11-42 presents a graphical summary of the relationships. The sales-mix constraint here is somewhat unusual. The X – Y   0 line is the one going upward at a 45° angle from the origin. Using the trial-and-error method:

Trial	Corner (X; Y)	Total Contribution Margin			
1	(0; 0)	$ 200(0)	+	$100(0)	= $ 0
2	(2; 2)	200(2)	+	100(2)	= 600
3	(2; 3)	200(2)	+	100(3)	= 700
4	(0; 6)	200(0)	+	100(6)	= 600

The optimal solution that maximizes operating income is 2 printers and 3 computers.

SOLUTION EXHIBIT 11-42
Graphic Solution to Find Optimal Mix, Information Technology, Inc.

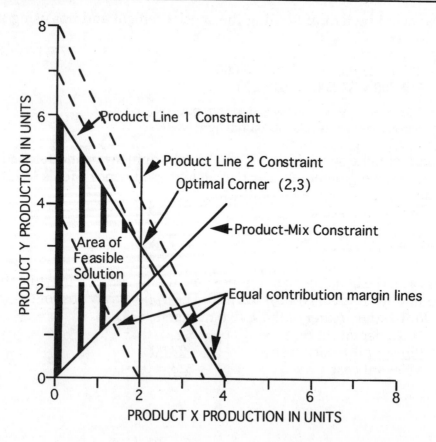

11-44 (30 min.)   **Make versus buy, ethics.**

1.   An analysis of relevant costs that shows whether or not Paibec Corporation should make MTR-2000 or purchase it from Marley Company for 2003 follows:

	Total Costs for 32,000 Units
Cost to purchase MTR-2000 from Marley	
Bid price from Marley, $17.30 × 32,000	$553,600
Equipment lease penalty	6,000
Total incremental cost to purchase	559,600
Cost for Paibec to make MTR-2000 in 2002	
Direct materials ($195,000 × 1.08) × $\frac{32,000}{30,000}$	224,640
Direct labour ($120,000 × 1.05) × $\frac{32,000}{30,000}$	134,400
Factory space rental	84,000
Equipment leasing costs	36,000
Variable manufacturing overhead ($225,000 × 40%) × $\frac{32,000}{30,000}$	96,000
Fixed manufacturing overhead (not relevant)	–
Total incremental cost to make MTR-2000	575,040
Savings if purchased from Marley	$ 15,440

2.   Based solely on the financial results, the 32,000 units of MTR-2000 for 2003 should be purchased from Marley. The total cost from Marley would be $559,600 or $15,440 less than if the units were made by Paibec.

At least three other factors that Paibec Corporation should consider before agreeing to purchase MTR-2000 from Marley Company are the following:

- The quality of the Marley component should be equal to, or better than, the quality of the internally made component, or else the quality of the final product might be compromised and Paibec's reputation affected.

- Marley's reliability as an on-time supplier is important, since late deliveries could hamper Paibec's production schedule and delivery dates for the final product.

- Layoffs may result if the component is outsourced to Marley. This could impact Paibec's other employees and cause labour problems or affect the company's position in the community. In addition, there may be termination costs which have not been factored into the analysis.

11-44 (cont'd)

3.   Lynn Hardt would consider the request of John Porter to be unethical for the following reasons:

- Prepare complete and clear reports and recommendations after appropriate analysis of relevant and reliable information. Adjusting cost is unethical.

- Refrain from either actively or passively subverting the attainment of the organization's legitimate and ethical objectives. Paibec has a legitimate objective of trying to obtain the component at the lowest cost possible, regardless of whether it is manufactured by Paibec or outsourced to Marley.

- Communicate unfavourable as well as favourable information and professional judgments or opinions. Hardt needs to communicate the proper and accurate results of the analysis, regardless of whether or not it is favourable to Paibec.

- Refrain from engaging in or supporting any activity that would discredit the profession. Falsifying the analysis would discredit Hardt and the profession.

- Communicate information fairly and objectively. Hardt needs to perform an objective make-versus-buy analysis and communicate the results fairly.

- Disclose fully all relevant information that could reasonably be expected to influence an intended user's understanding of the reports, comments, and recommendations presented. Hardt needs to disclose fully the analysis and the expected cost increases.

Hardt should indicate to Porter that the costs derived under the make alternative are correct. If Porter still insists on making the changes to lower the costs of making MTR-2000 internally, Hardt should raise the matter with Porter's superior, after informing Porter of her plans. If, after taking all these steps, there is continued pressure to understate the costs, Hardt should consider resigning from the company, rather than engage in unethical conduct.

CHAPTER 12
PRICING DECISIONS, PRODUCT PROFITABILITY DECISIONS, AND COST MANAGEMENT

12-2 Not necessarily. For a one-time-only special order the relevant costs are only those costs that will change as a result of accepting the order. In this case, full product costs will rarely be relevant. It is more likely that full product costs will be relevant costs for long-run pricing decisions.

12-4 Activity-based costing helps managers in pricing decisions in two ways.
(a) It gives managers more accurate product-cost information for making pricing decisions.
(b) It helps managers to manage costs during value engineering by identifying the cost impact of eliminating, reducing or changing various activities.

12-6 A target cost per unit is the estimated long-run cost per unit of a product (or service) that, when sold at the target price, enables the company to achieve the targeted operating income per unit.

12-8 A value-added cost is a cost that customers perceive as adding value, or utility, to a product or service. Examples are costs of materials, direct labour, tools, and machinery. Examples of nonvalue-added costs are costs of rework, scrap, expediting, and breakdown maintenance.

12-10 Cost-plus pricing is a pricing approach in which managers add a markup to cost in order to determine price.

12-12 Two examples where the difference in the incremental or outlay costs of two products or services is much smaller than the differences in their prices follow:
1. The difference in prices charged for a telephone call, hotel room, or car rental during busy versus slack periods is often much greater than the difference in costs to provide these services.
2. The difference in incremental or outlay costs for an airplane seat sold to a passenger travelling on business or a passenger travelling for pleasure is roughly the same. However, airline companies routinely charge business travellers—those who are likely to start and complete their travel during the same week excluding the weekend—a much higher price than pleasure travellers, who generally stay at their destinations over at least one weekend.

12-14 Three benefits of using a product life-cycle reporting format are:
1. The full set of revenues and costs associated with each product becomes more visible.
2. Differences among products in the percentage of total costs committed at early stages in the life cycle are highlighted.
3. Interrelationships among business function cost categories are highlighted.

12-16 (20-30 min.) **Relevant-cost approach to pricing decisions, special order.**

1.

Relevant revenues, $3.80 × 1,000		$3,800
Relevant costs		
Direct materials, $1.50 × 1,000	$1,500	
Direct manufacturing labour, $0.80 × 1,000	800	
Variable manufacturing overhead, $0.70 × 1,000	700	
Variable selling costs, 0.05 × $3,800	190	
Total		3,190
Increase in operating income		$ 610

This calculation assumes that:
  (a) The monthly fixed manufacturing overhead of $150,000 and $65,000 of monthly fixed marketing costs will be unchanged by acceptance of the 1,000 unit order.
  (b) The price charged and the volumes sold to other customers are not affected by the special order.

Chapter 12 uses the phrase "one-time-only special order" to describe this special case.

2. The president's reasoning is defective on at least two counts:
  (a) The inclusion of irrelevant costs—assuming the monthly fixed manufacturing overhead of $150,000 will be unchanged; it is irrelevant to the decision.
  (b) The exclusion of relevant costs—variable selling costs (5% of the selling price) are excluded.

3. Key issues are:
  (a) Will the existing customer base demand price reductions? If this 1,000-tape order is not independent of other sales, cutting the price from $5.00 to $3.80 can have a large negative effect on total revenues.
  (b) Is the 1,000-tape order a one-time-only order, or is there the possibility of sales in subsequent months? The fact that the customer is not in Dill Company's "normal marketing channels" does not necessarily mean it is a one-time-only order. Indeed, the sale could well open a new marketing channel. Dill Company should be reluctant to consider only short-run variable costs for pricing long-run business.

12-18 (25 min.) **Short-run pricing, capacity constraints.**

1.   With no constraints on availability of Pyrone or on plant capacity, Boutique would want to charge a minimum price for Seltium that would cover its incremental costs to manufacture Seltium. (Because there is excess capacity, there is no opportunity cost.) In this case, the incremental costs are the variable costs to manufacture a kilogram of Seltium:

Pyrone (2 kilograms × $4 per kilogram)	$ 8
Direct manufacturing labour	4
Variable manufacturing overhead costs	3
Total variable manufacturing costs	$15

Hence, the minimum price that Boutique should charge to manufacture Seltium is $15 per kilogram. For 3,000 kilograms of Seltium it should charge a minimum of $45,000 ($15 × 3,000).

2.   Now Pyrone is in short supply. Using it to make Seltium reduces the Bolzene that Boutique can make and sell. There is therefore an opportunity cost of manufacturing Seltium, the lost contribution from using the Pyrone to manufacture Bolzene. To make 3,000 kilograms of Seltium requires 6,000 (2 × 3,000) kilograms of Pyrone.

The 6,000 kilograms of Pyrone can be used to manufacture 4,000 (6,000 ÷ 1.5) kilograms of Bolzene, since each kilogram of Bolzene requires 1.5 kilograms of Pyrone.

The contribution margin from 4,000 kilograms of Bolzene is $24,000 ($6 per kilogram × 4,000 kilograms). This is the opportunity cost of using Pyrone to manufacture Seltium. The minimum price that Boutique should charge to manufacture Seltium should cover not only the incremental (variable) costs of manufacturing Seltium but also the opportunity cost:

	Costs of Manufacturing Seltium	
Relevant costs	**Total for 3,000 Kilograms** **(1)**	**Per Kilogram** **(2) = (1) ÷ 3,000**
Incremental (variable) costs of manufacturing Seltium	$45,000	$15
Opportunity cost of forgoing manufacture and sale of Bolzene	24,000	8
Minimum cost of order	$69,000	$23

The minimum price per kilogram that Boutique should charge for Seltium is $23 per kilogram. For 3,000 kilograms of Seltium, Boutique should charge a minimal of $69,000 ($23 × 3,000 kgs).

12-20 (25–30 min.) **Target operating income, value-added costs, service company.**

1.   The classification of total costs in 2002 into value-added, non-value added, or in the gray area in between follows.

	Value Added (1)	Gray Area (2)	Non-value added (3)	Total (4)= (1)+(2)+(3)
Doing calculations and preparing drawings 75% × $400,000	$300,000			$300,000
Checking calculations and drawings 4% × $400,000		$16,000		16,000
Correcting errors found in drawings 7% × $400,000			$28,000	28,000
Making changes in response to client requests 6% × $400,000	24,000			24,000
Correcting errors to meet government building code, 8% × $400,000			32,000	32,000
Total professional labour costs	324,000	16,000	60,000	400,000
Administration and support costs at 40% ($160,000 ÷ $400,000) of professional labour costs	129,600	6,400	24,000	160,000
Travel	18,000		–	18,000
Total	$471,600	$22,400	$84,000	$578,000

Doing calculations and responding to client requests for changes are value-added costs because customers perceive these costs as necessary for the service of preparing architectural drawings. Costs incurred in correcting errors in drawings and making changes because they were inconsistent with building codes are non-value-added costs. Customers do not perceive these costs as necessary and would be unwilling to pay for them. Carasco should seek to eliminate these costs. Checking calculations and drawings is in the gray area (some, but not all, checking may be needed). There is room for disagreement on these classifications. For example, checking calculations may be regarded as value added, and making changes to conform to the building code might be regarded as in the gray area.

Carasco's staff can reduce non-value-added costs by checking government building code requirements before drawing up the plans and taking more care when doing the actual work. To reduce value-added costs, Carasco's staff must work faster and more efficiently while at the same time maintaining quality. To achieve these goals, Carasco may want to consider investing in computer-aided drawing programs and training its professional staff to work with these tools.

12-20 (cont'd)

2.   Reduction in professional labour-hours by

(a) Correcting errors in drawings (7% × 8,000)	560 hours
(b) Correcting errors to conform to building code (8% × 8,000)	640 hours
Total	1,200 hours
Cost savings in professional labour costs (1,200 hours × $50)	$ 60,000
Cost savings in variable administration and support costs (40% × $60,000)	24,000
Total cost savings	$ 84,000

Current operating income in 2002	$102,000
Add: Cost savings from eliminating errors	84,000
Operating income in 2001 if errors are eliminated	$186,000

3.   Currently 85% × 8,000 hours = 6,800 hours are billed to clients generating revenues of $680,000. The remaining 15% of professional labour-hours (15% × 8,000 = 1,200 hours) is lost in making corrections. Carasco bills clients at the rate of $\frac{\$680,000}{6,800}$ = $100 per professional labour-hour. If the 1,200 professional labour-hours currently not being billed to clients were billed to clients, Carasco's revenues would increase by 1,200 hours × $100 = $120,000 from $680,000 to $800,000.

Costs remaining unchanged

Professional labour costs	$400,000
Administration and support (40% × $400,000)	160,000
Travel	18,000
Total costs	$578,000

Carasco's operating income would be

Revenues	$800,000
Total costs	578,000
Operating income	$222,000

12-22 (20 min.) **Cost-plus target return on investment pricing.**

1. Target operating income = target return on investment × invested capital

Target operating income , 25% of $960,000	$240,000
Total fixed costs	352,000
Target contribution margin	$592,000

Target contribution per room, ($592,000 ÷ 16,000)	$37
Add variable costs per room	3
Price to be charged per room	$40

Proof

Total room revenues ($40 × 16,000 rooms)		$640,000
Total costs:		
Variable costs ($3 × 16,000)	$ 48,000	
Fixed costs	352,000	
Total costs		400,000
Operating income		$240,000

The full cost of a room = variable cost per room + fixed cost per room
The full cost of a room = $3 + ($352,000 ÷ 16,000) = $3 + $22 = $25

Markup per room   =   Rental price per room – Full cost of a room
                      = $40 – $25 = $15
Markup percentage as a fraction of full cost = $15 ÷ $25 = 60%

2. If price is reduced by 10%, the number of rooms Beck could rent would increase by 10%.

The new price per room would be 90% of $40	= $36
The number of rooms Beck expects to rent is 110% of 16,000	= 17,600
The contribution margin per room would be $36 – $3	= $33
Contribution margin = $33 × 17,600	= $580,800

Since the contribution margin at the reduced price of $36 is less than the contribution margin at a price of $40, Beck should not reduce the price of the rooms. Note that the fixed costs of $352,000 will be the same under the $40 and the $36 price alternatives and are hence irrelevant to the analysis.

12-24 (25 min.)   **Target costs, effect of product-design changes on product costs.**

1. & 2. Indirect cost-allocation rates for 2002 and 2003 are as follows:

Indirect cost category	2002 Total Costs (1)	2002 Quantity of Cost-Allocation Base (2)	2002 Cost Allocation Rate (3)= (1) ÷ (2)	2003 Total Costs (4)	2003 Quantity of Cost-Allocation Base (5)	2003 Cost-Allocation Rate (6)= (4) ÷ (5)
Batch-level costs	$ 7,200,000	900	$ 8,000	$ 7,500,000	1,000	$ 7,500
Manuf. operations costs	12,100,000	220,000	55	12,500,000	250,000	50
Engineering change costs	2,640,000	220	12,000	2,000,000	200	10,000

Manufacturing costs of HJ6 in 2002 and 2003 are as follows:

	2002 Total (1)	2002 Per Unit (2)= (1) ÷ 3,500	2003 Total (3)	2003 Per Unit (4)= (3) ÷ 4,000
Direct materials, $1,200 × 3,500; $1,100 × 4,000	$4,200,000	$1,200	$4,400,000	$1,100
Batch-level costs, $8,000 × 70; $7,500 × 80	560,000	160	600,000	150
Manuf. operations costs, $55 × 21,000; $50 × 22,000	1,155,000	330	1,100,000	275
Engineering change costs, $12,000 × 15; $10,000 × 10	180,000	51	100,000	25
Total	$6,095,000	$1,741	$6,200,000	$1,550

3. $$\text{Target manufacturing cost per unit of HJ6 in 2001} = \text{Manufacturing cost per unit in 2000} \times 88\%$$

$$= \$1,741 \times 0.88 = \$1,532.08$$

Actual manufacturing cost per unit of HJ6 in 2003 was $1,550. Hence, Medical Instruments did not achieve its target manufacturing cost per unit of $1,532.08.

4.   To reduce the manufacturing cost per unit in 2003, Medical Instruments reduced the cost per unit in each of the four cost categories—direct materials costs, batch-level costs, manufacturing operations costs, and engineering change costs. It achieved this by reducing setup, production order, and materials handling costs per batch, the cost per machine hour, and cost per engineering change, perhaps by becoming more efficient in performing these activities. Efficiency improvements also helped Medical Instruments reduce the quantities of the cost allocation bases used to manufacture HJ6. For example, although production of HJ6 increased by 14.3% [(4,000 − 3,500) ÷ 3,500] between 2002 and 2003, machine-hours worked increased by only 4.8% [(22,000 ÷ 21,000) ÷ 21,000]. Medical Instruments achieved these gains through value engineering activities that retained only those product features that customers wanted while eliminating non-value-added activities and costs.

12-26 (30-40 min.)   **Life-cycle product costing, product emphasis.**

1.   A life-cycle income statement traces revenue and costs of each individual software package from its initial research and development to its final customer servicing and support in the marketplace. The two main differences from a calendar-based income statement are:
(a)   Costs incurred in different calendar periods are included in the same statement.
(b)   Costs and revenue of each package are reported separately rather than aggregated into company-wide categories.

The benefits of using a product life-cycle report are:
(a)   The full set of revenues and costs associated with each product becomes visible.
(b)   Differences among products in the percentage of total costs committed at early stages in the life cycle are highlighted.
(c)   Interrelationships among business function cost categories are highlighted. What is the effect, for example, of cutting back on R&D and product-design cost categories on customer-service costs in subsequent years?

2.

	EE-46		ME-83		IE-17	
Revenue ($000s)		$2,500		$1,500		$1,600
Costs ($000s)						
Research and development	$700		$450		$240	
Design	200		120		96	
Production	300		210		208	
Marketing	500		270		448	
Distribution	75		60		96	
Customer service	375	2,150	150	1,260	608	1,696
Operating income ($000s)		$ 350		$ 240		$ (96)

As emphasized in this chapter, the time value of money is not taken into account when summing life-cycle revenue or life-cycle costs. Chapters 21 and 22 discuss this topic in detail.

Rankings of the three packages on profitability (and relative profitability) are:

Operating income		**Operating income**
		Revenues
1. EE-46:	$350,000	1. ME-83: 16.0%
2. ME-83:	$240,000	2. EE-46: 14.0%
3. IE-17:	$ (96,000)	3. IE-17: (6.0%)

The EE-46 and ME-83 packages should be emphasized, and the IE-17 package should be de-emphasized. It is interesting that IE-17 had the lowest R&D costs but was the least profitable.

12-26 (cont'd)

3. The cost structures of the three software packages are:

	EE-46	ME-83	IE-17
Research and development	32.5%	35.7%	14.1%
Design	9.3	9.5	5.7
Production	14.0	16.7	12.3
Marketing	23.3	21.4	26.4
Distribution	3.5	4.8	5.7
Customer service	17.4	11.9	35.8
	100.0%	100.0%	100.0%

The major differences are:
   (a) EE-46 and ME-83 have over 40% of their costs in the R&D/product design categories compared to less than 20% (19.8%) for IE-17.
   (b) IE-17 has 35.8% of its costs in the customer-service category compared to 17.4% for EE-46 and 11.9% for ME-83.

There are several explanations for these differences:
   (a) EE-46 and ME-83 differ sizably from IE-17 in their R&D/product design intensity. For example, EE-46 and ME-83 may require considerably (a) more interaction with users, and (b) more experimentation with software algorithms than does IE-17.
   (b) The software division should have invested more in the R&D/product design categories for IE-17. The high percentage for customer service could reflect the correcting of problems that should have been corrected prior to manufacture. Life-cycle reports highlight possible causal relationships among cost categories.

12-28 (30 min.) **Relevant-cost approach to pricing decisions.**

1.

Revenues (1,000 crates at $100 per crate)		$100,000
Variable costs:		
Manufacturing	$40,000	
Marketing	14,000	
Total variable costs		54,000
Contribution margin		46,000
Fixed costs:		
Manufacturing	$20,000	
Marketing	16,000	
Total fixed costs		36,000
Operating income		$ 10,000

Normal markup percentage: $46,000 ÷ $54,000 = 85.19% of total variable costs.

2.   Only the manufacturing-cost category is relevant to considering this special order; no additional marketing costs will be incurred. The relevant manufacturing costs for the 200-crate special order are:

Variable manufacturing cost per unit	
$40 × 200 crates	$ 8,000
Special packaging	2,000
	$10,000

Any price above $50 per crate ($10,000 ÷ 200) will make a positive contribution to operating income.

The reasoning based on a comparison of $55 per-crate price with the $60 per-crate absorption cost ignores monthly cost-volume-profit relationships. The $60 per-crate absorption cost includes a $20 per-crate cost component that is irrelevant to the special order. The relevant range for the fixed manufacturing costs is from 500 to 1,500 crates per month; the special order will increase production from 1,000 to 1,200 crates per month. Furthermore, the special order requires no incremental marketing costs.

3.   If the new customer is likely to remain in business, Stardom should consider whether a strictly short-run focus is appropriate. For example, what is the likelihood of demand from other customers increasing over time? If Stardom accepts the 200-crate special order for more than one month, it may preclude accepting other customers at prices exceeding $55 per crate. Moreover, the existing customers may learn about Stardom's willingness to set a price based on variable cost plus a small contribution margin. The longer time frame over which Stardom keeps selling 200 crates of canned peaches at $55 a crate, the more likely that the existing customers will approach Stardom for their own special price reductions.

12-30 (50-60 min.) **Target cost, activity-based costing systems (continuation of 12-29).**

1.   A target cost per unit is the estimated long-run cost per unit of a product (or service) that, when sold at the target price, enables the company to achieve the target operating income per unit. A target cost per unit is the estimated unit long-run cost of a product that will enable a company to enter or to remain in the market and compete profitably against its competitors.

2.   The following table presents the manufacturing cost per unit for different cost categories for P-41REV and P-63 REV.

Cost Categories	P-41 REV	P-63 REV
Direct manufacturing product costs:		
Direct materials	$381.20	$263.10
Indirect manufacturing product costs:		
Materials handling		
(71 × $1.20; 39 × $1.20)	85.20	46.80
Assembly management		
(2.1 × $40; 1.6 × $40)	84.00	64.00
Machine-insertion of parts		
(59 × $0.70; 29 × $0.70)	41.30	20.30
Manual-insertion of parts		
(12 × $2.10; 10 × $2.10)	25.20	21.00
Quality testing		
(1.2 × $25; 0.9 × $25)	30.00	22.50
Total indirect manufacturing costs	265.70	174.60
Total manufacturing costs	$646.90	$437.70
Target cost	$680.00	$390.00

P-41 REV is $33.10 below its target cost. However, P-63 REV is $47.70 above its target cost. It appears that Executive Power will have major problems competing with the foreign printer costing $390.

12-30 (cont'd)

3.

P-41	=	$782.40		P-63	=	$504.00
P-41 REV	=	646.90		P-63 REV	=	437.70
Difference	=	$135.50		Difference	=	$ 66.30

The sources of the cost reductions in the redesigned products are:

		P-41	P-63
(a)	Reduction in direct materials costs	$ 26.30	$29.00
(b)	Changes in design:		
	Reduced materials handling costs because of fewer parts		
	(85 – 71); (46 – 39) × $1.20	16.80	8.40
	Reduced assembly time		
	(3.2 – 2.1); (1.9 – 1.6) × $40	44.00	12.00
	Reduced insertion of parts[1]		
	(49 – 59) × $0.70 + (36 – 12) × $2.10	43.40	
	(31 – 29) × $0.70 + (15 – 10) × $2.10		11.90
	Reduced quality testing		
	(1.4 – 1.2); (1.1 – 0.9) × $25	5.00	5.00
		$135.50	$66.30

[1] Note that the reduced costs for insertion of parts comes from two sources: (a) a reduction in total number of parts to be inserted, and (b) an increase in the percentage of parts inserted by the lower-cost machine method.

4.   The $12 reduction in cost per hour of assembly time (from $40 to $28) reduces product costs as follows:

P-41 REV: $12 × 2.1 hours = $25.20. The new total manufacturing product cost is $621.70 ($646.90 – $25.20)

P-63 REV: $12 × 1.6 hours = $19.20. The new total manufacturing product cost is $418.50 ($437.70 – $19.20)

The reduction in the assembly management activity rate further reduces the cost of P-41 REV below the target cost. It also makes it more likely that P-63 REV will achieve its target cost.

12-32 (25 min.)   **Cost-plus and market-based pricing.**

1.   Construction Temps' full cost per hour of supplying contract labour is:

Variable costs	$12
Fixed costs ($240,000 ÷ 80,000 hours)	3
Full cost per hour	$15

Price per hour at full cost plus 20% = $15 × 1.20 = $18 per hour.

2.   Contribution margins for different prices and demand realizations are as follows:

Price per Hour (1)	Variable Cost per Hour (2)	Contribution Margin per Hour (3)=(1)–(2)	Demand in Hours (4)	Total Contribution (5)=(3)×(4)
$16	$12	$4	120,000	$480,000
17	12	5	100,000	500,000
18	12	6	80,000	480,000
19	12	7	70,000	490,000
20	12	8	60,000	480,000

Fixed costs will remain the same regardless of the demand realizations. Fixed costs are therefore irrelevant since they do not differ among the alternatives.

The table above indicates that Construction Temps can maximize contribution margin and hence operating income by charging a price of $17 per hour.

3.   The cost-plus approach to pricing in requirement 1 does not explicitly consider the effect of prices on demand. The approach in requirement 2 models the interaction between price and demand and determines the optimal level of profitability using concepts of relevant costs. The two different approaches lead to two different prices in requirements 1 and 2. As the chapter describes, pricing decisions should consider both demand or market considerations and supply or cost factors. The approach in requirement 2 is the more balanced approach. In most cases, of course, managers use the cost-plus method of requirement 1 as only a starting point. They then modify the cost-plus price on the basis of market considerations—anticipated customer reaction to alternative price levels and the prices charged by competitors for similar products.

12-34 (35-40 min.) Life-cycle product costing, activity-based costing.

1. The budgeted life-cycle operating income for the new watch MX3 is $1,852,500 as shown below.

	Year 1 (1)	Year 2 (2)	Year 3 (3)	Life-Cycle (4)=(1)+(2)+(3)
Revenues $45 × 50,000; $40 × 200,000; $35 × 150,000	$2,250,000	$8,000,000	$5,250,000	$15,500,000
R&D and Design costs	900,000	100,000	0	1,000,000
Manufacturing costs:				
Variable $16 × 50,000; $15 × 200,000; $15 × 150,000	800,000	3,000,000	2,250,000	6,050,000
Batch $700 × 125[1]; $600 × 400[2]; $600 × 300[3]	87,500	240,000	180,000	507,500
Fixed	600,000	600,000	600,000	1,800,000
Marketing costs:				
Variable $3.60 × 50,000; $3.20 × 200,000; $2.80 × 150,000	180,000	640,000	420,000	1,240,000
Fixed	400,000	300,000	300,000	1,000,000
Distribution costs:				
Variable $1 × 50,000; $1 × 200,000; $1 × 150,000	50,000	200,000	150,000	400,000
Batch $120 × 250[4]; $120 × 1,250[5]; $100 × 1,250[6]	30,000	150,000	125,000	305,000
Fixed	240,000	240,000	240,000	720,000
Customer service costs:				
Variable $2 × 50,000; $1.50 × 200,000; $1.50 × 150,000	100,000	300,000	225,000	625,000
Total costs	3,387,500	5,770,000	4,490,000	13,647,500
Operating income	$(1,137,500)	$2,230,000	$ 760,000	$ 1,852,500

[1] 50,000 ÷ 400 = 125   [2] 200,000 ÷ 500 = 400   [3] 150,000 ÷ 500 = 300
[4] 50,000 ÷ 200 = 250   [5] 200,000 ÷ 160 = 1,250   [6] 150,000 ÷ 120 = 1,250

2.   Budgeted product life-cycle costs for R&D and design $1,000,000
       Total budgeted product life-cycle costs $13,647,500

$$\text{Percentage of budgeted product life-cycle costs incurred till the R\&D and design stages} = \frac{1,000,000}{13,647,500} = 7.33\%$$

3.   An analysis reveals that 80% of the total product life-cycle costs of the new watch will be locked in at the end of the R&D and design stages when only 7.33% of the costs have been incurred (requirement 2). The implication is that it will be difficult to alter or reduce the costs of MX3 once Destin finalizes the design of MX3. To reduce and manage total costs, Destin must act to modify the design before costs get locked in.

4.   The budgeted life-cycle operating income for MX3 if Destin reduces its price by $3 is $1,251,000 as shown on the next page. This is less than the operating income of $1,852,500 calculated in requirement 1. Therefore, Destin should not reduce MX3's price by $3.

12-34 (cont'd)

	Year 1 (1)	Year 2 (2)	Year 3 (3)	Life-Cycle (4)=(1)+(2)+(3)
Revenues $42 × 55,000; $37 × 220,000; $32 × 165,000	$2,310,000	$8,140,000	$5,280,000	$15,730,000
R&D and design costs	900,000	100,000	0	1,000,000
Manufacturing costs:				
Variable $16 × 55,000; $15 × 220,000; $15 × 165,000	880,000	3,300,000	2,475,000	6,655,000
Batch $700 × 125[1]; $600 × 400[2]; $600 × 300[3]	87,500	240,000	180,000	507,500
Fixed	600,000	600,000	600,000	1,800,000
Marketing costs:				
Variable $3.60 × 55,000; $3.20 × 220,000; $2.80 × 165,000	198,000	704,000	462,000	1,364,000
Fixed	400,000	300,000	300,000	1,000,000
Distribution costs:				
Variable $1 × 55,000; $1 × 220,000; $1 × 165,000	55,000	220,000	165,000	440,000
Batch $120 × 250[4]; $120 × 1,250[5]; $100 × 1,250[6]	30,000	150,000	125,000	305,000
Fixed	240,000	240,000	240,000	720,000
Customer service costs:				
Variable $2 × 55,000; $1.50 × 220,000; $1.50 × 165,000	110,000	330,000	247,500	687,500
Total costs	3,500,500	6,184,000	4,794,500	14,479,000
Operating income	$(1,190,500)	$1,956,000	$ 485,500	$ 1,251,000

[1] 55,000 ÷ 440 = 125   [2] 220,000 ÷ 550 = 400   [3] 165,000 ÷ 550 = 300
[4] 550,000 ÷ 220 = 250   [5] 220,000 ÷ 176 = 1,250   [6] 165,000 ÷ 132 = 1,250

12-36 (30 min.) **Airline pricing, considerations other than cost in pricing.**

1. If the fare is $2,000,
   (a) Air North would expect to have 190 business and 20 pleasure travellers.
   (b) Variable costs per passenger would be: food and beverages, $40; and ticket commissions of 8% × 2,000 = $160.
   (c) Contribution margin per passenger = $2,000 – $40 – $160 = $1,800.

   If the fare is $500,
   (a) Air North would expect to have 200 business and 100 pleasure travellers.
   (b) Variable costs per passenger would be: food and beverages, $40; and ticket commissions of 8% × $500 = $40.
   (c) Contribution margin per passenger = $500 – $40 – $40 = $420

   Contribution margin from business travellers at prices of $500 and $2,000 respectively follow:
   At a price of $500 : $420 × 200 passengers   = $84,000
   At a price of $2,000 : $1,800 × 190 passengers   = $342,000

   Air North would maximize contribution margin and operating income by charging business travellers a fare of $2,000. The reason is that the demand for business travel drops only slightly (from 200 passengers per flight to 190 passengers per flight) despite the large increase in fare. Also note that in deciding between the alternative prices all other costs such as fuel costs, allocated annual lease costs, allocated ground services costs, and allocated flight crew salaries are irrelevant. Why? Because these costs will not change, whatever price Air North chooses to charge.

   Contribution margin from pleasure travellers at prices of $500 and $2,000 respectively follow:
   At a price of $500 : $420 × 100 passengers   = $42,000
   At a price of $2,000 : $1,800 × 20 passengers   = $36,000

   Air North would maximize contribution margin and operating income by charging pleasure travellers a fare of $500. The reason is that the demand for pleasure travel drops significantly (from 100 passengers per flight to 20 passengers per flight) as a result of increasing the fare. Once again, in deciding between the alternative prices to charge pleasure travellers, all other costs such as fuel costs, allocated annual lease costs, allocated ground services costs, and allocated flight crew salaries are irrelevant.

   Air North would maximize contribution margin and operating income by a price differentiation strategy, where business travellers are charged $2,000 and pleasure travellers $500.

12-36 (cont'd)

2.   The elasticity of demand of the two classes of passengers drives the different demands of the travellers. Business travellers are relatively price insensitive because they must get to their destinations during the week (exclusive of weekends) and their fares are paid by their companies. A 300% increase in fares from $500 to $2,000 will deter only 5% of the business passengers from flying with Air North.

In contrast, a similar fare increase will lead to an 80% drop in pleasure travellers who are paying for their own travel costs, unlike business travellers, and who may have alternative vacation plans they could pursue instead.

3.   Since business travellers often want to return within the same week, while pleasure travellers often stay over weekends, a requirement that a Saturday night stay is needed to qualify for the $500 discount fare would discriminate between the passenger categories. This price discrimination is legal because airlines are service companies rather than manufacturing companies and because these practices do not, nor are they intended to, destroy competition.

CHAPTER 13
STRATEGY, BALANCED SCORECARD, AND STRATEGIC PROFITABILITY ANALYSIS

13-2 The five key forces to consider in industry analysis are: (a) competitors, (b) potential entrants into the market, (c) equivalent products, (d) bargaining power of customers, and (e) bargaining power of input suppliers.

13-4 The four key perspectives in the balanced scorecard are: (1) Financial perspective—this perspective evaluates the profitability of the strategy, (2) Customer perspective—this perspective identifies the targeted market segments and measures the company's success in these segments, (3) Internal business process perspective—this perspective focuses on internal operations that further both the customer perspective by creating value for customers and the financial perspective by increasing shareholder wealth, and (4) Learning and growth perspective—this perspective identifies the capabilities in which the organization must excel in order to achieve superior internal processes that create value for customers and shareholders.

13-6 A good balanced scorecard design has several features:
1. It tells the story of a company's strategy by articulating a sequence of cause-and-effect relationships.
2. It helps to communicate the strategy to all members of the organization by translating the strategy into a coherent and linked set of understandable and measurable operational targets.
3. It places strong emphasis on financial objectives and measures in for-profit companies. Nonfinancial measures are regarded as part of a program to achieve future financial performance.
4. It limits the number of measures to only those that are critical to the implementation of strategy.
5. It highlights suboptimal tradeoffs that managers may make when they fail to consider operational and financial measures together.

13-8 Three key components in doing a strategic analysis of operating income are:
1. The growth component which measures the change in operating income attributable solely to an increase in the quantity of output sold from one year to the next.
2. The price-recovery component which measures the change in operating income attributable solely to changes in the prices of inputs and outputs from one year to the next.
3. The productivity component which measures the change in costs attributable to a change in the quantity of inputs used in the current year relative to the quantity of inputs that would have been used in the previous year to produce current year output.

13-10 Engineered costs result from a cause-and-effect relationship between the cost driver, output, and the (direct or indirect) resources used to produce that output. Discretionary costs arise from periodic (usually) annual decisions regarding the maximum amount to be incurred. There is no measurable cause-and-effect relationship between output and resources used.

13-12 Downsizing (also called rightsizing) is an integrated approach configuring processes, products, and people in order to match costs to the activities that need to be performed for operating effectively and efficiently in the present and future.

13-14 Total factor productivity is the quantity of output produced divided by the costs of all inputs used, where the inputs are costed on the basis of current period prices.

13-16 (15 min.) Balanced scorecard.

1. La Quinta's 2003 strategy is a cost leadership strategy. La Quinta plans to grow by producing high-quality boxes at a low cost delivered to customers in a timely manner. La Quinta's boxes are not differentiated, and there are many other manufacturers who produce similar boxes. To succeed, La Quinta must achieve lower costs relative to competitors through productivity and efficiency improvements.

2. Measures that we would expect to see on La Quinta's balanced scorecard for 2003 are

Financial Perspective
(1) Operating income from productivity gain, (2) operating income from growth, (3) cost reductions in key areas.
   These measures evaluate whether La Quinta has successfully reduced costs and generated growth through cost leadership.

Customer Perspective
(1) Market share, (2) new customers, (3) customer satisfaction index, (4) customer retention, (5) time taken to fulfill customer orders.
   The logic is that improvements in these customer measures are leading indicators of superior financial performance.

Internal Business Process Perspective
(1) Yield, (2) productivity, (3) order delivery time, (4) on-time delivery.
   Improvements in these measures are expected to lead to more satisfied customers and in turn to superior financial performance.

Learning and Growth Perspective
(1) Percentage of employees trained in process and quality management, (2) employee satisfaction, (3) number of major process improvements.
   Improvements in these measures have a cause-and-effect relationship with improvements in internal business processes, which in turn lead to customer satisfaction and financial performance.

13-18 (15 min.) **Strategy, balanced scorecard.**

1.   Meredith Corporation follows a product differentiation strategy in 2003. Meredith's D4H machine is distinct from its competitors and generally regarded as superior to competitors' products. To succeed, Meredith must continue to differentiate its product and charge a premium price.

2.   Balanced Scorecard measures for 2003 follow:

Financial Perspective
(1) Increase in operating income from charging higher margins, (2) Price premium earned on products.

These measures indicate whether Meredith has been able to charge premium prices and achieve operating income increases through product differentiation.

Customer Perspective
(1) Market share in high-end special-purpose textile machines, (2) customer satisfaction, (3) new customers.

Improvements in these customer measures are leading indicators of superior financial performance.

Internal Business Process Perspective
(1) Manufacturing quality, (2) new product features added, (3) order delivery time.

Improvements in these measures are expected to result in more satisfied customers and in turn superior financial performance.

Learning and Growth Perspective
(1) Development time for designing new machines, (2) improvements in manufacturing processes, (3) employee education and skill levels, (4) employee satisfaction.

Improvements in these measures have a cause-and-effect relationship with improvements in internal business processes, which in turn lead to customer satisfaction and financial performance.

13-20 (20 min.) **Analysis of growth, price-recovery, and productivity components (continuation of 13-19).**

Effect of the industry-market-size factor

If the 10-unit increase in sales from 200 to 210 units, 3% or 6 (3% × 200) units is due to growth in market size, and 4 (10 − 6) units is due to an increase in market share. The change in Meredith's operating income from the industry-market-size factor rather than from specific strategic actions is:

$280,000 (the growth component in Exercise 13-19) $\times \dfrac{6}{10}$ $168,000 F

Effect of product differentiation

The change in operating income due to:

Increase in the selling price of D4H (revenue effect of price recovery)	$420,000 F
Increase in price of inputs (cost effect of price recovery)	184,500 U
Growth in market share due to product differentiation	

$280,000 (the growth component in Exercise 13-19) $\times \dfrac{4}{10}$ 112,000 F

Change in operating income due to product differentiation	$347,500 F

Effect of cost leadership

The change in operating income from cost leadership is:

Productivity component	$92,000 F

The change in operating income between 2002 and 2003 can be summarized as follows:

Change due to industry-market-size	$168,000 F
Change due to product differentiation	347,500 F
Change due to cost leadership	92,000 F
Change in operating income	$607,500 F

Meredith has been successful in implementing its product differentiation strategy. Nearly 57% ($347,500 ÷ $607,500) of the increase in operating income during 2003 was due to product differentiation. Meredith's operating income increase in 2003 was also helped by a growth in the overall market and some productivity improvements.

13-22 (15 min.) **Strategy, balanced scorecard, service company.**

1.   Snyder Corporation's strategy in 2002 is cost leadership. Snyder's consulting services for implementing sales management software is not distinct from its competitors. The market for these services is very competitive. To succeed, Snyder must deliver quality service at low cost. Improving productivity while maintaining quality is key.

2.   Balanced Scorecard measures for 2002 follow:

Financial Perspective
(1) Increase operating income from productivity gains and growth, (2) revenues per employee, (3) cost reductions in key areas, for example, software implementation and overhead costs.
       These measures indicate whether Snyder has been able to reduce costs and achieve operating income increases through cost leadership.

Customer Perspective
(1) Market share, (2) new customers, (3) customer responsiveness, (4) customer satisfaction.
       Improvements in these customer measures are regarded as leading indicators of superior financial performance.

Internal Business Process Perspective
(1) Time to complete customer jobs, (2) time lost due to errors, (3) quality of job (Is system running smoothly after job is completed?).
       Improvements in these measures are expected to lead to more satisfied customers, lower costs, and superior financial performance.

Learning and Growth Perspective
(1) Time required to analyze and design implementation steps, (2) time taken to perform key steps implementing the software, (3) skill levels of employees, (4) hours of employee training, (5) employee satisfaction and motivation.
       Improvements in these measures have a cause-and-effect relationship with improvements in internal business processes, customer satisfaction, and financial performance.

13-24 (25 min.) **Analysis of growth, price-recovery and productivity components (continuation of 13-23).**

Effect of industry-market-size factors
Of the 10-unit increase in sales from 60 to 70 units, 5% or 3 units (5% × 60) is due to growth in market size, and 7 (10 – 3) units is due to an increase in market share.
The change in Snyder's operating income from the industry market-size factor rather than from specific strategic actions is:

$200,000 (the growth component in Exercise 13-23) × $\frac{3}{10}$ $60,000 F

Effect of product differentiation
Of the $2,000 decrease in selling price, 1% or $500 (1% × $50,000) is due to a general decline in prices, and the remaining decrease of $1,500 ($2,000 – $500) is due to a strategic decision by Snyder's management to implement its cost leadership strategy of lowering prices to stimulate demand.

The change in operating income due to a decline in selling price (other than the strategic reduction in price included in the cost leadership component) $500 × 70 units	$ 35,000 U
Increase in prices of inputs (cost effect of price recovery)	129,000 U
Change in operating income due to product differentiation	$164,000 U

Effect of cost leadership

Productivity component	$189,000 F
Effect of strategic decision to reduce selling price, $1,500 × 70	105,000 U

Growth in market share due to productivity improvement
  and strategic decision to reduce selling price

$200,000 (the growth component in Exercise 13-23) × $\frac{7}{10}$	140,000 F
Change in operating income due to cost leadership	$224,000 F

The change in operating income between 2001 and 2002 can then be summarized as

Change due to industry-market-size	$ 60,000 F
Change due to product differentiation	164,000 U
Change due to cost leadership	224,000 F
Change in operating income	$120,000 F

Snyder has been very successful in implementing its cost leadership strategy. Due to a lack of product differentiation, Snyder was unable to pass along increases in labour costs by increasing the selling price—in fact selling price declined by $2,000 per work unit. However, Snyder was able to take advantage of its productivity gains to reduce price, gain market share, and increase operating income.

13-26 (20-30 min.) **Balanced scorecard.**

Perspectives	Strategic Objectives	Performance Measures
• Financial	• Increase shareholder value	• Earnings per share • Net income • Return on assets • Return on sales • Return on equity • Product cost per unit • Customer cost per unit
	• Increase profit generated by each salesperson	• Profit per salesperson
• Customer	• Acquire new customers	• Number of new customers
	• Retain customers	• Percentage of customers retained
	• Develop profitable customers	• Customer profitability
• Internal Business Processs	• Improve manufacturing quality	• Percentage of defective product units
	• Introduce new products	
	• Minimize invoice error rate	• Percentage of error-free invoices
	• On-time delivery by suppliers	• Percentage of on-time deliveries by suppliers
	• Increase proprietary products	• Number of patents
• Learning and Growth	• Increase information system capabilities	• Percentage of processes with real-time feedback
	• Enhance employee skills	• Employee turnover rate • Average job-related training hours per employee

13-28 (20 min.)   **Balanced scorecard.**

1.   Caltex's strategy is to focus on "service-oriented customers" who are willing to pay a higher price for services. Even though its product is largely a commodity product, gasoline, Caltex wants to differentiate itself through the service it provides at its retailing stations.

Does the scorecard represent Caltex's strategy? By and large it does. The focus of the scorecard is on measures of process improvement, quality, market share, and financial success from product differentiation. There are some deficiencies that the subsequent assignment questions raise but, abstracting from these concerns for the moment, the scorecard does focus on implementing a product differentiation strategy.

Having concluded that the scorecard has been reasonably well designed, how has Caltex performed relative to its strategy in 2001? It appears from the scorecard that Caltex was successful in implementing its strategy in 2001. It achieved all targets in the financial, internal business, and learning and growth perspectives. The only target it missed was the market share target in the customer perspective. At this stage, students may raise some questions about whether this is a good scorecard measure. Requirement 3 gets at this issue in more detail. The bottom line is that measuring "market share in the overall gasoline market" rather than in the "service-oriented customer market segment" is not a good scorecard measure, so not achieving this target may not be as big an issue as it may seem at first.

2.   Yes, Caltex should include some measure of employee satisfaction and employee training in the learning and growth perspective. Caltex's differentiation strategy and ability to charge a premium price is based on customer service. The key to good, fast, and friendly customer service is well-trained and satisfied employees. Untrained and dissatisfied employees will have poor interactions with customers and cause the strategy to fail. Hence, training and employee satisfaction are very important to Caltex for implementing its strategy. These measures are leading indicators of whether Caltex will be able to successfully implement its strategy and, hence, should be measured on the balanced scorecard.

3.   Caltex's strategy is to focus on the 60% of gasoline consumers who are service-oriented not on the 40% price-shopper segment. To evaluate if it has been successful in implementing its strategy, Caltex needs to measure its market share in its targeted market segment, "service-oriented customer," not its market share in the overall market. Given Caltex's strategy, it should not be concerned if its market share in the price-shopper segment declines. In fact, charging premium prices will probably cause its market share in this segment to decline. Caltex should replace "market share in overall gasoline market" with "market share in the service-oriented customer segment" in its balanced scorecard customer measure. Caltex may also want to consider putting a customer satisfaction measure on the scorecard. This measure should capture an overall evaluation of customer reactions to the facility, the convenience store, employee interactions, and quick turnaround. The customer satisfaction measure would serve as a leading indicator of market share in the service-oriented customer segment.

13-28 (cont'd)

4.   Although there is a cause-and-effect link between internal business process measures and customer measures on the current scorecard, Caltex should add more measures to tighten this linkage. In particular, the current scorecard measures focus exclusively on refinery operations and not on gas station operations. Caltex should add measures of gas station performance such as cleanliness of the facility, turnaround time at the gas pumps, the shopping experience at the convenience store, and the service provided by employees. Many companies do random audits of their facilities to evaluate how well their branches and retail outlets are performing. These measures would serve as leading indicators of customer satisfaction and market share in Caltex's targeted segments.

5.   Caltex is correct in not measuring changes in operating income from productivity improvements on its scorecard under the financial perspective. Caltex's strategy is to grow by charging premium prices for customer service. The scorecard measures focus on Caltex's success in implementing this strategy. Productivity gains per se are not critical to Caltex's strategy and, hence, should not be measured on the scorecard.

13-30 (35 min.) Analysis of growth, price-recovery, and productivity improvements.

1.   Halsey is following a product differentiation strategy. Halsey offers a wide selection of clothes and excellent customer service. Halsey's strategy is to distinguish itself from its competitors and to charge a premium price.

2.   Operating income for each year is as follows:

	2001	2002
Revenues ($60 × 40,000; $59 × 40,000)	$2,400,000	$2,360,000
Costs		
Materials costs ($40 × 40,000; $41 × 40,000)	1,600,000	1,640,000
Selling & customer service costs ($7 × 51,000); $6.90 × 43,000)	357,000	296,700
Purchasing & admin. costs ($250 × 980; $240 × 850)	245,000	204,000
Total costs	2,202,000	2,140,700
Operating income	$ 198,000	$ 219,300
Change in operating income	▲ $21,300 F ▲	

13-30 (cont'd)

3. **The Growth Component**

$$
\begin{array}{c}
\text{Revenue effect} \\
\text{of growth} \\
\text{component}
\end{array}
=
\left(
\begin{array}{c}
\text{Actual units of} \\
\text{output sold} \\
\text{in 2002}
\end{array}
-
\begin{array}{c}
\text{Actual units of} \\
\text{output sold} \\
\text{in 2001}
\end{array}
\right)
\times
\begin{array}{c}
\text{Output} \\
\text{price} \\
\text{in 2001}
\end{array}
$$

$$
= (40{,}000 - 40{,}000) \times \$60 = \$0
$$

$$
\begin{array}{c}
\text{Cost effect of} \\
\text{price - recovery} \\
\text{component}
\end{array}
=
\left(
\begin{array}{c}
\text{Actual units of input or} \\
\text{capacity that would} \\
\text{have been used to produce} \\
\text{year 2002 output assuming} \\
\text{the same input - output} \\
\text{relationship that existed in 2001}
\end{array}
-
\begin{array}{c}
\text{Actual units of} \\
\text{inputs or capacity} \\
\text{used to produce} \\
\text{2001 output}
\end{array}
\right)
\times
\begin{array}{c}
\text{Input} \\
\text{prices} \\
\text{in 2001}
\end{array}
$$

Materials costs that would be required in 2002 would be the same as that required in 2001 because output is the same between 2001 and 2002. Manufacturing conversion costs and selling and customer-service costs will not change since adequate capacity exists in 2001 to support year 2002 output and customers.

The cost effects of growth component are:

Materials costs	$(40{,}000 - 40{,}000)$	×	$\$60$ =	$\$0$
Selling & cust.-serv. costs	$(51{,}000 - 51{,}000)$	×	$\$7$ =	0
Purch. & admin. costs	$(980 - 980)$	×	$\$250$ =	$\underline{0}$
Cost effect of growth component				$\underline{\underline{\$0}}$

In summary, the net effect on operating income as a result of the growth component equals:

Revenue effect of growth component	$\$0$
Cost effect of growth component	$\underline{0}$
Change in operating income due to growth component	$\underline{\underline{\$0}}$

13-30 (cont'd)

The Price-Recovery Component

$$\begin{array}{c}\text{Revenue effect}\\\text{of price - recovery}\\\text{component}\end{array} = \left(\begin{array}{c}\text{Output price}\\\text{in 2002}\end{array} - \begin{array}{c}\text{Output price}\\\text{in 2001}\end{array}\right) \times \begin{array}{c}\text{Actual units}\\\text{of output}\\\text{sold in 2002}\end{array}$$

$$= \ (\$59 - \$60) \times 40{,}000 \ = \$40{,}000 \ U$$

$$\begin{array}{c}\text{Cost effect of}\\\text{price - recovery}\\\text{component}\end{array} = \left(\begin{array}{c}\text{Input}\\\text{prices}\\\text{in 2002}\end{array} - \begin{array}{c}\text{Input}\\\text{prices}\\\text{in 2001}\end{array}\right) \times \begin{array}{c}\text{Actual units of inputs or}\\\text{capacity that would}\\\text{have been used to produce}\\\text{year 2002 output assuming}\\\text{the same input - output}\\\text{relationship that existed in 2001}\end{array}$$

Materials costs	($41 – $40)	×	40,000	=	$40,000 U
Selling & cust.-serv. costs	($6.90 – $7)	×	51,000	=	5,100 F
Purchas. & admin. costs	($240 – $250)	×	980	=	9,800 F
Total cost effect of price-recovery component					$25,100 U

In summary, the net decrease in operating income as a result of the price-recovery component equals:

Revenue effect of price-recovery component	$40,000 U
Cost effect of price-recovery component	25,100 U
Change in operating income due to price-recovery component	$65,100 U

The Productivity Component

$$\begin{array}{c}\text{Productivity}\\\text{component}\end{array} = \left(\begin{array}{c}\text{Actual units of}\\\text{inputs or capacity}\\\text{used to produce}\\\text{year 2002 output}\end{array} - \begin{array}{c}\text{Actual units of inputs or}\\\text{capacity that would}\\\text{have been used to produce}\\\text{year 2002 output assuming}\\\text{the same input - output}\\\text{relationship that existed in 2001}\end{array}\right) \times \begin{array}{c}\text{Input}\\\text{prices}\\\text{in 2002}\end{array}$$

13-30 (cont'd)

The productivity component of cost changes are:

Materials costs	$(40,000 - 40,000) \times \$41$	=	0
Selling & cust.-serv. costs	$(43,000 - 51,000) \times \$6.90$	=	\$55,200 F
Purchasing & admin. costs	$(850 - 980) \times \$240$	=	31,200 F
Change in operating income due to productivity component			\$86,400 F

The change in operating income between 2001 and 2002 can be analyzed as follows:

	Income Statement Amounts in 1999 (1)	Revenue and Cost Effects of Growth Component in 2000 (2)	Revenue and Cost Effects of Price-Recovery Component in 2000 (3)	Cost Effect of Productivity Component in 2000 (4)	Income Statement Amounts in 2000 (5) = (1) + (2) + (3) + (4)
Revenues	\$2,400,000	\$0	\$40,000 U	—	\$2,360,000
Costs	2,202,000	0	25,100 U	\$ 86,400 F	2,140,700
Operating income	\$ 198,000	\$0	\$65,100 U	\$ 86,400 F	\$ 219,300

$21,300 F

Change in operating income

4. The analysis of operating income indicates that a significant amount of the increase in operating income resulted from productivity gains rather than product differentiation. The company was unable to charge a premium price for its clothes. Thus, the strategic analysis of operating income indicates that Halsey has not been successful at implementing its premium price, product differentiation strategy, despite the fact that operating income increased by more than 10% between 2001 and 2002. Halsey could not pass on increases in purchase costs to its customers via higher prices. Halsey must either reconsider its strategy or focus managers on increasing margins and growing market share by offering better product variety and superb customer service.

13-32 (20 min.) **Engineered and discretionary overhead costs, unused capacity, repairs and maintenance.**

1.   Rowland's repair and maintenance costs are indirect, engineered costs. The amount of repair and maintenance costs each year may not correlate directly to the quantity of gears produced. Over time, however, there is a clear cause-and-effect relationship between the output (quantity of gears produced) and repair and maintenance costs—the more gears that are produced, the greater the number of hours the machines will be run, and the greater the repairs and maintenance the machines will need.

2.   (1)   Available repair and maintenance capacity
              8 hours per day × 250 days × 4 workers   8,000 hours
       (2)   Repair and maintenance work actually done   6,000 hours
       (3) = (1) – (2) Hours of unused repair and maintenance capacity   2,000 hours
       (4)   Repair and maintenance cost per hour, $40,000 ÷ 2,000 $20 per hour
       (5) = (3) × (4) Cost of unused repair and maintenance capacity $40,000

Reasons why Rowland might want to downsize its repair and maintenance capacity are:
       a.   to reduce costs of carrying unused capacity
       b.   to create a culture of streamlining processes and operating efficiently

Reasons why Rowland might not want to downsize its repair and maintenance capacity are:
       a.   it projects greater demand for repairs and maintenance activity in the near future
       b.   it would negatively affect employee morale
       c.   it may want to use the expertise of the repairs and maintenance staff in other areas such as process improvements
       d.   it does not regard the unused capacity as particularly excessive

3.   If repair and maintenance costs are discretionary costs, calculating unused capacity is much more difficult. Repair and maintenance costs would be discretionary if repair and maintenance are mostly of a preventive type that management can choose when to do. In this case, the lack of a cause-and-effect relationship between output and repair and maintenance activity means that Rowland cannot determine the repair and maintenance resources used and, hence, the amount of unused capacity.

13-34 (20 min.) Partial productivity measurement.

1. Berkshire Corporation's partial productivity ratios in 2002 are as follows:

$$\text{Direct materials partial productivity} = \frac{\text{Quantity of output produced in 2002}}{\text{Kilograms of direct materials used in 2002}} = \frac{525,000}{610,000} = 0.86 \text{ units per kg}$$

$$\text{Direct manuf. labour partial productivity} = \frac{\text{Quantity of output produced in 2002}}{\text{Direct manuf. labour-hours used in 2002}} = \frac{525,000}{9,500} = 55.26 \text{ units per labour-hour}$$

$$\text{Manufacturing overhead partial productivity} = \frac{\text{Quantity of output produced in 2002}}{\text{Units of manuf. capacity in 2002}} = \frac{525,000}{582,000} = 0.90 \text{ units per unit of capacity}$$

To compare partial productivities in 2002 with partial productivities in 2001, we first calculate the inputs that would have been used in 2001 to produce year 2002's 525,000 units of output assuming the year 2001 relationship between inputs and outputs.

$$\text{Direct materials} = 450,000 \text{ kg (2001)} \times \frac{525,000 \text{ output units in 2002}}{375,000 \text{ output units in 2001}}$$

$$= 450,000 \times 1.4 = 630,000 \text{ kg}$$

$$\text{Direct manuf. labour} = 7,500 \text{ hours (2001)} \times \frac{525,000 \text{ output units in 2002}}{375,000 \text{ output units in 2001}}$$

$$= 7,500 \times 1.4 = 10,500 \text{ labour-hours}$$

Manufacturing capacity = 600,000 units of capacity, because manufacturing capacity is fixed, and adequate capacity existed in 2001 to produce year 2002 output.

Partial productivity calculations for 2001 based on year 2002 output (to make the partial productivities comparable across the two years)

$$\text{Direct materials partial productivity} = \frac{\text{Quantity of output produced in 2002}}{\substack{\text{Kilograms of direct materials that would} \\ \text{have been used in 2001 to produce} \\ \text{year 2002 output}}} = \frac{525,000}{630,000} = 0.83 \text{ units per kg}$$

$$\text{Direct manuf. labour partial productivity} = \frac{\text{Quantity of output produced in 2002}}{\substack{\text{Direct manuf. labour-hours that would} \\ \text{have been used in 2001 to produce} \\ \text{year 2002 output}}} = \frac{525,000}{10,500} = 50 \text{ units per labour-hour}$$

$$\text{Manufacturing overhead partial productivity} = \frac{\text{Quantity of output produced in 2002}}{\substack{\text{Units of manuf. capacity that would} \\ \text{have been used in 2001 to produce} \\ \text{year 2002 output}}} = \frac{525,000}{600,000} = 0.875 \text{ units per unit of capacity}$$

13-34 (cont'd)

The calculations indicate that Berkshire improved the partial productivity of all its inputs between 2001 and 2002 via improvements in efficiency of direct materials and direct manufacturing labour and by reducing unused manufacturing capacity.

2.   All partial productivity ratios increase from 2001 to 2002. We can therefore conclude that total factor productivity definitely increased from 2001 to 2002. Partial productivities cannot, however, tell us how much total factor productivity changed, because partial productivity measures cannot be aggregated over different inputs.

3.   Berkshire Corporation management can use the partial productivity measures to set targets for the next year. Partial productivity measures can easily be compared over multiple periods. For example, they may specify bonus payments if partial productivity of direct manufacturing labour increases to 60 units of output per direct manufacturing labour-hour and if partial productivity of direct materials improves to 0.90 units of output per kilogram of direct materials. A major advantage of partial productivity measures is that they focus on a single input; hence, they are simple to calculate and easy to understand at the operations level. Managers and operators can also examine these numbers to understand the reasons underlying productivity changes from one period to the next—better training of workers, lower absenteeism, lower labour turnover, better incentives, or improved methods. Management can then implement and sustain these factors in the future.

13-36   (25 min.)   Balanced scorecard, ethics.

1.   Yes, the Household Products Division (HPD) should include measures of employee satisfaction and customer satisfaction even if these measures are subjective. For a maker of kitchen dishwashers, employee and customer satisfaction are leading indicators of future financial performance. There is a cause-and-effect linkage between these measures and future financial performance. If HPD's strategy is correct and if the scorecard has been properly designed, employee and customer satisfaction information is very important in evaluating the implementation of HPD's strategy.

HPD should use employee and customer satisfaction measures even though these measures are subjective. One of the pitfalls to avoid when implementing a balanced scorecard is not to use only objective measures in the scorecard. Of course, HPD should guard against imprecision and potential for manipulation. Patricia Conley appears to be aware of this. She has tried to understand the reasons for the poor scores and has been able to relate these scores to other objective evidence such as employee dissatisfaction with the new work rules and customer unhappiness with missed delivery dates.

2.   Incorrect reporting of employee and customer satisfaction ratings to make divisions performance look good is unethical. In assessing the situation, a management accountant should consider the following:

13-36 (cont'd)

Clear reports using relevant and reliable information should be prepared. Preparing reports on the basis of incorrect employee and customer satisfaction ratings in order to make the division's performance look better than it is is unethical.

The management accountant has a responsibility to avoid actual or apparent conflicts of interest and advise all appropriate parties of any potential conflict. Conley may be tempted to report better employee and customer satisfaction ratings to please Emburey. The management accountant should communicate favourable as well as unfavourable information.

A management accountant should require that information be fairly and objectively communicated and that all relevant information should be disclosed.

Conley should indicate to Emburey that the employee and customer satisfaction ratings are, indeed, appropriate. If Emburey still insists on reporting better employee and customer satisfaction numbers, Conley should raise the matter with one of Emburey's superiors. If, after taking all these steps, there is continued pressure to overstate employee and customer satisfaction ratings, Conley should consider resigning from the company and not engage in unethical behaviour.

CHAPTER 14
COST ALLOCATION

14-2 The salary of a plant security guard would be a direct cost when the cost object is the security department or the plant. It would be an indirect cost when the cost object is a product.

14-4 Exhibit 14-2 lists four criteria used to guide cost allocation decisions:
1. Cause and effect.
2. Benefits received.
3. Fairness or equity.
4. Ability to bear.

Either the cause-and-effect criterion or the benefits received criterion is the dominant one when the purpose of the allocation is related to the economic decision purpose or the motivation purpose.

14-6 Cost-benefit considerations can affect costing choices in several ways:

(a) Classifying some immaterial costs as indirect when they could, at high cost, be traced to products, services or customers as direct costs.

(b) Using a small number of indirect cost pools when, at high cost, an increased number of indirect cost pools would provide more homogeneous cost pools.

(c) Using allocation bases that are readily available (or can be collected at low cost) when, at high cost, more appropriate cost allocation bases could be developed.

14-8 Examples of bases used to allocate corporate cost pools to operating divisions are:

Corporate Cost Pools	Possible Allocation Bases
Corporate executive dept.	Sales; assets employed; operating income
Treasury department	Sales; assets employed; estimated time or usage
Legal department	Estimated time or usage; sales; assets employed
Marketing department	Sales; number of sales personnel
Payroll department	Number of employees; payroll dollars
Personnel department	Number of employees; payroll dollars; number of new hires

14-10 Disagree. Allocating costs on "the basis of estimated long-run use by user department managers" means department managers can lower their cost allocations by deliberately underestimating their long-run use.

14-12 The *reciprocal method* is theoretically the most defensible method because it explicitly recognizes the mutual services rendered among all departments, irrespective of whether those departments are operating or support departments.

14-14 The basis for the cost allocation should be defined within the government contract.

14-16 (15-20 min.) **Single-rate versus dual-rate cost allocation methods.**

1.   The total costs in the single-cost pool are fixed ($1,000,000) and variable ($2,000,000) = $3,000,000. Ontario Company could use one of two allocation bases (budgeted usage or actual usage) given the information provided.

- Allocation to Ontario based on budgeted usage: $(60/200) \times \$3,000,000 = \$900,000$
- Allocation to Ontario based on actual usage: $(120/240) \times \$3,000,000 = \$1,500,000$

2.   Using the dual-rate method (with separate fixed and variable cost pools), several combinations of the budgeted and actual usage allocation bases are possible:

Fixed Cost Pool: Total costs of $1,000,000:
- Allocation to Ontario based on budgeted usage: $(60/200) \times \$1,000,000 = \$300,000$
- Allocation to Ontario based on actual usage: $(120/240) \times \$1,000,000 = \$500,000$

Variable Cost Pool: Total costs of $2,000,000:
- Allocation to Ontario based on budgeted usage: $(60/200) \times \$2,000,000 = \$600,000$
- Allocation to Ontario based on actual usage: $(120/240) \times \$2,000,000 = \$1,000,000$

The combinations possible are:

Combination	Fixed Cost Pool	Variable Cost Pool	Allocation Function
I	Budgeted Usage	Budgeted Usage	= $300,000 + $600,000 = $900,000
II	Budgeted Usage	Actual Usage	= $300,000 + $1,000,000 = $1,300,000
III	Actual Usage	Budgeted Usage	= $500,000 + $600,000 = $1,100,000
IV	Actual Usage	Actual Usage	= $500,000 + $1,000,000 = $1,500,000

Combinations I and IV give the same cost allocations as in requirement 1. Combination II is a frequently used dual-rate method. The fixed costs are allocated using budgeted usage on the rationale that it better captures the cost of providing capacity. The variable costs are allocated using actual usage on a cause-and-effect rationale. Combination III is rarely encountered in practice.

14-18 (30 min.) **Cost allocation to divisions.**

1.

	Hotel	Restaurant	Casino	Rembrandt
Revenue	$16,425,000	$5,256,000	$12,340,000	$34,021,000
Direct costs	9,819,260	3,749,172	4,284,768	17,853,200
Segment margin	$ 6,605,740	$1,506,828	$ 8,055,232	16,167,800
Indirect costs				14,550,000
Income before taxes				$ 1,617,800
Segment margin %	40.22%	28.67%	65.28%	

(handwritten notation: 9,819,260 / 16, .125)

2.

	Hotel	Restaurant	Casino	Rembrandt
Direct costs	$9,819,260	$3,749,172	$4,284,768	$17,853,200
Direct cost %	55.00%	21.00%	24.00%	100.00%
Square metres	80,000	16,000	64,000	160,000
Square metres %	50.00%	10.00%	40.00%	100.00%
# of employees	200	50	250	500
# of employees %	40.00%	10.00%	50.00%	100.00%

A: Cost allocation based on direct costs:

	Hotel	Restaurant	Casino	Rembrandt
Revenue	$16,425,000	$5,256,000	$12,340,000	$34,021,000
Direct costs	9,819,260	3,749,172	4,284,768	17,853,200
Segment margin	6,605,740	1,506,828	8,055,232	16,167,800
Allocated indirect costs	8,002,500	3,055,500	3,492,000	14,550,000
Segment pre-tax income	($1,396,760)	($1,548,672)	$ 4,563,232	$ 1,617,800
Segment pre-tax income %	−8.50%	−29.46%	36.98%	4.76%

B: Cost allocation based on floor space:

	Hotel	Restaurant	Casino	Rembrandt
Allocated indirect costs	$7,275,000	$1,455,000	$5,820,000	$14,550,000
Segment pre-tax income	($669,260)	$51,828	$2,235,232	$1,617,800
Segment pre-tax income %	−4.07%	0.99%	18.11%	4.76%

14-18 (cont'd)

C: Cost allocation based on # of employees

	Hotel	Restaurant	Casino	Rembrandt
Allocated indirect costs	$5,820,000	$1,455,000	$7,275,000	$14,550,000
Segment pre-tax income	$785,740	$51,828	$780,232	$1,617,800
Segment pre-tax income %	4.78%	0.99%	6.32%	4.76%

3. The segment fine-tax income percentages show the dramatic effect of choice of the cost allocation base on reported numbers:

Denominator	Hotel	Restaurant	Casino
Direct costs	−8.50%	−29.46%	36.98%
Floor space	−4.07	0.99	18.11
# of employees	4.78	0.99	6.32

The decision context should guide a. whether costs should be allocated, and b. the preferred cost allocation base. Decisions about, say, performance measurement may be made on a combination of financial and nonfinancial measures. It may well be that Rembrandt may prefer to exclude allocated costs from the financial measures to reduce areas of dispute.

Where cost allocation is required, the cause-and-effect and benefits-received criteria are recommended in Chapter 14. The $14,550,000 is a fixed overhead cost. This means that on a short-run basis, the cause-and-effect criterion is not appropriate. Rembrandt should look at how the $14,550,000 cost benefits the three divisions. This will help guide the choice of an allocation base.

4. The analysis in requirement 2 should not guide the decision on whether to shut down any of the divisions. Each division is not independent of the other two. A decision to shut down, say, the restaurant likely would negatively affect the attendance at the casino and possibly the hotel. Rembrandt should examine the future revenue and future cost implications of different resource investments in the three divisions. This is a future-oriented exercise, whereas the analysis in requirement 2 is an analysis of past costs.

14-20 (20 min.)   **Dual-rate cost allocation method, budgeted versus actual costs and quantities** (continuation of 14-19).

1.   Charges with Dual-Rate Method

Variable indirect cost rate   = $1,500 per trip

Fixed indirect cost rate   = $\dfrac{\$200,000 \text{ budgeted costs}}{250 \text{ budgeted trips}}$

= $800 per budgeted trip

Orange Juice Division
   Variable indirect costs, $1,500 × 200 $300,000
   Fixed indirect costs, $800 × 150   120,000
                              $420,000

Grapefruit Division
   Variable indirect costs, $1,500 × 100 $150,000
   Fixed indirect costs, $800 × 100   80,000
                              $230,000

2.

	Orange Juice Division	Grapefruit Juice Division
Single Rate I (budgeted rate × actual use)	$460,000	$230,000
Single Rate II (Actual rate × actual use)	430,000	215,000
Dual rate	420,000	230,000

If the dual-rate method used actual trips made as the allocation base, it would give the same answer as Single Rate I. The dual rate changes how the fixed indirect cost component is treated. By using budgeted trips made, the Orange Juice Division is unaffected by changes from its own budgeted usage or that of other divisions.

14-22 (30 min.) **Reciprocal cost allocation (continuation of 14-21).**

1.   The reciprocal allocation method explicitly includes the mutual services provided among all support departments. Interdepartmental relationships are fully incorporated into the support department cost allocations.

2.
$$AD = \$72,700 + .0833IS$$
$$IS = \$234,400 + .2308AD$$
$$AD = \$72,700 + [.0833(\$234,400 + .2308AD)]$$
$$= \$72,700 + [\$19,525.52 + 0.019226AD]$$
$$0.980774AD = \$92,225.52$$
$$AD = \$92,225.52 \div 0.980774$$
$$= \$94,033$$
$$IS = \$234,400 + (0.2308 \times \$94,033)$$
$$= \$256,103$$

14-22 (cont'd)

| | Support Depts | | Operating Depts | | |
	Admin.	Info. Systems	Corporate	Consumer	Total
Costs Incurred	$72,700	$234,400	$ 998,270	$489,860	$1,795,230
Alloc. of Admin. (21/91, 42/91, 28/91)	(94,033)	21,700	43,400	28,933	
Alloc. of Info. Syst. (320/3,840, 1,920/3,840, 1,600/3,840)	21,342	(256,103)	128,051	106,710	
	$ 9*	$ (3)*	$1,169,721	$625,503	$1,795,230

*Rounding causes not to be exactly $0.

3. The reciprocal method is more accurate than the direct and step-down methods when there is reciprocal relationships among support departments.

A summary of the alternatives is:

	Corporate Sales	Consumer Sales
Direct method	$1,169,745	$625,485
Step-down method (Admin. first)	1,168,830	626,400
Reciprocal method	1,169,721	625,503

The reciprocal method is the preferred method, although for September 2002 the numbers do not appear materially different across the alternatives.

14-24 (20-30 min.) **Allocation of common costs.**

1. The available criteria to guide cost allocations include:

   (a) Cause and effect. It is not possible to trace individual causes (either basic news <u>or</u> premium movies <u>or</u> premium sports) to individual effects (viewing by Sam or Sarah or Tony). The $70 total package is a bundled product.

   (b) Benefits received. There are various ways of operationalizing the benefits received:

       (i) Monthly service charge for their prime interest—basic news for Sam ($32), premium movies for Sarah ($25), and premium sports for Tony ($30). This measure captures the services available to be used by each person.

       (ii) Actual usage by each person. This would involve having a record of viewing by each person and then allocating the $70 on a % viewing time basis. This measure captures the services actually used by each person.

   (c) Ability to pay. This criteria requires the three people to agree upon their relative ability to pay. One measure here would be their respective salaries with the Toronto Fire Department.

   (d) Fairness or equity. This criteria is relatively nebulous. A straightforward approach would be to split the $70 equally among the three parties.

14-24 (cont'd)

2. Three methods of allocating the $70 are:

	Sam	Sarah	Tony
Stand-alone	$25.76	$20.09	$24.15
Incremental	13.00	25.00	32.00
Equal	23.33	23.33	23.33

(a) Stand-alone cost allocation method.

Sam: $\dfrac{\$32}{\$32 + \$25 + \$30} \times \$70 = 36.8\% \times \$70$
$= \$25.76$

Sarah: $\dfrac{\$25}{\$32 + \$25 + \$30} \times \$70 = 28.7\% \times \$70$
$= \$20.09$

Tony: $\dfrac{\$30}{\$32 + \$25 + \$30} \times \$70 = 34.5\% \times \$70$
$= \$24.15$

(b) Incremental cost allocation method:

Assume Tony (the owner) is the primary person, Sarah is first incremental party, and Sam the second incremental party.

Party	Cost Allocated	Cost Remaining to Be Allocated to Other Parties
Tony	$32	$38 ($70 − $32)
Sarah	25	13 ($70 − $32 − $25)
Sam	13	0
Total	$70	

This method is sure to generate disputes over the ranking of the three parties. Notice that Sam pays only $13 despite his prime interest in the most expensive basic news package.

(c) Equal sharing of the $70 amount. Sam, Sarah and Tony each pay $23.33.

Note: One student suggested the owner of the apartment (Tony) should pay the $70 and include the cable television service in the rental charge.

14-26 (30 min.) **Support department cost allocation, direct and step-down methods.**

			A/HR	IS	GOVT	CORP
1.	(a)	Direct Method				
		Costs	$600,000	$2,400,000		
		Alloc. of A/HR				
		(40/75, 35/75)	(600,000)		$ 320,000	$ 280,000
		Alloc. of I.S.				
		(30/90, 60/90)		(2,400,000)	800,000	1,600,000
			$ 0	$ 0	$1,120,000	$1,880,000
	(b)	Step-Down (A/HR first)				
		Costs	$600,000	2,400,000		
		Alloc. of A/HR				
		(0.25, 0.40, 0.35)	(600,000)	150,000	240,000	210,000
		Alloc. of I.S.				
		(30/90, 60/90)		(2,550,000)	850,000	1,700,000
			$ 0	$ 0	$1,090,000	$1,910,000
	(c)	Step-Down (I.S. first)				
		Costs	$600,000	2,400,000		
		Alloc. of I.S.				
		(0.10, 0.30, 0.60)	240,000	(2,400,000)	720,000	$1,440,000
		Alloc. of A/HR				
		(40/75, 35/75)	(840,000)		448,000	392,000
			$ 0	$ 0	$1,168,000	$1,832,000

		GOVT	CORP
2.	Direct method	$1,120,000	$1,880,000
	Step-Down (A/HR first)	1,090,000	1,910,000
	Step-Down (I.S. first)	1,168,000	1,832,000

The direct method ignores any services to other support departments. The step-down method partially recognizes support to other service departments. The information systems support group (with total budget of $2,400,000) provides 10% of its services to the A/HR group. The A/HR support group (with total budget of $600,000) provides 25% of its services to the information systems support group.

14-26 (cont'd)

3. Three criteria that could determine the sequence in the step-down method are:

    (a)   Allocate service departments on a ranking of the % of their total services provided to other service departments.

            1.   Administrative/HR   25%

            2.   Information Systems   10%

    (b)   Allocate service departments on a ranking of the total dollar amount in the service departments.

            1.   Information Systems $2,400,000

            2.   Administrative/HR $ 600,000

    (c)   Allocate service departments on a ranking of the dollar amounts of service provided to other service departments

            1.   Information Systems

                $(0.10 \times \$2,400,000)$ = $240,000

            2.   Administrative/HR

                $(0.25 \times \$600,000)$ = $150,000

14-28 (30 min.) **Support department cost allocation.**

1.   Using computer usage time as the allocation base for the Information Systems Department and square metres of floor space for the Facilities Department, the allocation of overhead from the support departments under the Direct and Step Methods, are presented below.

Direct Method

	Support Departments		Operating Departments		
	IS	Facilities	Programming	Consulting	Training
Budgeted overhead	$50,000	$25,000	$ 75,000	$110,000	$ 85,000
Proportion of service furnished:					
By IS:(1)			12/27	6/27	9/27
Allocation	(50,000)		$ 22,222	$ 11,111	$ 16,667
By Facilities:(2)			4/18	6/18	8/18
Allocation		(25,000)	$ 5,556	$ 8,333	$ 11,111
Totals	$ 0	$ 0	$102,778	$129,444	$112,778

(1) Allocated on the basis of 2,700 hours of computer usage.
(2) Allocated on the basis of 1,800 thousand square metres of floor space.

Step Method

	Support Departments		Operating Departments		
	IS	Facilities	Programming	Consulting	Training
Budgeted overhead	$50,000	$25,000	$ 75,000	$110,000	$ 85,000
Proportion of service furnished:					
By IS:(1)		3/30	12/30	6/30	9/30
Allocation	(50,000)	$ 5,000	$ 20,000	$ 10,000	$ 15,000
By Facilities:(2)			4/18	6/18	8/18
Allocation		($30,000)	$ 6,667	$ 10,000	$ 13,333
Totals	$ 0	$ 0	$101,667	$130,000	$113,333

(1) Allocated on the basis of 3,000 hours of computer usage.
(2) Allocated on the basis of 1,800 thousand square metres of floor space.

2.   The step method recognizes the services that Information Systems provides to the other support department (Facilities). In contrast, the direct method only recognizes services that support departments provide to operating departments.

The step-down method is conceptually preferable to the direct method. Birch might consider using the reciprocal method. This method fully recognizes the reciprocal services provided between the Information System and Facilities departments.

14-30 (40-60 min.) **Support department cost allocations; single-department cost pools; direct, step-down, and reciprocal methods.**

All the following computations are in dollars.
1.

Direct method:

	To X	To Y
A	250/400 × $100,000 = $62,500	150/400 × $100,000 = $37,500
B	100/500 × $40,000 = 8,000	400/500 × $40,000 = 32,000
Total	$70,500	$69,500

2. Step-down method, allocating B first:

	A	B	X	Y
Costs to be allocated	$100,000	$40,000	—	—
Allocate B: (0.5, 0.1, 0.4)	20,000	(40,000)	$ 4,000	$16,000
Allocate A: (250/400, 150/400)	(120,000)	—	75,000	45,000
Total	$ 0	$ 0	$79,000	$61,000

Step-down method, allocating A first:

	A	B	X	Y
Costs to be allocated	$100,000	$40,000	—	—
Allocate A: (0.2, 0.5, 0.3)	(100,000)	20,000	$50,000	$30,000
Allocate B: (0.2, 0.8)	—	(60,000)	12,000	48,000
Total	$ 0	$ 0	$62,000	$78,000

Note that these methods produce significantly different results, so the choice of method may frequently make a difference in the budgeted department overhead rates.

3. Reciprocal method:

Stage 1: Let   A = total costs of materials-handling department
            B = total costs of power-generating department
   (1)   A = $100,000 + 0.5B
   (2)   B = $ 40,000 + 0.2A

Stage 2: Substituting in (1): $A = \$100,000 + 0.5(\$40,000 + 0.2A)$
            $A = \$100,000 + \$20,000 + 0.1A$
         $0.9A = \$120,000$
            $A = \$133,333$

Substituting in (2): $B = \$40,000 + 0.2(\$133,333)$
            $B = \$66,666$

14-30 (cont'd)

Stage 3:

	A	B	X	Y
Original amounts	100,000	40,000	—	—
Allocation of A	(133,333)	26,666(20%)	66,667(50%)	40,000(30%)
Allocation of B	33,333(50%)	(66,666)	6,666(10%)	26,667(40%)
Totals accounted for	—	—	73,333	66,667

Comparison of methods:

Method of Allocation	X	Y
Direct method	$70,500	$69,500
Step-down: B first	79,000	61,000
Step-down: A first	62,000	78,000
Reciprocal method	73,333	66,667

Note that <u>in this case</u> the direct method produces answers that are the closest to the "correct" answers (that is, those from the reciprocal method), step-down allocating B first is next, and step-down allocating A first is least accurate.

2. At first glance, it appears that the cost of power is $40 per unit plus the material handling costs. If so, Manes would be better off by purchasing from the power company. However, the decision should be influenced by the effects of the interdependencies and the fixed costs. Note that the power needs would be less (students miss this) if they were purchased from the outside:

	Outside Power Units Needed
X	100
Y	400
A (500 units minus 20% of 500 units, because there is no need to service the nonexistent power department)	400
Total units	900

Total costs, 900 × $40 = $36,000

14-14

14-30 (cont'd)

In contrast, the total costs that would be saved by not producing the power inside would depend on the effects of the decision on various costs:

	Avoidable Costs of 100 Units of Power Produced Inside
Variable indirect labour and indirect material costs	$10,000
Supervision in power department	10,000
Materials handling, 20% of $70,000*	14,000
Probable minimum cost savings	$34,000
Possible additional savings:	
a. Can any supervision in materials handling be saved because of overseeing less volume? Minimum savings is probably zero; the maximum is probably 20% of $10,000 or $2,000.	?
b. Is any depreciation a truly variable, wear-and-tear type of cost?	?
Total savings by not producing 100 units of power	$34,000 + ?

*Materials-handling costs are higher because the power department uses 20% of materials handling. Therefore, materials-handling costs will decrease by 20%.

In the short-run (at least until a capital investment in equipment is necessary) the data suggest continuing to produce internally because the costs eliminated would probably be less than the comparable purchase costs.

14-32 (15 min.) Cost allocation and motivation.

Because corporate policy encourages line managers to seek legal counsel on pertinent issues from the Legal Department, any step in the direction of reducing costs of legal department services would be consistent with the corporate policy.

Currently a user department is charged a standard fee of $400 per hour based on actual usage. It is possible that some managers may not be motivated to seek the legal counsel they need due to the high-allocated cost of the service. It is also possible that those managers whose departments are currently experiencing budgetary cost overruns may be disinclined to make use of the service; it would save them from the Legal Department's cost allocation. However, it could potentially result in much costlier penalties for Environ later if the corporation inadvertently engaged in some activities that violated one or more laws.

It is quite likely that the line managers would seek legal counsel, whenever there were any pertinent legal issues, if the service were free. Making the service of the Legal Department free, however, might induce some managers to make excessive use of the service. To avoid any potential abuse, Environ may want to adjust the rate downward considerably, perhaps at a level lower than what it would cost if outside legal services were sought, but not eliminate it altogether. As long as the managers know that their respective departments would be charged for using the service, they would be disinclined to make use of it unnecessarily. However, they would be motivated to use it when necessary because it would be considered a "good value" if the standard hourly rate was low enough.

14-34 (20-30 min.)   **Cost allocation downward demand spiral.**

1.   Total costs, six months ended June 30, 2002 $64,800,000
      Fixed costs   16,200,000
      Variable costs $48,600,000

      Fixed costs per month per square metre

$$= \frac{\$16,200,000 \div 6}{2,250,000} = \$7.20/6 = \$1.20$$

      Variable costs per month per square metre

$$= \frac{\$48,600,000 \div 6}{2,250,000} = \$21.60/6 = \$3.60$$

2.   Variable costs per month per square metre   = $3.60

      Fixed costs per month per square metre

$$= \frac{\$36,000,000 \div 12}{2,500,000} \qquad = \qquad 1.20$$

      Total costs per month per square metre   = $4.80
      Total costs per day per square metre (assuming 30 days)   = $0.16

      The cost per square metre of $0.16 per day is above the competitive rate of $0.14. Thus it is not surprising that many of his internal clients are seeking external bids.

3.   Bubba should base his prices upon his total capacity of 5,000,000 square metres. This would result in costs as follows:

Variable costs per month per metre	=	$3.60
Fixed costs per month per metre		
($36,000,000 ÷ 12 ÷ 5,000,000 metres)	=	0.60
Total costs per month per metre	=	$4.20
Total costs per day per metre (assuming 30 days)	=	$0.14

      Thus to generate a profit, Bubba needs to operate closer to capacity and seek ways to reduce costs.

14-36 (20 min.) **Division managers' reactions to the allocation of central corporate costs to divisions (continuation of 14-35).**

The effect of the changes proposed by Dusty Rhodes for divisional income is:

	Oil & Gas Upstream	Oil & Gas Downstream	Chemical Products	Copper Mining
Divisional income—single-cost pool allocation scheme	$3,300	$(600)	$(200)	$(500)
Divisional income—four-cost pool allocation scheme	$2,522.4	$ 83.2	$(166.4)	$(439.2)

Given these changes, the reactions of the division managers are predictable. Rhodes should consider several general points when drafting his response:

- A controller is a staff function, while the division managers are line managers running multi-billion dollar enterprises.
- Cost allocation problems are ongoing issues in any organization, and ongoing refinements will likely occur continually in the future.
- Keep a clear distinction between evaluating the performance of a division and evaluating the performance of a division manager.

<u>Oil & Gas Upstream</u>: Observe that the proposed cost allocation scheme better captures cause-and-effect relationships than does the existing scheme. Note that the upstream division is highly capital intensive and that much of the debt was raised to acquire or develop those assets. Rhodes should also describe how Richfield Oil takes into account the Upstream's generation of a substantial positive cash flow in its performance evaluation of activities and managers.

<u>Oil & Gas Downstream</u>: Comment that you are glad that the proposed scheme was well received. However, stress that the changes are designed to capture cause-and-effect relationships. (You will be responding to the same manager in subsequent years and it is important that the motivations for the changes be understood. In subsequent years the same manager likely will argue the proposed changes are "unfair and inequitable.")

<u>Chemical Products</u>: Note that the manager's complaints are against cost allocation schemes in general and not against Rhodes' proposed changes. The appropriate response is to stress that the top management of Richfield Oil has decided to allocate central corporate costs (for reasons noted in requirement 1 of Problem 14-28). The manager should consider developing ways to improve the existing or proposed cost allocation schemes. Stress to the manager that top management distinguishes between the performance of a division and the performance of its manager. In evaluating the chemical products division, a better appreciation of the returns on Richfield Oil's investment can be obtained by considering the central corporate costs associated with the division. However, in evaluating managers, the

14-36 (cont'd)

ability to outperform competitors facing the same environment and to implement company-wide economy drives is highly valued (and hopefully rewarded by Richfield Oil).

Copper Mining: Agree with the manager that both the existing and the proposed schemes have imperfections. Specifically, admit that sometime in the future refinements in allocations of R&D may be made. One possible approach would be identification of R&D costs with projects done for each division; if no R&D is done for Copper Mining, no allocation of R&D cost would be made to Copper Mining. However, note that changes are being made gradually at Richfield Oil and that the current major issue is to get the proposed changes accepted. One point to stress is that the proposal recognizes the special problems of divisions with negative operating income (such as faced by the Copper Mining division). Rhodes proposes to allocate public affairs costs only to divisions with positive operating income.

Note: Richfield Oil may want to consider changes in its division compensation scheme if it makes changes in its cost allocation scheme. Major changes in one component of a management control system should not be made without considering changes in other components of the management control system.

14-38 (25 min.)   **Common costs.**

1. Miller $= \dfrac{900 \times \$1.00}{(900 \times \$1.00) + (600 \times \$1.00)} \times (\$1,200)$

$= \dfrac{\$900}{\$900 + \$600} \times \$1,200 = \$720$

Jackson $= \dfrac{600 \times \$1.00}{(600 \times \$1.00) + (900 \times \$1.00)} \times (\$1,200)$

$= \dfrac{\$600}{\$600 + \$900} \times \$1,200 = \$480$

2.

Party	Costs Allocated	Costs Remaining to be Allocated
Miller (primary)	$900	$300 ($1,200 – $900)
Jackson (incremental)	$300	$ 0

If Jackson is the primary party, the allocation would be

Party	Costs Allocated	Cost Remaining To be Allocated
Jackson (primary)	$600	$600 ($1,200 – $600)
Miller (incremental)	$600	$ 0

3.   Another approach is to use the Shapley value and consider each party as first the primary party and then the incremental party. Then the average of the two is computed to determine the allocation.

Miller:

Allocation as the primary party	$ 900
Allocation as the incremental party	600
Total	$1,500
Allocation ($1,500 ÷ 2)	$ 750

Jackson:

Allocation as the primary party	$ 600
Allocation as the incremental party	300
Total	$ 900
Allocation ($900 ÷ 2)	$ 450

14-38 (cont'd)

Using this approach, Miller is allocated $750 and Jackson is allocated $450 out of the total costs of $1,200. Miller and Jackson could also use the stand-alone cost allocation method to allocate the rent: Miller, $720; Jackson, $480. If they used the incremental cost-allocation method, Miller and Jackson would probably have disputes over who is the primary party because the primary party gets allocated all costs first.

14-40 (20 min.) Division cost allocation, R&D, ethics.

1. The overhead cost charged to each division for use of the Waterloo facility is:

$$\begin{bmatrix} \text{Budgeted \% use} \\ \text{by division of} \\ \text{Waterloo facility} \end{bmatrix} \times \begin{bmatrix} \text{Budgeted overhead costs} \\ \text{at Waterloo facility} \end{bmatrix}$$

If the ASD division understates its budgeted use of the Waterloo facility and all other divisions provide unbiased estimates of their budgeted use, the ASD division will have a lower budgeted % use factor for the Waterloo facility, and thus a lower overhead cost charge. If all divisions understate their budgeted use, those division(s) providing the greatest understatements will be those benefiting by their understatement.

2. Alternative approaches Waterloo might take include:
   a. Charging a division a penalty rate when it uses a higher number of hours than it submitted as its budgeted amount.
   b. Change the charge structure so that each hour of research scientist time used has a budgeted overhead charge component. (This approach only partially reduces the problem because the fixed overhead rate per hour must be determined.)
   c. Use actual costs per hour rather than budgeted costs per hour as the charge to each using division.

3. Goodwin's first response should be to develop a well-constructed argument to present to Roy Masters for using the 30,000 number. Masters should be given at least one more chance to respond to Goodwin's concerns. Ideally, Goodwin should give Masters a short time period (say one week) to think about her concerns. This is especially the case if there is already documentation at ASD for the 30,000 number. Goodwin might note that if internal control people at WS are called in to consider any allegations by other divisions that ASD is deliberately understating budgeted usage, the 30,000 figure likely will be observable.

If Masters continues with his threats about dropping Goodwin from "the ASD team," she should contact the corporate controller at WS to seek guidance on how to handle the situation.

CHAPTER 15
COST ALLOCATION: JOINT PRODUCTS AND BYPRODUCTS

15-2   A *joint cost* is a cost of a single process that yields multiple products simultaneously.

15-4   A *product* is any output that has a positive sales value (or an output that enables an organization to avoid incurring costs). In some joint-cost settings, outputs can occur that do not have a positive sales value. The offshore processing of hydrocarbons yields water that is recycled back into the ocean as well as yielding oil and gas. The processing of mineral ore to yield gold and silver also yields dirt as an output, which is recycled back into the ground.

15-6   The joint production process yields individual products that are either sold this period or held as inventory to be sold in subsequent periods. Hence the joint costs need to be allocated between total production rather than just those sold this period.

15-8   Both methods use market selling-price data in allocating joint costs, but they differ in which sales-price data they use. The *sales value at splitoff method* allocates joint costs on the basis of each product's relative sales value at the splitoff point. The *estimated net realizable value method* allocates joint costs on the basis of the relative estimated net realizable value (expected final sales value in the ordinary course of business minus the expected separable costs of production and marketing).

15-10   The estimated NRV method can be simplified by assuming (a) a standard set of post-splitoff point processing steps and (b) a standard set of selling prices. The use of (a) and (b) achieves the same benefits that the use of standard costs does in costing systems.

15-12   No. Any method used to allocate joint costs to individual products that is applicable to the problem of joint product-cost allocation should not be used for management decisions regarding whether a product should be sold or processed further. When a product is an inherent result of a joint process, the decision to process further should not be influenced by either the size of the total joint costs or the portion of the joint costs assigned to particular products. Joint costs are irrelevant for these decisions. The only relevant items for these decisions are the incremental revenue and the incremental costs beyond the splitoff point.

15-14   Two methods to account for byproducts are:
a.   Production method—recognizes byproducts in the financial statements at the time production is completed.
b.   Sales method—delays recognition of byproducts until the time of sale.

15-16 (20-30 min.) Joint-cost allocation, insurance settlement.

1.   (a)   Sales value at splitoff point method.

	Kilograms of Product	Wholesale Selling Price per Kilogram	Sales Value at Splitoff	Weighting: Sales Value at Splitoff	Joint Costs Allocated	Allocated Costs per Kilogram
Breasts	100	$1.10	$110	0.675	$ 67.50	0.6750
Wings	20	0.40	8	0.049	4.90	0.2450
Thighs	40	0.70	28	0.172	17.20	0.4300
Bones	80	0.20	16	0.098	9.80	0.1225
Feathers	10	0.10	1	0.006	0.60	0.0600
	250		$163	1.000	$100.00	

Costs of Destroyed Product

Breasts: $0.6750 × 20	=		$13.50
Wings: $0.2450 × 10	=		2.45
			$15.95

(b)   Physical measures method

	Kilograms of Product	Weighting: Physical Measures	Joint Costs Allocated	Allocated Costs per Kilogram
Breasts	100	0.400	$ 40.00	$0.400
Wings	20	0.080	8.00	0.400
Thighs	40	0.160	16.00	0.400
Bones	80	0.320	32.00	0.400
Feathers	10	0.040	4.00	0.400
	250	1.000	$100.00	

Costs of Destroyed Product

Breast: $0.40 × 20	=		$ 8
Wings: $0.40 × 10	=		4
			$12

15-16 (cont'd)

Note: Although not required, it is useful to highlight the individual product profitability figures:

Product	Sales Value	Sales Value at Splitoff Method		Physical Measures Method	
		Joint Costs Allocated	Gross Income	Joint Costs Allocated	Gross Income
Breasts	$110	$67.50	$42.50	$40.00	$70.00
Wings	8	4.90	3.10	8.00	0.00
Thighs	28	17.20	10.80	16.00	12.00
Bones	16	9.80	6.20	32.00	(16.00)
Feathers	1	0.60	0.40	4.00	(3.00)

2. The sales-value at splitoff method captures the benefits-received criterion of cost allocation. The costs of processing a chicken are allocated to products in proportion to the ability to contribute revenue. Chicken Little's decision to process chicken is heavily influenced by the revenues from breasts and thighs. The bones provide relatively few benefits to Chicken Little despite their high physical volume.

The physical measures method shows profits on breasts and thighs and losses on bones and feathers. Given that Chicken Little has to jointly process all the chicken products, it is non-intuitive to single out individual products that are being processed simultaneously as making losses while the overall operations make a profit.

15-18 (20-30 min.) **Net realizable value cost-allocation method, further process decision.**

A diagram of the situation is in Solution Exhibit 15-18.

1.

	Quantity in Kilograms	Sales Price per Kilogram	Final Sales Value	Separable Processing Costs	Estimated Net Realizable Value at Splitoff	Weighting
Alco	20,000	$20	$400,000	$100,000	$300,000	30/56
Devo	60,000	6	360,000	200,000	160,000	16/56
Holo	100,000	1	100,000	0	100,000	10/56
Totals			$860,000	$300,000	$560,000	

Allocation of $420,000 joint costs:

Alco	30/56 × $420,000	=	$225,000
Devo	16/56 × 420,000	=	120,000
Holo	10/56 × 420,000	=	75,000
			$420,000

	Joint Costs Allocated	Separable Processing Costs	Total Costs	Units	Unit Cost
Alco	$225,000	$100,000	$325,000	20,000	$16.25
Devo	120,000	200,000	320,000	60,000	5.33
Holo	75,000	0	75,000	100,000	0.75
Totals	$420,000	$300,000	$720,000	180,000	

The ending inventory is:

Alco	1,000 × $16.25	=	$16,250
Devo	1,000 × $ 5.33	=	5,330
Holo	1,000 × $ 0.75	=	750
			$22,330

15-18 (cont'd)

2.

	Unit Sales Price	Unit Cost	Gross Margin	Gross-Margin Percentage
Alco	$20	$16.25	$3.75	18.75%
Devo	6	5.33	0.67	11.17
Holo	1	0.75	0.25	25.00

3. Further processing of Devo yields incremental income of $40,000:

Incremental revenue of further processing Devo, ($6 – $2) × 60,000	$240,000
Incremental processing costs	200,000
Incremental operating income from further processing	$ 40,000

Tuscania should process Devo further. Note that joint costs are irrelevant to this decision; they remain the same, whichever alternative (sell at splitoff or process further) is selected.

SOLUTION EXHIBIT 15-18

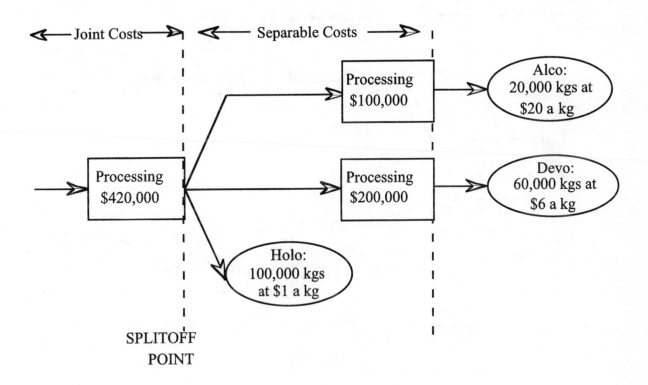

15-20 (10 min.) **Estimated net realizable value method.**

A diagram of the situation is in Solution Exhibit 15-20 (all numbers are in thousands).

	Cooking Oil	Soap Oil	Total
Expected final sales value of production, CO, 1,000 × $50; SO, 500 × $25	$50,000	$12,500	$62,500
Deduct expected separable costs to complete and sell	30,000	7,500	37,500
Estimated net realizable value at splitoff point	$20,000	$ 5,000	$25,000
Weighting	$\frac{\$20,000}{\$25,000} = 0.8$	$\frac{\$5,000}{\$25,000} = 0.2$	
Joint costs allocated, CO, 0.8 × $24,000; SO, 0.2 × $24,000	$19,200	$ 4,800	$24,000

SOLUTION EXHIBIT 15-20

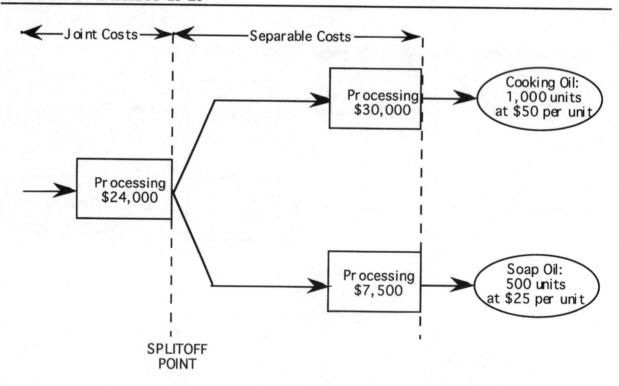

15-22 (20 min.) **Joint-cost allocation, physical measures method (continuation of 15-21).**

1.

	Crude Oil	NGL	Total
Expected final sales value of production	$2,700	$ 750	$ 3,450
Deduct expected separable costs	175	105	280
Estimated NRV at splitoff	$2,525	$ 645	$3,170
Weighting	0.7965	0.2035	1.000
Joint costs allocated (Weights × $1,800)	$1,433.70	$366.30	$1,800

	Crude Oil	NGL	Total
Sales	$2,700.00	$750.00	$3,450
Operating Costs			
Joint costs	1,433.70	366.30	1,800
Separable costs	175.00	105.00	280
Total operating costs	1,608.70	471.30	2,080
Operating margin	$1,091.30	$278.70	$1,370

2. The authorities' proposed method results in large profits on crude oil and large losses on gas:

	Crude Oil	NGL	Gas	Total
Sales	$2,700	$750	$0	$3,450
Operating Costs				
Joint costs	270	90	1,440	1,800
Separable costs	175	105	0	280
Total operating costs	445	195	1,440	2,080
Operating margin	$2,255	$555	$(1,440)	$1,370

The main points to note are:

(a) Gas is not a salable product. It is simply a recycled output that adds no revenues. Indeed, costs are incurred to recycle the gas.

(b) The physical measure method has all the problems alluded to in the literature—e.g., it ignores the revenue-earning potential of products and it may not have a consistent denominator.

15-24 (40 min.)   **Process further or sell, byproduct.**

1. The analysis shown below indicates that it would be more profitable for Newcastle Mining Company to continue to sell raw bulk coal without further processing. (This analysis ignores any value related to coal fines.)

Incremental sales revenues:

Sales revenue after further processing (9,500,000 tonnes × $36)	$342,000,000
Sales revenue from bulk raw coal (10,000,000 tonnes × $27)	270,000,000
Incremental sales revenue	72,000,000

Incremental costs:

Direct labour	600,000
Supervisory personnel	100,000
Heavy equipment costs ($25,000 × 12 months)	300,000
Sizing and cleaning (10,000,000 tonnes × $3.50)	35,000,000
Outbound rail freight (9,500,000 tonnes ÷ 60 tons) × $240 per car	38,000,000
Incremental costs	74,000,000
Incremental gain (loss)	$(2,000,000)

2. The analysis shown below indicates that the potential revenue from the coal fines byproduct would result in additional revenue, ranging between $5,250,000 and $9,000,000, depending on the market price of the fines.

a. Coal fines
   = 75% of 5% of raw bulk tonnage
   = 0.75 × (10,000,000 × 0.05)
   = 375,000 tonnes

Potential additional revenue:

	Market price	
	Minimum $14 per tonne	Maximum $24 per tonne
Additional revenue	$5,250,000	$9,000,000

Since the incremental loss is $2 million, as calculated in requirement 1, including the coal fines in the analysis indicates that further processing provides a positive result and is, therefore, favourable.

15-24 (cont'd)

b. Other factors that should be considered in evaluating a sell-or-process-further decision include:

- Stability of the current customer market and how it compares to the market for sized and cleaned coal.
- Storage space needed for the coal fines until they are sold and the handling costs of coal fines.
- Reliability of cost (e.g., rail freight rates) and revenue estimates, and the risk of depending on these estimates.
- Timing of the revenue stream from coal fines and impact on the need for liquidity.
- Possible environmental problems, i.e., dumping of waste and smoke from unprocessed coal.

15-26 (35-45 min.) **Joint costs and byproducts.**

A diagram of the situation is in Solution Exhibit 15-26.

1. Computing byproduct deduction to joint costs:

Marketing price of X, 100,000 × $3	$300,000
Deduct: Gross margin, 10% of sales	30,000
Marketing costs, 25% of sales	75,000
Department 3 separable costs	50,000
Estimated net realizable value of X	$145,000
Joint costs	$800,000
Deduct byproduct contribution	145,000
Net joint costs to be allocated	$655,000

	Quantity	Unit Sales Price	Final Sales Value	Deduct Separable Processing Cost	Est. Net Realizable Value at Splitoff	Weighting	Allocation of $655,000 Joint Costs
L	50,000	$10	$ 500,000	$100,000	$ 400,000	40%	$262,000
W	300,000	2	600,000	-	600,000	60%	393,000
Totals			$1,100,000	$100,000	$1,000,000		$655,000

15-26 (cont'd)

	Joint Costs Allocation	Add Separable Processing Costs	Total Costs	Units	Unit Cost
L	$262,000	$100,000	$362,000	50,000	$7.24
W	393,000	-	393,000	300,000	1.31
Totals	$655,000	$100,000	$755,000	350,000	

Unit cost for X: $1.45 + $0.50 = $1.95,
or $3.00 − $0.30 − $0.75 = $1.95.

2. If all three products are treated as joint products:

	Quantity	Unit Sales Price	Final Sales Value	Deduct Separable Processing Cost	Est. Net Realizable Value at Splitoff	Weighting	Allocation of $800,000 Joint Costs
L	50,000	$10	$ 500,000	$100,000	$ 400,000	40/125	$256,000
W	300,000	2	600,000	-	600,000	60/125	384,000
X	100,000	3	300,000	50,000	250,000	25/125	160,000
Totals			$1,400,000	$150,000	$1,250,000		$800,000

	Joint Costs Allocation	Add Separable Processing Costs	Total Costs	Units	Unit Cost
L	$256,000	$100,000	$356,000	50,000	$7.12
W	384,000	-	384,000	300,000	1.28
X	160,000	50,000	210,000	100,000	2.10
Totals	$800,000	$150,000	$950,000	450,000	

Call the attention of students to the differing unit "costs" between the two assumptions regarding the relative importance of Product X. The point is that costs of individual products depend heavily on which assumptions are made and which accounting methods and techniques are used.

15-26 (cont'd)

SOLUTION EXHIBIT 15-26

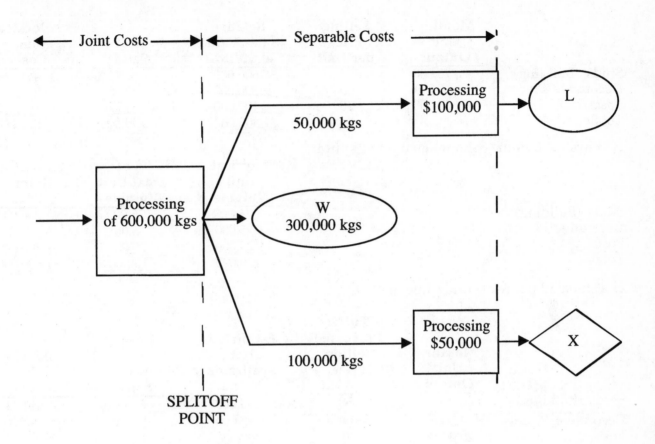

15-28 (30 min.)   **Joint-cost allocation, process further or sell.**

1.
   a. Relative sales value method at splitoff.

	Monthly Unit Output	Selling Price per Unit	Relative Sales Value at Splitoff	% of Sales	Allocated Joint Costs
Studs (Building)	75,000	$ 8	$ 600,000	46.15%	$ 461,539
Decorative Pieces	5,000	60	300,000	23.08	230,769
Posts	20,000	20	400,000	30.77	307,692
Totals			$1,300,000	100.00%	$1,000,000

   b. Physical output (volume) method at splitoff.

			Physical Unit Volume	% of Total Unit Volume	Allocated Joint Costs
Studs (Building)			75,000	75.00%	$ 750,000
Decorative Pieces			5,000	5.00	50,000
Posts			20,000	20.00	200,000
Totals			100,000	100.00%	$1,000,000

   c. Estimated net realizable value method.

	Monthly Unit Output	Fully Processed Selling Price per Unit	Estimated Net Realizable Value	% of Sales	Allocated Joint Costs
Studs (Building)	75,000	$8	$ 600,000	44.44%	$ 444,445
Decorative Pieces	4,500[a]	100	350,000[b]	25.93	259,259
Posts	20,000	20	400,000	29.63	296,296
Totals			$1,350,000	100.00%	$1,000,000

Notes:
a. 5,000 monthly units of output – 10% normal spoilage = 4,500 good units.
b. 4,500 good units × $100 = $450,000 – Further processing costs of $100,000 = $350,000

2.   Presented below is an analysis for Sonimad Sawmill Inc. comparing the processing of decorative pieces further versus selling the rough-cut product immediately at splitoff.

	Units	Dollars
Monthly unit output	5,000	
Less: Normal further processing shrinkage	500	
Units available for sale	4,500	
Final sales value (4,500 units @ $100 per unit)		$450,000
Less: Sales value at splitoff		300,000
Differential revenue		150,000
Less: Further processing costs		100,000
Additional contribution from further processing		$ 50,000

15-28 (cont'd.)

3. Assuming Sonimad Sawmill Inc. announces that in six months it will sell the rough-cut product at splitoff, due to increasing competitive pressure, at least three types of likely behaviour that will be demonstrated by the skilled labour in the planing and sizing process include the following.

- Poorer quality.
- Reduced motivation and morale.
- Job insecurity, leading to nonproductive employee time looking for jobs elsewhere.

Management actions that could improve this behaviour include the following.

- Improve communication by giving the workers a more comprehensive explanation as to the reason for the change in order to better understand the situation and bring out a plan for future operation of the rest of the plant.
- The company can offer incentive bonuses to maintain quality and production and align rewards with goals.
- The company could provide job relocation and internal job transfers.

SOLUTION EXHIBIT 15-28

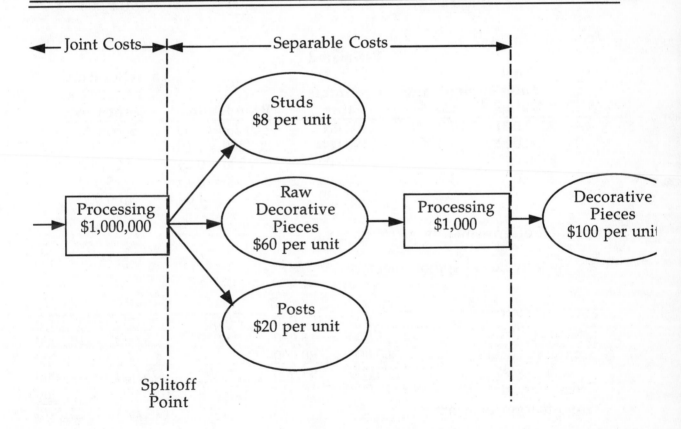

15-30 (40 min.) **Alternative methods of joint-cost allocation, product-mix decisions.**

A diagram of the situation is in Solution Exhibit 15-30.

1. Computation of joint-cost allocation proportions:

a.

	Sales Value at Splitoff	Proportions	Allocation of $100,000 Joint Costs
A	$ 50,000	50/200 = 0.25	$ 25,000
B	30,000	30/200 = 0.15	15,000
C	50,000	50/200 = 0.25	25,000
D	70,000	70/200 = 0.35	35,000
	$200,000	1.00	$100,000

b.

	Physical Measure	Proportions	Allocation of $100,000 Joint Costs
A	300,000 litres	300/500 = 0.60	$ 60,000
B	100,000 litres	100/500 = 0.20	20,000
C	50,000 litres	50/500 = 0.10	10,000
D	50,000 litres	50/500 = 0.10	10,000
	500,000 litres	1.00	$100,000

c.

	Final Sales Value	Separable Costs	Estimated Net Realizable Value	Proportions	Allocation of $100,000 Joint Costs
A	$300,000	$200,000	$100,000	100/200 =0.50	$ 50,000
B	100,000	80,000	20,000	20/200 = 0.10	10,000
C	50,000	–	50,000	50/200 = 0.25	25,000
D	120,000	90,000	30,000	30/200 = 0.15	15,000
			$200,000	1.00	$100,000

Computation of gross-margin percentages:

a. Sales value at splitoff method:

	Super A	Super B	C	Super D	Total
Sales	$300,000	$100,000	$50,000	$120,000	$570,000
Joint costs	25,000	15,000	25,000	35,000	100,000
Separable costs	200,000	80,000	0	90,000	370,000
Total costs	225,000	95,000	25,000	125,000	470,000
Gross margin	$ 75,000	$ 5,000	$25,000	$ (5,000)	$100,000
Gross-margin percentage	25%	5%	50%	(4.17%)	17.54%

15-30 (cont'd)

b. Physical-measure method:

	Super A	Super B	C	Super D	Total
Sales	$300,000	$100,000	$50,000	$120,000	$570,000
Joint costs	60,000	20,000	10,000	10,000	100,000
Separable costs	200,000	80,000	0	90,000	370,000
Total costs	260,000	100,000	10,000	100,000	470,000
Gross margin	$ 40,000	$ 0	$40,000	$ 20,000	$100,000
Gross-margin percentage	13.33%	0%	80%	16.67%	17.54%

c. Estimated net realizable value method:

	Super A	Super B	C	Super D	Total
Sales	$300,000	$100,000	$50,000	$120,000	$570,000
Joint costs	50,000	10,000	25,000	15,000	100,000
Separable costs	200,000	80,000	0	90,000	370,000
Total costs	250,000	90,000	25,000	105,000	470,000
Gross margin	$ 50,000	$ 10,000	$25,000	$ 15,000	$100,000
Gross-margin percentage	16.67%	10%	50%	12.5%	17.54%

Summary of gross-margin percentages:

Joint-Cost Allocation Method	Super A	Super B	C	Super D
Sales value at splitoff	25.00%	5%	50%	(4.17%)
Physical measure	13.33%	0%	80%	16.67%
Estimated net realizable value	16.67%	10%	50%	12.50%

15-30 (cont'd)

2.   Further Processing of A into Super A:

Incremental revenue, $300,000 – $50,000	$250,000
Incremental costs	200,000
Incremental operating income from further processing	$ 50,000

Further Processing of B into Super B:

Incremental revenue, $100,000 – $30,000	$ 70,000
Incremental costs	80,000
Incremental operating income from further processing	($ 10,000)

Further Processing of D into Super D:

Incremental revenue, $120,000 – $70,000	$ 50,000
Incremental costs	90,000
Incremental operating income from further processing	$ (40,000)

Operating income can be increased by $50,000 if both B and D are sold at their splitoff point.

SOLUTION EXHIBIT 15-30

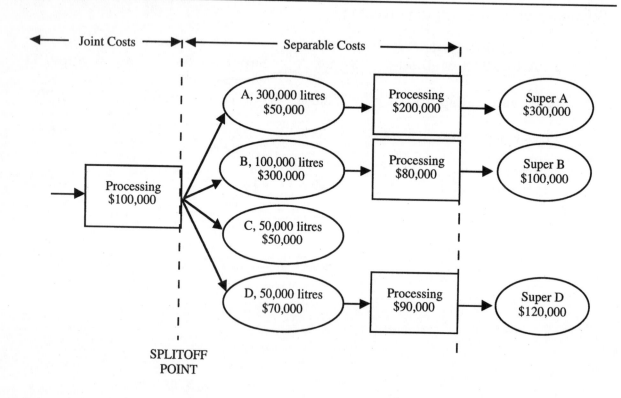

15-32 (25 min.) **Joint-cost allocation, relevant costs** (R. Capettini, adapted).

1.   The "four-day progressive product trimming" ignores the fundamental point that the $300 cost to buy the pig is a joint cost. A pig is purchased as a whole. The butcher's challenge is to maximize the total revenues minus incremental costs (assumed zero) from the sale of all products.

At each stage, the decision made ignores the general rule that product emphasis decisions should consider relevant revenues and relevant costs. Allocated joint costs are not relevant. For example, the Day 1 decision to drop bacon ignores the fact that the $300 joint cost has been paid to acquire the whole pig. The $144 of revenues are relevant inflows. This same position also holds for the Day 2 to Day 4 decisions.

2.   The revenue amounts are the figures to use in the sales value at splitoff method:

Product	Revenue	Joint Costs Weighting	Allocated
Pork chops	$120	0.2899	$ 86.97
Ham	150	0.3623	108.69
Bacon	144	0.3478	104.34
	$414	1.0000	$300.00

3.   No. The decision to sell or not sell individual products should consider relevant revenues and relevant costs. In the butcher's context, the relevant costs would be the additional time and other incidentals to take each pig part and make it a salable product. The relevant revenues would be the difference between the selling price at the consumer level for the pig parts and what the butcher may receive for the whole pig.

15-34 (30 min.) **Estimated net realizable value method, byproducts.**

1.

a. For the month of November 2002, Princess Corporation's output was:
- apple slices   89,100
- applesauce   81,000
- apple juice   67,500
- animal feed   27,000

These amounts were calculated as follows:

Product	Input	Proportion	Total Kilograms	Kilograms Lost	Net Kilograms
Slices	270,000 kg	0.33	89,100	–	89,100
Sauce	270,000	0.30	81,000	–	81,000
Juice	270,000	0.27	72,900	5,400	67,500*
Feed	270,000	0.10	27,000	–	27,000
		1.00	270,000	5,400	264,600

*Net kilograms: = 72,900 – (0.08 × net kilograms)
1.08 net kilograms   = 72,900
Net kilograms   = 67,500

b. The estimated net realizable value for each of the three main products is calculated below:

Product	Net Kilograms	Price	Revenue	Separable Costs	Estimated Net Realizable Value
Slices	89,100	$0.80	$ 71,280	$11,280	$ 60,000
Sauce	81,000	0.55	44,550	8,550	36,000
Juice	67,500	0.40	27,000	3,000	24,000
			$142,830	$22,830	$120,000

15-34 (cont'd)

c. and d.

The estimated net realizable value of the byproduct is deducted from the production costs prior to allocation to the joint products, as presented below:

Allocation of Cutting Department Costs
to Joint Products and Byproducts

Net realizable value
(NRV) of byproduct
- = By-product revenue − Separable costs
- = $0.10 (270,000 × 10%) − $700
- = $2,700 − $700
- = $2,000

Costs to be allocated
- = Joint costs − NRV of byproduct
- = $60,000 − $2,000
- = $58,000

Product	Revenue	Separable Costs	Joint Costs	Gross Margin
Slices	$ 71,280	$11,280	$29,000	$31,000
Sauce	44,550	8,550	17,400	18,600
Juice	27,000	3,000	11,600	12,400
	$142,830	$22,830	$58,000	$62,000

2.   The gross-margin dollar information by main product is determined by the arbitrary allocation of joint production costs. As a result, these cost figures and the resulting gross-margin information are of little significance for planning and control purposes. The allocation is made only for purposes of inventory costing and income determination.

15-36 (20 min.) **Byproduct, disposal costs, ethics.**

1. The comparative analysis prepared by the cost accountant is flawed. In the process further alternative, he has erroneously included the $250,000 allocated joint costs. Allocated joint costs are irrelevant because they are not incremental costs of the alternative being considered. If the joint costs allocated are taken out, it becomes clear that financially it would be to the advantage of the company to process further the product as it would increase the operating income by $150,000 [$500,000 − ($300,000 + $50,000)]. Furthermore, the dumping alternative does not consider potential future costs that may arise from environmental liabilities.

2. It appears that there would be no legal ramifications if the company decided to dump the hazardous product into the Gulf. The country either may have no laws against such dumping, or even if they exist, they are not enforced in accordance with the government policy. A more important consideration, however, is the ethical implications. To knowingly dump a hazardous material into the Gulf would certainly result in water pollution. This is an unacceptable action from a societal standpoint. *It is important to remember that an act that does not violate any laws is not necessarily an ethical act.* Ethical considerations go beyond legal considerations. In different parts of the world, legal systems are imperfect and not comprehensive. It is the responsibility of top management to take a broader, societal view when making decisions. In other words, a business should take its social responsibility seriously, by making it an integral part of the decision-making process. In the long run it is in the best interest of all stakeholders as well as the business itself.

CHAPTER 16
REVENUES, REVENUE VARIANCES, AND
CUSTOMER-PROFITABILITY ANALYSIS

16-2 The *stand-alone revenue-allocation method* uses information about individual products in their separate markets when allocating bundled revenues to individual products. The *incremental revenue-allocation method* ranks the individual products in a bundle and then uses this ranking to allocate the bundled revenues to these individual products.

16-4 A dispute over allocation of revenues of a bundled product could be resolved by (a) having an agreement that outlines the preferred method in the case of a dispute or (b) having a third party (such as the company president or an independent arbitrator) make a decision.

16-6 The total sales-mix variance for revenues arises from shifts in the revenues of individual products. The composite product unit concept enables the effect of individual product changes to be summarized in a single intuitive number.

16-8 The sales-quantity variance can be decomposed into (a) a market-size variance (the actual total market-size change from that budgeted) and (b) a market-share variance (the actual market-share change from that budgeted). Both variances use the budgeted average selling price per unit, when the focus is on revenues.

16-10 Customer profitability analysis highlights to managers how individual customers differentially contribute to total profitability. It helps managers to see whether customers who contribute sizably to total profitability are receiving a comparable level of attention from the organization.

16-12 No. A customer profitability profile highlights differences in current period's profitability across customers. Dropping customers should be the last resort. An unprofitable customer in one period may be highly profitable in subsequent future periods. Moreover, costs assigned to individual customers need not be purely variable with respect to short-run elimination of sales to those customers. Thus, when customers are dropped, costs assigned to those customers may not disappear in the short run.

16-14 A process where the inputs are nonsubstitutable leaves workers no discretion as to the components to use. A process where the inputs are substitutable means there is discretion about the exact number and type of inputs or about the weighting of inputs where the number and type is mandated.

16-16 (30 min.) **Revenue allocation, speaking fees.**

1. The total revenues from the seminar are:
   500 × $200 = $100,000.
   Revenues to be shared by speakers
   0.30 × $100,000 = $30,000.

The stand-alone revenue allocation method could guide the allocations. Possible weights are individual speaking fees, number of speeches, and speaking fee revenues:

	Individual Speaking Fee (1)	Relative Speaking Fee % (2)=(1)÷16,000	# of Speeches (3)	Relative Number of Speeches (4)=(3)÷96	Speaking Fee Revenues (5)=(1)×(3)	Relative Speaking Fee Revenues (6)=(5)÷34,000
Linda Young	$10,000	0.625	6	0.0625	$ 60,000	0.1765
Vince Rock	4,000	0.250	50	0.5208	200,000	0.5882
Juan Malvido	2,000	0.125	40	0.4167	80,000	0.2353
	$16,000	1.000	96	1.0000	$340,000	1.0000

These three weightings give the following allocation of $30,000:

	Relative Speaking Fee Weights (1)	Allocation of $30,000 (2)	Relative Number of Speeches Weights (3)	Allocation of $30,000 (4)	Relative Speaking Fee Revenues (5)	Allocation of $30,000 (6)
Linda Young	0.625	$18,750	0.0625	$ 1,875	0.1765	$ 5,295
Vince Rock	0.250	7,500	0.5208	15,624	0.5882	17,646
Juan Malvido	0.125	3,750	0.4167	12,501	0.2353	7,059
	1.000	$30,000	1.0000	$30,000	1.0000	$30,000

The incremental revenue-allocation method is not straightforward, as the sum of the individual speaking fees ($10,000 + $4,000 + $2,000 = $16,000) is less than the total $30,000 to be allocated.

2. Young could argue that she has the highest individual speaking fee and is high in demand. In contrast, the other two speakers have given numerous talks and likely will attract fewer people to the seminar. She could argue that Malvido should pay to be on the program, as he is marketing for the television network. The net of these arguments is that Young wants more than $10,000.

Rock could argue that he is in huge demand as a speaker, as is evidenced by his 50 speeches at $4,000. People pay this amount because he is both entertaining and dynamic. He could also claim his Olympic gold medal brings an aura of accomplishment to the seminar. The net of these arguments is that Rock wants more than $10,000.

Malvido could argue that he is the "television personality" everyone wants to meet and hear. He could also argue he could give the seminar invaluable publicity by promoting it on his television show. The net of these arguments is that Malvido wants more than $10,000.

16-18 (10-15 min.) **Revenue allocation, bundled products, additional complexities (continuation of 16-17).**

Alternatives include:

(a)   Use information about how each individual package is used to make the revenue allocations. Thus if one party uses only lodging and food, the $700 is allocated among those two groups. This would be the most accurate approach as it captures actual usage and non-usage of the facilities.

(b)   Use the average non-usage information to compute an "adjusted unit selling price:"

Lodging: $640 × 1.00	=	$ 640
Food: $160 × 0.95	=	152
Recreation: $300 × 0.90	=	270
		$1,062

These adjusted revenues can be used in either the stand-alone or incremental methods. For example, the stand-alone allocations are:

Lodging: $\dfrac{640}{\$1,062} \times \$700$ = $422

Food: $\dfrac{152}{\$1,062} \times \$700$ = $100

Recreation: $\dfrac{270}{\$1,062} \times \$700$ = $178

$700

16-20 (20 min.) **7-Up using variances to read the market.**

1. 7-Up should have conducted a Level 1 to 4 variance analysis that is focused on the U.S. soft-drink market. If information is available, individual 7-Up products (7-Up and Diet 7-Up) could be included to compute a sales mix-variance. The sales-quantity variance could be divided into a market-share variance and a market-size variance. 7-Up's market share has steadily declined from 3.2% to 2.4% over a 10-year period. This is a large decline.

    7-Up could also conduct more detailed analyses, including:
1) Changes in the market share and the market size of the citrus-flavoured category.
2) Changes in its market share and market size share by demographic segment (0-11 years, 12-24 years, and so on).

2. The brand objectives are critical to consider when evaluating 7-Up's strategy. The *Fortune* article has a negative tone. Much depends on whether 7-Up's management has attempted to make the brand investments required to compete in the soft drink market. If 7-Up's management has invested heavily in marketing, sales promotions, product extension, and so on, its decline in market share is a negative indicator. Suppose, however, 7-Up management has decided that they do not have the resources to compete with Coca-Cola or Pepsi-Cola. Their strategy is to budget for market declines, but extract higher profitability from the brand in the short run. This is a classic "milk-the-brand" strategy. Here, the issue is what is the optimal "milk-the-brand" strategy, which would consider the time period over which a market-share decline is predicted and the rate of decrease with alternative cutbacks in marketing outlays.

16-22 (30-40 min.) **Variance analysis of revenues, multiple countries.**

1.   All amounts are in thousands.

Budget for 2002

	Selling Price per Carton (1)	Units Sold (Cartons in 000s) (2)	Sales Mix (3)	Revenues (4) = (1) × (2)
Canada	$6.00	400,000	16%	$ 2,400,000
Mexico	4.00	600,000	24	2,400,000
U.S.	7.00	1,500,000	60	10,500,000
		2,500,000	100%	$15,300,000

Actual for 2002

	Selling Price per Carton (1)	Units Sold (Cartons in 000s) (2)	Sales Mix (3)	Revenues (4) = (1) × (2)
Canada	$6.20	480,000	16%	$ 2,976,000
Mexico	4.25	900,000	30	3,825,000
U.S.	6.80	1,620,000	54	11,016,000
		3,000,000	100%	$17,817,000

Solution Exhibit 16-22 summarizes the Level 1 to Level 3 variance analysis. Details of the underlying computations are presented below.

$$\text{Static-budget variance of revenue} = \text{Actual results} - \text{Static-budget amount}$$

Canada	= $ 2,976,000	– $ 2,400,000	=	$ 576,000 F
Mexico	= 3,825,000	– 2,400,000	=	1,425,000 F
United States	= 11,016,000	– 10,500,000	=	516,000 F
Total				$2,517,000 F

$$\text{Flexible-budget variance of revenue} = \text{Actual results} - \text{Flexible-budget amount}$$

Canada	= $ 2,976,000	– ($6.00 × 480,000)	=	$ 96,000 F
Mexico	= 3,825,000	– (4.00 × 900,000)	=	225,000 F
United States	= 11,016,000	– (7.00 × 1,620,000)	=	324,000 U
Total				$ 3,000 U

16-22 (cont'd)

$$\text{Sales-volume variance of revenue} = \left(\begin{array}{c}\text{Actual sales} \\ \text{quantity} \\ \text{in units}\end{array} - \begin{array}{c}\text{Budgeted sales} \\ \text{quantity} \\ \text{in units}\end{array}\right) \times \begin{array}{c}\text{Budgeted} \\ \text{revenue} \\ \text{per unit}\end{array}$$

Canada   = (480,000 –   400,000) × \$6.00   =   \$ 480,000 F
Mexico   = (900,000 –   600,000) × \$4.00   =   \$1,200,000 F
United States   = (1,620,000 – 1,500,000) × \$7.00   =   \$ 840,000 F
Total   \$2,520,000 F

$$\text{Sales-quantity variance of revenue} = \left(\begin{array}{c}\text{Actual units} \\ \text{of all products} \\ \text{sold}\end{array} - \begin{array}{c}\text{Budgeted units} \\ \text{of all products} \\ \text{sold}\end{array}\right) \times \begin{array}{c}\text{Budgeted} \\ \text{sales-mix} \\ \text{percentage}\end{array} \times \begin{array}{c}\text{Budgeted} \\ \text{revenue} \\ \text{per unit}\end{array}$$

Canada   = (3,000,000 – 2,500,000) × 0.16 × \$6.00   =   \$ 480,000 F
Mexico   = (3,000,000 – 2,500,000) × 0.24 × \$4.00   =   \$ 480,000 F
United States   = (3,000,000 – 2,500,000) × 0.60 × \$7.00   =   \$2,100,000 F
Total   \$3,060,000 F

$$\text{Sales-mix variance of revenue} = \begin{array}{c}\text{Actual units} \\ \text{of all} \\ \text{products sold}\end{array} \times \left(\begin{array}{c}\text{Actual} \\ \text{sales-mix} \\ \text{percentage}\end{array} - \begin{array}{c}\text{Budgeted} \\ \text{sales-mix} \\ \text{percentage}\end{array}\right) \times \begin{array}{c}\text{Budgeted} \\ \text{revenue} \\ \text{per unit}\end{array}$$

Canada   = 3,000,000 × (0.16 – 0.16) × \$6.00   =   \$ 0
Mexico   = 3,000,000 × (0.30 – 0.24) × \$4.00   =   \$ 720,000 F
United States   = 3,000,000 × (0.54 – 0.60) × \$7.00   =   \$1,260,000 U
Total   \$ 540,000 U

2.   There is a sizable favourable static-budget variance (Level 1) of revenue of \$2,517,000. The flexible-budget variance (Level 2) of \$3,000 U shows that the net effect of the selling price changes is minimal (Canada increases \$0.20 per carton, Mexico increases \$0.25 per carton, and U.S. decreases \$0.20 per carton).

     The Level 3 breakdown of the favourable sales-volume variance of \$2,520,000 for revenues shows that the biggest contributor is the 500,000 unit increase in sales. There is a partially offsetting unfavourable sales-mix variance.

16-6

SOLUTION EXHIBIT 16-22
Revenue Analysis for Cola-King

	Static-Budget Variance of Revenues
Canada	$ 576,000 F
Mexico	1,425,000 F
United States	516,000 F
Total	$2,517,000 F

Flexible-Budget Variance of Revenues		Sales-Volume Variance of Revenues	
Canada	$ 96,000 F	Canada	$ 480,000 F
Mexico	225,000 F	Mexico	1,200,000 F
United States	324,000 U	United States	840,000 F
Total	$ 3,000 U		$2,520,000 F

Sales-Mix Variance of Revenues		Sales-Quantity Variance of Revenues	
Canada	$ 0	Canada	$ 480,000 F
Mexico	720,000 F	Mexico	480,000 F
United States	1,260,000 U	United States	2,100,000 F
Total	$ 540,000 U		$3,060,000 F

16-24 (20-25 min.) **Customer profitability, distribution.**

1.   The activity-based costing for each customer is:

		Maple Pharmacy	Oak Pharmacy
1.	Order processing, $40 × 12; 10	$ 480	$ 400
2.	Line-item ordering, $3 × (12 × 10;10 × 18)	360	540
3.	Store deliveries, $50 × 6; 10	300	500
4.	Carton deliveries, $1 × (6 × 24; 10 × 20)	144	200
5.	Shelf-stocking, $16 × (6 × 0; 10 × 0.5)	0	80
	Operating costs	$1,284	$1,720

The operating income of each customer is:

	Maple Pharmacy	Oak Pharmacy
Revenues, $2,400 × 6; 1,800 × 10	$14,400	$18,000
Cost of goods sold, $2,100 × 6; $1,650 × 10	12,600	16,500
Gross margin	1,800	1,500
Operating costs	1,284	1,720
Operating income	$ 516	$ (220)

2.   Ways Figure Four could use this information include:
(a)   Pay increased attention to the top 20% of the customers. This could entail asking them for ways you can improve service. Alternatively, you may want to highlight to your own personnel the importance of these customers, e.g., it could entail stressing to delivery people the importance of never missing delivery dates for these customers.

(b)   Work out ways internally at Figure Four to reduce the rate per cost driver, e.g., reduce the cost per order by having better order placement linkages with customers. This cost reduction by Figure Four will improve the profitability of all customers.

(c)   Work with customers so that their behaviour reduces the total "system-wide" costs. At a minimum, this approach could entail having customers make fewer orders and fewer line items. This latter point is controversial with students; the rationale is that a reduction in the number of line items (diversity of products) carried by Ma and Pa stores may reduce the diversity of products Figure Four carries.

16-26 (35 min.)   **Direct materials price, efficiency, mix, and yield variances.**

1.   Solution Exhibit 16-26A presents the total price variance ($3,100F), the total efficiency variance ($2,560U) and the total flexible-budget variance ($540F).

Total direct materials price variance can also be computed as:

$$\begin{array}{c}\text{Direct materials} \\ \text{price variance} \\ \text{for each input}\end{array} = \left(\begin{array}{c}\text{Actual} \\ \text{Price}\end{array} - \begin{array}{c}\text{Budgeted} \\ \text{Price}\end{array}\right) \times \begin{array}{c}\text{Actual} \\ \text{Inputs}\end{array}$$

Tolman	=	($0.28 – $0.30) × 62,000	=	$1,240 F
Golden Delicious	=	($0.26 – $0.26) × 155,000	=	0
Ribston	=	($0.20 – $0.22) × 93,000	=	1,860 F
Total direct materials price variance				$3,100 F

Total direct materials efficiency variance can also be computed as:

$$\begin{array}{c}\text{Direct materials} \\ \text{efficiency variance} \\ \text{for each input}\end{array} = \left(\begin{array}{c}\text{Actual} \\ \text{inputs}\end{array} - \begin{array}{c}\text{Budgeted inputs allowed} \\ \text{for actual outputs achieved}\end{array}\right) \times \begin{array}{c}\text{Budgeted} \\ \text{prices}\end{array}$$

Tolman	=	(62,000 – 45,000) × $0.30	=	$5,100 U
Golden Delicious	=	(155,000 – 180,000) × $0.26	=	6,500 F
Ribston	=	(93,000 – 75,000) × $0.22	=	3,960 U
Total direct materials efficiency variance				$2,560 U

SOLUTION EXHIBIT 16-26A
Columnar Presentation of Direct Materials Price and Efficiency Variances for Greenwood Inc. for November 2002

	Actual Costs Incurred (Actual Inputs × Actual Prices) (1)		Actual Input × Budgeted Prices (2)		Flexible Budget (Budgeted Inputs Allowed for Actual Outputs Achieved × Budgeted Prices) (3)	
Tolman	62,000 × $0.28 =	$17,360	62,000 × $0.30 =	$18,600	45,000 × $0.30 =	$13,500
Golden Delicious	155,000 × $0.26 =	40,300	155,000 × $0.26 =	40,300	180,000 × $0.26 =	46,800
Ribston	93,000 × $0.20 =	18,600	93,000 × $0.22 =	20,460	75,000 × $0.22 =	16,500
		$76,260		$79,360		$76,800

$3,100 F
Total price variance

$2,560 U
Total efficiency variance

$540 F
Total flexible-budget variance

F = favourable effect on operating income; U = unfavourable effect on operating income

16-26 (cont'd)

2.   Solution Exhibit 16-26B presents the total direct materials yield and mix variances for Greenwood Inc. for November 2002.

The total direct materials yield variance can also be computed as the sum of the direct materials yield variances for each input:

$$\begin{pmatrix} \text{Direct} \\ \text{materials} \\ \text{yield variance} \\ \text{for each input} \end{pmatrix} = \begin{pmatrix} \text{Actual total} \\ \text{quantity of all} \\ \text{direct materials} \\ \text{inputs used} \end{pmatrix} - \begin{pmatrix} \text{Budgeted total quantity} \\ \text{of all direct materials} \\ \text{inputs allowed for} \\ \text{actual output achieved} \end{pmatrix} \times \begin{pmatrix} \text{Budgeted} \\ \text{direct materials} \\ \text{input mix} \\ \text{percentage} \end{pmatrix} \times \begin{pmatrix} \text{Budgeted} \\ \text{price of} \\ \text{direct materials} \\ \text{inputs} \end{pmatrix}$$

Tolman	$= (310,000 - 300,000) \times 0.15 \times \$0.30 = 10,000 \times 0.15 \times \$0.30 =$	\$ 450 U
Golden Delicious	$= (310,000 - 300,000) \times 0.60 \times \$0.26 = 10,000 \times 0.60 \times \$0.26 =$	1,560 U
Ribston	$= (310,000 - 300,000) \times 0.25 \times \$0.22 = 10,000 \times 0.25 \times \$0.22 =$	550 U
Total direct materials yield variance		$\underline{\$2,560}$ U

The total direct materials mix variance can also be computed as the sum of the direct materials mix variances for each input:

$$\begin{pmatrix} \text{Direct} \\ \text{materials} \\ \text{mix variance} \\ \text{for each input} \end{pmatrix} = \begin{pmatrix} \text{Actual} \\ \text{direct materials} \\ \text{input mix} \\ \text{percentage} \end{pmatrix} - \begin{pmatrix} \text{Budgeted} \\ \text{direct materials} \\ \text{input mix} \\ \text{percentage} \end{pmatrix} \times \begin{pmatrix} \text{Actual total} \\ \text{quantity of all} \\ \text{direct materials} \\ \text{inputs used} \end{pmatrix} \times \begin{pmatrix} \text{Budgeted} \\ \text{price of} \\ \text{direct materials} \\ \text{inputs} \end{pmatrix}$$

Tolman	$= (0.20 - 0.15) \times 310,000 \times \$0.30 = 0.05 \times 310,000 \times \$0.30 =$	\$4,650 U
Golden Delicious	$= (0.50 - 0.60) \times 310,000 \times \$0.26 = -0.10 \times 310,000 \times \$0.26 =$	8,060 F
Ribston	$= (0.30 - 0.25) \times 310,000 \times \$0.22 = 0.05 \times 310,000 \times \$0.22 =$	3,410 U
Total direct materials mix variance		$\underline{\$\quad 0}$ U

3.   Greenwood paid less for Tolman and Ribston apples and, so, had a favourable direct materials price variance of \$3,100. It also had an unfavourable efficiency variance of \$2,560. Greenwood would need to evaluate if these were unrelated events or if the lower price resulted from the purchase of apples of poorer quality that affected efficiency. The net effect in this case from a cost standpoint was favourable—the savings in price being greater than the loss in efficiency. Of course, if the applesauce is of poorer quality, Greenwood must also evaluate the potential effects on current and future revenues that have not been considered in the variances described in requirements 1 and 2.

16-26 (cont'd)

The unfavourable efficiency variance is entirely attributable to an unfavourable yield. The actual mix does deviate from the budgeted mix but at the budgeted prices, the greater quantity of Tolman and Ribston apples used in the actual mix exactly offsets the fewer Golden Delicious apples used. Again, management should evaluate the reasons for the unfavourable yield variance. Is it due to poor quality Tolman and Ribston apples (recall from requirement 1 that these apples were acquired at a price lower than the standard price)? Is it due to the change in mix (recall that the mix used is different from the budgeted mix, even though the mix variance is $0)? Isolating the reasons can lead management to take the necessary corrective actions.

SOLUTION EXHIBIT 16-26B
Columnar Presentation of Direct Materials, Yield, and Mix Variances
for Greenwood Inc. for November 2002

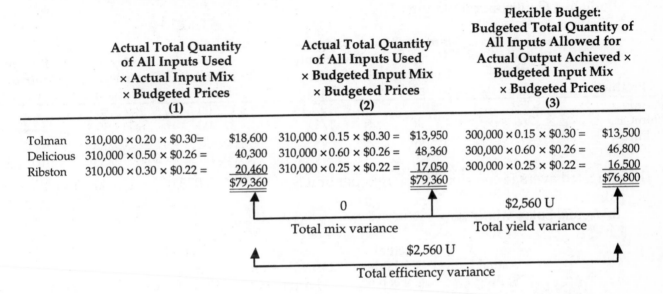

F = favourable effect on operating income; U = unfavourable effect on operating income

16-28 (60 min.)   **Variance analysis, sales-mix, and sales-quantity variances.**

1. Actual Contribution Margins

Product	Actual Selling Price	Actual Variable Costs per Unit	Actual Contribution Margin per Unit	Actual Sales Volume in Units	Actual Contribution Dollars	Actual Contribution Percent
PalmPro	$349	$178	$171	11,000	$ 1,881,000	16%
PalmCE	285	92	193	44,000	8,492,000	71%
PalmKid	102	73	29	55,000	1,595,000	13%
				110,000	$11,968,000	100%

The actual average contribution margin per unit is $108.80 ($11,968,000 ÷ 110,000 units).

Budgeted Contribution Margins

Product	Budgeted Selling Price	Budgeted Variable Costs per Unit	Budgeted Contribution Margin per Unit	Budgeted Sales Volume in Units	Budgeted Contribution Dollars	Budgeted Contribution Percent
PalmPro	$379	$182	$197	12,500	$ 2,462,500	19%
PalmCE	269	98	171	37,500	6,412,500	49%
PalmKid	149	65	84	50,000	4,200,000	32%
				100,000	$13,075,000	100%

The budgeted average contribution margin per unit is $130.75 ($13,075,000 ÷ 100,000 units).

2. Actual Sales Mix

Product	Actual Selling Price	Actual Variable Costs per Unit	Actual Contribution Margin per Unit	Actual Sales Volume in Units	Actual Sales Mix
PalmPro	$349	$178	$171	11,000	10.0%
PalmCE	285	92	193	44,000	40.0%
PalmKid	102	73	29	55,000	50.0%
				110,000	100%

Budgeted Sales Mix

Product	Budgeted Selling Price	Budgeted Variable Costs per Unit	Budgeted Contribution Margin per Unit	Budgeted Sales Volume in Units	Budgeted Sales Mix
PalmPro	$379	$182	$197	12,500	12.5%
PalmCE	269	98	171	37,500	37.5%
PalmKid	149	65	84	50,000	50.0%
				100,000	100%

16-28 (cont'd)

3. Flexible-budget variance of contribution margin:

$$= \begin{array}{c} \text{Actual} \\ \text{Results} \end{array} - \begin{array}{c} \text{Flexible-budget} \\ \text{amount} \end{array}$$

PalmPro = ($171 × 11,000) – ($197 × 11,000)

    = $1,881,000 – $2,167,000   = $ 286,000 U

PalmCE = (193 × 44,000) – ($171 × 44,000)

    = $8,492,000 – $7,524,000   =   968,000 F

PalmKid = ($29 × 55,000) – ($84 × 55,000)

    = $1,595,000 – $4,620,000   = 3,025,000 U

Total flexible-budget variance   = $2,343,000 U

Sales-volume variance of contribution margin:

$$= \left(\begin{array}{c} \text{Actual sales} \\ \text{quantity} \\ \text{in units} \end{array} - \begin{array}{c} \text{Budgeted sales} \\ \text{quantity} \\ \text{in units} \end{array} \right) \times \begin{array}{c} \text{Budgeted} \\ \text{contrib. margin} \\ \text{per unit} \end{array}$$

PalmPro = (11,000 – 12,500) × $197

    = –1,500 × $197   = $ 295,500 U

PalmCE = (44,000 – 37,500) × $171

    = 6,500 × $171   = 1,111,500 F

PalmKid = (55,000 – 50,000) × $84

    = 5,000 × $84   =   420,000 F

Total sales-volume variance   = $1,236,000 F

16-28 (cont'd)

Sales-mix variance of contribution-margin:

$$= \begin{pmatrix} \text{Actual units} \\ \text{of all} \\ \text{products sold} \end{pmatrix} \times \begin{pmatrix} \text{Actual} \\ \text{sales mix} \\ \text{percentage} \end{pmatrix} - \begin{pmatrix} \text{Budgeted} \\ \text{sales mix} \\ \text{percentage} \end{pmatrix} \times \begin{pmatrix} \text{Budgeted} \\ \text{contrib. margin} \\ \text{per unit} \end{pmatrix}$$

PalmPro = 110,000 × (0.10 − 0.125) × $197

      = 110,00 × −0.025 × $197   = $541,750 U

PalmCE = 110,000 × (0.40 − 0.375) × $171

      = 110,000 × 0.025 × $171   =   470,250 F

PalmKid = 110,000 × (0.50 − 0.50) × $84

      = 110,000 × 0.00 × $84   =   0 F

Total sales-mix variance   = $ 71,500 U

Sales-quantity variance of contribution margin:

$$= \begin{pmatrix} \text{Actual units} \\ \text{of all} \\ \text{products sold} \end{pmatrix} - \begin{pmatrix} \text{Budgeted units} \\ \text{of all} \\ \text{products sold} \end{pmatrix} \times \begin{pmatrix} \text{Budgeted} \\ \text{sales mix} \\ \text{percentage} \end{pmatrix} \times \begin{pmatrix} \text{Budgeted} \\ \text{contrib. margin} \\ \text{per unit} \end{pmatrix}$$

PalmPro = (110,000 − 100,000) × 0.125 × $197

      = 10,000 × 0.125 × $197   = $ 246,250 F

PalmCE = (110,000 − 100,000) × 0.375 × $171

      = 10,000 × 0.375 × $171   =   641,250 F

PalmKid = (110,000 − 100,000) × 0.50 × $84

      = 10,000 × 0.50 × $84   =   420,000 F

Total sales-quantity variance   = $1,307,500 F

16-28 (cont'd)

4.

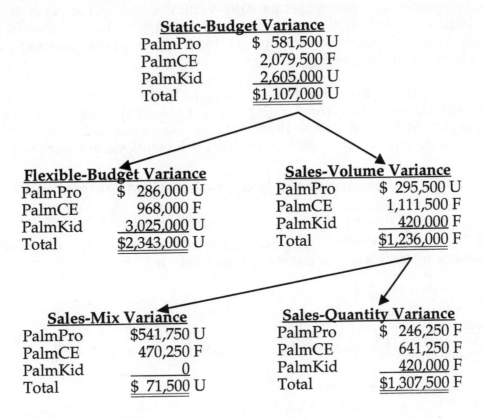

Static-Budget Variance

PalmPro	$ 581,500 U
PalmCE	2,079,500 F
PalmKid	2,605,000 U
Total	$1,107,000 U

Flexible-Budget Variance

PalmPro	$ 286,000 U
PalmCE	968,000 F
PalmKid	3,025,000 U
Total	$2,343,000 U

Sales-Volume Variance

PalmPro	$ 295,500 U
PalmCE	1,111,500 F
PalmKid	420,000 F
Total	$1,236,000 F

Sales-Mix Variance

PalmPro	$541,750 U
PalmCE	470,250 F
PalmKid	0
Total	$ 71,500 U

Sales-Quantity Variance

PalmPro	$ 246,250 F
PalmCE	641,250 F
PalmKid	420,000 F
Total	$1,307,500 F

5. Some factors to consider are:
- The difference in actual vs. budgeted contribution was $1,107,000. However, the contribution from the PalmCE exceeded budget by $2,079,500 while the contributions from the PalmPro and the PalmKid were lower than expected to an offsetting degree.
- In percentage terms, the PalmCE accounted for 71% of total contribution vs. a planned 49% contribution. However, the PalmPro accounted for 16% vs. planned 19% and the PalmKid accounted for only 13% vs. a planned 32%.
- In unit terms (rather than in contribution terms), the PalmKid accounted for 50% of the sales mix as planned. However, the PalmPro accounted for only 10% vs. a budgeted 12.5% and the PalmCE accounted for 40% vs. a planned 37.5%.
- Variance analysis for the PalmPro shows an unfavourable sales-mix variance outweighing a favourable sales-quantity variance and producing an unfavourable sales-volume variance of $295,500. The drop in sales-mix share was far larger than the gain from an overall greater quantity sold.
- The PalmCE gained both from an increase in share of the sales mix as well as from the increase in the overall number of units sold. These factors combined to a $1,111,500 favourable sales-volume variance.
- The PalmKid maintained sales-mix share—as a result, the sales-mix variance is zero. However, PalmKid sales did gain from the overall increase in units sold.

16-28 (cont'd)

- Overall, there was a favourable total sales-volume variance. However, the large drop in PalmKid's contribution margin per unit combined with a decrease in the number of PalmPro units purchased vs. budget, led to the total contribution margin being much lower than budgeted.

Other factors could be discussed here—for example, it seems that the PalmKid did not achieve much success with a three digit price point—selling price was budgeted at $149 but dropped to $102. At the same time, variable costs increased. This could have been due to a marketing push aimed at announcing the lower price in some markets.

16-30 (40 min.) Variance analysis of contribution margin, multiple products.

1, 2, and 3. Solution Exhibit 16-30 presents the sales-volume, sales-quantity, and sales-mix variances for each type of cookie and in total for Debbie's Delight Inc. in August 2002.

The sales-volume variances can also be computed as:

$$\begin{pmatrix} \text{Sales-volume} \\ \text{variance of} \\ \text{contribution margin} \end{pmatrix} = \begin{pmatrix} \text{Actual sales} \\ \text{quantity in kilograms} - \frac{\text{Budgeted sales}}{\text{quantity in kilograms}} \end{pmatrix} \times \begin{array}{c} \text{Budgeted contribution} \\ \text{margin per kilogram} \end{array}$$

The sales-volume variances are:

Chocolate chip	=	(57,600 – 45,000) × $2.00	=	$25,200 F
Oatmeal raisin	=	(18,000 – 25,000) × $2.30	=	16,100 U
Coconut	=	(9,600 – 10,000) × $2.60	=	1,040 U
White chocolate	=	(13,200 – 5,000) × $3.00	=	24,600 F
Macadamia nut	=	(21,600 – 15,000) × $3.10	=	20,460 F
All cookies				$53,120 F

The sales-quantity variance can also be computed as :

$$\begin{pmatrix} \text{Sales-quantity} \\ \text{variance of} \\ \text{contribution margin} \end{pmatrix} = \begin{pmatrix} \text{Actual kilograms} & \text{Budgeted kilograms} \\ \text{of all cookies} - \text{of all cookies} \\ \text{sold} & \text{sold} \end{pmatrix} \begin{array}{c} \text{Budgeted} \\ \times \text{sales-mix} \\ \text{percentage} \end{array} \times \begin{array}{c} \text{Budgeted} \\ \text{contribution} \\ \text{margin per kilogram} \end{array}$$

The sales-quantity variances are:

Chocolate chip	=	(120,000 – 100,000) × 0.45 × $2.00 =	$18,000 F
Oatmeal raisin	=	(120,000 – 100,000) × 0.25 × $2.30 =	11,500 F
Coconut	=	(120,000 – 100,000) × 0.10 × $2.60 =	5,200 F
White chocolate	=	(120,000 – 100,000) × 0.05 × $3.00 =	3,000 F
Macadamia nut	=	(120,000 – 100,000) × 0.15 × $3.10 =	9,300 F
All cookies			$47,000 F

The sales-mix variance can also be computed as:

$$\begin{pmatrix} \text{Sales-mix} \\ \text{variance of} \\ \text{contribution margin} \end{pmatrix} = \begin{pmatrix} \text{Actual sales-} \\ \text{mix percentage} - \frac{\text{Budgeted sales-}}{\text{mix percentage}} \end{pmatrix} \times \begin{array}{c} \text{Actual kilograms} \\ \text{of all cookies} \\ \text{sold} \end{array} \times \begin{array}{c} \text{Budgeted} \\ \text{contribution} \\ \text{margin per kilogram} \end{array}$$

16-30 (cont'd)

The sales-mix variances are:

Chocolate chip	=	(0.48 – 0.45) × 120,000 × $2.00	=	$ 7,200 F
Oatmeal raisin	=	(0.15 – 0.25) × 120,000 × $2.30	=	27,600 U
Coconut	=	(0.08 – 0.10) × 120,000 × $2.60	=	6,240 U
White chocolate	=	(0.11 – 0.05) × 120,000 × $3.00	=	21,600 F
Macadamia nut	=	(0.18 – 0.15) × 120,000 × $3.10	=	11,160 F
All cookies				$ 6,120 F

A summary of the variances is:

Sales-Volume Variance of C.M.

Chocolate chip	$25,200 F
Oatmeal raisin	16,100 U
Coconut	1,040 U
White chocolate	24,600 F
Macadamia nut	20,460 F
All cookies	$53,120 F

Sales-Mix Variance of C.M.

Chocolate chip	$ 7,200 F
Oatmeal raisin	27,600 U
Coconut	6,240 U
White chocolate	21,600 F
Macadamia nut	11,160 F
All cookies	$ 6,120 F

Sales-Quantity Variance of C.M.

Chocolate chip	$18,000 F
Oatmeal raisin	11,500 F
Coconut	5,200 F
White chocolate	3,000 F
Macadamia nut	9,300 F
All cookies	$47,000 F

4.   Debbie's Delight shows a favourable sales-quantity variance because it sold more cookies in total than was budgeted. Together with the higher quantities, Debbie's also sold more of the high-contribution margin white chocolate and macadamia nut cookies relative to the budgeted mix—hence Debbie's also showed a favourable total sales-mix variance.

16-30 (cont'd)

SOLUTION EXHIBIT 16-30
Columnar Presentation of Sales-Volume, Sales-Quantity and Sales-Mix Variances for Debbie's Delight Inc.

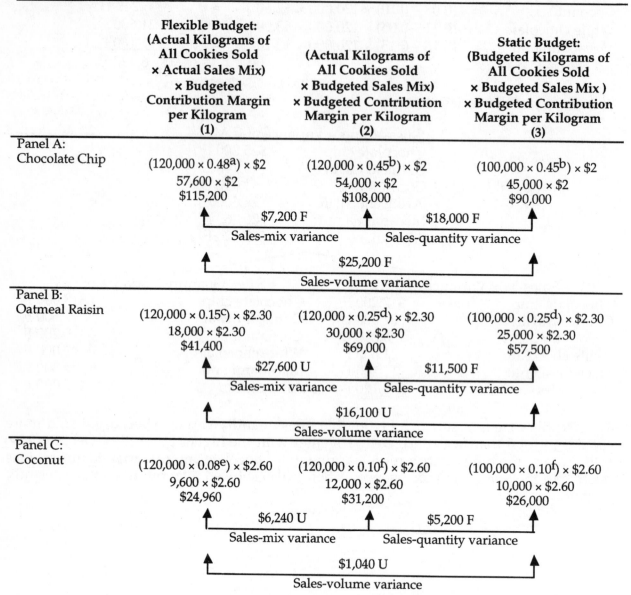

	Flexible Budget: (Actual Kilograms of All Cookies Sold × Actual Sales Mix) × Budgeted Contribution Margin per Kilogram (1)	(Actual Kilograms of All Cookies Sold × Budgeted Sales Mix) × Budgeted Contribution Margin per Kilogram (2)	Static Budget: (Budgeted Kilograms of All Cookies Sold × Budgeted Sales Mix) × Budgeted Contribution Margin per Kilogram (3)
Panel A: Chocolate Chip	$(120{,}000 \times 0.48^a) \times \$2$ $57{,}600 \times \$2$ $\$115{,}200$	$(120{,}000 \times 0.45^b) \times \$2$ $54{,}000 \times \$2$ $\$108{,}000$	$(100{,}000 \times 0.45^b) \times \$2$ $45{,}000 \times \$2$ $\$90{,}000$

$7,200 F — Sales-mix variance

$18,000 F — Sales-quantity variance

$25,200 F — Sales-volume variance

Panel B: Oatmeal Raisin	$(120{,}000 \times 0.15^c) \times \$2.30$ $18{,}000 \times \$2.30$ $\$41{,}400$	$(120{,}000 \times 0.25^d) \times \$2.30$ $30{,}000 \times \$2.30$ $\$69{,}000$	$(100{,}000 \times 0.25^d) \times \$2.30$ $25{,}000 \times \$2.30$ $\$57{,}500$

$27,600 U — Sales-mix variance

$11,500 F — Sales-quantity variance

$16,100 U — Sales-volume variance

Panel C: Coconut	$(120{,}000 \times 0.08^e) \times \$2.60$ $9{,}600 \times \$2.60$ $\$24{,}960$	$(120{,}000 \times 0.10^f) \times \$2.60$ $12{,}000 \times \$2.60$ $\$31{,}200$	$(100{,}000 \times 0.10^f) \times \$2.60$ $10{,}000 \times \$2.60$ $\$26{,}000$

$6,240 U — Sales-mix variance

$5,200 F — Sales-quantity variance

$1,040 U — Sales-volume variance

F = favourable effect on operating income; U = unfavourable effect on operating income.

Actual Sales Mix:				Budgeted Sales Mix:			
[a]Chocolate Chip	=	$57{,}600 \div 120{,}000$	= 48%	[b]Chocolate Chip	=	$45{,}000 \div 100{,}000$	= 45%
[c]Oatmeal Raisin	=	$18{,}000 \div 120{,}000$	= 15%	[d]Oatmeal Raisin	=	$25{,}000 \div 100{,}000$	= 25%
[e]Coconut	=	$9{,}600 \div 120{,}000$	= 8%	[f]Coconut	=	$10{,}000 \div 100{,}000$	= 10%

16-30 (cont'd)

SOLUTION EXHIBIT 16-30 (Cont'd.)
Columnar Presentation of Sales-Volume, Sales-Quantity, and Sales-Mix Variances for Debbie's Delight Inc.

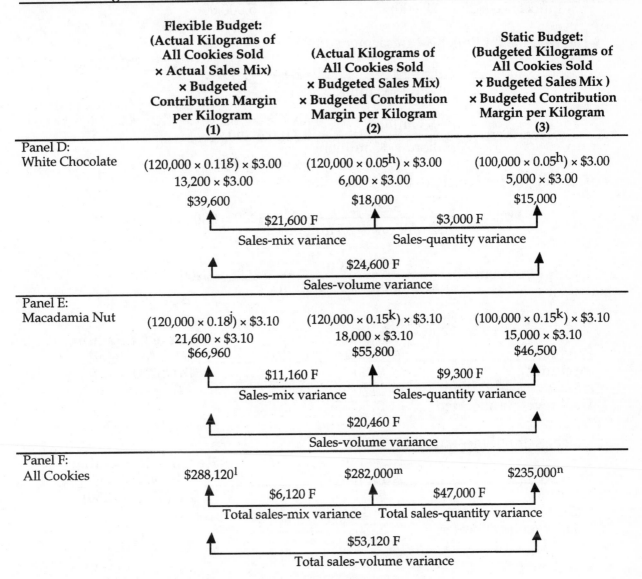

F = favourable effect on operating income; U = unfavourable effect on operating income.

Actual Sales Mix:
[g]White Chocolate = 13,200 ÷ 120,000 = 11%
[j]Macadamia Nut = 21,600 ÷ 120,000 = 18%

[l]$115,200 + $41,400 + $24,960
$\qquad$ + $39,600 + $66,960 = $288,120

Budgeted Sales Mix:
[h]White Chocolate = 5,000 ÷ 100,000 = 5%
[k]Macadamia Nut = 15,000 ÷ 100,000 = 15%

[m]$108,000 + $69,000 + $31,200
$\qquad$ + $18,000 + $55,800 = $282,000

[n]$90,000 + $57,500 + $26,000
$\qquad$ + $15,000 + $46,500 = $235,000

16-32 (50-60 min.) **Revenue allocation, bundled products.**

1a.   Stand-alone revenues in 2003:

Fraîche ($100 × 20,000)	$2,000,000
Désarmer ($80 × 37,500)	3,000,000
Innocence ($250 × 20,000)	5,000,000

The weights for Fraîche + Désarmer suite:

$$\text{Fraîche:} \quad \frac{\$2 \text{ million}}{\$2 \text{ million} + \$3 \text{ million}} \times \$150 = \$60$$

$$\text{Désarmer:} \quad \frac{\$3 \text{ million}}{\$2 \text{ million} + \$3 \text{ million}} \times \$150 = \$90$$

The weights for Fraîche + Innocence suite:

$$\text{Fraîche:} \quad \frac{\$2 \text{ million}}{\$2 \text{ million} + \$5 \text{ million}} \times \$280 = \$80$$

$$\text{Innocence:} \quad \frac{\$5 \text{ million}}{\$2 \text{ million} + \$5 \text{ million}} \times \$280 = \$200$$

b.   Fraîche + Désarmer suite:

Product	Revenue Allocated	Revenue Remaining to be Allocated
Désarmer	$ 80	$70 ($150 – $80)
Fraîche	70	0
Total revenue allocated	$150	

Fraîche + Innocence suite:

Product	Revenue Allocated	Revenue Remaining to be Allocated
Innocence	$250	$30 ($280 – $250)
Fraîche	30	0
Total revenue allocated	$280	

16-32 (cont'd)

2. Each product will be considered as a primary product and first incremental product. An average revenue is the final revenue allocation to the product. This approach is illustrated below.

Fraîche + Désarmer suite:

Fraîche

Allocation as the primary product	$100
Allocation as the incremental product ($150 – $80)	70
Total	$170
Allocation ($170 ÷ 2)	$ 85

Désarmer

Allocation as the primary product	$ 80
Allocation as the incremental product ($150 – $100)	50
Total	$130
Allocation ($130 ÷ 2)	$ 65

According to this approach, Fraîche's revenue allocation is $85 and Désarmer's revenue allocation is $65 out of the total suite revenue of $150.

Fraîche + Innocence suite:

Fraîche

Allocation as the primary product	$100
Allocation as the incremental product ($280 – $250)	30
Total	$130
Allocation ($130 ÷ 2)	$ 65

Innocence

Allocation as the primary product	$250
Allocation as the incremental product ($280 – $100)	180
Total	$430
Allocation ($430 ÷ 2)	$215

Fraîche is allocated $65 revenue and Innocence is allocated $215 revenue out of the total suite revenue of $280.

An alternative approach is to take into account both the price and the units sold, that is, total revenues from each product when calculating the weights.

On a stand-alone basis, the price of Fraîche plus Désarmer is $100 + $80 = $180.

On a stand-alone basis the revenues are

Fraîche	$2,000,000
Désarmer	3,000,000
Total	$5,000,000

16-32 (cont'd)

So Fraîche accounts for 40% ($2,000,000 ÷ $5,000,000) and Désarmer 60% ($3,000,000 ÷ 5,000,000) of total revenues from Fraîche and Désarmer.

Applying these percentages to the total stand-alone price of $180, we get revenue-weighted prices of $180 × 40% = $72 for Fraîche and $180 × 60% = $108 for Désarmer.

Using these revenue-weighted prices and considering each product as the primary product and then the incremental product:

Fraîche and Désarmer suite:

<u>Fraîche</u>

Allocation as the primary product	$ 72
Allocation as the incremental product ($150 – $108)	42
Total	$114
Allocation ($114 ÷ 2)	$ 57

<u>Désarmer</u>

Allocation as the primary product	$108
Allocation as the incremental product ($150 – $72)	78
Total	$186
Allocation ($186 ÷ 2)	93

On a stand-alone basis, the price of Fraîche + Innocence is $100 + $250 = $350.
On a stand-alone basis, the revenues are

Fraîche	$2,000,000
Innocence	$5,000,000
Total	$7,000,000

So Fraîche accounts for 2/7 ($2,000,000 ÷ $7,000,000) and Innocence 5/7 ($5,000,000 ÷ $7,000,000) of total revenues from Fraîche and Innocence.

Applying these percentages to the total stand-alone price of $350, we get revenue-weighted prices of $350 × 2/7 = $100 for Fraîche and $350 × 5/7 = $250 for Innocence.

Using these revenue-weighted prices and considering each product as the primary product and then the incremental product:

Fraîche and Innocence suite:

<u>Fraîche</u>

Allocation as the primary product	$100
Allocation as the incremental product ($280 – $250)	30
Total	$130
Allocation ($130 ÷ 2)	$ 65

<u>Innocence</u>

Allocation as the primary product	$250
Allocation as the incremental product ($280 – $100)	$180
Total	$430
Allocation ($430 ÷ 2)	$215

16-32 (cont'd)

A summary of the price allocations for the bundled products under different methods follows

	Stand-alone Revenue Allocation (1)	Incremental With Fraîche Primary (2)	Incremental With Désarmer/ Innocence Primary (3)	Shapley Value Based on Price (4)	Shapely Value Based on Revenue-Weighted Price (5)
Fraîche	$ 60	$100	$ 70	$ 85	$ 57
Désarmer	90	50	80	65	93
Total	$150	$150	$150	$150	$150
Fraîche	$ 80	$100	$ 30	$ 65	$ 65
Innocence	200	180	250	215	215
Total	$280	$280	$280	$280	$280

Note that the Shapley value calculations based on price and revenue-weighted prices are the same for Fraîche and Innocence because the same number of units of each of these products is sold (20,000 units). In general, the Shapely value calculations based on revenue-weighted prices gives the most fair allocation of prices to each product in the bundle because it considers not only the prices of each product sold but also the units. Thus, if one of the products in the bundle sells very few units, it gets very few revenues allocated to it even if it sells for a high price. The table above also indicates that the stand-alone revenue allocation method closely approximates the Shapley value calculations based on revenue-weighted prices. Note that columns 2, 3, and 4 in the above table all allocate more revenues with Fraîche-Désarmer bundle to Fraîche because Fraîche sells for a higher price ($100 versus $80). But the allocations in these columns ignore the important fact that Fraîche sells far fewer units than Désarmer (20,000 versus 37,500).

16-34 (60 min.) **Customer-profitability analysis**

1. Solution Exhibit 16-34 shows the customer-profitability analysis. Alternative rankings are:
   a. Customer-level operating income
      1. Brothers $507,440
      2. April   459,390
      3. Suitors   123,140

   b. Gross margin/Net revenues
      1. Suitors, $304,800 ÷ $863,600   35.29%
      2. Brothers, $572,000 ÷ $1,830,400   31.25
      3. April, $501,600 ÷ $2,340,800   21.43

   c. Customer-level operating income/Net revenues
      1. Brothers, $507, 440 ÷ $1,830,400   27.72%
      2. April, $459,390 ÷ $2,340,800   19.63
      3. Suitors, $123,140 ÷ $863,600   14.26

A breakdown of the revenues at list prices is:

	April	Brothers	Suitors
Revenues at list prices	100.00%	100.00%	100.00%
Discount	30.00	20.00	15.00
Sales returns	3.50	6.20	17.11
Cost of goods sold	52.25	50.74	43.93
Gross margin	14.25	23.06	23.96
Customer-level costs	1.20	2.60	14.28
Customer-level operating Income	13.05%	20.46%	9.68%

The following conclusions relate to these percentages:

April – has high price discounting as its major differential to Brothers
Brothers – has lower price discounting than April and lower sales returns than Suitors
Suitors – has highest sales returns and highest customer-level costs

2. Key challenges facing Sims are:
   a. Reduce level of price discounting, especially by April,
   b. Reduce level of sales returns, especially by Suitors, and
   c. Reduce level of customer-level costs, especially by Suitors.

The ABC cost system highlights areas where the Suitors account is troublesome—it has a high number of orders, a high number of customer visits, a high number of rushed deliveries, and a high number of sales returns. Sims needs to consider whether this high level of activity can be reduced without reducing customer revenues.

16-34 (cont'd)

SOLUTION EXHIBIT 16-34
Customer-Profitability Analysis for Zoot's Suits

	April	Brothers	Suitors
Revenues at list prices			
$44 \times 400 \times \$200; 62 \times 200 \times \$200; 212 \times 30 \times \$200$	$3,520,000	$2,480,000	$1,272,000
Discount			
$44 \times 400 \times \$60^a; 62 \times 200 \times \$40^b; 212 \times 30 \times \$30^c$	1,056,000	496,000	190,800
Net revenues before returns	2,464,000	1,984,000	1,081,200
Sales returns			
$880 \times \$140; 960 \times \$160; 1,280 \times \$170$	123,200	153,600	217,600
Net revenues	2,340,800	1,830,400	863,600
Cost of goods sold			
$16,720^d \times 110; 11,440^e \times 110; 5,080^f \times 110$	1,839,200	1,258,400	558,800
Gross margin	501,600	572,000	304,800
Customer-level costs			
Order processing			
$44, 62, 212 \times \$245$	10,780	15,190	51,940
Customer visits			
$8, 12, 22 \times \$1,430$	11,440	17,160	31,460
Delivery—regular			
$41, 48, 166 \times \$300$	12,300	14,400	49,800
Delivery—rushed			
$3, 14, 46 \times \$850$	2,550	11,900	39,100
Returns processing			
$4, 6, 16 \times \$185$	740	1,110	2,960
Return stocking fee			
$880, 960, 1,280 \times \$5$	4,400	4,800	6,400
Total customer-level costs	42,210	64,560	181,660
Customer-level operating income	$ 459,390	$ 507,440	$ 123,140

[a] $\$200 - \$140 = \$60$
[b] $\$200 - \$160 = \$40$
[c] $\$200 - \$170 = \$30$
[d] $(44 \times 400) - 880 = 16,720$
[e] $(62 \times 200) - 960 = 11,440$
[f] $(212 \times 30) - 1,280 = 5,080$

16-36 (40 min.) **Customer loyalty clubs and profitability analysis.**

1.

Gold Program

Revenues

2,430 × 20 × ($200 × 0.90)	$ 8,748,000
2,430 × 30 × ($200 × 0.80)	11,664,000
2,430 × 10 × ($200 × 0.70)	3,402,000
Total revenues	23,814,000

Variable Costs

Hotel variable costs, 2,430 × 60 × $65	9,477,000

Wine Costs

2,430 × 50 × $5	607,500
2,430 × 10 × $20	486,000

Restaurant costs

2,430 × 20 × $10	486,000
2,430 × 30 × $15	1,093,500
2,430 × 10 × $20	486,000
Total variable costs	12,636,000
Contribution margin	$11,178,000

Silver Program

Revenues

8,340 × 20 × ($200 × 0.90)	$30,024,000
8,340 × 15 × ($200 × 0.80)	20,016,000
Total revenues	50,040,000

Variable Costs

Hotel variable costs, 8,340 × 35 × $65	18,973,500
Wine costs, 8,340 × 35 × $5	1,459,500

Restaurant Costs

8,340 × 20 × $10	1,668,000
8,340 × 15 × $15	1,876,500
Total variable costs	23,977,500
Contribution margin	$26,062,500

Bronze Program

Revenues, 80,300 × 10 × ($200 × 0.90)	$144,540,000

Variable costs

Hotel variable costs, 80,300 × 10 × $65	52,195,000
Wine costs 80,300 × 10 × $5	4,015,000
Restaurant costs 80,300 × 10 × $10	8,030,000
Total variable costs	64,240,000
Contribution margin	$ 80,300,000

16-36 (cont'd)

No Program

Revenues, 219,000 × 1 × $200	$43,800,000
Variable costs, 219,000 × 1 × $65	14,235,000
Contribution margin	$29,565,000

Loyalty Program	Total Revenues	Variable Costs	Contribution Margin	Contrib. Margin Total Revenues
Gold	$ 23,814,000	$ 12,636,000	$ 11,178,000	46.94%
Silver	50,040,000	23,977,500	26,062,500	52.08
Bronze	144,540,000	64,240,000	80,300,000	55.56
No program	43,800,000	14,235,000	29,565,000	67.50
Total	$262,194,000	$115,088,500	$147,105,500	

The no-program group of customers has the highest contribution margin per revenue dollar. However, it comprises only 16.71% ($43,800,000 ÷ $262,194,000) of total revenues. The gold program has the lowest contribution margin per revenue dollar. However, it is misleading to evaluate each program in isolation. A key aim of loyalty programs is to promote a high frequency of return business. The contribution margin to total revenue ratio of each program in isolation does not address this issue.

2.

Revenues	$262,194,000
Variable costs	115,088,500
Contribution margin	147,105,500
Fixed costs	140,580,000
Operating income	$ 6,525,500

3. Number of room nights

Gold, 2,430 × 60	145,800
Silver, 8,340 × 35	291,900
Bronze, 80,300 × 10	803,000
No program, 219,000 × 1	219,000
	1,459,700

Average room rate per night: $\dfrac{\$262,194,000}{1,459,700} = \$179.62$

Average variable cost per night: $\dfrac{\$115,088,500}{1,459,700} = \$78.84$

16-36 (cont'd)

4. Sherriton Hotels has fixed costs of $140,580,000. A key challenge is to attract a high number of repeat business customers. Loyalty programs aim to have customers return to Sherriton multiple times. Their aim is increasing the revenues beyond what they would be without the program. It is to be expected that the higher the level of nights stayed, the greater the inducements necessary to keep attracting the customer to return. However, given the low level of variable costs to room rates, there is considerable cushion available for Sherriton to offer high inducements for frequent stayers.

Sherriton could adopt a net present value analysis of customers who are in the different loyalty clubs. It would be informative for Sherriton to have information on how much of each customer's total lodging industry expenditures it captures. It may well want to give higher levels of inducements to frequent stayers if the current program attracts only, say, 30% of each of its frequent customer's total business in cities where it has lodging properties available.

16-38 (15-20 min.) **Customer profitability, responsibility for environmental clean-up, ethics.**

1. Customer-profitability analysis examines how individual customers differ in their profitability. The revenues and costs of each customer can be estimated with varying degrees of accuracy. Revenues of IF typically would be known at the time of sale. Many costs also would be known, e.g., the cost of materials used to manufacture the fluids sold to each customer. A major area of uncertainty is future costs associated with obligations arising from the sale. There are several issues here:

(a) Uncertainty as to the existence and extent of legal liability. Each customer has primary responsibility to dispose of their own toxic waste. Papandopolis needs to determine the extent of IF's liability. It would be necessary to seek legal guidance on this issue.

(b) Uncertainty as to when the liability will occur. The further in the future, the lower the amount of the liability (assuming discounting for the time value of money occurs.)

(c) Uncertainty as to the amount of the liability given that the liability exists and the date of the liability can be identified. Papandopolis faces major difficulties here—see the answer to requirement 2.

Many companies argue that uncertainties related to (a), (b), and (c) make the inclusion of "hard-dollar estimates meaningless." However, at a minimum, a contingent liability should be recognized and included in the internal customer-profitability reports.

2. Papandopolis' controller may believe that if estimates of future possible legal exposure are sufficiently uncertain they should not be recorded. His concern about "smoking guns" may have a very genuine basis—that is, if litigation arises, third parties may misrepresent Papandopolis' concerns to the detriment of IF. Any written comments that she makes may surface 5 or 10 years later and be interpreted as "widespread knowledge" within IF that they have responsibility for large amounts of environmental clean-up.

Given this background, Papandopolis still has the responsibility to prepare a report in an objective and competent way. Moreover, she has visited 10 customer sites and has details as to their toxic-waste-handling procedures. If Acme goes bankrupt and has no liability insurance, one of the "deep pockets" available to meet toxic-waste-handling costs is likely to be IF. At a minimum, she should report the likely bankruptcy and the existence of IF's contingent liability for toxic-waste clean-up in her report. Whether she quantifies this contingent liability is a more difficult question. Papandopolis has limited information available to make a meaningful quantification. She is not an employee of Acme Metal and has no information about Acme's liability insurance. Moreover, she does not know what other parties (such as other suppliers) are also jointly liable to pay Acme's clean-up costs.

The appropriate course appears to be to highlight the contingent liability but not to attempt to quantify it.

CHAPTER 17
PROCESS COSTING SYSTEMS

17-2   Process-costing systems separate costs into cost categories according to the timing of when costs are introduced into the process. Often, only two cost classifications, direct materials and conversion costs, are necessary. Direct materials are frequently added at one point in time, often the start or the end of the process and all conversion costs are added at about the same time, but in a pattern different from direct materials costs.

17-4   The five key steps in process costing follow:
Step 1: Summarize the flow of physical units of output.
Step 2: Compute output in terms of equivalent units.
Step 3: Compute equivalent unit costs.
Step 4: Summarize total costs to account for.
Step 5: Assign these costs to units completed and to units in ending Work in Process.

17-6   Three inventory methods associated with process costing are:
• Weighted average.
• First-in, first-out.
• Standard costing.

17-8   FIFO computations are distinctive because they assign the cost of the earliest equivalent units available (starting with equivalent units in beginning work in process inventory) to units completed and transferred out, and the cost of the most recent equivalent units worked on during the period to ending work in process inventory. In contrast, the weighted-average method costs units completed and transferred out and in ending work in process at the same average cost.

17-10   A major advantage of FIFO is that managers can judge the performance in the current period independently from the performance in the preceding period.

17-12   Standard-cost procedures are particularly appropriate to process-costing systems where there are various combinations of materials and operations. Standard-cost procedures avoid the intricacies involved in detailed tracking with weighted-average or FIFO methods when there are frequent price variations over time.

17-14   No. Transferred-in costs or previous department costs are costs incurred in a previous department that have been charged to a subsequent department. These costs may be costs incurred in that previous department during this accounting period or a preceding accounting period.

17-16 (25 min.)   **Equivalent units: no beginning inventory.**

1.   Direct materials cost per unit ($720,000 ÷ 10,000) $ 72
     Conversion cost per unit ($760,000 ÷ 10,000)   76
     Assembly Department cost per unit $148

2.   Solution Exhibit 17-16A calculates the equivalent units of direct materials and conversion costs in the Assembly Department of International Electronics in February 2000.

Solution Exhibit 17-16B computes equivalent units costs

Direct materials cost per unit $ 72
Conversion cost per unit   80
Assembly Department cost per unit $152

3.   The difference in the Assembly Department cost per unit calculated in requirements 1 and 2 arises because the costs incurred in January and February are the same but fewer equivalent units of work are done in February relative to January. In January, all 10,000 units introduced are fully completed resulting in 10,000 equivalent units of work done with respect to direct materials and conversion costs. In February, of the 10,000 units introduced, 10,000 equivalent units of work is done with respect to direct materials but only 9,500 equivalent units of work is done with respect to conversion costs. The Assembly Department cost per unit is therefore higher.

17-16 (cont'd)

SOLUTION EXHIBIT 17-16A
Steps 1 and 2: Summarize Output in Physical Units and Compute Equivalent Units
Assembly Department of International Electronics for February 2002

	(Step 1) Physical Units	(Step 2) Equivalent Units	
Flow of Production		Direct Materials	Conversion Costs
Completed and transferred out during current period	9,000	9,000	9,000
Add work in process, ending* 1,000 × 100%; 1,000 × 50%	1,000	1,000	500
Total accounted for	10,000	10,000	9,500
Deduct work in process, beginning	0	0	0
Started during current period	10,000		
Work done in current period only		10,000	9,500

*Degree of completion in this department: direct materials, 100%; conversion costs, 50%.

SOLUTION EXHIBIT 17-16B
Step 3: Compute Equivalent Unit Costs
Assembly Department of International Electronics for February 2002

	Direct Materials	Conversion Costs
Costs added during February (given)	$720,000	$760,000
Divide by equivalent units of work done in February 2002 (from Soln Exh 17-16A)	÷ 10,000	÷ 9,500
Cost per equivalent unit of work done in February 2002	$ 72	$ 80

17-18 (25 min.) **No beginning inventory, materials introduced in middle of process.**

1.   Solution Exhibit 17-18A shows equivalent units of work done in the current period of Chemical P, 50,000; Chemical Q, 35,000; Conversion costs, 45,000.

2(a)   Solution Exhibit 17-18B calculates cost per equivalent unit of work done in the current period for chemical P, Chemical Q, and conversion costs.

2(b)   Solution Exhibit 17-18C summarizes the total Mixing Department costs for July 2002, and assigns these costs to units completed (and transferred out) and to units in ending work in process.

SOLUTION EXHIBIT 17-18A
Steps 1 and 2: Summarize Output in Physical Units and Compute Equivalent Units
Mixing Department of Vaasa Chemicals for July 2002

Flow of Production	(Step 1) Physical Units	(Step 2) Equivalent Units		
		Chemical P	Chemical Q	Conversion Costs
Completed and transferred out during current period	35,000	35,000	35,000	35,000
Add work in process, ending*	15,000†			
15,000 × 100%; 15,000 × 0%; 15,000 × 66 2/3%		15,000	0	10,000
Total accounted for	50,000	50,000	35,000	45,000
Deduct work in process, beginning	0	0	0	0
Started during current period	50,000			
Work done in current period only		50,000	35,000	45,000

*Degree of completion in this department: chemical P, 100%; chemical Q, 0%; conversion costs, 66 2/3%.

Note that chemical Q has not been included in the ending work in process, since the ending WIP is 66 2/3% complete and chemical Q is only added when the units are 75% or three-fourths complete.

†Ending work in process   = Beginning work in process + Units started – Units completed
        = 0 + 50,000 – 35,000 = 15,000 units

SOLUTION EXHIBIT 17-18B
Step 3 : Compute Equivalent Unit Costs
Mixing Department of Vaasa Chemicals for July 2002

	Chemical P	Chemical Q	Conversion Costs
Costs added during July (given)	$250,000	$70,000	$135,000
Divide by equivalent units of work done in July 2002 (from Solution Exhibit 17-18A)	÷ 50,000	÷35,000	÷45,000
Cost per equivalent unit of work done in July 2002	$ 5	$ 2	$ 3

SOLUTION EXHIBIT 17-18C

Step 4: Summarize Total Costs to Account For and Assign These Costs to Units Completed, and Units in Ending Work in Process
Mixing Department of Vaasa Chemicals for July 2002

	Chemical P			Chemical Q			Conversion Costs			Total Production Costs
	Equivalent Unit (1)	Cost per Equivalent Unit (2)	Total Costs (3)=(1) × (2)	Equivalent Unit (4)	Cost per Equivalent Unit (5)	Total Costs (6)=(4) × (5)	Equivalent Unit (7)	Cost per Equivalent Unit (8)	Total Costs (9)=(7) × (8)	(10)= (3)+(6)+(9)
Panel A: Total Costs to Account For Work done in July (from Solution Exhibit 17-18B)	50,000	$5	$250,000	35,000	$2	$70,000	45,000	$3	$135,000	$455,000
Panel B: Assignment of Costs Completed and transferred out: (35,000 physical units)	35,000[1]	$5	$175,000	35,000[1]	$2	$70,000	35,000[1]	$3	$105,000	$350,000
Work in process, ending (15,000 physical units)	15,000[1]	$5	75,000	0[1]	$2	0	10,000[1]	$3	30,000	105,000
Accounted for	50,000	$5	$250,000	35,000		$70,000	45,000		$135,000	$455,000

[1] From Solution Exhibit 17-18A.

17-20 (25 min.) FIFO method. See Solution Exhibit 17-20 below.

SOLUTION EXHIBIT 17-20
Step 4: Summarize Total Costs to Account For and Assign These Costs to Units Completed, and Units in Ending Work in Process Using the FIFO Method
Chatham Company for July 2002

	Direct Materials			Conversion Costs			Total Production Costs
	Equivalent Units (1)	Cost per Equivalent Unit (2)	Total Costs (3)=(1)×(2)	Equivalent Units (4)	Cost per Equivalent Unit (5)	Total Costs (6)=(4)×(5)	(7)=(3)+(6)
Panel A: Total Costs to Account For							
Work in process, beginning	20,000	$6.00	$120,000	14,000	$10.00	$140,000	$260,000
Work done in current period only	30,000	$7.00	210,000	28,000	$10.75	301,000	511,000
To account for	50,000		$330,000	42,000		$441,000	$771,000
Panel B: Assignment of Costs							
Completed and transferred out:							
Work in process, beginning	20,000	$6.00	$120,000	14,000	$10.00	$140,000	$260,000
Work done in current period to complete beginning work in process	0*	$7.00	0	6,000†	$10.75	64,500	64,500
Total from beginning inventory	20,000		120,000	20,000		204,500	324,500
Started and completed	14,000‡	$7.00	98,000	14,000‡	$10.75	150,500	248,500
Total completed and transferred out	34,000		218,000	34,000		355,000	573,000
Work in process, ending	16,000	$7.00	112,000	8,000	$10.75	86,000	198,000
Accounted for	50,000		$330,000	42,000		$441,000	$771,000

*Beginning work in process is 100% complete as to direct materials so zero equivalent units of direct materials need to be added to complete beginning work in process.
†Beginning work in process is 70% complete, which equals 14,000 equivalent units of conversion costs. To complete the 20,000 physical units of beginning work in process, 6,000 (20,000 – 14,000) equivalent units of conversion costs need to be added.
‡34,000 total equivalent units completed and transferred out minus 20,000 equivalent units completed and transferred from beginning inventory equals 14,000 equivalent units.

17-22 (15 min.) **Weighted-average method, equivalent units and unit costs.**

Under the weighted-average method, equivalent units are calculated as the equivalent units of work done to date. Solution Exhibit 17-22 shows equivalent units of work done to date for the Satellite Assembly Division of Aerospatiale for direct materials and conversion costs.

SOLUTION EXHIBIT 17-22

Steps 1 and 2: Summarize Output in Physical Units and Compute Equivalent Units Weighted-Average Method of Process Costing, Satellite Assembly Division of Aerospatiale for May 2002

Flow of Production	(Step 1) Physical Units (given)	(Step 2) Equivalent Units Direct Materials	Conversion Costs
Work in process beginning	8		
Started during current period	50		
To account for	58		
Completed and transferred out during current period	46	46.0	46.0
Work in process, ending* (12 × 60%; 12 × 30%)	12	7.2	3.6
Accounted for	58		
Work done to date		53.2	49.6

*Degree of completion in this department: direct materials, 60%; conversion costs, 30%.

17-24 (15 min.) FIFO method, equivalent units and unit costs.

1.   Under the FIFO method, equivalent units are calculated as the equivalent units of work done in the current period only. Solution Exhibit 17-24 shows equivalent units of work done in May 2002 in the Assembly Department of Aerospatiale for direct materials and conversion costs.

SOLUTION EXHIBIT 17-24
Steps 1 and 2: Summarize Output in Physical Units and Compute Equivalent Units FIFO Method of Process Costing, Satellite Assembly Division of Aerospatiale for May 2002

Flow of Production	(Step 1) Physical Units	(Step 2) Equivalent Units Direct Materials	(Step 2) Equivalent Units Conversion Costs
Work in process, beginning (given)	8	(work done before current	
Started during current period (given)	50	period)	
To account for	58		
Completed and transferred out during current period:			
From beginning work in process§	8		
8 × (100% − 90%); 8 × (100% − 40%)		0.8	4.8
Started and completed	38†		
38 × 100%, 38 × 100%		38.0	38.0
Work in process, ending* (given)	12		
12 × 60%; 12 × 30%		7.2	3.6
Accounted for	58		
Work done in current period only		46.0	46.4

§Degree of completion in this department: direct materials, 90%; conversion costs, 40%.
†46 physical units completed and transferred out minus 8 physical units completed and transferred out from beginning work-in-process inventory.
*Degree of completion in this department: direct materials, 60%; conversion costs, 30%.

2.

Direct material costs	$32,200,000
Equivalent units	46
Cost per equivalent unit	$700,000
Conversion costs	$13,920,000
Equivalent units	46.4
Cost per equivalent units	$300,000

17-26 (25-30 min.) **Standard-costing method, assigning costs.**

1.   The calculations of equivalent units for direct materials and conversion costs are identical to the calculations of equivalent units under the FIFO method. Solution Exhibit 17-24 shows the equivalent unit calculations under standard costing given by the equivalent units of work done in May 2002 in the Assembly Department.

2.   Solution Exhibit 17-26 summarizes the total costs to account for, and assigns these costs to, units completed and transferred out, and to units in ending work in process.

3.   Solution Exhibit 17-26 shows the direct materials and conversion cost variances for

Direct materials	$230,000 U
Conversion costs	$232,000 U

17-26 (cont'd)

SOLUTION EXHIBIT 17-26

Steps 3, 4, and 5: Compute Equivalent Unit Costs, Summarize Total Costs to Account For, and Assign Costs to Units Completed and to Units in Ending Work in Process

Use of Standard Costs in Process Costing, Satellite Assembly Division of Aerospatiale for May 2002.

	Total Production Costs	Direct Materials	Conversion Costs
(Step 3) Standard cost per equivalent unit (given)		$ 695,000	$ 295,000
Work in process, beginning (given)			
Direct materials, 7.2 × $695,000; Conversion costs, 3.2 × $295,000	$ 5,948,000		
Costs added in current period at standard costs			
Direct materials, 46.0 × $695,000; Conversion costs, 46.4 × $295,000	45,658,000	$31,970,000	$13,688,000
(Step 4) Costs to account for	$51,606,000		
(Step 5) Assignment of costs at standard costs:			
Completed and transferred out (46 units):			
Work in process, beginning (8 units)	$ 5,948,000		
Direct materials added in current period	556,000	0.8* × $695,000	
Conversion costs added in current period	1,416,000		4.8* × $295,000
Total from beginning inventory	7,920,000		
Started and completed (38 units)	37,620,000	38† × $695,000	+ 38† × $295,000
Total costs of units transferred out	45,540,000		
Work in process, ending (12 units)			
Direct materials	5,004,000	7.2# × $695,000	
Conversion costs	1,062,000		3.6# × $295,000
Total work in process, ending	6,066,000		
Total costs accounted for	$51,606,000		
Summary of variances for current performance:			
Costs added in current period at standard prices (see above)		$31,970,000	$13,688,000
Actual costs incurred (given)		32,200,000	13,920,000
Variance		$ 230,000 U	$ 232,000 U

*Equivalent units to complete beginning work in process from Solution Exhibit 17-24, Step 2.
†Equivalent units started and completed from Solution Exhibit 17-24, Step 2.
#Equivalent units in work in process, ending from Solution Exhibit 17-24, Step 2.

17-28 (35-40 min.) Transferred-in costs, FIFO method.

1. The calculations for equivalent tonnes of solvent completed and ending work in process for each cost element are exactly as in requirement 1 of Exercise 17-27 shown in Solution Exhibit 17-27A.

2. Solution Exhibit 17-28A presents computations of equivalent unit costs under the FIFO method.

3. Solution Exhibit 17-28B presents a summary of total costs to account for and assigns these costs to tonnes completed and to tonnes in ending work in process using the FIFO method.

SOLUTION EXHIBIT 17-28A
Step 3: Compute Equivalent Unit Costs Under the FIFO Method
Cooking Department of Hideo Chemicals for June 2002

	Transferred-in Costs	Direct Materials	Conversion Costs
Equivalent unit costs of beginning work in process			
Work in process, beginning (given)	$39,200	—	$18,000
Divide by equivalent units of beginning work in process (from Solution Exhibit 17-27A)	÷ 40	—	÷ 30
Cost per equivalent unit of beginning work in process	$ 980	—	$ 600
Equivalent unit costs of work done in current period only			
Costs added in current period (given)	$85,600	$36,000	$49,725
Divide by equivalent units of work done in current period (from Solution Exhibit 17-27A)	÷ $80	÷ 90	÷ 75
Cost per equivalent unit of work done in current period only	$ 1,070	$ 400	$ 663

17-11

17-28 (cont'd)

SOLUTION EXHIBIT 17-28B

Step 4: Summarize Total Costs to Account For and Assign These Costs to Units Completed, and Units in Ending Work in Process Using the FIFO Method Cooking Department of Hideo Chemicals June 2002

	Transferred-in Costs			Direct Materials			Conversion Costs			Total Production Costs
	Equivalent Units (1)	Cost per Equivalent Unit (2)	Total Costs (3)=(1)×(2)	Equivalent Units (4)	Cost per Equivalent Unit (5)	Total Costs (6)=(4)×(5)	Equivalent Units (7)	Cost per Equivalent Unit (8)	Total Costs (9)=(7)×(8)	(10)= (3)+(6)+(9)
Panel A: Total Costs to Account For										
Work in process, beginning (from Solution Exhibit 17-28A)	40	$980	$ 39,200	0	—	$ 0	30	$600	$18,000	$ 57,200
Work done in current period only (from Solution Exhibit 17-28A)	80	$1,070	85,600	90	$400	36,000	75	$663	49,725	172,925
To account for	120		$124,800	90		$36,000	105		$67,725	$228,525
Panel B: Assignment of Costs										
Completed and transferred out: (90 physical tons)										
Work in process, beginning (40 physical tons)	40	$980	$ 39,200	0	—	$ 0	30	$600	$18,000	$57,200
Work done in current period to complete beginning work in process	0*		0	40†	$400	16,000	10‡	$663	6,630	22,630
Total from beginning inventory	40		39,200	40		16,000	40		24,630	79,830
Started and completed (50 physical tons)	50‖	$1,070	53,500	50‖	$400	20,000	50‖	$663	33,150	106,650
Total completed and transferred out (90 physical tons)	90§		92,700	90§		36,000	90§		57,780	186,480
Work in process, ending (30 physical tons)	30§	$1,070	32,100	0§	$400	0	15§	$663	9,945	42,045
Accounted for	120		$124,800	90		$36,000	105		$67,725	$228,525

*Beginning work in process is 100% complete as to transferred-in costs so zero equivalent tons of transferred-in costs need to be added to complete beginning work in process.

†Beginning work in process is 0% complete as to direct materials, which equals 0 equivalent tons of direct materials. To complete the 40 physical tons of direct materials need to be added.

‡Beginning work in process is 75% complete as to conversion costs, which equals 30 equivalent tons of conversion costs. To complete the 40 physical tons of beginning work in process, 10 (40 − 30) equivalent tons of conversion costs need to be added.

‖90 total equivalent tons completed and transferred out (Solution Exhibit 17-28A) minus 40 equivalent tons completed and transferred from beginning inventory equals 50 equivalent tons.

§From Solution Exhibit 17-28A.

17-30 (25 min.) Weighted-average method.

1.   Solution Exhibit 17-30A shows equivalent units of work done in the current period of

| Direct materials | 80 equivalent units |
| Conversion costs | 85 equivalent units |

2.   Solution Exhibit 17-30B calculates cost per equivalent unit of beginning work in process and of work done in the current period for direct materials and conversion costs.

3.   Solution Exhibit 17-30C summarizes the total Assembly Department costs for October 2002, and assigns these costs to units completed (and transferred out) and to units in ending work in process using the weighted-average method.

SOLUTION EXHIBIT 17-30A
Steps 1 and 2: Summarize Output in Physical Units and Compute Equivalent Units
Assembly Department of Global Defence Inc. for October 2002

Flow of Production	(Step 1) Physical Units	(Step 2) Equivalent Units Direct Materials	Conversion Costs
Completed and transferred out during current period		9090	90
Add work in process, ending*	10		
10 × 100†%; 10 × 70%		10	7
Total accounted for	100	100	97
Deduct work in process, beginning§	20		
20 × 100†%; 20 × 60%		20	12
Started during current period	80	—	—
Work done in current period only		80	85

†Direct materials are 100% complete in work in process inventories since all direct materials are introduced at the beginning of the Assembly Process.

*Degree of completion in this department: direct materials, 100%; conversion costs, 50%.

§Degree of completion in this department: direct materials, 100%; conversion costs, 60%.

17-30 (cont'd)

SOLUTION EXHIBIT 17-30B
Step 3: Compute Equivalent Unit Costs:
Assembly Department of Global Defence Inc. for October 2002

	Direct Materials	Conversion Costs
Equivalent unit costs of beginning work in process		
Work in process, beginning (given)	$ 460,000	$120,000
Divide by equivalent units of beginning work in process (from Solution Exhibit 17-27A)	÷ 20	÷ 12
Cost per equivalent unit of beginning work in process	$ 23,000	$ 10,000
Equivalent unit costs of work done in current period only		
Costs added in current period (given)	$2,000,000	$935,000
Divide by equivalent units of work done in current period (from Solution Exhibit 17-30A)	÷ 80	÷ 85
Cost per equivalent unit of work done in current period only	$ 25,000	$ 11,000

SOLUTION EXHIBIT 17-30C

Step 4: Summarize Total Costs to Account For and Assign These Costs to
Units Completed, and Units in Ending Work in Process Using the Weighted-Average Method
Assembly Department of Global Defence Inc. for October 2002

		Direct Materials				Conversion Costs			Total Production Costs
	Equivalent Units (1)	Cost per Equivalent Unit (2)	Total Costs (3)=(1)×(2)	Equivalent Units (4)	Cost per Equivalent Unit (5)	Total Costs (6)=(4)×(5)			(7)=(3)+(6)
Panel A: Total costs to account for									
Work in process, beginning from Solution Exhibit 17-28B)	20	$23,000	$ 460,000	12	$10,000	$ 120,000			$ 580,000
Work done in current period only (from Solution Exhibit 17-28B)	80	$25,000	2,000,000	85	$11,000	935,000			2,935,000
To account for	100	$24,600*	2,460,000	97	$10,876.29†	$1,055,000			$3,515,000
Panel B: Assignment of costs									
Complete and transferred out: (90 physical units)	90‡	$24,600	$2,214,000	90‡	$10,876.29	$ 978,866			$3,192,866
Work in process, ending (10 physical units)	10‡	$24,600	246,000	7‡	$10,876.29	76,134			322,134
Accounted for	100		$2,460,000	97		$1,055,000			$3,515,000

*Weighted-average cost per equivalent unit of direct materials = Total direct materials costs divided by total equivalent units of direct materials
$2,460,000 ÷ 100 = $24,600
†Weighted-average cost per equivalent unit of conversion costs = Total conversion costs divided by total equivalent units of conversion costs
$1,055,000 ÷ 97 = $10,876.29
‡From Solution Exhibit 17-30A.

17-32 (20 min.) **FIFO method (continuation of 17-30 and 17-31).**

1.   The equivalent units of work done in the Assembly Department in October 2002 for direct materials and conversion costs are the same as in Problem 17-30 and are shown in Solution Exhibit 17-30A.

2.   The cost per equivalent unit of work done in the Assembly Department in October 2002 for direct materials and conversion costs are calculated in Problem 17-30 in Solution Exhibit 17-30B.

3.   Solution Exhibit 17-32 summarizes the total Assembly Department costs for October 2002, and assigns these costs to units completed (and transferred out) and units in ending work in process under the FIFO method.

The cost per equivalent unit of beginning inventory and of work done in the current period differ:

	Beginning Inventory	Work Done in Current Period
Direct materials	$23,000	$25,000
Conversion costs	$10,000	$11,000

The following table summarizes the costs assigned to units completed and those still in process under the weighted-average and FIFO process-costing methods for our example.

	Weighted Average (Solution Exhibit 17-30C)	FIFO (Solution Exhibit 17-32)	Difference
Cost of units completed and transferred out	$3,192,866	$3,188,000	−$4,866
Work in process, ending	322,134	327,000	+$4,866
Total costs accounted for	$3,515,000	$3,515,000	

The FIFO ending inventory is higher than the weighted-average ending inventory by $4,866. This is because, FIFO assumes that all the lower-cost prior-period units in work in process are the first to be completed and transferred out while ending work in process consists of only the higher-cost current-period units. The weighted-average method, however, smoothes out cost per equivalent unit by assuming that more of the higher-cost units are completed and transferred out, while some of the lower-cost units in beginning work in process are placed in ending work in process. Hence, in this case, the weighted-average method results in a higher cost of units completed and transferred out and a lower ending work-in-process inventory relative to FIFO.

17-32 (cont'd)

SOLUTION EXHIBIT 17-32

Step 4: Summarize Total Costs to Account For and Assign These Costs to Units Completed, and Units in Ending Work in Process Using the FIFO Method Testing Department of Global Defence Inc. for October 2002

	Direct Materials			Conversion Costs			Total Production Costs
	Equivalent Units (1)	Cost per Equivalent Unit (2)	Total Costs (3)=(1)×(2)	Equivalent Units (4)	Cost per Equivalent Unit (5)	Total Costs (6)=(4)×(5)	(7)=(3)+(6)
Panel A: Total costs to account for							
Work in process, beginning (from Solution Exhibit 17-30B)	20	$23,000	$ 460,000	12	$10,000	$ 120,000	$ 580,000
Work done in current period only (from Solution Exhibit 17-30B)	80	$25,000	2,000,000	85	$11,000	935,000	2,935,000
To account for	100		2,460,000	97		$1,055,000	$3,515,000
Panel B: Assignment of costs							
Completed and transferred out: (90 physical units)							
Work in process, beginning (20 physical units)	20	$23,000	$460,000	12	$10,000	$ 120,000	$ 580,000
Work done in current period to complete beginning work in process	0*	$25,000	0	8†	$11,000	88,000	88,000
Total from beginning inventory	20		460,000	20		208,000	668,000
Started and completed (70 physical units)	70†	$25,000	1,750,000	70‡	$11,000	770,000	2,520,000
Total completed and transferred out (90 physical units)	90		2,210,000	90		978,000	3,188,000
Work in process, ending (10 physical units)	10§	$25,000	250,000	7§	$11,000	77,000	327,000
Accounted for	100		$2,460,000	97		$1,055,000	$3,515,000

*Beginning work in process is 100% complete as to direct materials so zero equivalent units of direct materials need to be added to complete beginning work in process.

†Beginning work in process is 60% complete as to conversion costs, which equals 12 equivalent units of conversion costs. To complete the 20 physical units of beginning work in process, 8 (20 − 12) equivalent units of conversion costs need to be added.

‡90 total equivalent units completed and transferred out (Solution Exhibit 17-30) minus 20 equivalent units completed and transferred from beginning inventory equals 70 equivalent units.

§From Solution Exhibit 17-30A.

17-34 (30 min.) Transferred-in costs, FIFO costing (continuation of 17-33).

1.   As explained in Problem 17-33, requirement 1, transferred-in costs are 100% complete and direct materials are 0% complete in both beginning and ending work in process inventory.

2.   The equivalent units of work done in October 2002 in the Testing Department for transferred-in costs, direct materials and conversion costs are exactly as in Solution Exhibit 17-33A.

3.   Solution Exhibit 17-34A calculates the cost per equivalent unit of beginning work in process and of work done in October 2002 in the Testing Department for transferred-in costs, direct materials, and conversion costs.

4.   Solution Exhibit 17-34B summarizes total Testing Department costs for October 2002, and assigns these costs to units completed and transferred out and to units in ending work in process using the FIFO method.

5.   Journal entries:
   i.   Work in Process—Testing Department   3,188,000
            Work in Process—Assembly Department   3,188,000
         Cost of goods completed and transferred out
            during October from the Assembly Dept. to
            the Testing Dept.

   ii. Finished Goods   9,281,527
            Work in Process—Testing Department   9,281,527
         Cost of goods completed and transferred out
            during October from the Testing Department
            to Finished Goods inventory

17-34 (cont'd)

SOLUTION EXHIBIT 17-34A
Step 3: Compute Equivalent Unit Costs Under the FIFO Method
Testing Department of Global Defence Inc. for October 2002

	Transferred-in Costs	Direct Materials	Conversion Costs
Equivalent unit costs of beginning work in process			
Work in process, beginning (given)	$ 980,060	—	$ 331,800
Divide by equivalent units of beginning work in process (from Solution Exhibit 17-33A)	÷ 30	—	÷ 21
Cost per equivalent unit of beginning work in process	$ 32,668.67	—	$ 15,800
Equivalent unit costs of work done in current period only			
Costs added in current period (given)	$3,188,000	$3,885,000	$1,581,000
Divide by equivalent units of work done in current period (from Solution Exhibit 17-33A)	÷ 90	÷ 105	÷ 93
Cost per equivalent unit of work done in current period only	$35,422.22	$ 37,000	$ 17,000

17-34 (cont'd)

SOLUTION EXHIBIT 17-34B

Step 4: Summarize Total Costs to Account For and Assign These Costs to Units Completed, and Units in Ending Work in Process Using the FIFO Method Testing Department of Global Defence Inc. for October 2002

	Transferred-in Costs			Direct Materials			Conversion Costs			Total Production Costs
	Equivalent Units	Cost per Equivalent Unit	Total Costs	Equivalent Units	Cost per Equivalent Unit	Total Costs	Equivalent Units	Cost per Equivalent Unit	Total Costs	
	(1)	(2)	(3)=(1)×(2)	(4)	(5)	(6)=(4)×(5)	(7)	(8)	(9)=(7)×(8)	(10)=(3)+(6)+(9)
Panel A: Total Costs to Account For										
Work in process, beginning (from Solution Exhibit 17-34A)	30	$32,668.67	$ 980,050	0	—	$ 0	21	$15,800	$ 331,800	$1,311,860
Work done in current period only (from Solution Exhibit 17-34A)	90	$35,422.22	3,188,000	105	$37,000	3,885,000	93	$17,000	1,581,000	8,654,000
To account for	120		$4,168,060	105		$3,885,000	114		$1,912,800	$9,965,860
Panel B: Assignment of Costs										
Completed and transferred out (105 physical units)										
Work in process, beginning (30 physical units)	30	$32,668.67	$ 980,060	0		$ 0	21	$15,800	$ 331,800	$1,311,860
Work done in current period to complete beginning work in process	0*		0	30†	$37,000	1,110,000	9‡	$17,000	153,000	1,263,000
Total from beginning inventory	30		980,060	30		1,110,000	30		153,000	2,574,860
Started and completed (75 physical units)	75||	$35,422.22	2,656,667	75||	$37,000	2,775,000	75||	$17,000	1,275,000	6,706,667
Total completed and transferred out (105 physical units)	105§		3,636,727	105§		3,885,000	105§		1,759,800	9,281,527
Work in process, ending (15 physical tons)	15§	$35,422.22	531,333	0§	$37,000	0	9§	$17,000	153,000	684,333
Accounted for	120		$4,168,060	105		$3,885,000	114		$1,912,800	$9,965,860

*Beginning work in process is 100% complete as to transferred-in costs so zero equivalent tons of transferred-in costs need to be added to complete beginning work in process.

†Beginning work in process is 0% complete as to direct materials, which equals 0 equivalent tons of direct materials. To complete the 30 physical tons of beginning work in process, 30 equivalent tons of direct materials need to be added.

‡Beginning work in process is 70% complete as to conversion costs, which equals 21 equivalent tons of conversion costs. To complete the 30 physical tons of beginning work in process, 9 (30 − 21) equivalent tons of conversion costs need to be added.

||105 total equivalent tons completed and transferred out (Solution Exhibit 17-31A) minus 30 equivalent tons completed and transferred from beginning inventory equals 75 equivalent tons.

§From Solution Exhibit 17-33A.

17-36 (5-10 min.) **Journal entries (continuation of 17-35).**

1. Work in Process—Forming Department   70,000
            Accounts Payable   70,000
       To record direct materials purchased and
            used in production during April

2. Work in Process—Forming Department   42,500
            Various Accounts   42,500
       To record Forming Department conversion
            costs for April

3. Work in Process—Finishing Department   104,000
            Work in Process—Forming Department   104,000
       To record cost of goods completed and transferred out
            in April from the Forming Department
            to the Finishing Department

Work in Process—Forming Department		
Beginning inventory, April 1	9,625	3. Transferred out to
1. Direct materials	70,000	Work in Process–finishing 104,000
2. Conversion costs	42,500	
Ending inventory, April 30	18,125	

17-38 (30 min.)   **Transferred-in costs, weighted average (related to 17-35 through 17-37) (Chapter Appendix I).**

1.   Solution Exhibit 17-38A computes the equivalent units of work done in April 2002 in the Finishing Department for transferred-in costs, direct materials, and conversion costs.

Solution Exhibit 17-38B calculates the cost per equivalent unit of beginning work in process and of work done in April 2002 in the Finishing Department for transferred-in costs, direct materials, and conversion costs.

Solution Exhibit 17-38C summarizes total Finishing Department costs for April 2002, and assigns these costs to units completed and transferred out and to units in ending work in process using the weighted-average method.

2.   Journal entries:

i.	Work in Process—Finishing Department	104,000	
	Work in Process—Forming Department		104,000
	Cost of goods completed and transferred out during April from the Forming Department to the Finishing Department		
ii.	Finished Goods	168,552	
	Work in Process—Finishing Department		168,552
	Cost of goods completed and transferred out during April from the Finishing Department to Finished Goods inventory		

17-38 (cont'd)

SOLUTION EXHIBIT 17-38A
Steps 1 and 2: Summarize Output in Physical Units and Compute Equivalent Units
Finishing Department of Star Toys for April 2002

| | (Step 1) | (Step 2) Equivalent Units | | |
Flow of Production	Physical Units	Transferred-in Costs	Direct Materials	Conversion Costs
Completed and transferred out during current period	2,100	2,100	2,100	2,100
Add work in process, ending*	400			
(400 × 100%; 400 × 0%; 400 × 60%)		400	0	120
Total accounted for	2,500	2,500	2,100	2,220
Deduct work in process, beginning‖	500			
(500 × 100%; 500 × 0%; 500 × 60%)		500	0	300
Transferred in during current period	2,000			
Work done in current period only		2,000	2,100	1,920

*Degree of completion in this department: transferred-in costs, 100%; direct materials, 0%; conversion costs, 30%.

‖Degree of completion in this department: transferred-in costs, 100%; direct materials, 0%; conversion costs, 60%.

SOLUTION EXHIBIT 17-38B
Step 3: Compute Equivalent Unit Costs Under the Weighted-Average Method
Finishing Department of Star Toys for April 2002

	Transferred-in Costs	Direct Materials	Conversion Costs
Equivalent unit costs of beginning work in process			
Work in process, beginning (given)	$ 17,750	—	$ 7,250
Divide by equivalent units of beginning work in process (from Solution Exhibit 17-38A)	÷ 500	—	÷ 300
Cost per equivalent unit of beginning work in process	$ 35.50	—	$24.167
Equivalent unit costs of work done in current period only			
Costs added in current period (given)	$104,000	$23,100	$38,400
Divide by equivalent units of work done in current period (from Solution Exhibit 17-38A)	÷ 2,000	÷ 2,100	÷ 1,920
Cost per equivalent unit of work done in current period only	$ 52	$ 11	$ 20

17-23

17-38 (cont'd)

SOLUTION EXHIBIT 17-38C

Step 4: Summarize Total Costs to Account For and Assign These Costs to Units Completed, and Units in Ending Work in Process Using the Weighted-Average Method Finishing Department of Star Toys for April 2002

	Transferred-in Costs			Direct Materials			Conversion Costs			Total Production Costs
	Equivalent Unit (1)	Cost per Equivalent Unit (2)	Total Costs (3)=(1)×(2)	Equivalent Unit (4)	Cost per Equivalent Unit (5)	Total Costs (6)=(4)×(5)	Equivalent Unit (7)	Cost per Equivalent Unit (8)	Total Costs (9)=(7)×(8)	(10)=(3)+(6)+(9)
Panel A: Total Costs to Account for:										
Work in process, beginning (from Solution Exhibit 17-38B)	500	$35.50	$ 17,750	0	—	$ 0	300	$24.167	$ 7,250	$ 25,000
Work done in current period only (from Solution Exhibit 17-38B)	2,000	$52.00	104,000	2,100	$11	23,100	1,920	$20	38,400	165,500
To account for	2,500	$48.70*	$121,750	2,100	$11†	$23,100	2,220	$20.563‡	$45,650	$190,500
Panel B: Assignment of Costs Completed and transferred out: (2,100 physical units)	2,100**	$48.70	$102,270	2,100**	$11	$23,100	2,100**	$20.563	$43,182	$168,552
Work in process, ending (400 physical units)	400**	$48.70	19,480	0**	—	0	120**	$20.563	2,468	21,948
Accounted for	2,500		$121,750	2,100		$23,100	2,220		$45,650	$190,500

*Weighted-average cost per equivalent unit of transferred-in costs = Total transferred-in costs divided by total equivalent units of transferred-in costs
= $121,750 ÷ 2,500 = $48.70

†Weighted average costs per equivalent unit of direct materials = Total direct materials costs divided by total equivalent units of direct materials
= $23,100 ÷ 2,100 = $11.

‡Weighted-average cost per equivalent unit of conversion costs = Total conversion costs divided by total equivalent units of conversion costs
= $45,650 ÷ 2,220 = $20.563

*From Exhibit 17-38A.

17-40 (45 min.)   **Transferred-in costs, weighted average and FIFO (Chapter Appendix I).**

1.   Solution Exhibit 17-40A computes the equivalent units of work done in week 37 in the Drying and Packaging Department for transferred-in costs, direct materials, and conversion costs.

2.   Solution Exhibit 17-40B calculates the cost per equivalent unit of beginning work in process and of work done in week 37 in the Drying and Packaging Department for transferred-in costs direct materials, and conversion costs.

Solution Exhibit 17-40C summarizes total drying and packaging Department costs for week 37, and assigns these costs to units completed and transferred out and to units in ending work in process using the weighted-average method.

3.   Solution Exhibit 17-40D calculates the cost per equivalent unit of beginning work in process and of work done in week 37 in the Drying and Packaging Department for transferred-in costs, direct materials, and conversion costs.

Solution Exhibit 17-40E summarizes total Drying and Packaging Department costs for week 37, and assigns these costs to units completed and transferred out and to units in ending work in process using the FIFO method.

17-40 (cont'd)

SOLUTION EXHIBIT 17-40A
Steps 1 and 2: Summarize Output in Physical Units and Compute Equivalent Units
Drying and Packaging Department of Frito-Lay Inc. for Week 37

Flow of Production	(Step 1) Physical Units	(Step 2) Equivalent Units		
		Transferred-in Costs	Direct Materials	Conversion Costs
Completed and transferred out during current period	5,250	5,250	5,250	5,250
Add work in process, ending*	1,000			
(1,000 × 100%; 1,000 × 0%;1,000 × 40%)		1,000	0	400
Total accounted for	6,250	6,250	5,250	5,650
Deduct work in process, beginning ‖	1,250			
(1,250 × 100%; 1,250 × 0%; 1,250 × 80%)		1,250	0	1,000
Transferred in during current period	5,000			
Work done in current period only		5,000	5,250	4,650

*Degree of completion in this department: transferred-in costs, 100%; direct materials, 0%; conversion costs, 40%.

‖Degree of completion in this department: transferred-in costs, 100%; direct materials, 0%; conversion costs, 80%.

SOLUTION EXHIBIT 17-40B
Step 3: Compute Equivalent Unit Costs Under the Weighted-Average Method
Drying and Packaging Department of Frito-Lay Inc. for Week 37

	Transferred-in Costs	Direct Materials	Conversion Costs
Equivalent unit costs of beginning work in process			
Work in process, beginning (given)	$29,000	—	$ 9,060
Divide by equivalent units of beginning work in process (from Solution Exhibit 17-40A)	÷ 1,250	—	÷ 1,000
Cost per equivalent unit of beginning work in process	$ 23.20	—	$ 9.06
Equivalent unit costs of work done in current period only			
Costs added in current period (given)	$96,000	$25,200	$38,400
Divide by equivalent units of work done in current period (from Solution Exhibit 17-40A)	÷ 5,000	÷ 5,250	÷ 4,650
Cost per equivalent unit of work done in current period only	$ 19.20	$ 4.80	$ 8.258

17-40 (cont'd)

SOLUTION EXHIBIT 17-40C

Step 4: Summarize Total Costs to Account For and Assign These Costs to Units Completed, and Units in Ending Work in Process Using the Weighted-Average Method Drying and Packaging Department of Frito-Lay for Week 37

	Transferred-in Costs			Direct Materials			Conversion Costs			Total Production Costs
	Equivalent Units	Cost per Equivalent Unit	Total Costs	Equivalent Units	Cost per Equivalent Unit	Total Costs	Equivalent Units	Cost per Equivalent Unit	Total Costs	
	(1)	(2)	(3)=(1)×(2)	(4)	(5)	(6)=(4)×(5)	(7)	(8)	(9)=(7)×(8)	(10)=(3)+(6)+(9)
Panel A: Total Costs to Account for Work in process, beginning (from Solution Exhibit 17-40B)	1,250	$23.20	$ 29,000	0	—	$ 0	1,000	$9.060	$ 9,060	38,060
Work done in current period only (from Solution Exhibit 17-40B)	5,000	$19.20	96,000	5,250	$4.80	25,200	4,650	$8.258	38,400	159,600
To account for	6,250	$20.00*	$125,000	5,250	$4.80†	$25,200	5,650	$8.400‡	$47,460	$197,660
Panel B: Assignment of Costs Completed and transferred out: (5,250 physical units)	5,250**	$20.00	$105,000	5,250**	$4.80	$25,200	5,250**	$8.400	$44,100	$174,300
Work in process, ending (1,000 physical units)	1,000**	$20.00	20,000	0**	—	0	400**	$8.400	3,360	23,360
Accounted for	6,250		$125,000	5,250		$25,200	5,650		$47,460	$197,660

*Weighted-average cost per equivalent unit of transferred-in costs = Total transferred-in costs divided by total equivalent units of transferred-in costs = $125,000 ÷ 6,250 = $20.

†Weighted-average costs per equivalent unit of direct materials = Total direct materials costs divided by total equivalent units of direct materials = $25,200 ÷ 5,250 = $4.80.

‡Weighted-average cost per equivalent unit of conversion costs = Total conversion costs divided by total equivalent units of conversion costs = $47,460 ÷ 5,650 = $8.40.

**From Solution Exhibit 17-40A.

17-40 (cont'd)

SOLUTION EXHIBIT 17-40D
Step 3: Compute Equivalent Unit Costs Under the FIFO Method
Drying and Packaging Department of Frito-Lay Inc. for Week 37

	Transferred-in Costs	Direct Materials	Conversion Costs
Equivalent unit costs of beginning work in process			
Work in process, beginning (given)	$28,920	—	$ 9,060
Divide by equivalent units of beginning work in process (from Solution Exhibit 17-40A)	÷ 1,250	—	÷ 1,000
Cost per equivalent unit of beginning work in process	$23.136	—	$ 9.06
Equivalent unit costs of work done in current period only			
Costs added in current period (given)	$94,000	$25,200	$38,400
Divide by equivalent units of work done in current period (from Solution Exhibit 17-40A)	÷ 5,000	÷ 5,250	÷ 4,650
Cost per equivalent unit of work done in current period only	$ 18.80	$ 4.80	$ 8.258

17-40 (cont'd)

SOLUTION EXHIBIT 17-40E

Step 4: Summarize Total Costs to Account For and Assign These Costs to Units Completed, and Units in Ending Work in Process Using the FIFO Method Drying and Packaging Department of Frito-Lay for Week 37

	Transferred-in Costs			Direct Materials			Conversion Costs			Total Production Costs
	Equivalent Units (1)	Cost per Equivalent Unit (2)	Total Costs (3)=(1)×(2)	Equivalent Units (4)	Cost per Equivalent Unit (5)	Total Costs (6)=(4)×(5)	Equivalent Units (7)	Cost per Equivalent Unit (8)	Total Costs (9)=(7)×(8)	(10)=(3)+(6)+(9)
Panel A: Total Costs to Account for Work in process, beginning (from Solution Exhibit 17-40D)	1,250	$23.18¢	$ 28,920	0	—	$ 0	1,000	$9.06	$ 9,060	$37,980
Work done in current period only (from Solution Exhibit 17-40D)	5,000		94,000	5,250		25,200	4,650		38,400	157,600
To account for	6,250	$18.80	$122,920	5,250	$4.80	$25,200	5,650	$8.258	$47,460	$195,580
Panel B: Assignment of Costs Completed and transferred out (5,250 physical units):										
Work in process, beginning (1,250 physical units)	1,250	$23.13¢	$ 28,920	0	—	$ 0	1,000	$9.06	$ 9,060	$ 37,980
Work done in current period to complete beginning work in process	0*		0	1,250†	$4.80	6,000	250‡	$8.258	2,065	8,065
Total from beginning inventory	1,250		28,920	1,250		6,000	1,250		11,125	46,045
Started and completed (4,000 physical units)	4,000¹¹	$18.80	75,200	4,000¹¹	$4.80	19,200	4,000¹¹	$8.258	33,032	127,432
Total completed and transferred out (5,250 physical units)	5,250§		104,120	5,250§		25,200	5,250§		44,157	173,477
Work in process, ending (1,000 physical units)	1,000§	$18.80	18,800	0§		0	400§	$8.258	3,303	22,103
Accounted for	6,250		$122,920	5,250		$25,200	5,650		$47,460	$195,580

*Beginning work in process is 100% complete as to transferred-in costs so zero equivalent units of transferred-in costs need to be added to complete beginning work in process.

†Beginning work in process is 0% complete as to direct materials, which equals 0 equivalent units of direct materials. To complete the 1,250 physical units of beginning work in process, 1,250 equivalent units of direct materials need to be added.

‡Beginning work in process is 80% complete as to conversion costs, which equals 1,000 equivalent units of conversion costs. To complete the 1,250 physical units of beginning work in process, 250 (1,250 – 1,000) equivalent units of conversion costs need to be added.

¹¹5,250 total equivalent units completed and transferred out (Solution Exhibit 17-40A) minus 1,250 equivalent units completed and transferred from beginning inventory equals 4,000 equivalent units.

§From Solution Exhibit 17-40A.

17-42 (15 min.) **Operation costing (Chapter Appendix II).**

Costs of Work Order 815 and Work Order 831 are as follows:

	Work Order 815	Work Order 831
Number of units (pairs)	1,000	5,000
Direct materials costs	$30,000	$50,000
Conversion costs:		
Cutting (1,000; 5,000 × $10)	10,000	50,000
Sewing (1,000; 5,000 × $15)	15,000	75,000
Lining (1,000; 0 × $8)	8,000	—
Packing (1,000; 5,000 × $2)	2,000	10,000
Total costs	$65,000	$185,000

Total cost per unit

$$\frac{\$65,000}{1,000} = \$65$$

$$\frac{\$185,000}{5,000} = \$37$$

17-44 (20-25 min.) **Equivalent unit computations, benchmarking, ethics.**

1.   The reported monthly cost per equivalent unit of either direct materials or conversion costs is lower when the plant manager overestimates the percentage of completion of ending work in process; the overestimate increases the denominator and thus decreases the cost per equivalent whole unit. By reporting a lower cost per equivalent unit, the plant manager increases the likelihood of being in the top three ranked plants for the benchmarking comparisons.

A plant manager can manipulate the monthly estimate of percentage of completion by understating the number of steps yet to be undertaken before a suit becomes a finished good.

2.   There are several options available:
   a.   Major shows the letters to the line executive to whom the plant managers report in a hard-line way (say, the corporate manager of manufacturing). This approach is appropriate if the letters allege it is the plant managers who are manipulating the percentage of completion estimates.
   b.   Major herself shows the letters to the plant managers. This approach runs the danger of the plant managers ignoring or reacting negatively to someone to whom they do not report in a line-mode questioning their behaviour. Much will depend here on how Major raises the issue. Unsigned letters need not have much credibility unless they contain specific details.

17-44 (cont'd)

c. Major discusses the letters with the appropriate plant controllers without including the plant manager in the discussion. While the plant controller has responsibility for preparing the accounting reports from the plant, the plant controller in most cases reports hard-line to the plant manager. If this reporting relationship exists, Major may create a conflict of interest situation for the plant controller. Only if the plant controller reports hard-line to the corporate controller and dotted-line to the plant manager should Major show the letters to the plant controller without simultaneously showing them to the plant manager.

3. The plant controller's ethical responsibilities to Major and to Leisure Suits should be the same. These include:
   - The plant controller is expected to have the competence to make equivalent unit computations. This competence does not always extend to making estimates of the percentage of completion of a product. In Leisure Suits' case, however, the products are probably easy to understand and observe. Hence, a plant controller could obtain reasonably reliable evidence on percentage of completion at a specific plant.
   - The plant controller should not allow the possibility of the division being written-up favourably in the company newsletter to influence the way equivalent unit costs are computed.

4. Major could seek evidence on possible manipulations as follows:
   a. Have plant controllers report detailed breakdowns on the stages of production and then conduct end-of-month audits to verify the actual stages completed for ending work in process.
   b. Examine trends over time in ending work in process. Divisions that report low amounts of ending work in process relative to total production are not likely to be able to greatly affect equivalent cost amounts by manipulating percentage of completion estimates. Divisions that show sizable quantities of total production in ending work in process are more likely to be able to manipulate equivalent cost computations by manipulating percentage of completion estimates.

CHAPTER 18
SPOILAGE, REWORK, AND SCRAP

18-2   Spoilage—unacceptable units of production that are discarded or sold for net disposal proceeds.

Reworked units—unacceptable units of production that are subsequently reworked and sold as acceptable finished goods.

Scrap—product that has minimal (frequently zero) sales value compared with the sales value of the main or joint product(s).

18-4   Abnormal spoilage is spoilage that is not expected to arise under efficient operating conditions. Costs of abnormal spoilage are losses, measures of inefficiency that should be written off directly as losses for the accounting period.

18-6   Normal spoilage typically is expressed as a percentage of good units passing the inspection point. Given actual spoiled units, we infer abnormal spoilage as follows:

Abnormal spoilage = Actual spoilage − Normal spoilage

18-8   Yes. Normal spoilage rates should be computed from the good output or from the <u>normal</u> input, not the <u>total</u> input. Normal spoilage is a given percentage of a certain output base. This base should never include abnormal spoilage, which is included in total input. Abnormal spoilage does not vary in direct proportion to units produced, and to include it would cause the normal spoilage count to fluctuate irregularly but not vary in direct proportion to the output base.

18-10   No. If abnormal spoilage is detected at a different point in the production cycle than normal spoilage, then unit costs would differ. If, however normal and abnormal spoilage are detected at the same point in the production cycle, their unit costs would be the same.

18-12   No. Unless there are special reasons for charging rework to jobs that contained the bad units, the costs of extra materials, labour, and so on are usually charged to manufacturing overhead and allocated to all jobs.

18-14   A company is justified in inventorying scrap when its estimated net realizable value is significant and the time between storing it and selling or reusing it may be quite long.

18-16 (25 min.) **Weighted-Average Method, spoilage**

1.   Solution Exhibit 18-16A calculates the equivalent units of work done for each cost element in September 2002.

2.   Solution Exhibit 18-16B presents computations of the cost per equivalent unit of beginning inventory and of work done in the current period for each cost element under the weighted-average method.

3.   Solution Exhibit 18-16C presents a summary of total costs to account for and assigns these costs to units completed, normal spoilage, abnormal spoilage, and to units in ending work in process using the weighted-average method.

SOLUTION EXHIBIT 18-16A
Steps 1 and 2: Summarize Output in Physical Units and Compute Equivalent Units
Microchip Department of Superchip Company for September 2002

Flow of Production	(Step 1) Physical Units	(Step 2) Equivalent Units	
		Direct Materials	Conversion Costs
Good units completed and transferred out during current period	1,400	1,400	1,400
Normal spoilage†	210		
210 × 100%; 210 × 100%		210	210
Abnormal spoilage‡	190		
190 × 100%; 190 × 100%		190	190
Work in process, ending§	300		
300 ×100%; 300 × 40%		300	120
Total accounted for	2,100	2,100	1,920
Deduct work in process, beginning	400		
400 × 100%; 400 × 30%		400	120
Started during current period	1,700		
Work done in current period only		1,700	1,800

† Normal spoilage is 15% of good units transferred out: 15% × 1,400 = 210 units; Degree of completion of normal spoilage in this department: direct materials, 100%; conversion costs, 100%.

‡ Abnormal spoilage = Actual spoilage – Normal spoilage = 400 – 210 = 190 units; Degree of completion of abnormal spoilage in this department: direct materials, 100%; conversion costs, 100%.

§ Degree of completion in this department: direct materials, 100%; conversion costs, 40%.

  Degree of completion in this department: direct materials, 100%; conversion costs, 30%.

18-16 (cont'd)

SOLUTION EXHIBIT 18-16B
Step 3: Compute Equivalent Unit Costs:
Microchip Department of Superchip Company for September 2002

	Direct Materials	Conversion Costs
Equivalent unit costs of beginning work in process		
Work in process, beginning (given)	$ 64,000	$ 10,200
Divide by equivalent units in beginning work in process (from Solution Exhibit 18-16A)	÷ 400	÷ 120
Cost per equivalent unit of beginning work in process	$ 160	$ 85
Equivalent unit costs of work done in current period only		
Costs added in current period (given)	$378,000	$153,600
Divide by equivalent units of work done in current period (from Solution Exhibit 18-16A)	÷ 1,700	÷ 1,800
Costs per equivalent unit of work done in current period only	$ 222.35	$ 85.33

18-16 (cont'd)

SOLUTION EXHIBIT 18-16C

Step 4: Summarize Total Costs to Account For and Assign These Costs to Units Completed, Units Spoiled and Units in Ending Work in Process Using the Weighted-Average Method, Microchip Department of Superchip for September 2002

	Direct Materials			Conversion Costs			Total Production Costs
	Equivalent Units (1)	Cost per Equivalent Unit (2)	Total Costs (3)=(1)x(2)	Equivalent Units (4)	Cost per Equivalent Unit (5)	Total Costs (6)=(4)x(5)	(7)=(3)+(6)
Panel A: Total Costs to Account For							
Work in process, beginning (from Solution Exhibit 18-16B)	400	$160	$ 64,000	120	$85	$ 10,200	$ 74,200
Work done in current period only (from Solution Exhibit 18-16B)	1,700	$222.35	378,000	1,800	$85.33	153,600	531,600
To account for	2,100	$210.476*	$442,000	1,920	$85.3125†	$163,800	$605,800
Panel B: Assignment of costs							
Good units completed and transferred out (1,400 units):							
Costs before adding normal spoilage	1,400‡	$210.476	$294,667	1,400‡	$85.3125	$119,437	$414,104
Normal spoilage (15% of good units)	210‡	$210.476	44,200	210‡	$85.3125	17,916	62,116
Total costs of good units transferred out			338,867			137,353	476,220
(A)							
Abnormal spoilage (4,000 – normal spoilage)	190‡	$210.476	39,990	190‡	$85.3125	16,209	56,199
(B)							
Work in process, ending	300‡	$210.476	63,143	120‡	$85.3125	10,238	73,381
(C)							
Accounted for	2,100		$442,000	1,920		$163,800	$605,800
(A)+(B)+(C)							

*Weighted-average cost per equivalent unit of direct materials = Total costs of direct materials divided by total equivalent units of direct materials = 442,000 ÷ 2,100 = $210.4762

†Weighted-average cost per equivalent unit of conversion costs = Total conversion costs divided by total equivalent units of conversion costs = 163,800 ÷ 1,920 = $85.3125

‡From Solution Exhibit 18-16A.

18-18 (30 min.) **Standard costing method, spoilage.**

1.   Solution Exhibit 18-16A shows the computation of the equivalent units of work done in September 2002 for direct materials (1,700 units) and conversion costs (1,800 units).

2.   The direct materials cost per equivalent unit of beginning work in process and of work done in September 2002 is the standard cost of $205 given in the problem.
       The conversion cost per equivalent of beginning work in process and of work done in September 2002 is the standard cost of $80 given in the problem.

3.   Solution Exhibit 18-18 summarizes the total costs to account for, and assigns these costs to units completed, normal spoilage, abnormal spoilage and ending work in process using the standard costing method.

SOLUTION EXHIBIT 18-18

Step 4: Summarize Total Costs to Account For and Assign These Costs to Units Completed, Units Spoiled and Units in Ending Work in Process Using Standard Costs, Microchip Department of Superchip for September 2002

	Direct Materials			Conversion Costs			Total Production Costs
	Equivalent Units (Solution Exhibit 18-16A) (1)	Cost per Equivalent Unit (2)	Total Costs (3)=(1)x(2)	Equivalent Units (Solution Exhibit 18-16A) (4)	Cost per Equivalent Unit (5)	Total Costs (6)=(4)x(5)	(7)=(3)+(6)
Panel A: Total Costs to Account For							
Work in process, beginning	400	$205	$ 82,000	120	$80	$ 9,600	$ 91,600
Work done in current period only	1,700	$205	348,500	1,800	$80	144,000	574,500
To account for	2,100	$205	$430,500	1,920	$80	$153,600	$584,100
Panel B: Assignment of Costs							
Good units completed and transferred out (1,400 units):							
Costs before adding normal spoilage	1,400	$205	$287,000	1,400	$80	$112,000	$399,000
Normal spoilage (15% of good units)	210	$205	43,050	210	$80	16,800	59,850
(A) Total costs of good units transferred out			330,050			128,800	458,850
(B) Abnormal spoilage (400 – normal spoilage)	190	$205	38,950	190	$80	15,200	54,150
(C) Work in process, ending	300	$205	61,500	120	$80	9,600	71,100
(A)+(B)+(C) Accounted for	2,100		$430,500	1,920		$153,600	$584,100

18-20 (5-10 min.) **Normal and abnormal spoilage in units.**

1. Total spoiled units   12,000
    Normal spoilage in units 5% × 132,000   6,600
    Abnormal spoilage in units   5,400

2. Abnormal spoilage, 5,400 × $10 $ 54,000
    Normal spoilage, 6,600 × $10   66,000
    Potential savings, 12,000 × $10 $120,000

Regardless of the targeted normal spoilage, abnormal spoilage is non-recurring and avoidable. The targeted normal spoilage rate is subject to change. Many companies have reduced their spoilage to almost zero, which would realize all potential savings. Of course, zero spoilage usually means higher-quality products, more customer satisfaction, more employee satisfaction, and various effects on nonmanufacturing (for example, purchasing) costs of direct materials.

18-22 (25 min.) FIFO method.

1.   The calculation of the cost per equivalent unit of beginning work in process and of work done in the current period for direct materials and conversion costs is the same as in Solution Exhibit 18-21A, since this calculation does not depend on the specific weighted-average or FIFO cost-flow assumption.

2.   Solution Exhibit 18-22 summarizes the total costs to account for, and assigns these costs to units completed, normal spoilage, abnormal spoilage and ending work in process using the FIFO method.

3.   From Solution Exhibit 18-22, under the FIFO method,

$$\text{Cost of a good unit completed (and transferred out)} = \frac{\text{Total production costs of good units transferred out}}{\text{Number of good units completed}}$$

$$= \frac{\$423,950}{20,000} = \$21.1975$$

Note that this cost is higher than the cost per equivalent unit of $18.75 (direct materials, $8.25 and conversion costs, $10.50). Why? Because the cost of good units completed and transferred out also includes the cost of normal spoilage of 15%.

18-22 (cont'd)

SOLUTION EXHIBIT 18-22

Step 4: Summarize Total Costs to Account For, and Assign These Costs to, Units Completed, Units Spoiled and Units in Ending Work in Process Using the FIFO Method
Molding Department of Anderson Plastics for April 2002

		Direct Materials			Conversion Costs			Total
	Equivalent Units (1)	Cost per Equivalent Unit (2)	Total Costs (3)=(1)x(2)	Equivalent Units (4)	Cost per Equivalent Unit (5)	Total Costs (6)=(4)x(5)	Total Production Costs (7)=(3)+(6)
Panel A: Total Costs to Account For							
Work in process, beginning (from Solution Exhibit 18-21A)	15,000	$8.00	$120,000	14,000	$10.00	$140,000	$260,000
Work done in current period only (from Solution Exhibit 18-21A)	25,000	$8.40	210,000	28,000	$10.75	301,000	511,000
To account for	40,000		$330,000	42,000		$441,000	$771,000
Panel B: Assignment of Costs							
Good units completed and transferred out (20,000 physical units):							
Work in process, beginning	15,000	$8.00	$120,000	14,000	$10.00	$140,000	$260,000
Work done in current period to complete beginning work in process	0*	$8.40	0	1,000†	$10.75	10,750	10,750
Total from beginning inventory before normal spoilage			120,000	15,000		150,750	270,750
Started and completed before normal spoilage (5,000 units)	5,000‡	$8.40	42,000	5,000‡	$10.75	53,750	95,750
Normal spoilage (15% of good units = 3,000)	3,000	$8.40	25,200	3,000	$10.75	32,250	57,450
(A) Total costs of good units transferred out			187,200			236,750	423,950
(B) Abnormal spoilage (4,000 – normal spoilage)	1,000	$8.40	8,400	1,000	$10.75	10,750	19,150
(C) Work in process, ending (20,000 units)	16,000	$8.40	134,400	18,000	$10.75	193,500	327,900
(A)+(B)+(C) Accounted for	40,000		$330,000	42,000		$441,000	$771,000

*Beginning work in process is 100% complete as to direct materials so zero equivalent units of direct materials need to be added to complete beginning work in process.

†Beginning work in process is 14/15 complete, as to conversion costs which equals 14,000 equivalent units of conversion costs. To complete the 15,000 physical units of beginning work in process, 1,000 (15,000 – 14,000) equivalent units of conversion costs need to be added.

‡20,000 total equivalent units completed and transferred out (given) minus 15,000 equivalent units completed and transferred out from beginning inventory equal to 5,000 equivalent units.

18-24 (20 min.) Equivalent units, equivalent unit costs, spoilage.

1.   Solution Exhibit 18-24A calculates equivalent units of work done in the current period for direct materials and conversion costs.

2.   Solution Exhibit 18-24B calculates cost per equivalent unit of beginning work in process and of work done in the current period for direct materials and conversion costs.

SOLUTION EXHIBIT 18-24A
Step 1 and Step 2: Summarize Output in Physical Units and Compute Equivalent Units, Gray Manufacturing Company for November 2002

Flow of Production	(Step 1) Physical Units	(Step 2) Equivalent Units	
		Direct Materials	Conversion Costs
Good units completed and transferred out during November 2002	9,000	9,000	9,000
Normal spoilage[†]	100		
100 × 100%; 100 × 100%		100	100
Abnormal spoilage[‡]	50		
50 × 100%; 50 × 100%		50	50
Work in process, ending[§]	2,000		
2,000 × 100%; 2,000 × 30%		2,000	600
Total accounted for	11,150	11,150	9,750
Deduct work in process, beginning [≠]	1,000	1,000	500
1,000 × 100%; 1,000 × 50%			
Started during current period	10,150		
Work done in current period only		10,150	9,250

[†] Degree of completion of normal spoilage: direct materials, 100%; conversion costs, 100%.
[‡] Degree of completion of abnormal spoilage: direct materials, 100%; conversion costs, 100%.
[§] Degree of completion of ending work in process: direct materials, 100%; conversion costs, 30%.
[≠] Degree of completion of beginning work in process: direct materials, 100%; conversion costs, 50%.

18-24 (cont'd)

SOLUTION EXHIBIT 18-24B
Step 3: Compute Equivalent Unit Costs:
Gray Manufacturing Company Inc. for November 2002

	Direct Materials	Conversion Costs
<u>Equivalent unit costs of beginning work in process</u>		
Work in process, beginning (given)	$ 1,300	$ 1,250
Divide by equivalent units in beginning work in process (from Solution Exhibit 18-24A)	÷1,000	÷ 500
Cost per equivalent unit of beginning work in process	$ 1.30	$ 2.50
<u>Equivalent unit costs of work done in current period only</u>		
Costs added in current period (given)	$12,180	$27,750
Divide by equivalent units of work done in current period (from Solution Exhibit 18-24A)	÷10,150	÷ 9,250
Costs per equivalent unit of work done in current period only	$ 1.20	$ 3.00

18-26 (15 min.) **FIFO method, spoilage, equivalent units.**

Solution Exhibit 18-26 calculates equivalent units of work done in the current period for direct materials and conversion costs and the costs per equivalent unit for direct materials and conversion costs.

SOLUTION EXHIBIT 18-26
Summarize Output in Physical Units and Compute Equivalent Units.
First-in, First-out (FIFO) Method of Process Costing with Spoilage
Gray Manufacturing Company for November 2002

Flow of Production	(Step 1) Physical Units	(Step 2) Equivalent Units	
		Direct Materials	Conversion Costs
Work in process, beginning (given)	1,000		
Started during current period (given)	10,150		
To account for	11,150		
Good units completed and transferred out during current period:			
From beginning work in process[II]	1,000	0	500
1,000 × (100% −100%); 1,000 × (100% − 50%)	8,000#	8,000	8,000
Started and completed			
8,000 × 100%; 8,000 × 100%	100	100	100
Normal spoilage*			
100 × 100%; 100 × 100%	50	50	50
Abnormal spoilage[†]			
50 × 100%; 50 × 100%	2,000	2,000	600
Work in process, ending[‡]			
2,000 × 100%; 2,000 × 30%	11,150		
Accounted for		10,150	9,250
Work done in current period only			

[II]Degree of completion in this department: direct materials, 100%; conversion costs, 50%.
#9,000 physical units completed and transferred out minus 1,000 physical units completed and transferred out from beginning work-in-process inventory.
*Degree of completion of normal spoilage in this department: direct materials, 100%; conversion costs, 100%.
[†]Degree of completion of abnormal spoilage in this department: direct materials, 100%; conversion costs, 100%.
[‡]Degree of completion in this department: direct materials, 100%; conversion costs, 30%.

Cost of direct materials	$12,180
Equivalent units	10,150
Cost per equivalent unit	$1.20
Cost of conversion costs	$27,750
Equivalent units	9,250
Cost per equivalent unit	$3.00

18-28 (15 min.) **Reworked units, costs of rework.**

1.   The two alternative approaches to accounting for the materials costs of reworked units are:
    (a)   To charge the costs of rework to the current period as a separate expense item. This approach would highlight to White Goods the costs of the supplier problem.
    (b)   To charge the costs of the rework to manufacturing overhead.

2.   The $50 tumbler cost is the cost of the actual tumblers included in the washing machines. The $44 tumbler units from the new supplier units were never used in any washing machine and that supplier is now bankrupt.

3.   The total costs of rework due to the defective tumbler units include:
    (a)   The labour and other conversion costs spent on substituting the new tumbler units.
    (b)   The costs of any extra negotiations to obtain the replacement tumbler units.
    (c)   Any higher price the existing supplier may have charged to do a rush order for the replacement tumbler units.

18-30 (30 min.) Weighted-average method, spoilage.

1. Solution Exhibit 18-30, Panel A, calculates the equivalent units of work done to date for each cost category in March 2004.

2. & 3. Solution Exhibit 18-30, Panel B, calculates the cost per equivalent unit for each cost category, summarizes total costs to account for, and assigns these costs to units completed (including normal spoilage), to abnormal spoilage, and to units in ending work in process using the weighted-average method.

SOLUTION EXHIBIT 18-30
Weighted-Average Method of Process Costing with Spoilage
Wang Manufacturing Company, March 2004

PANEL A: Steps 1 and 2—Summarize Output in Physical Units and Compute Eqvlt. Units

Flow of Production	(Step 1) Physical Units (given)	Step (2) Equivalent Units Direct Materials	Conversion Costs
Work in process, beginning	30,000		
Started during current period	50,000		
To account for	80,000		
Good units completed and transferred out during current period:	40,000	40,000	40,000
Normal spoilage*			
6,000 × 100%; 6,000 × 100%	6,000	6,000	6,000
Abnormal spoilage†			
2,000 × 100%; 2,000 × 100%	2,000	2,000	2,000
Work in process ending ‡			
32,000 × 100%; 32,000 × 75%	32,000	32,000	24,000
Accounted for	80,000		
Work done to date		80,000	72,000

*Degree of completion of normal spoilage in this department: direct materials, 100%; conversion costs, 100%.

† Degree of completion of abnormal spoilage in this department: direct materials, 100%; conversion costs, 100%.

‡ Degree of completion in this department: direct materials, 100%; conversion costs, 75%.

18-13

18-30 (cont'd)

PANEL B: Steps 3, 4, and 5—Compute Equivalent Unit Costs, Summarize Total Costs to Account For, and Assign Costs to Units Completed, to Spoilage Units, and to Units in Ending Work in Process

Conversion	Total Production Costs	Direct Materials	Costs
(Step 3) Work in process, beginning (given)	$ 420,000	$240,000	$180,000
Costs added in current period (given)	1,003,200	420,000	583,200
Costs incurred to date		660,000	763,200
Divide by equiv. units of work to date		÷ 80,000	÷ 72,000
Equivalent unit costs of work done to date		$8.25	$10.60
(Step 4) Total costs to account for	$1,423,200		
(Step 5) Assignment of costs			
Good units completed and transferred out (40,000 units)			
Costs before adding normal spoilage	$ 754,000	$(40,000^{\#} \times \$8.25)$ +	$(40,000^{\#} \times \$10.6$
Normal spoilage (6,000 units)	113,100	$(6,000^{\#} \times \$8.25)$ +	$(6,000^{\#} \times \$10.6$
Total cost of good units			
(A) completed and transferred out	867,100		
(B) Abnormal spoilage (2,000 units)	37,700	$(2,000^{\#} \times \$8.25)$ +	$(2,000^{\#} \times \$10.6$
Work in process, ending (32,000 units)			
Direct materials	264,000	$32,000^{\#} \times \$8.25$	
Conversion costs	254,400		$24,000^{\#} \times \$10.6$
(C) Total work in process, ending	518,400		
(A)+(B)+(C) Total costs accounted for	$1,423,200		

$^{\#}$ Equivalent units of direct materials and conversion costs calculated in Step 2 in Panel A.

18-32 (30 min.)   Standard-costing method, spoilage
(Refer to the information in 18-30).

1. The equivalent units of work done in the current period for direct materials and conversion costs are calculated in Solution Exhibit 18-31, Panel A.
2. The cost per equivalent unit for direct materials and conversion costs equals the standard cost per unit given in the problem: $8.00 per equivalent unit for direct materials in both beginning inventory and work done in the current period, and $10.00 per equivalent unit for conversion costs in both beginning inventory and work done in the current period.
3. Solution Exhibit 18-32 summarizes the total costs to account for and assigns these costs to units completed and transferred out (including normal spoilage), to abnormal spoilage and to ending work in process using the standard costing method.

18-32 (cont'd)

SOLUTION EXHIBIT 18-32
Standard Costing Method of Proven Costing with Spoilage
Wang Manufacturing Company, March 2004

Compute Equivalent Unit Costs, Summarize Total Costs to Account For, and Assign Costs to Units Completed, to Spoilage Units, and to Units in ending Work in Process.

		Total Production Costs	Direct Materials	Conversi Costs
(Step 3) (given)	Standard cost per equivalent unit	$ 18	$ 8	$ 10
	Work in process, beginning*	$ 420,000		
	Costs added in current period at at standard prices Direct materials 50,000 × $8; Conversion costs 54,000 × $10	940,000	$400,000	$540,000
(Step 4)	Costs to account for	$1,360,000		
(Step 5)	Assignment of costs at standard costs: Goods units completed and transferred out (40,000 units) Work in process, beginning (30,000 units)	$ 420,000		
	Direct materials added in Current period	0	$0^{\S} \times \$8$	
	Conversion costs added in Current period	120,000		$12,000^{\S} \times \$$
	Total from beginning inventory before normal spoilage	540,000		
	Started and completed before normal spoilage (10,000 units)	180,000	$(10,000^{\S} \times \$8) +$	$(10,000^{\S} \times \$$
	Normal spoilage (6,000 units)	108,000	$(6,000^{\S} \times \$8) +$	$(6,000^{\S} \times \$$
(A)	Total cost of good units transferred out	828,000		
(B)	Abnormal spoilage (2,000 units)	36,000	$(2,000^{\S} \times \$8) +$	$(2,000^{\S} \times \$$
	Work in process, ending (32,000 units) Direct materials	256,000	$32,000^{\S} \times \$8$	
	Conversion costs	240,000		$24,000^{\S} \times \$$
(C)	Total work in process, ending	496,000		
(A)+(B)+(C)	Total costs accounted for	$1,360,000		

*Work in process, beginning has 30,000 equivalent units (30,000 physical units × 100%) of direct materials and 18,000 equivalent units (30,000 physical units × 60%) of conversion costs. Hence work in process, beginning inventory at standard cost equals ($8 × 30,000) + ($10 × 18,000) = $240,000 + $180,000 = $420,000.

§ Equivalent units of direct materials and conversion costs calculated in Step 2 in Solution Exhibit 18-31 Panel A.

18-34 (25 min.) **FIFO method, spoilage.**

The equivalent units of work done in the Cleaning Department of the Alston Company in May for direct materials and conversion costs are the same as in problem 18-33 and are shown in Solution Exhibit 18-33A. The cost per equivalent unit of beginning inventory and of work done in the Cleaning Department in May for direct materials and conversion costs are calculated in problem 18-33 in Solution Exhibit 18-33B. Solution Exhibit 18-34 summarizes the total Cleaning Department costs for May, and assigns these costs to units completed (and transferred out), normal spoilage, abnormal spoilage, and units in ending work in process under the FIFO method.

SOLUTION EXHIBIT 18-34

Step 4: Summarize Total Costs to Account For, and Assign These Costs to Units Completed, Units Spoiled and Units in Ending Work in Process Using the FIFO Method Cleaning Department of Alston for May

	Direct Materials			Conversion Costs			Total Production Costs
	Equivalent Units (1)	Cost per Equivalent Unit (2)	Total Costs (3)=(1)×(2)	Equivalent Units (4)	Cost per Equivalent Unit (5)	Total Costs (6)=(4)×(5)	(7)=(3)+(6)
Panel A: Total Costs to Account For							
Work in process, beginning (from Solution Exhibit 18-33B)	1,000	$1	$ 1,000	800	$1	$ 800	$ 1,800
Work done in current period only (from Solution Exhibit 18-33B)	9,000	$1	9,000	8,000	$1	8,000	17,000
To account for	10,000		$10,000	8,800		$8,800	$18,800
Panel B: Assignment of Costs							
Good units completed and transferred out (7,400 physical units):							
Work in process, beginning (1,000 physical units)		$1	$ 1,000		$1	$ 800	$ 1,800
Work done in current period to complete beginning work in process	0*	$1	0	200†	$1	200	200
Total from beginning inventory before normal spoilage			1,000			1,000	2,000
Started and completed before normal spoilage (6,400 units)	6,400‡	$1	6,400	6,400‡	$1	6,400	12,800
Normal spoilage (740 units)	740§	$1	740	740§	$1	740	1,480
(A) Total costs of good units transferred out			8,140			8,140	16,280
(B) Abnormal spoilage (260 units)	260§	$1	260	260§	$1	260	520
(C) Work in process, ending (1,600 units)	1,600§	$1	1,600	400§	$1	400	2,000
(A)+(B)+(C) Accounted for	10,000		$10,000	8,800		$8,800	$18,800

*Beginning work in process is 100% complete as to direct materials so zero equivalent units of direct materials need to be added to complete beginning work in process.

†Beginning work in process is 80% complete as to conversion costs, which equals 800 equivalent units of conversion costs. To complete the 1,000 physical units of beginning work in process, 200 (1,000 – 800) equivalent units of conversion costs need to be added.

‡7,400 total equivalent units completed and transferred out (Solution Exhibit 18-33A) minus 1,000 equivalent units completed and transferred out from beginning inventory equal to 6,400 equivalent units.

§From Solution Exhibit 18-33A.

18-36 (25 min.) **FIFO method, Milling Department.**

The equivalent units of work done in the Milling Department in January for transferred-in costs, direct materials and conversion costs are the same as in problem 18-35 and are shown in Solution Exhibit 18-35A. The cost per equivalent unit of beginning inventory and of work done in the Cooking Department in January for transferred-in costs, direct materials and conversion costs are calculated in problem 18-35 in Solution Exhibit 18-35B. Solution Exhibit 18-36 summarizes the total Milling Department costs for May, and assigns these costs to units completed (and transferred out), normal spoilage, abnormal spoilage, and units in ending work in process under the FIFO method.

18-36 (cont'd)

SOLUTION EXHIBIT 18-36

Step 4: Summarize Total Costs to Account for, and Assign These Costs to Units Completed, Units Spoiled, and Units in Ending Work in Process Using the FIFO Method Milling Department of Alston for May

	Transferred-in Costs			Direct Materials			Conversion Costs			Total Production Cost
	Equivalent Unit	Cost per Equivalent Unit	Total Costs	Equivalent Unit	Cost per Equivalent Unit	Total Costs	Equivalent Unit	Cost per Equivalent Unit	Total Costs	
	(1)	(2)	(3)=(1)x(2)	(4)	(5)	(6)=(4)x(5)	(7)	(8)	(9)=(7)x(8)	(10)=(3)+(6)+(9)
Panel A: Total Costs to Account For:										
Work in process, beginning (from Solution Exhibit 18-35B)	3,000	$2.15	$ 6,450	—	—	—	2,400	$1.021	$2,450	$ 8,900
Work done in current period only (from Solution Exhibit, 18-35B)	7,400	$2.20	16,280	6,400	$0.10	$640	5,000	$0.99	4,950	21,870
To account for	10,400		$22,730	6,400		$640	7,400		$7,400	$30,770
Panel B: Assignment of Costs										
Good units completed and transferred out (6,000 physical units):										
Work in process, beginning (3,000 physical units)	3,000	$2.15	$ 6,450	—	—	—	2,400	$1.021	$2,450	$ 8,900
Work done in current period to complete beginning WIP	0#	$2.20	0	3,000*	$0.10	$300	600†	$0.99	594	894
Total from beginning inventory before normal spoilage			6,450			300	3,000		3,044	9,794
Started and completed before normal spoilage (3,000 units)	3,000‡	$2.20	6,600	3,000‡	$0.10	300	3,000‡	$0.99	2,970	9,870
Normal spoilage (300 units)	300§	$2.20	660	300§	$0.10	30	300§	$0.99	297	987
(A) Total costs of good units tfd out			13,710			630			6,311	20,651
(B) Abnormal spoilage (100 units)	100§	$2.20	220	100§	$0.10	10	100§	$0.99	99	329
(C) Work in process, ending	4,000§	$2.20	8,800	0§	$0.10	0	1,000§	$0.99	990	9,790
(A)+(B)+(C) Accounted for	10,400		$22,730	6,400		$640	7,400		$7,400	$30,770

Beginning work in process is 100% complete as to transferred-in costs so zero equivalent units of transferred-in costs need to be added to complete beginning work in process.

* Beginning work in process is 0% complete as to direct materials so 3,000 equivalent units of direct materials need to be added to complete the 3,000 physical units of beginning work in process.

† Beginning work in process is 80% complete as to conversion costs, which equals 2,400 equivalent units of conversion costs. To complete the 3,000 physical units of beginning work in process, 600 (3,000 – 2,400) equivalent units of conversion costs need to be added.

‡ 6,000 total equivalent units completed and transferred out (Solution Exhibit 18-35A) minus 3,000 equivalent units completed and transferred out from beginning inventory equal to 3,000 equivalent units.

§ From Solution Exhibit 18-35A.

18-38 (30 min.) **Job costing, rework.**

1.

Work in Process Control (SM-5 motors) ($550 × 80)	44,000	
Materials Control ($300 × 80)		24,000
Wages Payable ($60 × 80)		4,800
Manufacturing Overhead Allocated ($190 × 80)		15,200

(Total costs assigned to 80 spoiled units of SM-4
Motors before considering rework costs.)

Manufacturing Department Overhead Control (rework)	9,000	
Materials Control ($60 × 50)		3,000
Wages Payable ($45 × 50)		2,250
Manufacturing Overhead Allocated ($75 × 50)		3,750

(Normal rework attributable specifically to the SM-5
motor batches or jobs.)

Loss from Abnormal Rework ($180 × 30)	5,400	
Materials Control ($60 × 30)		1,800
Wages Payable ($45 × 30)		1,350
Manufacturing Overhead Allocated ($75 × 30)		2,250

(Total costs assigned to 80 spoiled units of SM-4
Motors before considering rework costs.)

Work in Process Control (SM-5 motors)	6,000	
Work in Process Control (RW-8 motors)	3,000	
Manufacturing Department Overhead Allocated (rework)		9,000

(Allocating manufacturing department rework costs
to SM-5 and RW-8 in the proportion 1,000:500 since
each motor requires the same number of machine
hours.)

2.   Total rework costs for SM-5 motors in February 2000 are as follows:

Normal rework costs allocated to SM-5	$6,000
Abnormal rework costs for SM-5	5,400
Total rework costs	$11,400

We emphasize two points:

(i)   Only $6,000 of the normal rework costs are allocated to SM-5 even though the normal rework costs of the 50 SM-5 motors reworked equal $9,000. The reason is that the normal rework costs are not specifically attributable to SM-5. For example, the machines happened to malfunction when SM-5 was being made but the rework was not caused by the specific requirements of SM-5. If it were, then all $9,000 would be charged to SM-5.

(ii)   Abnormal rework costs of $5,400 are pegged to SM-5 in the management control system, even though for financial reporting purposes, the abnormal rework costs are written off to the income statement.

18-40 (15-20 min.) **Physical units, inspection at various stages of completion (Chapter Appendix).**

	Inspection at 15%	Inspection at 40%	Inspection at 100%
Work in process, beginning (20%)*	14,000	14,000	14,000
Started during March	120,000	120,000	120,000
To account for	134,000	134,000	134,000
Good units completed and transferred out	113,000a	113,000a	113,000a
Normal spoilage	7,440b	6,600c	6,780d
Abnormal spoilage			
(10,000 – normal spoilage)	2,560	3,400	3,220
Work in process, ending (70%)*	11,000	11,000	11,000
Accounted for	134,000	134,000	134,000

*Degree of completion for conversion costs of the forging process at the dates of the work in process inventories

a 14,000 beginning inventory +120,000 –10,000 spoiled – 11,000 ending inventory = 113,000

b $6\% \times (113,000 + 11,000) = 6\% \times 124,000 = 7,440$

c $6\% \times (113,000 – 14,000 + 11,000) = 6\% \times 110,000 = 6,600$

d $6\% \times (113,000) = 6,780$

18-42 (40 min.) **Job Costing, Spoilage.**

1. Analysis of the 5,000 units rejected by Richport Company for Job No. N1192-122 yields the following breakdown between normal and abnormal spoilage.

	Units
Normal spoilage*	3,000
Abnormal spoilage:	
Design defect	900
Other [5,000 – (3,000 + 900)]	1,100
Total units rejected	5,000

$$* \text{ Normal spoilage} = 0.025 \text{ of normal input}$$
When output equals 117,000 units,
$$\begin{aligned} \text{Normal input} &= 117,000 \div (1 - 0.025) \\ &= 120,000 \text{ units} \\ \text{Normal spoilage} &= 120,000 \times 0.025 \\ &= 3,000 \text{ units} \end{aligned}$$

2. The journal entries required to properly account for Job No. N1192-122 are presented below and use an average cost per unit of $57 ($6,954,000 ÷ 122,000).

Materials control (or A/R or cash)[1]	28,700	
Abnormal loss[2]	107,500	
WIP control[3]		135,000
Cash[4]		1,200

To account for 5,000 units rejected.

Finished good inventory	6,819,000	
WIP control		6,819,000

To transfer 117,000 units to finished goods inventory.

[1] Units for sale 4,100 units sold at $7 each.
[2] Loss from abnormal spoilage:

2,000 units at $57	$114,000
Disposal cost	1,200
Cost recovery (1,100 × $7)	(7,700)
	$107,500

[3] WIP control:

900 defective units at $57	$51,300
1,100 other rejected units at $57	62,700
3,000 normal units at $57	21,000
	$135,000

[4] Additional cost to dispose of 900 units rejected because of design defect.

18-42 (cont'd)

3a.   If all spoilage were considered normal, the journal entries to account for Job No. N1192-122 would be as follows:

Materials Control (or A/R or cash)	136,200	
WIP Control		135,000
Cash		1,200

To account for 5,000 units of normal spoilage.

Finished Goods Control	6,919,000	
WIP Control		6,919,000

To transfer 117,000 units to finished-goods inventory (costs incurred on job and debited to WIP Control, $6,954,000, minus $35,000 credited to WIP Control).

By considering all spoilage as normal, Richport will show no abnormal loss but instead will add $107,500 to the finished-goods inventory. Hence, showing all spoilage as normal will increase Richport's operating income by $107,500.

3b.   Incorrect reporting of spoilage as normal instead of abnormal with the goal of increasing operating income is unethical. In assessing the situation, the management accountant should consider the following:

- Spoilage should be accounted for using relevant and reliable information. Accounting for spoilage incorrectly to make the company's operating performance look better than it is violates competence standards. It is unethical for Rutherford to suggest that Gonzales change abnormal spoilage to normal spoilage in order to make operating performance look good.

- The management accountant has a responsibility to avoid actual or apparent conflicts of interest and advise all appropriate parties of any potential conflict. Rutherford's motivation for wanting Gonzales to revise the quality figures could well have been motivated by Rutherford's desire to please senior management. In this regard, both Rutherford's and Gonzales's behaviour (if Gonzales agrees to modify the spoilage classification) could be viewed as unethical.

- The management accountant should require that information be fairly and objectively communicated and that all relevant information should be disclosed. From a management accountant's standpoint, showing abnormal spoilage as normal spoilage to make operating performance look good would be unethical.

Gonzales should indicate to Rutherford that the classification of normal and abnormal spoilage established by Richport Company is, indeed, appropriate. If Rutherford still insists on modifying the spoilage classification for this job to report higher operating income figures, Gonzales should raise the matter with one of Rutherford's superiors. If, after taking all these steps, there is continued pressure to overstate operating income, Gonzales should consider resigning from the company, and not engage in unethical behaviour.

CHAPTER 19
COST MANAGEMENT: QUALITY, TIME, AND
THE THEORY OF CONSTRAINTS

19-2   Quality of design measures how closely the characteristics of products or services match the needs and wants of customers. Conformance quality measures whether the product has been made according to design, engineering and manufacturing specifications.

19-4   An internal failure cost differs from an external failure cost on the basis of when the nonconforming product is detected. An internal failure is detected *before* a product is shipped to a customer whereas an external failure is detected *after* a product is shipped to a customer.

19-6   No, companies should emphasize financial as well as nonfinancial measures of quality, such as yield and defect rates. Nonfinancial measures are not directly linked to bottom-line performance but they indicate and direct attention to the specific areas that need improvement. Tracking nonfinancial measures over time directly reveals whether these areas have, in fact, improved over time. Nonfinancial measures are easy to quantify and easy to understand.

19-8   Examples of nonfinancial measures of internal performance are:
1. The number of defects for each product line.
2. Process yield (rates of good output to total output at a particular process).
3. Manufacturing lead time (the time taken to convert direct materials into finished output).
4. Employee turnover (ratio of the number of employees who left the company in a year, say, to the total number of employees who worked for the company in that year).

19-10   No. There is a trade-off between customer-response time and on-time performance. Simply scheduling longer customer-response time makes achieving on-time performance easier. Companies should, however, attempt to reduce uncertainty of arrival of orders, manage bottlenecks, reduce setup and processing time and run smaller batches. This would have the effect of reducing both customer-response time and improving on-time performance.

19-12   No. Adding a product when capacity is constrained and the timing of customer orders is uncertain causes delays in delivering all existing products. If the revenue losses from delays in delivering existing products and the increase in carrying costs of the existing products exceeds the positive contribution earned by the product that was added, then it is not worthwhile to make and sell the new product, despite its positive contribution margin. The chapter describes the negative effects (negative externalities) that one product can have on others when products share manufacturing facilities.

19-14 The four key steps in managing bottleneck resources are:

Step 1: Recognize that the bottleneck operation determines throughput contribution.
Step 2: Search for and find the bottleneck.
Step 3: Keep the bottleneck busy and subordinate all nonbottleneck operations to the bottleneck operation.
Step 4: Increase bottleneck efficiency and capacity.

19-16 (30 min.) Costs of quality.

1. The ratio of each COQ category to revenues for each period is as follows:

Semi-annual Costs of Quality Report Bergen, Inc.
(in thousands)

	6/30/2002	% of Rev. (2) = (1) ÷ 4,120	12/31/2002	% of Rev. (4) = (3) ÷ 4,540	6/30/2003	% of Rev. (6) = (5) ÷ 4,650	12/31/2003	% of Rev. (8) = (7) ÷ 4,510
	(1)		(3)		(5)		(7)	
Prevention costs								
Machine maintenance	$ 215		$ 215		$ 190		$ 160	
Training suppliers	5		45		20		15	
Design reviews	20		102		100		95	
	240	5.8%	362	8.0%	310	6.7%	270	6.0%
Appraisal costs								
Incoming inspection	45		53		36		22	
Final testing	160		160		140		94	
	205	5.0%	213	4.7%	176	3.8%	116	2.6%
Internal failure costs								
Rework	120		106		88		62	
Scrap	68		64		42		40	
	188	4.6%	170	3.7%	130	2.8%	102	2.2%
External failure costs								
Warranty repairs	69		31		25		23	
Customer returns	262		251		116		80	
	331	8.0%	282	6.2%	141	3.0%	103	2.3%
Total quality costs	$ 964	23.4%	$1,027	22.6%	$ 757	16.3%	$ 591	13.1%
Total production and revenues	$4,120		$4,540		$4,650		$4,510	

From an analysis of the Cost of Quality Report, it would appear that Bergen Inc.'s program has been successful since

- Total quality costs as a percentage of total revenues have declined from 23.4% to 13.1%.
- External failure costs, those costs signalling customer dissatisfaction have declined from 8% of total revenues to 2.3%. These declines in warranty repairs and customer returns should translate into increased revenues in the future.
- Internal failure costs have been reduced from 4.6% to 2.2% of revenues
- Appraisal costs have decreased from 5.0% to 2.6%. Preventing defects from occurring in the first place is reducing the demand for final testing.
- Quality costs have shifted to the area of prevention where problems are solved before production starts. Maintenance, training, and design reviews have increased from 5.8% of total revenues to 6% and from 25% of total quality costs (240 ÷ 964) to 45.7% (270 ÷ 591). The $30,000 increase in these costs is more than offset by decreases in other quality costs.

19-16 (cont'd)

Because of improved designs, quality training, and additional pre-production inspections, scrap and rework costs have declined. Production does not have to spend an inordinate amount of time with customer service since they are now making the product right the first time and warranty repairs and customer returns have decreased.

2.   To measure the opportunity cost of not implementing the quality program, Bergen Inc. could assume that

- Sales and market share would continue to decline if the quality program had not been implemented and then calculate the loss in revenue and contribution margin.
- The company would have to compete on price rather than quality and calculate the impact of having to lower product prices.

Opportunity costs are not recorded in accounting systems because they represent the results of what might have happened if Bergen had not improved quality. Nevertheless, opportunity costs of poor quality can be significant. It is important for Bergen to take these costs into account when making decisions about quality.

19-18   (30-40 min.)   **Costs of quality analysis, nonfinancial quality measures.**

1. and 2.   **Sales, Costs of Quality and Costs of Quality as a Percentage of Sales for Olivia**

Sales = $2,000 × 10,000 units = $20,000,000

Costs of Quality	Cost (1)	Percentage of Sales (2) = (1) ÷ $20,000,000
<u>Prevention costs</u>		
Design engineering ($75 × 6,000 hours)	$ 450,000	2.25%
<u>Appraisal costs</u>		
Testing and inspection ($40 × 1 hour × 10,000 units)	400,000	2.00%
<u>Internal failure costs</u>		
Rework ($500 × 5% × 10,000 units)	250,000	1.25%
<u>External failure costs</u>		
Repair ($600 × 4% × 10,000 units)	<u>240,000</u>	<u>1.20</u>%
Total costs of quality	<u>$1,340,000</u>	<u>6.70</u>%

**Sales, Costs of Quality and Costs of Quality
as a Percentage of Sales for Solta**

Sales: $1,500 × 5,000 units = $7,500,000

Costs of Quality	Costs (1)	Percentage of Sales (2)=(1)÷$7,500,000
Prevention costs		
Design engineering ($75 × 1,000 hours)	$ 75,000	1.00%
Appraisal costs		
Testing and inspection ($40 × 0.5 × 5,000 units)	100,000	1.33%
Internal failure costs		
Rework ($400 × 10% × 5,000 units)	200,000	2.67%
External failure costs		
Repair ($450 × 8% × 5,000 units)	180,000	2.40%
Estimated forgone contribution margin on lost sales [($1,500 – $800) × 300]	210,000	2.80%
Total external failure costs	390,000	5.20%
Total costs of quality	$765,000	10.20%

Costs of quality as a percentage of sales are significantly different for Solta (10.20%) compared with Olivia (6.70%). Ontario spends very little on prevention and appraisal activities for Solta, and incurs high costs of internal and external failures. Ontario follows a different strategy with respect to Olivia, spending a greater percentage of sales on prevention and appraisal activities. The result: fewer internal and external failure costs and lower overall costs of quality as a percentage of sales compared with Solta.

3.   Examples of nonfinancial quality measures that Ontario Industries could monitor as part of a total-quality-control effort are
    (a)   Outgoing quality yield for each product.
    (b)   Returned refrigerator percentage for each product.
    (c)   On-time delivery.
    (d)   Employee turnover.

19-20 (25 min.) **Quality improvement, relevant costs, and relevant revenues.**

1. Incremental costs over the next year of choosing the new lens = $50 × 20,000 copiers = $1,000,000.

2.

	Incremental Benefits over the Next Year of Choosing the New Lens
Costs of quality items	
Savings on rework costs	
$40 × 12,000 rework hours	$ 480,000
Savings in customer-support costs	
$20 × 800 customer-support hours	16,000
Savings in transportation costs for parts	
$180 × 200 fewer loads	36,000
Savings in warranty repair costs	
$45 × 8,000 repair hours	360,000
Opportunity costs	600,000
Contribution margin from increased sales	
	$1,492,000

Cost savings and additional contribution margin

3. Since the expected benefits of $1,492,000 (requirement 2) exceed the costs of the new lens of $1,000,000 (requirement 1), Photon should introduce the new lens. Note that the opportunity cost benefits in the form of higher contribution margin from increased sales is an important component for justifying the investment in the new lens. The incremental costs of the new lens of $1,000,000 is greater than the incremental savings in rework and repair costs of $892,000. Investing in the new lens is beneficial provided it generates additional contribution margin of, at least, $108,000 ($1,000,000 – $892,000), that is, additional sales of at least $108,000 ÷ $6,000 = 18 copiers.

19-22 (20 min.) **Waiting time, banks.**

1. If the branch expects to receive 40 customers each day and it takes 5 minutes to serve a customer, the average time that a customer will wait in line before being served is:

$$= \frac{\left(\begin{matrix}\text{Average number} \\ \text{of customers}\end{matrix}\right) \times \left(\begin{matrix}\text{Time taken to} \\ \text{serve a customer}\end{matrix}\right)^2}{2 \times \left[\begin{matrix}\text{Available time} \\ \text{counter is open}\end{matrix} - \left[\left(\begin{matrix}\text{Average number} \\ \text{of customers}\end{matrix}\right) \times \left(\begin{matrix}\text{Time taken to} \\ \text{serve a customer}\end{matrix}\right)\right]\right]}$$

$$= \frac{[40 \times (5)^2]}{2 \times [300 - (40 \times 5)]} = \frac{(40 \times 25)}{2 \times (300 - 200)} = \frac{1{,}000}{2 \times 100} = \frac{1{,}000}{200} = 5 \text{ minutes}$$

2. If the branch expects to receive 50 customers each day and the time taken to serve a customer is 5 minutes, the average time that a customer will wait in line before being served is:

$$= \frac{[50 \times (5)^2]}{2 \times [300 - (50 \times 5)]} = \frac{(50 \times 25)}{2 \times (300 - 250)} = \frac{50 \times 25}{2 \times 50} = \frac{1{,}250}{100} = 12.5 \text{ minutes}$$

3. If the branch expects to receive 50 customers each day and the time taken to serve a customer is 4 minutes, the average time that a customer will wait in line before being served is:

$$= \frac{[50 \times (4)^2]}{2 \times [300 - (50 \times 4)]} = \frac{(50 \times 16)}{2 \times (300 - 200)} = \frac{50 \times 16}{2 \times 100} = \frac{800}{200} = 4 \text{ minutes}$$

19-24 (15 min.) **Theory of constraints, throughput contribution, relevant costs.**

1.   Finishing is a bottleneck operation. Hence, producing 1,000 more units will generate additional throughput contribution and operating income.

Increase in throughput contribution ($72 − $32) × 1,000	$40,000
Incremental costs of the jigs and tools	30,000
Net benefit of investing in jigs and tools	$10,000

Mayfield should invest in the modern jigs and tools because the benefit of higher throughput contribution of $40,000 exceeds the cost of $30,000.

2.   The Machining Department has excess capacity and is not a bottleneck operation. Increasing its capacity further will not increase throughput contribution. There is therefore no benefit from spending $5,000 to increase the Machining Department's capacity by 10,000 units. Mayfield should not implement the change to do setups faster.

19-26 (15 min.) **Theory of constraints, throughput contribution, quality.**

1.   Cost of defective unit at machining operation which is not a bottleneck operation is the loss in direct materials (variable costs) of $32 per unit. Producing 2,000 units of defectives does not result in loss of throughput contribution. Despite the defective production machining can produce and transfer 80,000 units to finishing. Therefore cost of 2,000 defective units at the machining operation is $32 × 2,000 = $64,000.

2.   A defective unit produced at the bottleneck finishing operation costs Mayfield materials costs plus the opportunity cost of lost throughput contribution. Bottleneck capacity not wasted in producing defective units could be used to generate additional sales and throughput contribution. Cost of 2,000 defective units at the finishing operation is

Loss of direct materials $32 × 2,000	$ 64,000
Forgone throughput contribution ($72 − $32) × 2,000	80,000
Total cost of 2,000 defective units	$144,000

Alternatively, the cost of 2,000 defective units at the finishing operation can be calculated as the lost revenue of $72 × 2,000 = $144,000. That is, the direct materials costs of $32 × 2,000 = $64,000 and all fixed operating costs in the machining and finishing operations are irrelevant since these costs would be incurred anyway whether a defective or good unit is produced. The cost of producing a defective unit is the revenue lost of $144,000.

19-28 (30 min.) **Quality improvement, relevant costs, and relevant revenues.**

1. By implementing the new method, Tan would incur additional direct materials costs on all the 200,000 units started at the molding operation.

Additional direct materials costs = $3 per lamp × 200,000 lamps	$600,000

2. The relevant benefits of adding the new material are:

(a)	Increased revenue from selling 30,000 more lamps $40 per lamp × 30,000 lamps	$1,200,000
(b)	Additional variable costs incurred in the welding department on the good lamps $2.50 × 30,000 lamps	(75,000)
	Total benefits to Tan of adding new material to improve quality	$1,125,000

Note that Tan Corporation continues to incur the same total variable costs of direct materials, direct manufacturing labour, setup labour, and materials handling labour and the same fixed costs of equipment, rent, and allocated overhead that it is currently incurring even when it improves quality. Since these costs do not differ among the alternatives of adding the new material or not adding the new material, they are excluded from the analysis. The relevant benefit of adding the new material is the extra revenue that Tan would get from producing 30,000 good lamps minus the additional variable welding costs it would incur on these lamps in the welding department.

An alternative approach to analyzing the problem is to focus on scrap costs and the benefits of reducing scrap.

The relevant benefits of adding the new material are:

(a)	Cost savings from eliminating scrap: Variable costs per lamp, $19[a] × 30,000 lamps	$ 570,000
(b)	Additional contribution margin from selling another 30,000 lamps because 30,000 lamps will no longer be scrapped:	
	Unit contribution margin $18.50[b] × 30,000 lamps	555,000
	Total benefits to Tan of adding new material to improve quality	$1,125,000

[a]Note that only the variable scrap costs of $19 per lamp (direct materials, $16 per lamp and direct manufacturing labour, setup labour, and materials handling labour, $3 per lamp) are relevant because improving quality will save these costs. Fixed scrap costs of equipment, rent, and allocated overhead are irrelevant because these costs will be incurred whether Tan Corporation adds or does not add the new material.

19-28 (cont'd)

[b]Unit contribution margin

Selling price		$40.00
Variable costs:		
Direct materials costs per lamp	$16.00	
Molding department variable manufacturing costs per lamp (direct manufacturing labour, setup labour, and materials handling labour)	3.00	
Welding department variable manufacturing costs per lamp	2.50	
Variable costs		21.50
Unit contribution margin		$18.50

3. On the basis of quantitative considerations alone, Tan should use the new material. Relevant benefits of $1,125,000 exceeds the relevant costs of $600,000 by $525,000.

4. Other nonfinancial and qualitative factors that Tan should consider in making a decision include the effects of quality improvement on:

  (a) Gaining manufacturing expertise that could lead to further cost reductions in the future.

  (b) Enhanced reputation and increased customer goodwill which could lead to higher future revenues through greater unit sales and higher sales prices.

  (c) More worker empowerment and higher employee morale.

19-30 (30-40 min.) **Compensation linked with profitability, on-time delivery, and external quality performance measures; balanced scorecard.**

1.

Detroit	Jan.-March	April-June	July-Sept.	Oct.-Dec.
Add: Profitability				
2% of operating income	$16,000	$17,000	$14,000	$18,000
Add: On-time delivery				
$10,000 if above 98%	10,000	10,000	0	0
Deduct: Quality				
50% of cost of sales returns	(9,000)	(13,000)	(5,000)	(12,500)
Total: Bonus paid	$17,000	$14,000	$ 9,000	$ 5,500
Los Angeles				
Add: Profitability				
2% of operating income	$32,000	$30,000	$36,000	$38,000
Add: On-time delivery				
$10,000 if above 98%	0	0	0	10,000
Deduct: Quality				
50% of cost of sales returns	(17,500)	(17,000)	(14,000)	(11,000)
Total: Bonus paid	$14,500	$13,000	$22,000	$37,000

2. Operating income as a measure of profitability

Operating income does capture revenue and cost-related factors. However, there is no recognition of investment differences between the two plants. Los Angeles sales are approximately double that of Detroit. This difference gives the Los Angeles plant manager the opportunity to earn a larger bonus due to investment size alone. An alternative approach would be to use return on investment (perhaps relative to the budgeted ROI).

98% on-time benchmark as a measure of on-time delivery performance

This measure does reflect the ability of Pacific-Dunlop to meet a benchmark for on-time delivery. Several concerns arise with this specific measure:

(a)   It is a yes-or-no cut-off. A 10% on-time performance earns no bonus, but neither does a 97.9% on-time performance. Moreover, no extra bonus is paid for performance above 98.0%. An alternative is to have the bonus be a percentage of the on-time delivery percentage.

(b)   It can be manipulated by management. The Pacific-Dunlop plant manager may quote conservative delivery dates to salespeople in an effort to "guarantee" that the 98% target is achieved.

(c)   It reflects performance only relative to scheduled delivery date. It does not consider how quickly Pacific-Dunlop can respond to customer orders.

19-30 (cont'd)

<u>50% of cost of sales returns as a measure of quality</u>

This measure does incorporate one cost that arises with defective goods. However, there are several concerns with its use:

(a) Not all sales returns are due to defective work by the plant manager. Some returns are due to tampering by the customer. Other returns arise from breakage during delivery and installation.

(b) It does not systematically incorporate customer opinion about quality. Not all customers return defective goods.

(c) It ignores important categories of the cost of defective goods. For example, dissatisfied customers may decline to make any subsequent purchases.

3.   Most companies use both financial and nonfinancial measures to evaluate performance, sometimes presented in a single report called a <u>balanced scorecard</u>. Using multiple measures of performance enables top management to evaluate whether lower-level managers have improved one area at the expense of others. For example, did the on-time delivery performance of the Detroit plant manager decrease in the October-December period relative to the April-June period because the manager emphasized shipment of high-margin products to increase operating income?

4.   If on-time delivery were dropped as a performance evaluation measure, managers will concentrate on increasing operating income and decreasing sales returns but will give less attention to on-time delivery. Consider the following situation. Suppose a manager must choose between (1) delivering a high-margin order that will add to operating income while delaying a number of other orders and adversely affecting on-time performance or (2) delaying the high-margin order and sacrificing some operating income to achieve better on-time performance. What action will the manager take? If on-time performance is excluded as a performance evaluation measure, the manager will almost certainly choose (1). Only if on-time performance is included in the manager's performance evaluation will the manager consider choosing option (2).

19-32 (20-30 min.) **Waiting times, relevant revenues and relevant costs (continuation of 19-31).**

1. The direct approach is to look at incremental revenues and incremental costs.

Average selling price per order for Y28, which has average operating throughput time of 350 hours	$ 8,000
Variable costs per order	5,000
Additional contribution per order from Y28	3,000
Multiply by expected number of orders	× 25
Increase in expected contribution from Y28	$75,000

Expected loss in revenues and increase in costs from introducing Y28

Product (1)	Expected Loss in Revenues from Increasing Average Manufacturing Lead Times for All Products (2)	Expected Increase in Carrying Costs from Increasing Average Manufacturing Lead Times for All Products (3)	Expected Loss in Revenues Plus Expected Increases in Costs of Introducing Y28 (4) = (2) + (3)
Z39	$25,000.00[a]	$6,375.00[b]	$31,375.00
Y28	–	2,187.50[c]	2,187.50
Total	$25,000.00	$8,562.50	$33,562.50

[a]50 orders × ($27,000 – $26,500)
[b](410 hours – 240 hours) × $0.75 × 50 orders
[c](350 hours – 0) × $0.25 × 25

Increase in expected contribution from Y28 of $75,000 is greater than increase in expected costs of $33,562.50 by $41,437.50. Therefore, SRG should introduce Y28.

19-32 (cont'd)

Alternative calculations of incremental revenues and incremental costs of introducing Y28.

	Alternative 1: Introduce Y28 (1)	Alternative 2: Do Not Introduce Y28 (2)	Relevant Revenues and Relevant Costs (3) = (1) – (2)
Expected revenues	$1,525,000.00[a]	$1,350,000.00[b]	$175,000.00
Expected variable costs	875,000.00[c]	750,000.00[d]	125,000.00
Expected carrying costs	17,562.50[e]	9,000.00[f]	8,562.50
Expected total variable and carrying costs	892,562.50	759,000.00	133,562.50
Expected revenues minus expected costs	$ 632,437.50	$ 591,000.00	$ 41,437.50

[a]$(50 \times \$26,500) + (25 \times \$8,000)$
[b]$50 \times \$27,000$
[c]$(50 \times \$15,000) + (25 \times \$5,000)$
[d]$50 \times \$15,000$

[e]$(50 \times \$0.75 \times 410) + (25 \times \$0.25 \times 350)$
[f]$50 \times \$0.75 \times 240$

2. Introducing Y28 results in an incremental cost of $33,562.50. To break even, we need to earn a total contribution of $33,562.50 over the 25 orders, or a contribution per order of $33,562.50 ÷ 25 = $1,342.50.

Variable costs per order of Y28	$5,000.00
Required contribution to break even	1,342.50
Selling price per dollar of Y28 to break even	$6,342.50

If Y28 sells above $6,342.50 per order, SRG should manufacture and sell Y28. If Y28 sells below $6,342.50 per order, SRG should not manufacture and sell Y28.

19-34 (20 min.) **Theory of constraints, throughput contribution, relevant costs.**

1. It will cost Columbia $50 per unit to reduce manufacturing time. But manufacturing is not a bottleneck operation, installation is. Therefore manufacturing more equipment will not increase sales and throughput contribution. Columbia Industries should not implement the new manufacturing method.

2. Additional relevant costs of new direct materials, $2,000 × 320 units $640,000
   Increase in throughput contribution, $25,000 × 20 units $500,000

The additional incremental costs exceed the benefits from higher throughput contribution by $140,000, so Columbia Industries should not implement the new design.

Alternatively, compare throughput contribution under each alternative.

Current throughput contribution is $25,000 × 300 $7,500,000
With the modification, throughput contribution is $23,000 × 320 $7,360,000

The current throughput contribution is greater than the throughput contribution resulting from the proposed change in direct materials. Hence, Columbia Industries should not implement the new design.

3. Increase in throughput contribution, $25,000 × 10 units $250,000
   Increase in relevant costs $ 50,000

The additional throughput contribution exceeds incremental costs by $200,000 so Columbia Industries should implement the new installation technique.

4. Motivating installation workers to increase productivity is worthwhile because installation is a bottleneck operation and any increase in productivity at the bottleneck will increase throughput contribution. On the other hand, motivating workers in the manufacturing department to increase productivity is not worthwhile. Manufacturing is not a bottleneck operation, so any increase in output will only result in extra inventory of equipment. Columbia Industries should only encourage manufacturing to produce as much equipment as the installation department needs, not to produce as much as it can. Under these circumstances, it would not be a good idea to evaluate and compensate manufacturing workers on the basis of their productivity.

19-36 (25 min.)   **Quality improvement, Pareto charts, fishbone diagrams.**

1.   Examples of failures in accounts receivable management are:
   (a)   Uncollectible amounts or bad debts.
   (b)   Delays in receiving payments.

2.   Prevention activities that could reduce failures in accounts receivable management include:
   (a)   Credit checks on customers
   (b)   Shipping the correct copier to the customer
   (c)   Supporting installation of the copier and answering customer questions
   (d)   Sending the correct invoice, in the correct amount and to the correct address promptly
   (e)   Following up to see if the machine is functioning smoothly

3.   A Pareto diagram for the problem of delays in receiving customer payments might look like the following:

SOLUTION EXHIBIT 19-36A
Pareto Diagram for Failures in Accounts Receivables at Murray Corporation

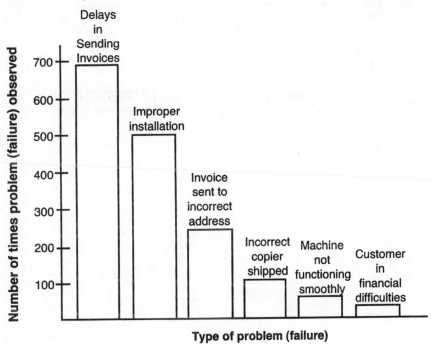

19-36 (cont'd)

A cause-and-effect or fishbone diagram for the problem of delays in sending invoices may appear as follows:

SOLUTION EXHIBIT 19-36B
Cause-and-Effect Diagram for Problem of Delays in Sending Invoices at Murray Corporation

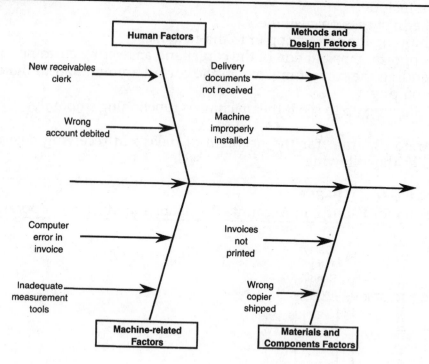

CHAPTER 20
INVENTORY MANAGEMENT, JUST-IN-TIME, AND BACKFLUSH COSTING

20-2 Five cost categories important in managing goods for sale in a retail organization are:
1. Purchase costs.
2. Ordering costs.
3. Carrying costs.
4. Stockout costs.
5. Quality costs.

20-4 Costs included in the carrying costs of inventory are *incremental costs* for such items as insurance, rent, obsolescence, spoilage, and breakage plus the *opportunity cost* of capital (or required return on investment).

20-6 The steps in computing the costs of a prediction error when using the EOQ decision model are:
Step 1: Compute the monetary outcome from the best action that could have been taken, given the actual amount of the cost input.
Step 2: Compute the monetary outcome from the best action based on the incorrect amount of the predicted cost input.
Step 3: Compute the difference between the monetary outcomes from Steps 1 and 2.

20-8 Just-in-time (JIT) purchasing is the purchase of goods or materials such that a delivery immediately precedes demand or use. Benefits include lower inventory holdings (reduced warehouse space required and less money tied up in inventory) and less risk of inventory obsolescence and spoilage.

20-10 The sequence of activities involved in placing a purchase order can be facilitated by use of the Internet. For example, Cisco is streamlining the procurement process for its customers—e.g., having online a complete price list, information about expected shipment dates, and a service order capability that is available 24 hours a day with e-mail or fax confirmation.

20-12 Obstacles to companies adopting a supply-chain approach include:
* Communication obstacles—the unwillingness of some parties to share information.
* Trust obstacles—includes the concern that all parties will not meet their agreed-upon commitments.
* Information system obstacles—includes problems due to the information systems of different parties not being technically compatible.
* Limited resources—includes problems due to the people and financial resources given to support a supply-chain initiative not being adequate.

20-14 Traditional normal and standard costing systems use sequential tracking, which is any product-costing method where recording of the journal entries occurs in the same order as actual purchases and progress in production.

Backflush costing omits the recording of some or all of the journal entries relating to the cycle from purchase of direct materials to sale of finished goods. Where journal entries for one or more stages in the cycle are omitted, the journal entries for a subsequent stage use normal or standard costs to work backward to flush out the costs in the cycle for which journal entries were not made.

20-16 (20 min.)   **Economic order quantity for retailer.**

1.   D = 10,000, P = $225, C = $10

$$\text{EOQ} = \sqrt{\frac{2\,DP}{C}} = \sqrt{\frac{2(10,000)\$225}{10}}$$

$$= 670.82$$

$$\cong 671 \text{ jerseys}$$

2.   Number of orders per year $= \dfrac{D}{\text{EOQ}} = \dfrac{10,000}{671}$

$$= 14.90$$

$$\cong 15 \text{ orders}$$

3. $\dfrac{\text{Demand each}}{\text{working day}} = \dfrac{D}{\text{Number of working days}}$

$$= \frac{10,000}{365}$$

$$= 27.40 \text{ jerseys per day}$$

Purchase lead time = 7 days

Reorder point   = 27.40 × 7

$$= 191.80 \cong 192 \text{ jerseys}$$

20-18 (15 min.) **EOQ for a retailer.**

1. $D = 20,000$, $P = \$160$, $C = 20\% \times \$8 = \$1.60$

$$EOQ = \sqrt{\frac{2DP}{C}} = \sqrt{\frac{2(20,000)\$160}{\$1.60}} = 2,000 \text{ metres}$$

2. Number of orders per year: $\dfrac{D}{EOQ} = \dfrac{20,000}{2,000} = 10 \text{ orders}$

3. Demand each working day $= \dfrac{D}{\text{Number of working days}}$

$= \dfrac{20,000}{250}$

$= 80 \text{ metres per day}$

$= 400 \text{ metres per week}$

Purchasing lead time = 2 weeks
Reorder point = $400 \times 2 = 800$ metres

20-20 (20 min.) **Sensitivity of EOQ to changes in relevant ordering and carrying costs.**

1. A straightforward approach to the requirement is to construct the following table for EOQ at relevant carrying and ordering costs. Annual demand is 10,000 units. The formula for the EOQ model is:

$$EOQ = \sqrt{\frac{2DP}{C}}$$

where   D = demand in units for a specified period of time

        P = relevant ordering costs per purchase order

        C = relevant carrying costs of one unit in stock for the time period used for D (one year in this problem).

Relevant Carrying Costs Per Unit Per Year	Relevant Ordering Costs Per Purchase Order	
	$300	$200
$10	$\sqrt{\dfrac{2 \times 10,000 \times \$300}{\$10}} = 775$	$\sqrt{\dfrac{2 \times 10,000 \times \$200}{\$10}} = 632$
15	$\sqrt{\dfrac{2 \times 10,000 \times \$300}{\$15}} = 632$	$\sqrt{\dfrac{2 \times 10,000 \times \$200}{\$15}} = 516$
20	$\sqrt{\dfrac{2 \times 10,000 \times \$300}{\$20}} = 548$	$\sqrt{\dfrac{2 \times 10,000 \times \$200}{\$20}} = 447$

2.   For a given demand level, as relevant carrying costs increase, EOQ becomes smaller. For a given demand level, as relevant order costs increase, EOQ increases.

20-22 (20-30 min.) **Purchase-order size for retailer, EOQ, just-in-time purchasing.**

1. $EOQ = \sqrt{\dfrac{2DP}{C}}$

(a) $D = 6{,}000$; $P = \$30$; $C = \$1$

$$EOQ = \sqrt{\dfrac{2(6{,}000)\,(\$30)}{\$1}} = \sqrt{360{,}000} = 600 \text{ cases}$$

(b) $D = 6{,}000$; $P = \$30$; $C = \$1.50$

$$EOQ = \sqrt{\dfrac{2(6{,}000)\,(\$30)}{\$1.50}} = \sqrt{240{,}000} = 489.9 \text{ cases} \approx 490 \text{ cases}$$

(c) $D = 6{,}000$; $P = \$5$; $C = \$1.50$

$$EOQ = \sqrt{\dfrac{2(6{,}000)\,(\$5)}{\$1.50}} = \sqrt{40{,}000} = 200 \text{ cases}$$

2. A just-in-time purchasing policy involves the purchase of goods such that their delivery immediately precedes their demand. Given the purchase order sizes calculated in requirement 1, the number of purchase orders placed each month is (D ÷ EOQ):

(a) $\dfrac{D}{EOQ} = \dfrac{6{,}000}{600} = 10$ orders per month or ≈ 1 every 3 days

(b) $\dfrac{D}{EOQ} = \dfrac{6{,}000}{490} = 12.25$ orders per month or ≈ 1 every 2.45 days

(c) $\dfrac{D}{EOQ} = \dfrac{6{,}000}{200} = 30$ orders per month or ≈ 1 every day

An increase in C and a decrease in P led to increases in the optimal frequency of orders. The 24-Hour Mart has increased the frequency of delivery from every third day (1a: P = \$30; C = \$1) to a delivery every day (1c: P = \$5; C = \$1.50). There is a reduction of 200 cases in the average inventory level: (600 – 200) ÷ 2 = 200.

20-24 (30 min.) **Backflush costing and JIT production.**

1.

(a) Purchases of raw materials	Inventory: Raw and In-Process Control	2,754,000	
	Accounts Payable Control		2,754,000
(b) Incur conversion costs	Conversion Costs Control	723,600	
	Various Accounts		723,600
(c) Completion of finished goods	Finished Goods Control[a]	3,484,000	
	Inventory: Raw and In-Process Control		2,733,600
	Conversion Costs Allocated		750,400
(d) Sale of finished goods	Cost of Goods Sold[b]	3,432,000	
	Finished Goods Control		3,432,000

[a]$26,800 \times (\$102 + \$28) = \$3,484,000$
[b]$26,400 \times (\$102 + \$28) = \$3,432,000$

2.

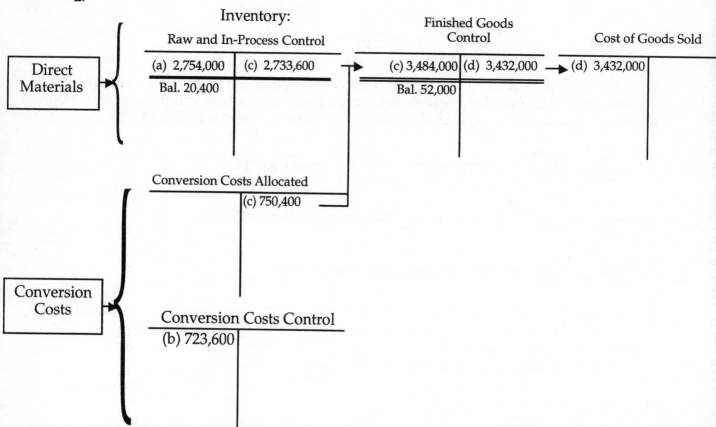

3. Under an ideal JIT production system, there could be zero inventories at the end of each day. Entry (c) would be $3,432,000 finished goods production, not $3,484,000.

20-26 (20 min.) **Backflush costing, two trigger points, production completion and sale (continuation of 20-24).**

(a) Purchases of raw materials	No entry		
(b) Incur conversion costs	Conversion Costs Control	723,600	
	Various Accounts		723,600
(c) Completion of finished goods	Finished Goods Control	3,484,000	
	Accounts Payable Control		2,733,600
	Conversion Costs Allocated		750,400
(d) Sale of finished goods	Cost of Goods Sold	3,432,000	
	Finished Goods Control		3,432,000
(e) Underallocated or overallocated conversion costs	Conversion Costs Allocated	750,400	
	Costs of Goods Sold		26,800
	Conversion Costs Control		723,600

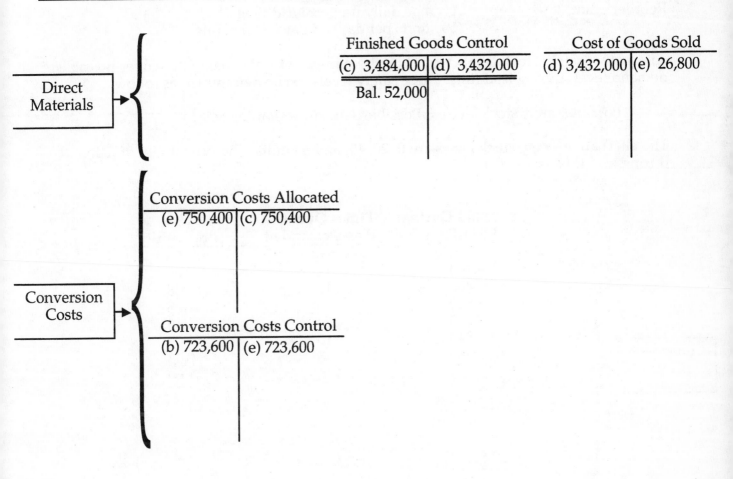

Finished Goods Control

(c) 3,484,000	(d) 3,432,000	
Bal. 52,000		

Cost of Goods Sold

(d) 3,432,000	(e) 26,800

Conversion Costs Allocated

(e) 750,400	(c) 750,400

Conversion Costs Control

(b) 723,600	(e) 723,600

Direct Materials

Conversion Costs

20-28 (30-45 min.) **EOQ, uncertainty, safety stock, reorder point.**

1. The Starr Company is searching for the safety stock level that will minimize the expected total of the costs of carrying additional inventory and the costs associated with insufficient inventories (stockout costs). The present reorder point, alternative safety stock levels, and probability of usage during lead time have to be computed before this level can be determined.

The present reorder point is calculated as follows:

$$\text{Average daily usage} = \frac{\text{Annual demand}}{\text{Number of working days}}$$

$$= \frac{30{,}000 \text{ units}}{300 \text{ days}}$$

$$\text{Reorder point} = \text{Average daily usage} \times \text{Lead time}$$
$$= (100 \text{ units per day}) \times 5 \text{ days} = 500 \text{ units}$$

Alternative safety stock levels would be the number of units needed to cover possible demand levels during lead time. These safety levels can be determined as follows:

$$\text{Possible safety stock levels} = \text{Possible demand} - \text{Reorder point}$$

The alternative safety stock levels are 0, 20, 40, and 60 units. The probability of demand during lead time is:

Demand During Lead Time	Number of Times Quantity Was Demanded	Probability
440	6	.03
460	12	.06
480	16	.08
500	130	.65
520	20	.10
540	10	.05
560	6	.03
	200	1.00

Safety Stock Level in Units (1)	Demand Realizations Resulting in Stockouts (2)	Stockout in Units[a] (3)=(2)– 500–(1)	Probability of Stockout (4)	Relevant Stockout Costs[b] (5)=(3)×$20	Number of Orders Per Year[c] (6)	Expected Stockout Costs[d] (7)= (4)×(5)×(6)	Relevant Carrying Costs[e] (8)= (1) × $10	Total Relevant Costs (9)=(7)+(8)
0	520	20	0.10	$ 400	10	$ 400		
	540	40	0.05	800	10	400		
	560	60	0.03	1,200	10	360		
						$1,160	$ 0	$1,160
20	540	20	0.05	400	10	$ 200		
	560	40	0.03	800	10	240		
						$ 440	$200	$ 640
40	560	20	0.03	400	10	$ 120	$400	$ 520
60	—	—	—	—	—	$ 0[f]	$600	$ 600

a Realized demand – inventory available during lead time (excluding safety stock), 500 units – safety stock.

b Stockout units × relevant stockout costs of $20 per motor.

c Annual demand 30,000 ÷ 3,000 EOQ = 10 orders per year.

d Probability of stockout × relevant stockout costs × number of orders per year.

e Safety stock × annual relevant carrying costs of $10 per motor (assumes that safety stock is on hand at all times and that there is no overstocking caused by decreases in expected usage).

f At a safety stock level of 60 motors, no stockouts will occur and hence expected stockout costs = $0.

Safety stock of 40 units would minimize Starr Company's total stockout and carrying costs.

2.   The new reorder point would be:

Present reorder point (demand during lead time: 100 × 5)	500 units
Safety stock	40 units
New reorder point	540 units

20-28 (cont'd)

3. The factors Starr Company should have considered when estimating the stockout costs include:
   (a) Possible lost contribution margin on motors not sold.
   (b) Costs associated with disruption or idle time.
   (c) Forgone contribution margin on future sales from possible loss of customers and customer goodwill.
   (d) Additional clerical costs involved in keeping records of back orders.
   (e) How valid is the past empirical distribution of demand when predicting the future demand distribution.

20-30 (30 min.) JIT purchasing, relevant benefits, relevant costs.

1. Solution Exhibit 20-30 presents the $37,500 cash savings that would result if Margro Corporation adopted the just-in-time inventory system in 2002.

2. Conditions that should exist in order for a company to install "just-in-time" inventory successfully include the following.

   - Top management must be committed and provide the necessary leadership support in order to ensure a company-wide, coordinated effort.

   - A detailed system for integrating the sequential operations of the manufacturing process needs to be developed and implemented. Direct materials must arrive when needed for each subassembly so that the production process functions smoothly.

   - Accurate sales forecasts are needed for effective finished goods planning and production scheduling.

   - Products should be designed to use standardized parts to reduce manufacturing time and reduce costs.

   - Reliable vendors who can deliver quality direct materials on time with minimum lead time must be obtained.

20-30 (cont'd)

SOLUTION EXHIBIT 20-30
Annual Relevant Costs of Current Purchasing Policy and JIT Purchasing Policy for Margro Corporation

	Incremental Costs Under Current Purchasing Policy	Incremental Costs Under JIT Purchasing Policy
Required return on investment		
20% per year × $600,000 of average inventory per year	$120,000	
20% per year × $0 inventory per year		$ 0
Annual insurance costs	14,000	0
Warehouse rent	60,000	(13,500)[a]
Overtime costs		
No overtime	0	
Overtime premium		40,000
Stockout costs		
No stockouts	0	
$6.50[b] contribution margin per unit × 20,000 units		130,000
Total incremental costs	$194,000	$156,500
Difference in favour of JIT purchasing	$37,500	

[a]$(13,500) = Warehouse rental revenues, [(75% × 12,000) × $1.50].

[b]Calculation of unit contribution margin:

Selling price		
($10,800,000 ÷ 900,000 units)		$12.00
Variable costs per unit :		
Variable manufacturing costs per unit		
($4,050,000 ÷ 900,000 units)	$4.50	
Variable marketing and distribution costs per unit		
($900,000 ÷ 900,000 units)	1.00	
Total variable costs per unit		5.50
Contribution margin per unit		$ 6.50

Note that the incremental costs of $40,000 for overtime premiums to make the additional 15,000 units are less than the contribution margin from losing these sales equal to $97,500 ($6.50 × 15,000). Margro would rather incur overtime than lose 15,000 units of sales.

20-32 (20–25 min.) **Backflush, two trigger points, materials purchase and sale (continuation of 20-31).**

1.

(a) Purchase of raw materials	Inventory Control	5,300,000	
	Accounts Payable Control		5,300,000

(b) Incur conversion costs	Conversion Costs Control	3,080,000	
	Various Accounts		3,080,000

(c) Completion of finished goods   No entry

(d) Sale of finished goods	Cost of Goods Sold	7,872,000	
	Inventory Control		4,992,000
	Conversion Costs Allocated		2,880,000

(e) Underallocated or overallocated conversion costs	Conversion Costs Allocated	2,880,000	
	Cost of Goods Sold	200,000	
	Conversion Costs Control		3,080,000

2.

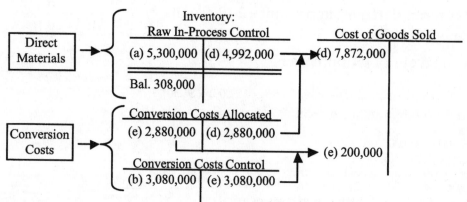

The $308,000 ending balance of Inventory Control consists of the $100,000 direct materials still on hand (same as shown in the solution to Problem 20-31) and the $26 × 8,000 = $208,000 direct materials embodied in the 8,000 units manufactured but not sold during June.

20-32 (cont'd)

3. Entry (e) in requirement 1 would be revised so that some conversion costs would be included in Inventory, 8,000 units × \$15 conversion cost per unit = \$120,000:

Conversion Costs Allocated	2,880,000	
Inventory Control		120,000
Cost of Goods Sold		80,000
Conversion Costs Control		3,080,000

If you assigned Problem 20-31, compare the answer here with the answer in the solution to Problem 20-31. Note that the underallocated conversion costs are \$80,000 in both answers. Note especially that the monthly writeoffs of all conversion costs may not be acceptable for external reporting purposes if inventories are materially understated. This variation of backflush costing is suitable for production systems that have minimal finished goods inventories. It is less feasible otherwise.

20-34 (25 min.) **Relevant benefits and relevant costs of JIT purchasing.**

Solution Exhibit 20-34 presents the $724.50 cash savings that would result if Hardesty Medical Instruments adopted the Just-in-time inventory system in 2003.

SOLUTION EXHIBIT 20-34

Annual Relevant Costs of Current Purchasing Policy and JIT Purchasing Policy for Hardesty Medical Instruments

	Relevant Costs Under	
Relevant Item	Current Purchasing Policy	JIT Purchasing Policy
Purchasing costs		
$10 per unit × 20,000 units	$200,000.00	
$10.05 per unit × 20,000 units		$201,000.00
Ordering costs		
$5 per order × 20 orders per year	100.00	
$5 per order × 200 orders per year		1,000.00
Opportunity carrying costs, required return on investment		
20% per year × $10 cost per unit × 500[a] units of average inventory per year	1,000.00	
20% per year × $10.05 cost per unit × 50[b] units of average inventory per year		100.50
Other carrying costs		
$4.50 per unit per year × 500[a] units of average inventory per year	2,250.00	
$4.50 per unit per year × 50[b] units of average inventory per year		225.00
Stockout costs		
No stockouts	0	
$3 per unit × 100 units per year		300.00
Total annual relevant costs	$203,350.00	$202,625.50

Annual difference in favor of JIT purchasing $724.50

[a] Order quantity ÷ 2 = 1,000 ÷ 2 = 500
[b] Order quantity ÷ 2 = 100 ÷ 2 = 50

2. Hardesty may benefit from Morrison managing its inventories if there is high order variability caused by randomness in when consumers purchase surgical scalpels or trade promotions that prompt retailers to stock for the future. By coordinating their activities and sharing information about retail sales and inventory held throughout the supply chain, Morrison can plan its manufacturing activities to ensure adequate supply of product while keeping inventory low. For this to succeed, Hardesty and Morrison must have compatible information systems, build trust, and communicate freely.

20-36 (25 min.) **Supplier evaluation and relevant costs of quality and timely deliveries.**

Solution Exhibit 20-36 presents the $1,450 annual relevant costs difference in favour of purchasing from Quality Sports. Copeland should buy the footballs from Quality Sports.

SOLUTION EXHIBIT 20-36
Annual Relevant Costs of Purchasing from Big Red and Quality Sports

	Relevant Costs of Purchasing from	
Relevant Item	**Big Red**	**Quality Sports**
Purchasing costs		
$ 50 per unit × 12,000 units per year	$600,000	
$ 51 per unit × 12,000 units per year		$612,000
Ordering costs		
$6 per order × 60[a] orders per year	360	
$6 per order × 60[a] orders per year		360
Inspection costs		
$0.02 per unit × 12,000 units	240	
No inspection necessary		0
Opportunity carrying costs, required return on investment,		
15% per year × $50 cost per unit × 100 units of average inventory per year;	750	
15% per year × $51 cost per unit × 100 units of average inventory per year		765
Other carrying costs (insurance, material handling, and so on)		
$4 per unit × 100 units of average inventory per year	400	
$4.50 per unit × 100 units of average inventory per year		450
Stockout costs		
$20 per unit × 350 units per year	7,000	
$10 per unit × 60 units per year		600
Customer returns costs		
$25 per unit × 300 units	7,500	
$25 per unit × 25 units		625
Total annual relevant costs	$616,250	$614,800

Annual difference in favor of Quality Sports ⬆ $1,450 ⬆

[a] Number of orders placed:
    Average inventory per year 100 units
    Average order size = 100 × 2 = 200 units
    Annual demand = 12,000 units
    Number of orders placed = 12,000 units/200 units per order = 60 orders

20-38 (20 min.) **Backflush, two trigger points, materials purchase and sale (continuation of 20-37).**

1.

(a) Purchases of raw materials	Inventory Control	550,000	
	Accounts Payable Control		550,000
(b) Incur conversion costs	Conversion Costs Control	440,000	
	Various Accounts (such as Accounts Payable) Payable Control and Wages		440,000
(c) Completion of finished goods	No entry		
(d) Sale of finished goods	Cost of Goods Sold	900,000	
	Inventory Control		500,000
	Conversion Costs Allocated		400,000
(e) Underallocated or overallocated conversion costs	Conversion Costs Allocated	400,000	
	Cost of Goods Sold	40,000	
	Conversion Costs Control		440,000

2.

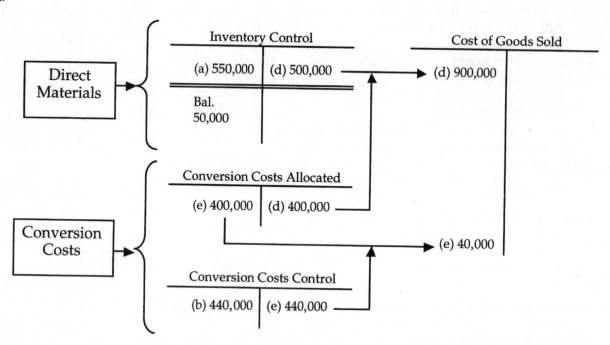

20-40 (20 min.)　　**Supply-chain analysis, company viewpoints.**

1. The major benefits to adopting a supply-chain approach include:

   a. Overall reduction in inventory levels across the supply chain:
      - "receiving better information has allowed us to forecast and reduce inventory levels ..."
      - "The inventory levels are lower ... by not overstocking the warehouses"

   b. Fewer stockouts at the retail level.

   c. Reduced manufacturing of items not subsequently demanded by retailers:
      - "You produce only what you need"
      - "We have less waste by not overstocking the warehouses"

   d. Lower manufacturing costs due to better production scheduling and fewer expedited orders:
      - "We can fine tune our production scheduling"

These benefits can both increase revenues (fewer stockouts) and decrease costs (lower manufacturing costs, lower holding costs, and lower distribution costs).

2. Key obstacles to a manufacturer adopting a supply-chain approach are:

   a. Communication obstacles—includes the unwillingness of some parties to share information.

   b. Trust obstacles—includes the concern that all parties will not meet their agreed-upon commitments.

   c. Information system obstacles—includes problems due to the information systems of different parties not being technically compatible.

   d. Limited resources—includes problems due to the people and financial resources given to support a supply-chain initiative not being adequate.

CHAPTER 21
CAPITAL BUDGETING AND COST ANALYSIS

21-2   The six stages in capital budgeting are:

1.   An *identification stage* to distinguish which capital expenditure projects will accomplish organization objectives.
2.   A *search stage* that explores several potential capital expenditure investments that will achieve organization objectives.
3.   An *information-acquisition stage* to consider the consequences of alternative capital investments.
4.   A *selection stage* to choose projects for implementation.
5.   A *financing stage* to obtain project financing.
6.   An *implementation and control* stage to put the project in motion and monitor its performance.

21-4   No. Only quantitative outcomes are formally analyzed in capital-budgeting decisions. Many effects of capital-budgeting decisions, however, are difficult to quantify in financial terms. These nonfinancial or qualitative factors, for example, the number of accidents in a manufacturing plant, or employee morale, are important to consider in making capital-budgeting decisions.

21-6   The payback method measures the time it will take to recoup, in the form of net cash inflows, the total dollars invested in a project. The payback method is simple and easy to understand. It is a handy method when precision in estimates of profitability is not crucial and when predicted cash flows in later years are highly uncertain. The main weakness of the payback method is its neglect of profitability and the time value of money.

21-8   No. The discounted cash-flow techniques implicitly consider depreciation in rate of return computations; the compound interest tables automatically allow for recovery of investment. The net initial investment of an asset is usually regarded as a lump-sum outflow at time zero.

21-10   No. If managers are evaluated on the accrual accounting rate of return, they may not use the NPV method for capital-budgeting decisions. Instead, managers will choose investments that maximize the accrual accounting rate of return.

21-12   Four critical success factors that managers focus on when controlling job projects are (a) scope (b) quality (c) time schedule and (d) costs.

21-14   Exercises in compound interest.

The answers to these exercises are printed after the last problem, at the end of the chapter.

21-16 (30 min.) **Comparison of approaches to capital budgeting.**

The table for the present value of annuities (Appendix B, Table 4) shows: 10 periods at 14% = 5.216

1. Payback period $= \dfrac{\$110,000}{\$28,000} = 3.93$ years

2. Net present value
   $= \$28,000(5.216) - \$110,000$
   $= \$146,048 - \$110,000 = \$36,048$

3. Internal rate of return:

   $\$110,000 =$ Present value of annuity of \$28,000 at X% for 10 years, or what factor (F) in the table of present values of an annuity (Appendix B, Table 4) will satisfy the following equation.

   $\$110,000 = \$28,000F$

   $F = \dfrac{\$110,000}{\$28,000} = 3.929$

On the ten-year line in the table for the present value of annuities (Appendix B, Table 4) find the column closest to 3.929; 3.929 is between a rate of return of 20% and 22%.

Interpolation can be used to determine the exact rate:

	Present Value Factors	
20%	4.192	4.192
IRR rate	—	3.929
22%	3.923	—
Difference	0.269	0.263

Internal rate of return $= 20\% + \left[\dfrac{0.263}{0.269}\right](2\%)$

$= 20\% + (0.978)(2\%) = 21.96\%$

4. Accrual accounting rate of return based on net initial investment:

   Net initial investment $= \$110,000$
   Estimated useful life $= 10$ years
   Annual straight-line depreciation $= \$110,000 \div 10 = \$11,000$

   Accrual accounting rate of return $= \dfrac{\$28,000 - \$11,000}{\$110,000}$

   $= \dfrac{\$17,000}{\$110,000} = 15.46\%$

21-18 (20-30 min.)   **Net present value, internal rate of return, sensitivity analysis.**

1a.   The table for the present value of annuities (Appendix B) shows:
16 periods at 14%   = 3.88

Net present value   = $40,000 (3.889) − $120,000

= $155,560 − $120,000 = $35,560

1b.   Internal rate of return:
$120,000 = Present value of annuity of $40,000 at X% for 6 years, or what factor (F) in the table of present values of an annuity (Appendix B, Table 4) will satisfy the following equation.

$120,000 = $40,000F

$$F \quad = \frac{\$120,000}{\$40,000} = 3.0$$

On the six-year line in the table for the present value of annuities (Appendix B), find the column closest to 3.0; 3.0 is between a rate of return of 24% and 26%.

Interpolation is necessary:

	Present Value Factors	
24%	3.020	3.020
IRR rate	—	3.000
26%	2.885	—
Difference	0.135	0.020

$$\text{Internal rate of return} \quad = 24\% + \left[\frac{0.020}{0.135}\right](2\%)$$

$$= 24\% + (0.148)(2\%) = 24.30\%$$

2.   Let the minimum annual cash savings be $X.
Then we want $X (3.889)   = $120,000

$$X \quad = \frac{\$120,000}{3.889} \quad = \quad \$30,856$$

Johnson Corporation would want annual cash savings of at least $30,856 for the net present value of the investment to equal zero. This amount of cash savings would justify the investment in financial terms.

3.   When the manager is uncertain about future cash flows, the manager would want to do sensitivity analysis, a form of which is described in requirement 2. Calculating the minimum cash flows necessary to make the project desirable gives the manager a feel for whether the investment is worthwhile or not. If the manager were quite certain about the future cash-operating cost savings, the approaches in requirement 1 would be preferred.

21-20 (30 min.) **Payback and NPV methods, no income taxes.**

1. a. Payback measures the time taken to recoup, in the form of expected future cash flows, the net investment in a project. Payback emphasizes the early recovery of cash as a key aspect of project ranking. Some managers argue that this emphasis on early recovery of cash is appropriate if there is a high level of uncertainty about future cash flows. Projects with shorter paybacks give the organization more flexibility because funds for other projects become available sooner.

Strengths

- Easy to understand
- One way to capture uncertainty about expected cash flows in later years of a project (although sensitivity analysis is a more systematic way)

Weaknesses

- Fails to incorporate the time value of money
- Does not consider a project's cash flows after the payback period

b.

Project A

Outflow, $200,000
Inflow, $50,000^1 + $50,000^2 + $50,000^3 + $50,000^4

Payback = 4 years

Project B

Outflow, $190,000

Inflow, $40,000^1 + $50,000^2 + $70,000^3 + $\dfrac{\$30,000^4}{\$75,000}$

Payback = $3 + \dfrac{\$30,000}{\$75,000} = 3.4$ years

Project C

Outflow, $250,000

Inflow, $75,000^1 + $75,000^2 + $60,000^3 + $\dfrac{\$40,000^4}{\$80,000}$

Payback = $3 + \dfrac{\$40,000}{\$80,000} = 3.5$ years

21-20 (cont'd)

Project D

Outflow, $210,000
Inflow, $75,000(Year 1) + $75,000(Year 2) + $60,000(Year 3)

Payback = 3 years

2. Solution Exhibit 21-22 shows the following ranking:

	NPV
1. Project C	$27,050
2. Project B	$25,635
3. Project D	$(3,750)
4. Project A	$(19,750)

3. Using NPV, Project C is the preferred project despite its having the longest payback. Project C has sizable cash inflows after the payback period. Nonfinancial qualitative factors should also be considered. For example, are there differential worker safety issues across the projects? Are there differences in the extent of learning that can benefit other projects? Are there differences in the customer relationships established with different projects that can benefit Cording Manufacturing in future projects?

SOLUTION EXHIBIT 21-20

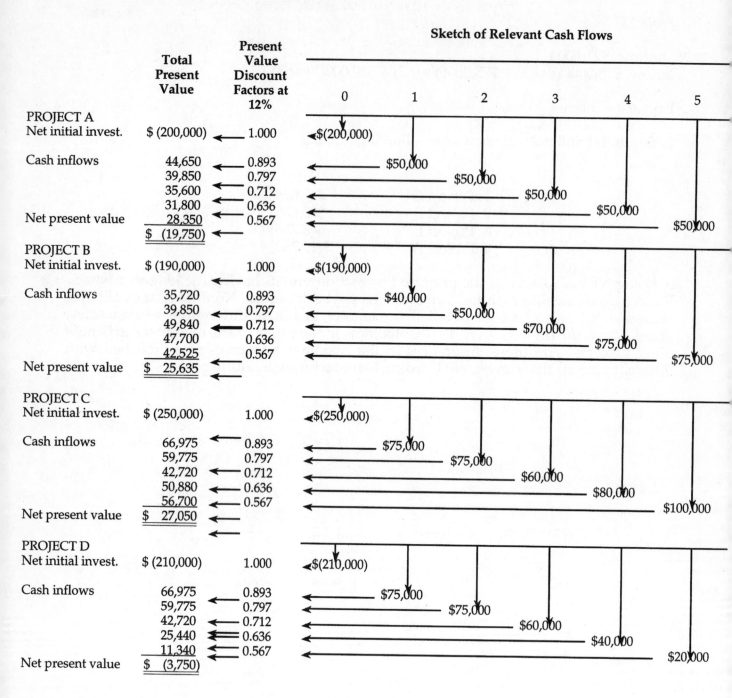

Sketch of Relevant Cash Flows

	Total Present Value	Present Value Discount Factors at 12%	0	1	2	3	4	5
PROJECT A								
Net initial invest.	$ (200,000)	1.000	$(200,000)					
Cash inflows	44,650	0.893		$50,000				
	39,850	0.797			$50,000			
	35,600	0.712				$50,000		
	31,800	0.636					$50,000	
Net present value	28,350	0.567						$50,000
	$ (19,750)							
PROJECT B								
Net initial invest.	$ (190,000)	1.000	$(190,000)					
Cash inflows	35,720	0.893		$40,000				
	39,850	0.797			$50,000			
	49,840	0.712				$70,000		
	47,700	0.636					$75,000	
	42,525	0.567						$75,000
Net present value	$ 25,635							
PROJECT C								
Net initial invest.	$ (250,000)	1.000	$(250,000)					
Cash inflows	66,975	0.893		$75,000				
	59,775	0.797			$75,000			
	42,720	0.712				$60,000		
	50,880	0.636					$80,000	
	56,700	0.567						$100,000
Net present value	$ 27,050							
PROJECT D								
Net initial invest.	$ (210,000)	1.000	$(210,000)					
Cash inflows	66,975	0.893		$75,000				
	59,775	0.797			$75,000			
	42,720	0.712				$60,000		
	25,440	0.636					$40,000	
	11,340	0.567						$20,000
Net present value	$ (3,750)							

21-22 (21-30 min.) **DCF, accrual accounting rate of return, working capital, evaluation of performance.**

1a. A summary of cash inflows and outflows (in thousands) are:

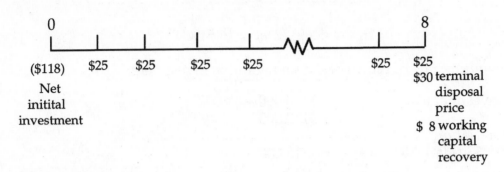

Present value of annuity of savings in cash operating costs
($25,000 per year for 8 years at 14%): $25,000 × 4.639 .... $115,975
Present value of $30,000 terminal disposal price of machine at
end of year 8: $30,000 × 0.351 10,530
Present value of $8,000 recovery of working capital at
end of year 8: $8,000 × 0.351 2,808
Gross present value 129,313
Deduct net initial investment:
  Special-purpose machine, initial investment $110,000
    Additional working capital investment 8,000   118,000
Net present value .... $ 11,313

1b. Use a trial and error approach. First, try a 16% discount rate:

$25,000 × 4.344	$108,600
($30,000 + $8,000) × .305	11,590
Gross present value	120,190
Deduct net initial investment	(118,000)
Net present value	$ 2,190

Second, try an 18% discount rate:

$25,000 × 4.078	$101,950
($30,000 + $8,000) × .266	10,108
Gross present value	112,058
Deduct net initial investment	(118,000)
Net present value	$ (5,942)

21-22 (cont'd)

By interpolation:

Internal rate of return $= 16\% + \left(\dfrac{2{,}190}{2{,}190 + 5{,}942} \right)(2\%)$

$$= 16\% + (.269)\,(2\%) = 16.54\%$$

2. Accrual accounting rate of return based on net initial investment:

Net initial investment $= \$110{,}000 + \$8{,}000$
$= \$118{,}000$

Annual depreciation
$(\$110{,}000 - \$30{,}000) \div 8$ years $= \$10{,}000$

Accrual accounting rate of return $= \dfrac{\$25{,}000 - \$10{,}000}{\$118{,}000} = 12.71\%$

3. If your decision is based on the DCF model, the purchase would be made because the net present value is positive, and the 16.54% internal rate of return exceeds the 14% required rate of return. However, you may believe that your performance may actually be measured using accrual accounting. This approach would show a 12.71% return on the initial investment, which is below the required rate. Your reluctance to make a "buy" decision would be quite natural unless you are assured of reasonable consistency between the decision model and the performance evaluation method.

21-24 (40 min.) **NPV and customer profitability, no income taxes.**

1.

Homebuilders	2002	2003	2004	2005	2006	2007
Revenues (5%)*	$45,000	$47,250	$49,612	$52,093	$54,698	$57,433
COGS (4%)*	22,000	22,880	23,795	24,747	25,737	26,766
Op. Costs (4%)*	10,000	10,400	10,816	11,249	11,699	12,167
Total costs	32,000	33,280	34,611	35,996	37,436	38,933
Cash flow from operations	$13,000	$13,970	$15,001	$16,097	$17,262	$18,500
Kitchen						
Revenues (15%)*	$325,000	$373,750	$429,812	$494,284	$568,427	$653,691
COGS (4%)*	180,000	187,200	194,688	202,476	210,575	218,998
Op. Costs (4%)*	75,000	78,000	81,120	84,365	87,740	91,250
Total costs	255,000	265,200	275,808	286,841	298,315	310,248
Cash flow from operations	$ 70,000	$108,550	$154,004	$207,443	$270,112	$343,443
Subdivision						
Revenues (8%)*	$860,000	$928,800	$1,003,104	$1,083,352	$1,170,020	$1,263,622
COGS (4%)*	550,000	572,000	594,880	618,675	643,422	669,159
Op. Costs (4%)*	235,000	244,400	254,176	264,343	274,917	285,914
Total costs	785,000	816,400	849,056	883,018	918,339	955,073
Cash flow from operations	$75,000	$112,400	$154,048	$200,334	$251,681	$308,549

*Annual increases given in question.

2.

		Homebuilders		Kitchen		Subdivision	
		Cash Flow		**Cash Flow**		**Cash Flow**	
	P.V. Factor	**from**	**Present**	**from**	**Present**	**from**	**Present**
Year	**for 10%**	**Operations**	**Value**	**Operations**	**Value**	**Operations**	**Value**
2001	0.909	$13,970	$12,699	$108,550	$98,672	$112,400	$102,172
2002	0.826	15,001	12,391	154,004	127,207	154,048	127,244
2003	0.751	16,097	12,089	207,443	155,790	200,334	150,451
2004	0.683	17,262	11,790	270,112	184,486	251,681	171,898
2005	0.621	18,500	11,488	343,443	213,278	308,549	191,609
			$60,457		$779,433		$743,374

Customer NPVs

Homebuilders	$ 60,457
Kitchen Constructors	779,433
Subdivision Erectors	743,374

21-24 (cont'd)

3. Assume the 20% discount is given in 2003

	2002	2003	2004	2005	2006	2007
Revenues (5%)	$325,000	$260,000[a]	$273,000[b]	$286,650[b]	$300,982[b]	$316,031[b]
Total costs (4%)	255,000	265,200	275,808	286,841	298,315	310,248
Cash flow from operations	$70,000	$ (5,200)	$ (2,808)	$ (191)	$ 2,667	$ 5,783

[a] 20% price discount
[b] 5% annual increase

Net present value:

Year	P.V. Factor at 10%	Cash Flow from Operations	Present Value
2001	0.909	$(5,200)	$(4,727)
2002	0.826	(2,808)	(2,319)
2003	0.751	(191)	(143)
2004	0.683	2,667	1,822
2005	0.621	5,783	3,591
			$(1,776)

The 20% discount and reduced subsequent annual revenue reduces the NPV from $779,433 to ($1,776). This is a drop of $781,209 in NPV.

Christen should consider whether the price discount demanded by Kitchen need be met in full to keep the account. The implication of meeting the full demand is that the account is minimally profitable at best. An equally serious concern is whether Christen's other two customers will demand comparable price discounts if Kitchen's full demands are met. The consequence would be very large reductions in the NPVs of all its customers.

Christen should also consider the reliability of the growth estimates used in computing the NPVs. Are the predicted differences in revenue growth rates based on reliable information? Many revenue growth estimates by salespeople turn out to be overestimates or occur over a longer time period than initially predicted.

21-26 (20-30 min.) **Relevant costs, replacement decisions, performance evaluation.**

All amounts are in thousands.

1. Old cash flow: Cash revenues, $120 – Cash costs, $124 $(4)
    New cash flow: 10% of $80 8
    Expected increase in recurring operating
        cash flows for 10 years $12

2. Initial machine investment $64
    Deduct current disposal price of old equipment (4)
    Net initial investment $60

    Payback period: $60 ÷ $12 = 5 years

3. NPV of cash inflows and outflows (in thousands):

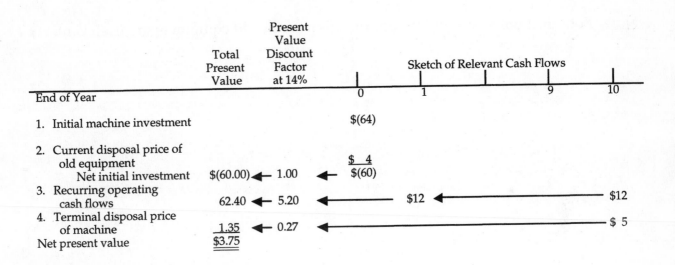

End of Year	Total Present Value	Present Value Discount Factor at 14%	Sketch of Relevant Cash Flows
			0 1 9 10
1. Initial machine investment			$(64)
2. Current disposal price of old equipment			$ 4
Net initial investment	$(60.00) ← 1.00		← $(60)
3. Recurring operating cash flows	62.40 ← 5.20		← $12 ———— $12
4. Terminal disposal price of machine	1.35 ← 0.27		———————— $ 5
Net present value	$3.75		

21-26 (cont'd)

4. Let X = Annual gross vending machine receipts.

$$(.10X + \$4)(5.20) + \$1.35 = \$60$$
$$0.52X + \$20.80 = \$60 - \$1.35$$
$$0.52X = \$58.65 - \$20.80 = \$37.85$$
$$X = \$37.85 \div 0.52$$
$$= \$72.788 \text{ (or } \$72{,}788)$$

Proof:		
	$72,788 × 10%	$ 7,278.80
	Add	4,000.00
	Total	11,278.80
	Multiply by	5.20
	Total	58,650.00
	Disposal price, $5,000 × 0.27	1,350.00
	Total	60,000.00
	Deduct investment	(60,000.00)
	Difference	$ 0

Note: Both the book value and the amortization on the old equipment are irrelevant.

21-28 (30 min.) **Special order, relevant costs, capital budgeting.**

1.   Relevant cash inflow from accepting the special order

	Relevant Cash Flows	
	Per Car (1)	Total (2)=(1) × 100,000
Incremental revenues (cash inflows)	$50	$5,000,000
Incremental costs (cash outflows)		
Neon paint	6	600,000
Boxes	3	300,000
Direct manufacturing labour	8	800,000
Total incremental costs	17	1,700,000
Net incremental benefit	$33	$3,300,000

Notes
(a)   The costs of plastic cars are irrelevant because these cars have already been purchased and so entail no incremental cash flow.

(b)   Vat depreciation is irrelevant because it is a past cost.

(c)   Allocated plant manager's salary is irrelevant because it will not change whether or not the special order is accepted.

(d)   Variable marketing costs are not deducted because they will not be incurred on the special order.

(e)   Fixed marketing costs are irrelevant because they will not change whether or not the special order is accepted.

If it must offer the same $50 price to its other customers, Toys Inc. will lose cash flow of $9 × 130,000 = $1,170,000 per year for 4 years from its existing customers.

Note that whatever incremental costs Toys incurs on sales to its existing customers is irrelevant. These costs would continue to be incurred whether Toys prices the cars at $50 or $59. You can verify that Toys generates positive contribution margin at a price of $50 and so should continue to sell to its existing customers.

21-28 (cont'd)

From Appendix B, the present value of a stream of $1,170,000 payments for 4 years discounted at 16% is $1,170,000 × 2.798 = $3,273,660.

The net relevant benefit of accepting the special order is $3,300,000 – $3,273,660 = $26,340. Therefore, Toys, Inc. should accept the special order.

2. Let the dollar discount from the current $59 price offered to existing customers be $X

Then $X (130,000) (2.798) = 3,300,000

$$X = \frac{3,300,000}{(130,000)(2.798)} = \$9.0724$$

At a price of $49.9276 ($59 – $9.0724) per car to its existing customers, Toys would just be indifferent between accepting and rejecting Tiny Tot's special order.

21-30 (25 min.) **Capital budgeting, computer-integrated manufacturing, sensitivity.**

1.   The net present value analysis of the CIM proposal follows. We consider the differences in cash flows if the machine is replaced. All values in millions.

		Relevant Cash Flows	Present Value Discount Factors at 14%	Total Present Value
1.	Initial investment in CIM today	$(45)	1.000	$(45.000)
2a.	Current disposal price of old production line	5	1.000	5.000
2b.	Current recovery of working capital ($6 – $2)	4	1.000	4.000
3.	Recurring operating cash savings $4[1] each year for 10 years	4	5.216	20.864
4a.	Higher terminal disposal price of machines ($14 – $0) in year 10	14	0.270	3.780
4b.	Reduced recovery of working capital ($2 – $6) in year 10	(4)	0.270	(1.080)
	Net present value of CIM investment			$(12.436)

On the basis of this formal financial analysis, Dynamo should not invest in CIM—it has a negative net present value of $(12.436) million.

[1]Recurring operating cash flows are as follows:

Cost of maintaining software programs and CIM equipment	$(1.5)
Reduction in lease payments due to reduced floor-space requirements	1.0
Fewer product defects and reduced rework	4.5
Annual recurring operating cash flows	$ 4.0

2.   Requirement 1 only looked at cost savings to justify the investment in CIM. Burns estimates additional cash revenues net of cash operating costs of $3 million a year as a result of higher quality and faster production resulting from CIM.

From Appendix B, the net present value of the $3 million annuity stream for 10 years discounted at 14% is $3 × 5.216 = $15.648. Taking these revenue benefits into account, the net present value of the CIM investment is $3.212 ($15.648 – $12.436) million. On the basis of this financial analysis, Dynamo should invest in CIM.

3. Let the annual cash flow from additional revenues be $X. Then we want the present value of this cash flow stream to overcome the negative NPV of $(12.436) calculated in requirement 1. Hence,

$$X (5.216) = 12.436$$

$$X = \$2.384 \text{ million}$$

An annuity stream of $2.384 million for 10 years discounted at 14% gives an NPV of $2.384 × 5.216 = 12.436 (rounded).

4.

		Relevant Cash Flows	Present Value Discount Factors at 14%	Total Present Value
1.	Initial investment in CIM today	$(45)	1.000	$(45.000)
2a.	Current disposal price of old production line	5	1.000	5.000
2b.	Current recovery of working capital ($6 – $2)	4	1.000	4.000
3a.	Recurring operating cash savings $4 each year for 5 years	4	3.433	13.732
3b.	Recurring cash flows from additional revenues of $3 each year for 5 years	3	3.433	10.299
4a.	Higher terminal disposal price of machines ($20 – $4) in year 5	16	0.519	8.304
4b.	Reduced recovery of working capital ($2 – $6) in year 5	(4)	0.519	(2.076)
	Net present value of CIM investment			$ (5.741)

The use of too short a time horizon such as 5 years biases against the adoption of CIM projects. Before finally deciding against CIM in this case, Burns should consider other factors including

(a) Sensitivity to different estimates of recurring cash savings or revenue gains.
(b) Accuracy of the costs of implementing and maintaining CIM.
(c) Benefits of greater flexibility that results from CIM and the opportunity to train workers for the manufacturing environment of the future.
(d) Potential obsolescence of the CIM equipment. Dynamo should consider how difficult the CIM equipment would be to modify if there is a major change in CIM technology.
(e) Alternative approaches to achieving the major benefits of CIM such as changes in process or implementation of just-in-time systems.
(f) Strategic factors. CIM may be the best approach to remain competitive against other low-cost producers in the future.

CHAPTER 22
CAPITAL BUDGETING: A CLOSER LOOK

22-2   Yes. To apply a consistent set of regulations and to provide for implementation of government initiatives, the federal government has implemented its own system of capital cost allowance (CCA). The Income Tax Act (ITA) does not permit a company to deduct amortization expense in determining taxable income but rather a company is allowed to deduct CCA. Therefore, the accounting amortization method will have no effect on taxes payable.

22-4   The total project approach calculates the present value of *all* cash outflows and inflows associated with each alternative. The incremental approach analyzes only those cash outflows and inflows that differ between alternatives.

22-6   No. Income taxes also affect the cash-operating flows from an investment and the cash flows from current and terminal disposal of machines in the capital-budgeting decision. When a company has positive cash-operating flows, income taxes reduce the cash flows available to the company from these sources.

22-8   The *real rate of return* is the rate of return required to cover only investment risk. This rate is made up of two elements: (a) a risk-free element and (b) a business-risk element. The *nominal rate of return* is the rate of return required to cover investment risk and the anticipated decline, due to inflation, in general purchasing power of the cash that the investment generates. This rate is made up of two elements: (a) the real rate of return and (b) an inflation element.

The *nominal rate of return* and the *real rate of return* are related as follows:

$$\text{Nominal rate} = [(1 + \text{Real rate})(1 + \text{Inflation rate})] - 1$$

22-10   The chapter outlines five approaches used to recognize risk in capital budgeting:

1.   Varying the required payback time.
2.   Adjusting the required rate of return.
3.   Adjusting the estimated future cash flows.
4.   Sensitivity ("what-if") analysis.
5.   Estimating the probability distribution of future cash inflows and outflows for each project.

22-12   No. Discounted cash-flow analysis applies to both profit-seeking and nonprofit organizations. Nonprofit organizations must also decide which long-term assets will accomplish various tasks at the least cost. Nonprofit organizations incur an opportunity cost of funds.

22-14 NPV and IRR will not always rank projects identically. Different rankings occur when projects have unequal lives or unequal initial investments. The difference arises because the IRR method assumes a reinvestment rate equal to the indicated rate of return for the shortest-lived project. NPV assumes that funds can be reinvested at the required rate of return.

22-16 (15-20 min.) Multiple choice.

1. (a)

Before-tax annual cash flow	$10,000
Amortization ($30,000 ÷ 6)	(5,000)
Net income before tax	5,000
Income tax expense	2,000
Accounting income	$ 3,000

After-tax accrual accounting rate of return = $3,000 ÷ 30,000 = 10%

2. (b)

Year	CCA	Tax Shield	Operating-Cash Flows	Total Cash Flows	Cummulative Cash Flows
1	$ 3,000	$ 1,200	$10,000	$11,200	$11,200
2	5,400	2,160	10,000	12,160	23,360
3	4,320	1,728	10,000	11,728	35,088

Payback period = 2 + ((30,000 − 23,360)/11,728) = 2.6 years

3. (b)

	Relevant Cash Flows	Present-Value Discount Factors at 15%	Total Present Value
Initial investment	$(30,000)	1.000	$(30,000)
Recurring after-tax operating savings*	6,000	3.785	22,710
Tax shield from CCA**	6,405	1.000	6,405
Net present value			$ (885)

*10,000 × (1 − 0.40) = 6,000
**(30,000 × 0.4) × (0.20/(0.20 + 0.15)) × (2 + 0.15)/2(1 + 0.15)) = 6,405

4. (b) Only one payment will be made which 5 years later must yield $30,000. Therefore, deduct the value of an annuity of four payments from the value of an annuity of five payments:

$$3.353 - 2.856 = 0.497$$

Note that 3.353 − 2.856 = 0.497 is the present value of a cash outflow of $1 occurring at the end of period 5. Alternatively stated, $1 is the future value of $0.497 invested five years ago. Therefore, to have $30,000 now, we need to invest its present value 5 years ago discounted at 15% equal to:

$$\$30,000 \times 0.497 = \$14,910$$

22-18 (40 min.) **Total project versus differential approach, income taxes.**

(a)   Total Project Approach

Replace machine

	Relevant Cash Flows	Present-Value Discount Factors at 14%	Total Present Value
Initial new machine investment	$(63,000)	1.000	$(63,000)
Disposal of old machine	29,000	1.000	29,000
Recurring after-tax cash operating costs*	(28,000)	2.322	(65,016)
Tax shield from CCA**	5,632	1.000	5,632
Net Present Value			$(93,384)

$*40,000 \times (1 - 0.3) = 28,000$

$**((63,000 - 29,000) \times 0.3) \times (0.2 / (0.2 + 0.14)) \times ((2 + 0.14) / ((2(1 + 0.14)))) = 5,632$

Keep machine

	Relevant Cash Flows	Present-Value Discount Factors at 14%	Total Present Value
Disposal of old machine at end of useful life	$6,000	0.675	$4,050
Recurring after-tax cash operating costs*	(42,000)	2.322	(97,524)
Tax shield from CCA**	(1,059)	0.675	(715)
Net Present Value			$(94,189)

$*60,000 \times (1 - 0.3) = 42,000$

$**((-6,000 \times 0.3) \times (0.2 / (0.2 + 0.14)) = -1,059$

Net present value different in favour of replacement $805

(b)   Total Project Approach

	Relevant Cash Flows	Present-Value Discount Factors at 14%	Total Present Value
Initial new machine investment	$(63,000)	1.000	$(63,000)
Disposal of old machine	29,000	1.000	29,000
Recurring after-tax cash operating costs*	14,000	2.322	32,508
Tax shield from CCA**	5,632	1.000	5,632
Difference in terminal value	(6,000)	0.675	(4,050)
Tax shield lost from terminal value	1,059	0.675	715
Net Present Value			$ 805

$*(60,000 - 40,000) \times (1 - 0.3) = 14,000$

22-20 (40 min.)   **Project risk, required rate of return.**

Drilling equipment project

1.

		Relevant Cash Flows	Present-Value Discount Factors at 12%	Total Present Value
1.	Initial drilling equipment investment	$(1,000,000)	1.000	$(1,000,000)
2.	Tax shield rated by CCA*	191,822	1.000	191,822
3.	Recurring cash-operating flows	$ 370,000		
	Additional income taxes at 30%	(111,000)		
	Recurring after-tax cash-operating flows each year for 5 years (excl. amort. effects)	$ 259,000	3.605	933,695
	Net present value			$ 125,517

$*(1,000,000 \times 0.3) \times (0.25/(0.25 + 0.12)) \times ((2 + 0.12)/2(1 + 0.12)) = 191,822$

Production equipment project

	Relevant Cash Flows	Present-Value Discount Factors	Total Present Value
Initial production equipment investment	$ (800,000)	1.000	$(800,000)
Tax shield created by CCA*	153,475	1.000	153,475
Recurring operating cash flows**	210,000	3.037	637,770
Net Present Value			$ (8,755)

$*(800,000 \times 0.3) \times (0.25/(0.25 + 0.12)) \times ((2 + 0.12)/2(1 + 0.12)) = 153,475$
$**300,000 \times (1 - 0.3) = 210,000$

At a 12% discount rate for both projects, the drilling equipment project has the higher NPV and would be preferred.

2.   We calculate the NPV of the high-risk drilling equipment project assuming a required rate of return of 18%.

		Relevant Cash Flows	Present-Value Discount Factors at 18%	Total Present Value
1.	Initial drilling equipment investment	$(1,000,000)	1.000	$(1,000,000)
2.	Tax shield created by CCA*	$ 161,006	1.000	161,006
3.	Recurring cash-operating flows	$ 370,000		
	Additional income taxes at 30%	(111,000)		
	Recurring after-tax cash-operating flows each year for 5 years (excl. amort. effects)	$ 259,000	3.127	809,893
	Net present value			$ (29,101)

$*(1,000,000 \times 0.3) \times (0.25/(0.25 + 0.18)) \times ((2+0.18)/2(1 + 0.18)) = 161,006$

22-20 (cont'd)

The lower-risk production equipment project for the refinery discounted at 12% has an NPV of $8,755 (requirement 1) that is greater than the NPV of $(29,101) for the higher-risk drilling equipment project for oil exploration discounted at 18%.

3.   Esso should favour the investment in the production equipment for the refinery because it has a positive NPV. It should not invest in the drilling equipment because this project has a negative NPV when discounted at the risk adjusted 18% required rate of return.

22-22 (25 min.) **Inflation and nonprofit institution, no tax aspects.**

1.   The university official calculated the following NPV using the 18.8% discount rate and real cash-operating savings.

Year	Relevant Cash-Operating Savings in Real Dollars as of 12-31-2000 (1)	Present-Value Discount Factors at 18.8% (2)	Present Value of Cash Flows (3) = (1) × (2)
2003	$1,000	0.842	$ 842
2004	1,000	0.709	709
2005	1,000	0.596	596
2006	1,000	0.502	502
2007	1,000	0.423	423
Present value of recurring cash-operating savings			3,072
Net initial investment			3,500
Net present value			$ (428)

On the basis of these calculations, the university official would reject the proposal to invest in the photocopying machine. This approach is incorrect because it discounts real cash flows using a nominal discount rate. I would redo the analysis after restating the real cash savings into nominal cash savings as shown below.

Year	Relevant Cash-Operating Savings in Nominal Dollars (1)	Present-Value Discount Factors at 18.8% (2)	Present Value of Nominal Cash Flows (3) = (1) × (2)
2003	$1,000 × 1.10 = $1,100	0.842	$ 926
2004	1,000 × (1.10)^2 = 1,210	0.709	858
2005	1,000 × (1.10)^3 = 1,331	0.596	793
2006	1,000 × (1.10)^4 = 1,464	0.502	735
2007	1,000 × (1.10)^5 = 1,611	0.423	681
Present value of recurring cash-operating savings			3,993
Net initial investment			3,500
Net present value			$ 493

22-22 (cont'd)

The net present value using nominal cash flows and a nominal rate of return is positive, $493. Eastern University should invest in the photocopying machine on the basis of financial considerations.

2a. The real rate of return required by Eastern University can be computed using the following relationship:

$$(1 + \text{real rate}) = \frac{1 + \text{nominal rate}}{1 + \text{inflation rate}} = \frac{1 + 0.188}{1 + 0.10} = \frac{1.188}{1.10} = 1.08$$

Real rate of return required = 0.08 or 8%

2b. The net present value using real operating cash savings and real rates of return are as follows:

Year	Relevant Cash-Operating Savings in Real Dollars as of 12-31-2000	Present-Value Discount Factors at 8% (2)	Present Value of Real Cash Flows (3) = (1) × (2)
1	$1,000	0.926	$ 926
2	1,000	0.857	857
3	1,000	0.794	794
4	1,000	0.735	735
5	1,000	0.681	681
Present value of recurring cash-operating savings			3,993
Net initial investment			3,500
Net present value			$ 493

3. Requirements 1 and 2 when correctly done give the same NPV of $493. Consistency is key in capital budgeting. Requirement 1 uses nominal cash flows and nominal rates of return. Requirement 2 uses real cash flows and real rates of return. Both are valid approaches.

22-24 (20-30 min.) **Comparison of projects with unequal lives.**

1. Internal rate of return

Project 1

Let F = Present-value factor of $1 at X% received at the end of 1 year, Appendix B, Table 2

$$\$10,000 = \text{PV of } \$12,000 \text{ at } X\% \text{ to be received at the end of year 1}$$

$$F = \frac{\$10,000}{\$12,000} = 0.833$$

$$\text{IRR} = 20\%$$

Project 2

Let F = Present-value factor of $1 at X% received at the end of year 4, Appendix B, Table 2

$$\$10,000 = \text{PV of } \$17,500 \text{ at } X\% \text{ to be received at the end of year 4}$$

$$F = \frac{\$10,000}{\$17,500} = 0.571$$

The internal rate of return can be calculated by interpolation:

	Present-Value Factors for $1 Received after 4 years	
14%	0.592	0.592
IRR rate	–	0.571
16%	0.552	–
Difference	0.040	0.021

$$\text{IRR rate: } 14\% + \left(\frac{0.021}{0.040}\right)(2\%) = 15.05\%$$

Project 1 is preferable to Project 2 using the IRR criterion.

2. Net present value

Project 1:

Gross present value	= PV of $12,000 at 10% to be received at the end of year 1		
	= $12,000 (0.909)	=	$10,908
Net present value	= $10,908 – $10,000	=	$908

22-24 (cont'd)

Project 2:

Gross present value   =   PV of $17,500 at 10% to be received at the end of year 4
                          = $17,500 (0.683)   = $11,952.50

Net present value   = $11,952.50 – $10,000 = $1,952.50

Project 2 is preferable to Project 1 using the net present-value criterion.

3.   This problem contrasts the implied reinvestment rates of return under the internal rate of return and net present-value methods. Where the economic lives of mutually exclusive projects are unequal, this clash of reinvestment rates may give different conclusions under the two methods. This result occurs because the internal rate of return method assumes that the reinvestment rate is at least equal to the computed rate of return on the project. The net present-value method assumes that the funds obtainable from competing projects can be reinvested at the rate of the company's required rate of return. Comparisons follow:

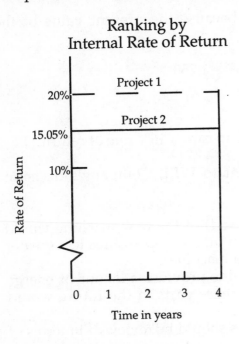

Ranking by
Internal Rate of Return

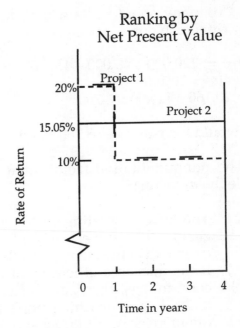

Ranking by
Net Present Value

Assumption: Project 1 funds can be reinvested at 20% over the life of the shorter-lived project.

Assumption: Project (1) funds can be reinvested at 10%, the required rate of return.

22-9

22-26 (40 min.) Replacement of a machine, income taxes, sensitivity.

1.

	Relevant Cash Flows	Present-Value Discount Factors at 16%	Total Present Value
Initial machine investment	$ (120,000)	1.000	$ (120,000)
Proceeds from disposal of old machine	40,000	1.000	40,000
Tax shield created by CCA*	18,167	1.000	18,167
Recurring operating savings**	11,400	2.798	31,897
Proceeds from disposal of machine***	13,000	0.552	7,176
Lost tax shield because of disposal****	(3,171)	0.552	(1,750)
Net Present Value			$ (24,510)

$*((120{,}000 - 40{,}000) \times 0.4) \times (0.25/(0.25 + 0.16)) \times ((2 + .16)/(2(1 + 0.16))) = 18{,}167$

$**300{,}000 \times (0.2 - 0.14) \times (1 - 0.4) + (15{,}000 - 14{,}000)0.6 = 11{,}400$

$***20{,}000 - 7{,}000 = 13{,}000$

$****(-13{,}000 \times 0.4) \times (0.25/(0.25 + 0.16)) = -3{,}171$

WRL Company should retain the old equipment because the present value of the incremental cash flows is negative.

2. $0 = -120{,}000 + 40{,}000 + 18{,}167 + 2.798atcs + 7{,}176 - 1{,}750$
$atcs = 20{,}160$
$20{,}160 - 11{,}400 = 8{,}760$

WRL would have to save $8,760 more after-tax dollars to earn a 16% rate of return.

3.   The nonquantitative factors that are important to WRL Company's decision include the following:

(a)   The lower operating costs (variable and fixed) of the new machine would enable WRL to meet future competitive or inflationary pressures to a greater degree than the business could using the old machine.

(b)   If the increased efficiency of the new machine provides a labour or energy cost savings, then additional increases in these costs in the future would make the new machine more attractive.

(c)   Maintenance and servicing of both machines should be reviewed in terms of reliability of the manufacturer and the costs.

(d)   Potential technological advances in machinery over the next four years should be evaluated.

(e)   Space requirements for the new machine should be reviewed and compared with the space requirements of the present equipment to determine if more or less space is required.

22-28 (35 min.) Capital budgeting, inventory changes.

1.   A schedule of relevant cash flows follows:

Sketch of Relevant Cash Flows

	Year 0	Year 1	Year 2	Year 3	Year 4
Acquire machines	($109,200)				
Sales					
6,000 × $25		$150,000			
6,200 × $25			$155,000		
7,700 × $24				$184,800	
3,100 × $22					$68,200
Manufacturing Costs					
7,000 × $12		(84,000)			
6,500 × $13			(84,500)		
6,500 × $14				(91,000)	
3,000 × $15					(45,000)
Marketing, distribution & customer service costs					
6,000 × $3		(18,000)			
6,200 × $3			(18,600)		
7,700 × $3				(23,100)	
3,100 × $3					(9,300)
Disposal of machine					18,000
Taxes (see schedule)		(18,540)	(13,165)	(14,914)	(7,425)
Net cash flow after tax	($109,200)	$ 29,460	$ 38,735	$ 55,786	$ 30,275

	Year 1	Year 2	Year 3	Year 4
Sales	$150,000	$155,000	$184,800	$ 68,200
COGS*	72,000	79,600	106,500	46,400
Mkt, Dist. & Cust. serv.	18,000	18,600	23,100	9,300
CCA	13,650	23,888	17,916	8,937
Taxable income	$ 46,350	$ 32,912	$ 37,284	$ 3,563
Tax Rate	40%	40%	40%	40%
Taxes	$ 18,540	$ 13,165	$ 14,914	$ 1,425

*Year 1: 6,000 × 12 = 72,000
  Year 2: (1,000 × 12) + (5,200 × 13) = 79,600
  Year 3: (1,300 × 13) + (6,400 × 14) = 106,500
  Year 4: (100 × 14) + (3,000 × 15) = 46,400

22-28 (cont'd)

2.

	Relevant Cash Flows	Present-Value Discount Factors at 16%	Total Present Value
Year 0	$ (109,200)	1.000	$ (109,200)
Year 1	29,460	0.862	25,395
Year 2	38,735	0.743	28,780
Year 3	55,786	0.641	35,759
Year 4	30,275	0.552	16,712
Remaining CCA tax shield*	6,539	0.476	3,113
Net Present Value			$ 558

*$((109,200 - 13,650 - 23,888 - 17,916 - 8,937 - 18,000) \times 0.4) \times (0.25/(0.25 + 0.16)) = 6,539$

22-30 (40 min.) **Mining, income taxes, inflation, sensitivity analysis.**

1. <u>Annual cash flow (Years 1-5)</u>

Revenue ($350 × 4,800[a])		$1,680,000
Cash-operating costs		
Variable costs ($100 × 4,800)	480,000	
Technicians ($110,000)	110,000	
Maintenance	50,000	
Total cash-operating costs		640,000
Recurring cash-operating flows		1,040,000
Additional income taxes at 40%		416,000
Recurring after-tax cash-operating flows		
each year for 5 years (excl. amort. effects)		$624,000

Year	CCA	Tax Shield	Operating Cash Flows	Total Cash Flows	Cummulative Cash Flows
1	$450,000	$180,000	$624,000	$804,000	$ 804,000
2	765,000	306,000	624,000	930,000	1,734,000
3	535,500	214,200	624,000	838,200	2,572,200
4	374,850	149,940	624,000	773,940	3,346,140

Payback period = 3 + ((3,000,000 – 2,572,200)/773,940) = 3.55 years

2. The net present value of VanDyk Enterprises' proposed acquisition of the extraction equipment is $60,745, as shown in the following calculation:

	Relevant Cash Flows	Present-Value Discount Factors at 12%	Total Present Value
Initial equipment investment	$ (3,000,000)	1.000	$ (3,000,000)
Recurring cash-operating savings*	624,000	3.605	2,249,520
Tax shield created by CCA**	811,225	1.000	811,225
Net Present Value			$ 60,745

*1,040,000 × (1 – 0.4) = 624,000
**((3,000,000 × 0.4) × 0.3/(0.3 + 0.12)) × ((2 + 0.12) (2(1 + 0.12))) = 811,125

3. In order for VanDyk Enterprises' acquisition of the extraction equipment to break even from a net present-value perspective, the revenue per ounce of gold must be at least $344.15, calculated as follows.

0	=	–3,000,000 + 811,225 + 3.605os
os	=	607,150
607,150	=	(4,800 × (rev – 100) – 110,000 – 50,000) × (1 – 0.4)
rev	=	344.15

Therefore the minimum revenue per ounce is $344.15.

22-30 (cont'd)

4.   Under the assumptions given here, requirement 2 has already calculated NPV using nominal cash flows and nominal rates of return. It has already taken inflationary effects into consideration. Hence no new calculations are necessary. The after-tax net present value is $60,745 as calculated in requirement 2. Some students may question whether the assumptions specified in requirement 4 are appropriate since despite the 2% inflation per year, the revenues and cash-operating costs are assumed to be the same each year for the 5 years. There is no inconsistency here. Despite the 2% increase in general price levels, the specific revenues per ounce of gold and the specific cash-operating costs in this industry could well be the same either because of contractual reasons or because of the general economic conditions of supply and demand.

22-32 (40 min.) **Ranking projects.**

1. Project B

Let F = Present-value factor for an annuity of $1 for 10 years in Appendix B, Table 4

$100,000 = $20,000 F
F = 5.000 for ten-year life

The internal rate of return can be calculated by interpolation:

	Present-Value Factors for Annuity of $1 for 10 years	
14%	5.216	5.216
IRR	–	5.000
16%	4.833	–
Difference	0.383	0.216

$$\text{IRR} = 14\% + \left(\frac{0.216}{0.383}\right)(2\%) = 15.1\%$$

Project C

$200,000 = $70,000 F

Let F = Present-value factor for an annuity of $1 for 5 years in Appendix B, Table 4

F = 2.857 for five-year life

The internal rate of return can be calculated by interpolation:

	Present-Value Factors for Annuity of $1 for 5 years	
22%	2.864	2.864
IRR	–	2.857
24%	2.745	–
Difference	0.119	0.007

$$\text{IRR} = 22\% + \left(\frac{0.007}{0.119}\right)(2\%) = 22.1\%$$

22-32 (cont'd)

<u>Project D</u>

$200,000 = PV of a four-year annuity of $200,000 per year deferred five years

Trial and error:

	At 18%	At 20%	At 22%
$1 per year for 4 years	2.690	2.589	2.494
Multiply by $200,000, the total value of the annuity	$538,000	$517,800	$498,800
Multiply by the present value of $1 five years hence	0.437	0.402	0.370
PV of annuity in arrears	$235,106	$208,156	$184,556

$$IRR = 20\% + \left(\frac{\$208,156 - \$200,000}{\$208,156 - \$184,556}\right)(2\%)$$

$$= 20\% + \left(\frac{\$8,156}{\$23,600}\right)(2\%) = 20.7\%$$

<u>Ranking of Projects</u>

Rank	Project	IRR	Initial Investment
1	C	22.1%	$200,000
2	D	20.7	200,000
3	B	15.1	100,000
4	A	14.0	100,000
5	E	12.6	200,000
6	F	12.0	50,000

2. <u>Budget limit:</u>

<u>$500,000</u>	<u>$550,000</u>	<u>$650,000</u>
C	C	C
D	D	D
B	B	B
	F	A
		F

3. <u>Ranking by net present value, discounting at 16%:</u>

Rank	Project	Net Present Value
1	D	$ 66,370
2	C	29,180
3	B	(3,340)
4	F	(3,384)
5	A	(13,170)
6	E	(35,965)

22-32 (cont'd)

Because 16% is the implicit reinvestment rate, these rankings are different from the rankings made on the basis of internal rates of return in requirement 1.

Computations

Project D

PV of $200,000 per year for four years at 16% = $200,000 (2.798)	$559,600
It is in arrears five years, so PV = $559,600 (0.476)	266,370
Net initial investment	(200,000)
Net present value	$ 66,370

Project C

PV of $70,000 per year for five years at 16% = $70,000 (3.274)	$229,180
Net initial investment	(200,000)
Net present value	$ 29,180

Project B

PV of $20,000 per year for ten years at 16% = $20,000 (4.833)	$ 96,660
Net initial investment	(100,000)
Net present value	$ (3,340)

Project F

PV at 16%:	$23,000 × 0.862	$ 19,826
	20,000 × 0.743	14,860
	10,000 × 0.641	6,410
	10,000 × 0.552	5,520
	Total PV	46,616
Net initial investment		(50,000)
Net present value		$ (3,384)

Project A

PV of annuity of $20,000 for 15 years	= $20,000 × 5.575	$111,500
Deduct deferral of 2 years	= 20,000 × 1.605	(32,100)
PV of annuity in arrears		79,400
PV of $10,000 due in 2 years	= 10,000 × 0.743	7,430
Total PV		86,830
Net initial investment		(100,000)
Net present value		$ (13,170)

22-32 (cont'd)

Project E

PV of annuity of $50,000 for 10 years	= $50,000	×	4.833	$241,650
Deduct deferral of 3 years	= 50,000	×	2.246	(112,300)
PV of annuity in arrears				129,350
PV of $30,000 due in 3 years	= 30,000	×	0.641	19,230
PV of $15,000 due in 2 years	= 15,000	×	0.743	11,145
PV of $ 5,000 due in 1 year	= 5,000	×	0.862	4,310
Total PV				164,035
Net initial investment				(200,000)
Net present value				$ (35,965)

4. Other influential factors include:

(a) The risk linked with a given proposal may prompt management to judge it more or less attractive than other proposals that promise a comparable internal rate of return.

(b) Future investment opportunities may affect the current relative attractiveness of alternative proposals. For example, if management expects that in five years hence the best available alternatives will bring less than 20%, Project D (which promises an internal rate of return of 20.7% for 9 years) may be preferable to Project C (which promises 22.1% for 5 years). However, if future opportunities are expected to bring equal or higher internal rates of return, a shorter-lived project may be more attractive, even though a longer-lived project may yield a higher rate of return. Thus, if a choice must be made now between E and F, Project F (12.0% for 4 years) may be chosen instead of Project E (12.6%, but it locks in capital for 10 years and necessitates a much larger investment).

22-34 (40-50 min.) Ethics, discounted cash-flow analysis.

1.

	Relevant Cash Flows	Present-Value Discount Factors at 12%	Total Present Value
Initial equipment investment	$ (900,000)	1.000	$ (900,000)
Initial working capital investment	(200,000)	1.000	(200,000)
Tax shield created by CCA*	207,191	1.000	207,191
Cash flow from canceling lease**	(19,200)	1.000	(19,200)
Additional working capital investment	(200,000)	0.797	(159,400)
Recurring rent cash flow forgone***	(28,800)	4.111	(118,397)
Recurring operating cash flows****			1,200,448
Market research and sales promotion cash flows*****	(192,000)	0.893	(171,456)
Recovery of working capital	400,000	0.507	202,800
Proceeds from disposal of equipment	300,000	0.507	152,100
Lost tax shield from disposal******	(72,973)	0.507	(36,997)
Net Present Value			$ 157,089

$*(900,000 \times 0.36) \times (0.25/(0.25 + 0.12)) \times ((2 + 0.12)/(2(1 + 0.12))) = 207,191$

$**-30,000 \times (1 - 0.36) = -19,200$

$***-45,000 \times (1 - 0.36) = -28,800$

****Recurring after-tax cash-operating flows

Year (1)	Cash-Operating Flows (2)	After-Tax Cash-Operating Flows (3) = 0.64 × (2)	Present-Value Discount Factors at 12%	Total Present Value
1	$400,000	$256,000	0.893	$ 228,608
2	400,000	256,000	0.797	204,032
3	600,000	384,000	0.712	273,408
4	600,000	384,000	0.636	244,224
5	600,000	384,000	0.567	217,728
6	100,000	64,000	0.507	32,448
				$1,200,448

$*****-300,000 \times (1 - 0.36) = -192,000$

$******(-300,000 \times 0.36) \times (0.25/(0.25 + 0.12)) = -72,973$

Dudley should launch the new household product because investing in the product has a positive net present value.

2.

	Relevant Cash Flows	Present-Value Discount Factors at 12%	Total Present Value
Initial equipment investment	$ (1,150,000)	1.000	$ (1,150,000)
Initial working capital investment	(200,000)	1.000	(200,000)
Tax shield created by CCA*	264,744	1.000	264,744
Cash flow from canceling lease**	(19,200)	1.000	(19,200)
Additional working capital investment	(200,000)	0.797	(159,400)
Recurring rent cash flow forgone***	(28,800)	4.111	(118,397)
Recurring operating cash flows (see above)			1,200,448
Market research and sales promotion cash flows****	(192,000)	0.893	(171,456)
Recovery of working capital	400,000	0.507	202,800
Proceeds from disposal of equipment	300,000	0.507	152,100
Lost tax shield from disposal*****	(72,973)	0.507	(36,997)
Net Present Value			$ (35,358)

$*(1,150,000 \times 0.36) \times (0.25/(0.25 + 0.12)) \times ((2 + 0.12)/(2(1 + 0.12))) = 264,744$

$**-30,000 \times (1 - 0.36) = -19,200$

$***-45,000 \times (1 - 0.36) = -28,800$

$****-300,000 \times (1 - 0.36) = -192,000$

$*****(-300,000 \times 0.36) \times (0.25/(0.25 + 0.12)) = -72,973$

The overall NPV of the project would then be $(35,358). Griffey is unhappy with Chen's revised analysis because the NPV of the project is now negative, possibly leading to the project being rejected. He would like to resume production in the plant, and reemploy his friends who had been laid off earlier. There is also the possibility that Griffey may be hired as a consultant by the new plant management after he retires next year.

Considering the ethical issues, Andrew Chen should evaluate Eric Griffey's directives as follows:

1. Chen should present complete and clear reports and recommendations after appropriate analyses of relevant and reliable information. Griffey does not wish the report to be complete or clear, and has provided some information which is not totally reliable.

2. Chen should not disclose confidential information outside of the organization; but it also appears that Griffey wants to refrain from disclosing information to senior management that it should know about.

3. In evaluating Griffey's directive as it affects Chen, Chen has an obligation to communicate unfavourable as well as favourable information and professional judgments or opinions.

22-34 (cont'd)

The responsibility to communicate information fairly and objectively, as well as to disclose fully all relevant information that could reasonably be expected to influence an intended user's understanding of the reports and recommendations presented, is being hampered. Management will not have the full scope of information they should have when they are presented with the analysis.

Andrew Chen should take the following steps to resolve this situation:

- Chen should first investigate and see if Dudley Company has an established policy for resolution of ethical conflicts and follow those procedures.
- If this policy does not resolve the ethical conflict, the next step would be for Chen to discuss the situation with his supervisor, Griffey, and see if he can obtain resolution. One possible solution may be to present a "base case" and sensitivity analysis of the investment. Chen should make it clear to Griffey that he has a problem and is seeking guidance.
- If Chen cannot obtain a satisfactory resolution with Griffey, he could take the situation up to the next layer of management, and inform Griffey that he is doing this. If this is not satisfactory, Chen should progress to the next, and subsequent, higher levels of management until the issue is resolved (i.e., the president, Audit Committee, or Board of Directors).
- Chen may want to have a confidential discussion with an objective advisor to clarify relevant concepts and obtain an understanding of possible courses of action.
- If Chen cannot satisfactorily resolve the situation within the organization, he may resign from the company and submit an informative memo to an appropriate person in Dudley (i.e., the president, Audit Committee, or Board of Directors).

CHAPTER 23
CONTROL SYSTEMS, TRANSFER PRICING,
AND MULTINATIONAL CONSIDERATIONS

23-2   To be effective, management control systems should be (a) closely aligned to an organization's strategies and goals, (b) designed to fit the organization's structure and the decision-making responsibility of individual managers, and (c) able to motivate managers and employees to put in effort to attain selected goals desired by top management.

23-4   The chapter cites five benefits of decentralization:
1.   Creates greater responsiveness to local needs.
2.   Leads to quicker decision making.
3.   Increases motivation.
4.   Aids management development and learning.
5.   Sharpens the focus of managers.

The chapter cites four costs of decentralization:
1.   Leads to suboptimal decision making.
2.   Results in duplication of activities.
3.   Decreases loyalty toward the organization as a whole.
4.   Increases costs of gathering information.

23-6   No. A transfer price is the price one subunit of an organization charges for a product or service supplied to another subunit of the same organization. The two segments can be cost centres, profit centres, or investment centres. For example, the allocation of service department costs to production departments that are set up as either cost centres or investment centres is an example of transfer pricing.

23-8   Transfer prices should have the following properties. They should
1.   promote goal congruence,
2.   promote a sustained high level of management effort,
3.   promote a high level of subunit autonomy in decision making.

23-10   Transferring products or services at market prices generally leads to optimal decisions when (a) the intermediate market is perfectly competitive, (b) interdependencies of subunits are minimal, and (c) there are no additional costs or benefits to the corporation as a whole in using the market instead of transacting internally.

23-12   Reasons why a dual-pricing approach to transfer pricing is not widely used in practice include:
1.   The manager of the division using a cost-based method does not have sufficient incentives to control costs.
2.   This approach does not provide clear signals to division managers about the level of decentralization top management wants.
3.   This approach tends to insulate managers from the frictions of the marketplace.

23-14 Yes. The general transfer-pricing guideline specifies that the minimum transfer price equals the additional *outlay costs* per unit incurred up to the point of transfer *plus* the *opportunity costs* per unit to the supplying division. When the supplying division has idle capacity, its opportunity costs are zero; when the supplying division has no idle capacity, its opportunity costs are positive. Hence the minimum transfer price will vary depending on whether the supplying division has idle capacity or not.

23-16 (25 min.) **Decentralization, responsibility centres**.

1.   The manufacturing plants in the Manufacturing Division are cost centres. Senior management determines the manufacturing schedule based on the quantity of each type of lighting product specified by the sales and marketing division and detailed studies of the time and cost to manufacture each type of product. Manufacturing managers are accountable only for costs. They are evaluated based on achieving target output within budgeted costs.

2a.   If manufacturing and marketing managers were to directly negotiate the prices for manufacturing various products, Quinn should evaluate manufacturing plant managers as profit centres—revenues received from marketing minus the costs incurred to produce and sell output.

2b.   Quinn Corporation would be better off decentralizing its marketing and manufacturing decisions and evaluating each division as a profit centre. Decentralization would encourage plant managers to increase total output to achieve the greatest profitability, and motivate plant managers to cut their costs to increase margins. Manufacturing managers would be motivated to design their operations according to the criteria that meet the marketing managers' approval, thereby improving cooperation between manufacturing and marketing.

     Under Quinn's existing system, manufacturing managers had every incentive not to improve. Manufacturing managers' incentives were to get as high a cost target as possible so that they could produce output within budgeted costs. Any significant improvements could result in the target costs being lowered for the next year, increasing the possibility of not achieving budgeted costs. By the same line of reasoning, manufacturing managers would also try to limit their production so that production quotas would not be increased in the future. Decentralizing manufacturing and marketing decisions overcomes these problems.

23-18 (30 min.)   **Effect of alternative transfer-pricing methods on division operating income.**

1.

	Internal Transfers at Market Prices Method B	Internal Transfers at 110% of Full Costs Method A
MINING DIVISION		
Revenues:		
$90, $66[1] × 400,000 units	$36,000,000	$26,400,000
Deduct:		
Division variable costs:		
$52[2] × 400,000 units	20,800,000	20,800,000
Division fixed costs:		
$8[3] × 400,000 units	3,200,000	3,200,000
Division operating income	$12,000,000	$ 2,400,000
METALS DIVISION		
Revenues:		
$150 × 400,000 units	$60,000,000	$60,000,000
Deduct:		
Transferred-in costs:		
$90, $66 × 400,000 units	36,000,000	26,400,000
Division variable costs:		
$36[4] × 400,000 units	14,400,000	14,400,000
Division fixed costs:		
$15[5] × 400,000 units	6,000,000	6,000,000
Division operating income	$ 3,600,000	$13,200,000

[1]$66 = $60 × 110%

[2]Variable cost per unit in Mining Division = Direct materials + Direct manufacturing labour + 75% of Manufacturing overhead = $12 + $16 + 75% × $32 = $52

[3]Fixed cost per unit = 25% of Manufacturing overhead = 25% ×$32 = $8

[4]Variable cost per unit in Metals Division = Direct materials + Direct manufacturing labour + 40% of Manufacturing overhead = $6 + $20 + 40% × $25 = $36

[5]Fixed cost per unit in Metals Division = 60% of Manufacturing overhead = 60% × $25 = $15

23-18 (cont'd)

2.   Bonus paid to division managers at 1% of division operating income will be as follows:

	Method B Internal Transfers at Market Prices	Method A Internal Transfers at 110% of Full Costs
Mining Division manager's bonus (1% × $12,000,000; 1% × $2,400,000)	$120,000	$ 24,000
Metals Division manager's bonus (1% × $3,600,000; 1% × $13,200,000)	36,000	132,000

The Mining Division manager will prefer Method A (transfer at market prices) because this method gives $120,000 of bonus rather than $24,000 under Method B (transfers at 110% of full costs). The Metals Division manager will prefer Method B because this method gives $132,000 of bonus rather than $36,000 under Method A.

3.   Brian Jones, the manager of the Mining Division will appeal to the existence of a competitive market to price transfers at market prices. Using market prices for transfers in these conditions leads to goal congruence. Division managers acting in their own best interests make decisions that are also in the best interests of the company as a whole.

      Jones will further argue that setting transfer prices based on cost will cause Jones to pay no attention to controlling costs since all costs incurred will be recovered from the Metals Division at 110% of full costs.

23-20 (25 min.)   **General guideline, transfer price range.**

1.   If the Screen Division sells screens in the outside market, it will receive, for each screen, the market price of the screen minus variable marketing and distribution costs per screen = $110 − $4 = $106. The incremental cost of manufacturing each screen is $70. The Screen Division is operating at capacity. Hence, the opportunity cost per screen of selling the screen to the Assembly Division rather than in the outside market is the contribution margin the Screen Division would forgo if it transferred screens internally rather than sold them in the outside market.

Contribution margin per screen = $106 − $70 = $36.

Using the general guideline,

$$\text{Minimum transfer price per screen} = \text{Incremental costs per screen up to the point of transfer} + \text{Opportunity costs per screen to the selling division}$$

That is,   Minimum transfer price per screen = $70 + $36 = $106

2.   If the two division managers were to negotiate a transfer price, the range of possible transfer prices is between $106 and $112 per screen. As calculated in requirement 1, the Screen Division will be willing to supply screens to the Assembly Division only if the transfer price equals or exceeds $106 per screen.

If the Assembly Division were to purchase the screens in the outside market, it will incur a cost of $112, the cost of the screen equal to $110 plus variable purchasing costs of $2 per screen. Hence, the Assembly Division will be willing to buy screens from the Screen Division only if the price does not exceed $112 per screen. Within the price range of $106 and $112 per screen, each division will be willing to transact with the other. The exact transfer price between $106 and $112 will depend on the bargaining strengths of the two divisions.

23-22 (30 min.)   **Multinational transfer pricing, goal-congruence (continuation of 23-21).**

1.   After tax operating income if Mornay Company sold all 1,000 units of Product 4A36 in Canada is

Revenues, $600 × 1,000 units	$600,000
Full manufacturing costs, $500 × 1,000 units	500,000
Operating income	100,000
Income taxes at 40%	40,000
After-tax operating income	$ 60,000

From requirement 1, Mornay Company's after-tax operating income if it transfers 1,000 units of Product 4A36 to Austria at full manufacturing cost and sells the units in Austria is $112,000. Therefore Mornay should sell the 1,000 units in Austria.

2.   Transferring Product 4A36 at the full manufacturing cost of the Canadian Division minimizes import duties and taxes (requirement 2), but creates zero operating income for the Canadian Division. Acting autonomously, the Canadian Division manager would maximize division operating income by selling Product 4A36 in the Canadian market which results in $60,000 in after-tax division operating income as calculated in requirement 3, rather than by transferring Product 4A36 to the Austrian division at full manufacturing cost.

3.   The minimum transfer price at which the Canadian Division manager acting autonomously will agree to transfer Product 4A36 to the Austrian division is $600 per unit. Any transfer price less than $600 will leave the Canadian Division's performance worse than selling directly in the Canadian market. Since the Canadian Division can sell as many units of Product 4A36 in the Canadian market, there is an opportunity cost of transferring the product internally.

This transfer price will result in Mornay Company as a whole paying more import duties and taxes than the answer to requirement 2 as calculated below:

CANADIAN DIVISION

Revenues, $600 × 1,000 units	$600,000
Full manufacturing costs	500,000
Division operating income	100,000
Division income taxes at 40%	40,000
Division after-tax operating income	$ 60,000

23-22 (cont'd)

AUSTRIAN DIVISION

Revenues, $750 × 1,000 units`	$750,000
Transferred in costs, $600 × 1,000 units	600,000
Import duties at 10% of transferred-in price, $60 × 1,000 units	60,000
Division operating income	90,000
Division income taxes at 44%	39,600
Division after-tax operating income	$ 50,400

Total import duties and income taxes at transfer prices of $500 and $600 per unit for 1,000 units of Product 4A36 follow:

		Transfer Price of $500 per Unit (Requirement 2)	Transfer Price of $600 per Unit
(a)	Canadian income taxes	$ 0	$ 40,000
(b)	Austrian import duties	50,000	60,000
(c)	Austrian income taxes	88,000	39,600
		$138,000	$139,600

The minimum transfer price that the Canadian division manager acting autonomously would agree to results in Mornay Company paying $1,600 in additional import duties and income taxes.

A student who has done the calculations shown in requirement 2 can calculate the additional taxes from a $600 transfer price more directly as follows:

Every $1 increase in the transfer price per unit over $500 results in additional import duty and taxes of $0.016 per unit

So a $100 increase ($600 – $500) per unit will result in additional import duty and taxes of $0.016 × 100 = $1.60

For 1,000 units transferred, this equals $1.60 × 1,000 = $1,600

23-24 (35 min.) **Multinational transfer pricing, effect of alternative transfer-pricing methods, global income tax minimization.**

1.   This is a three-country, three-division transfer pricing problem with three alternative transfer-pricing methods. Summary data in Canadian dollars are:

China Plant
        Variable costs: 1,000 Yuan ÷ 8 Yuan per $ = $125 per subunit
        Fixed costs: 1,800 Yuan ÷ 8 Yuan per $ = $225 per subunit

South Korea Plant
        Variable costs: 240,000 Won ÷ 800 Won per $ = $300 per unit
        Fixed costs: 320,000 Won ÷ 800 Won per $ = $400 per unit

Canadian Plant
        Variable costs: = $100 per unit
        Fixed costs: = $200 per unit

Market prices for private label sale alternatives:
        China Plant: 3,600 Yuan ÷ 8 Yuan per $ = $450 per subunit
        South Korea Plant: 1,040,000 Won ÷ 800 Won per $ = $1,300 per unit

The transfer prices under each method are: $\longrightarrow$

   (a)   Market price
         • China to South Korea   = $450 per subunit
         • South Korea to Canadian Plant = $1,300 per unit

   (b)   200% of full costs
         • China to South Korea
              2.0 ($125 + $225) = $700 per subunit
         • South Korea to Canadian Plant
              2.0 ($700 + $300 + $400) = $2,800 per unit

   (c)   300% of variable costs
         • China to South Korea
              3.0 ($125) = $375 per subunit
         • South Korea to Canadian Plant
              3.0 ($375 + $300) = $2,025 per unit

23-24 (cont'd)

	Method A Internal Transfers at Market Price	Method B Internal Transfers at 200% of Full Costs	Method C Internal Transfers at 300% of Variable Costs
1. CHINA DIVISION			
Division revenues per unit	$ 450	$ 700	$ 375
Deduct :			
Division variable costs per unit	125	125	125
Division fixed costs per unit	225	225	225
Division operating income per unit	100	350	25
Income tax at 40%	40	160	10
Division net income per unit	$ 60	$ 190	$ 15
2. SOUTH KOREA DIVISION	$1,300	$2,800	$2,025
Division revenues per unit			
Deduct:	450	700	375
Transferred-in costs per unit	300	300	300
Division variable costs per unit	400	400	400
Division fixed costs per unit	150	1,400	950
Division operating income per unit	30	280	190
Income tax at 20%	$ 120	$1,120	$ 760
Division net income per unit			
	$3,200	$3,200	$3,200
3. CANADIAN DIVISION			
Division revenues per unit	1,300	2,800	2,025
Deduct:	100	100	100
Transferred-in costs per unit	200	200	200
Division variable costs per unit	1,600	100	875
Division fixed costs per unit	480	30	
Division operating income per unit	$ 1,120	$ 70	262.5
			$ 612.5
Income tax at 30%			
Division net income per unit			

2. Division net income:

	Market Price	200% of Full Costs	300% of Variable Cost
China Division	$ 60	$ 190	$ 15.00
South Korea Division	120	1,120	760.00
Canadian Division	1,120	70	612.50
User Friendly Computer Inc.	$1,300	$1,380	$1,387.50

User Friendly will maximize its net income by using the 300% of variable cost, transfer-pricing method. This is because the 300% of full cost method sources most income in the country with the lower income tax rates.

23-26 (5 min.) **Transfer-pricing problem (continuation of 23-25).**

The company as a whole would benefit in this situation if C purchased from outside suppliers. The $15,000 disadvantage to the company as a whole by purchasing from the outside supplier would be more than offset by the $30,000 contribution margin of A's sale of 1,000 units to other customers.

Purchase costs from outside supplier, 1,000 units × $135	$135,000
Deduct variable cost savings, 1,000 units × $120	120,000
Net cost to company as a whole by buying from outside	$ 15,000

A's sales to other customers, 1,000 units × $155		$155,000
Deduct:		
Variable manufacturing costs, $120 × 1,000 units	$120,000	
Variable marketing costs, $5 × 1,000 units	5,000	
Variable costs		125,000
Contribution margin from selling A to other customers		$ 30,000

23-28 (30 min.)   **Goal-congruence problems with cost-plus transfer-pricing methods, dual-pricing methods.**

1. Two examples of goal congruence problems are:
   (a) Division managers using an outside supplier when Oceanic Products' operating income is maximized by buying from an internal division.
   (b) Division managers selling to an outside purchaser when it is better for Oceanic Products to further process internally.

2. <u>Transfers to buying divisions at market price</u>
   Harvesting Division to Processing Division = $1.00 per kilogram of raw tuna
   Processing Division to Marketing Division = $5.00 per kilogram of
                                                              processed tuna

   <u>Transfers out to selling divisions at 150% of full costs</u>
   Harvesting Division to Processing Division
          = 1.5 ($0.20 + $0.40) = $0.90 per kilogram of raw tuna
   Processing Division to Marketing Division
          = 1.5 [($1.00 × 2)* + $0.80 + $0.60] = $5.10 per kilogram
            of processed tuna

   *The transferred-in cost is $1.00 per kilogram of raw tuna. It takes two kilograms of raw tuna to produce one kilogram of tuna fillets.

   <u>Tuna Harvesting Division</u>
Division revenues: $0.90 × 1,000	$ 900
Division variable costs: $0.20 × 1,000	200
Division fixed costs: $0.40 × 1,000	400
Division total costs	600
Division operating income	$ 300

   <u>Tuna Processing Division</u>
Division revenues: $5.10 × 500	$2,550
Transferred-in costs: $1.00 × 1,000	1,000
Division variable costs: $0.80 × 500	400
Division fixed costs: $0.60 × 500	300
Division total costs	1,700
Division operating income	$ 850

   <u>Tuna Marketing Division</u>
Division revenues: $12 × 300	$3,600
Transferred-in costs: $5 × 500	2,500
Division variable costs: $0.30 × 300	90
Division fixed costs: $0.70 × 300	210
Division total costs	2,800
Division operating income	$ 800

23-28 (cont'd)

3.

	Division Operating Income
Tuna Harvesting Division	$ 300
Tuna Processing Division	850
Tuna Marketing Division	800
Oceanic Products	$1,950

The overall company operating income from harvesting 1,000 kilograms of raw tuna and its further processing and marketing is $2,000 (see Problem 23-27, requirement 1).

A dual transfer-pricing method entails using different transfer prices for transfers into the buying division and transfers out of the supplying division. There is no reason why the sum of division operating incomes should equal the total company operating income.

4. Problems which may arise if Oceanic Products uses the dual-transfer pricing system include:
   (a) It may reduce the incentives of the supplying division to control costs since every $1 of cost of the supplying division is transferred out to the buying division at $1.50. It may also reduce the incentives of the supplying divisions to keep abreast of market conditions.
   (b) A dual transfer-pricing system does not provide clear signals to the individual divisions about the level of decentralization top management seeks.

23-30 (30-40 min.) **Pricing in imperfect markets (continuation of 23-29).**

An alternative presentation, which contains the same numerical answers, can be found at the end of this solution.

1. Potential contribution from external intermediate
       sale is 1,000 × ($195 – $120) $75,000
    Contribution through keeping price at $200 is
       800 × $80.   64,000
    Forgone contribution by transferring 200 units $11,000

    Opportunity cost per unit to the supplying division by transferring internally:

    $$\frac{\$11,000}{200} = \$55$$

    Transfer price = $120 + $55 = $175

An alternative approach to obtaining the same answer is to recognize that the incremental or outlay cost is the same for all 1,000 units in question. Therefore, the total revenue desired by A would be the same for selling outside or inside.

   Let X equal the transfer price at which Division A is indifferent between selling all units outside versus transferring 200 units inside
$$1,000\ (\$195) = 800\ (\$200) + 200X$$
$$X = \$175$$

The $175 price will lead to the correct decision. Division B will not buy from Division A because its total costs of $175 + $150 will exceed its prospective selling price of $300. Division A will then sell 1,000 units at $195 to the outside; Division A and the company will have a contribution margin of $75,000. Otherwise, if 800 units were sold at $200 and 200 units were transferred to Division B, the company would have a contribution of $64,000 plus $6,000 (200 units of final product × $30), or $70,000.

A comparison might be drawn regarding the computation of the appropriate transfer prices between the preceding problem and this problem:

$$\text{Minimum transfer price} = \left(\begin{array}{c}\text{Additional } \textit{incremental costs}\\ \text{per unit incurred up}\\ \text{to the point of transfer}\end{array}\right) + \left(\begin{array}{c}\textit{Opportunity costs}\\ \text{per unit to}\\ \text{Division A}\end{array}\right)$$

   Perfect markets: = $120 + (Selling price – Outlay costs per unit)
                       = $120 + ($200 – $120) = $200

23-13

23-30 (cont'd)

$$\text{Imperfect markets:} \quad = \$120 + \frac{\text{Marginal revenues} - \text{Outlay costs}}{\text{Number of units transferred}}$$

$$= \$120 + \frac{\$35,000^a - \$24,000^b}{200} = \$175$$

[a] Marginal revenues of Division A from selling 200 units outside rather than transferring to Division B
= ($195 × 1,000) − ($200 × 800) = $195,000 − $160,000 = $35,000.

[b] Incremental (outlay) costs incurred by Division A to produce 200 units
= $120 × 200 = $24,000.

Therefore, selling price ($195) and marginal revenues per unit ($175 = $35,000 ÷ 200) are not the same.

The following discussion is optional. These points should be explored only if there is sufficient class time:

Some students will erroneously say that the "new" market price of $195 is the appropriate transfer price. They will claim that the general guideline says that the transfer price should be $120 + ($195 − $120) = $195, the market price. This conclusion assumes a perfect market. But here there are imperfections in the intermediate market. That is, the market price is <u>not</u> a good approximation of alternative revenue. If a division's sales are heavy enough to reduce market prices, marginal revenue will be less than market price.

It is true that <u>either</u> $195 or $175 will lead to the correct decision by B in this case. But suppose that B's variable costs were $120 instead of $150. Then B would buy at a transfer price of $175 (but not at a price of $195, because then B would earn a negative contribution of $15 per unit [$300 − ($195 + $120)]. Note that if B's variable costs were $120, transfers would be desirable:

Division A contribution is:
800 × ($200 − $120) + 200 ($175 − $120)   = $75,000
Division B contribution is:
200 × [$300 − ($175 + $120)]   =   <u>1,000</u>
Total contribution   <u>$76,000</u>

Or the same facts can be analyzed for the company as a whole:

Sales of intermediate product,
800 × ($200 − $120)   = $64,000
Sales of final products,
200 × [300 − ($120 + $120)]   =   <u>12,000</u>
Total contribution   <u>$76,000</u>

23-30 (cont'd)

If the transfer price were $195, B would not accept the transfer and would not earn any contribution. As shown above, Division A and the company as a whole will earn a total contribution of $75,000 instead of $76,000.

2. (a) Division A can sell 900 units at $195 to the outside market and 100 units to Division B, or 800 at $200 to the outside market and 200 units to Division B. Note that, under both alternatives, 100 units can be transferred to Division B at no opportunity cost to A.

    Using the general guideline, the minimum transfer price of <u>the first 100 units</u> [901-1,000] is:

    $$TP_1 = \$120 + 0 = \$120$$

    If Division B needs 100 additional units, the opportunity cost to A is not zero, because Division A will then have to sell only 800 units to the outside market for a contribution of $800 \times (\$200 - \$120) = \$64,000$ instead of 900 units for a contribution of $900 (\$195 - \$120) = \$67,500$. Each unit sold to B in addition to the first 100 units has an opportunity cost to A of $(\$67,500 - \$64,000) \div 100 = \$35$.

    Using the general guideline, the minimum transfer price of <u>the next 100 units</u> [801-900] is:

    $$TP_2 = \$120 + \$35 = \$155$$

    Alternatively, the computation could be:

Increase in contribution from 100 more units, $100 \times \$75$	$7,500
Loss in contribution on 800 units, $800 \times (\$80 - \$75)$	<u>4,000</u>
Net "marginal revenue"	<u>$3,500</u> $\div100$ units $= \$35$

(Minimum) transfer price applicable to first 100 units offered by A is $120 + $0	=	$120 per unit
(Minimum) transfer price applicable to next 100 units offered by A is $120 + ($3,500 ÷ 100)	=	$155 per unit
(Minimum) transfer price applicable to next 800 units	=	$195 per unit

    (b) The manager of Division B will not want to purchase more than 100 units because the units at $155 would decrease his contribution ($155 + $150 > $300). Because the manager of B does not buy more than 100 units, the manager of A will have 900 units available for sale to the outside market. The manager of A will strive to maximize the contribution by selling them all at $195.

23-30 (cont'd)

This solution maximizes the company's contribution:

$$900 \times (\$195 - \$120) = \$67,500$$
$$100 \times (\$300 - \$270) = \underline{3,000}$$
$$\$70,500$$

which compares favourably to:

$$800 \times (\$200 - \$120) = \$64,000$$
$$200 \times (\$300 - \$270) = \underline{6,000}$$
$$\$70,000$$

ALTERNATIVE PRESENTATION (by James Patell)

1. Company Viewpoint

a: Sell 1,000 outside at $195		b: Sell 800 outside at $200, transfer 200	
Price	$195	Transfer price	$200
Variable costs	120	Variable costs	120
Contribution	$ 75 × 1,000 = $75,000	Contribution	$ 80 × 800 = $64,000

Total contribution given up if transfer occurs[*]
= $75,000 − $64,000 = $11,000

On a per-unit basis, the relevant costs are:

$$\underset{\text{point of transfer}}{\text{Incremental costs to}} + \underset{\text{Division A of transfer}}{\text{Opportunity costs to}} = \text{Transfer price}$$

$$\$120 + \frac{\$11,000}{200} = \$175$$

By formula, costs are:

$$\begin{bmatrix} \text{Incremental costs} \\ \text{to point} \\ \text{of transfer} \end{bmatrix} + \begin{bmatrix} \text{Lost opportunity to} \\ \text{sell 200 at \$195, for} \\ \text{contribution of \$75} \end{bmatrix} - \begin{bmatrix} \text{Gain when 1st 800} \\ \text{sell at \$200} \\ \text{instead of \$195} \end{bmatrix}$$

$$= \quad \$120 + \frac{200 \times \$75}{200} - \frac{[(\$200 - \$195) \times 800]}{200}$$

$$= \quad\quad\quad \$120 + \$75 - \$20 = \$175$$

[*]Contribution of $30 per unit by B is not given up if transfer occurs, so it is not relevant here.

23-30 (cont'd)

2.   (a)   At most, Division A can sell only 900 units and can produce 1,000. Therefore, at least 100 units should be transferred, at a transfer price no less than $120. The question is whether or not a second 100 units should be transferred.

Company Viewpoint

a: Sell 900 outside at $195		b: Sell 800 outside at $200, transfer 100	
Transfer price	$195	Transfer price	$200
Variable cost	120	Variable cost	120
Contribution	$ 75 × 900 = $67,500	Contribution	$ 80 × 800 = $64,000

Total contribution forgone if transfer of 100 units occurs
= $67,500 − $64,000 = $3,500 (or $35 per unit)

$$\begin{matrix} \text{Incremental costs to} \\ \text{point of transfer} \end{matrix} + \begin{matrix} \text{Opportunity costs to} \\ \text{Division A of transfer} \end{matrix} = \text{Transfer price}$$

$$\$120 \quad + \quad \$35 \quad = \quad \$155$$

(b)   By formula:

$$\begin{bmatrix} \text{Incremental costs} \\ \text{to point} \\ \text{of transfer} \end{bmatrix} + \begin{bmatrix} \text{Lost opportunity to} \\ \text{sell 100 at \$195, for} \\ \text{contribution of \$75} \end{bmatrix} - \begin{bmatrix} \text{Gain when 1st 800} \\ \text{sell at \$200} \\ \text{instead of \$195} \end{bmatrix}$$

$$= \quad \$120 + \frac{100 \times \$75}{100} - \frac{[(\$200 - \$195) \times 800]}{100}$$

$$= \quad \$120 + \$75 - \$40 = \$155$$

Transfer Price Schedule (minimum acceptable transfer price)

Units	Transfer Price
0-100	$120
101-200	$155
201-1,000	$195

23-32 (30-40 min.) **Multinational transfer pricing and taxation.**

1.   Anita Corporation and its subsidiaries' operating income if it manufactures the machine and sells it in Brazil or in Switzerland follows:

	If Sold in Brazil	If Sold in Switzerland
Revenue	$1,000,000	$950,000
Costs		
Manufacturing costs	500,000	500,000
Transportation and modification costs	200,000	250,000
Total costs	700,000	750,000
Operating income	$ 300,000	$200,000

Anita Corporation maximizes operating income by manufacturing the machine and selling it in Brazil.

2.   Anita Corporation will not sell if the transfer price is less than $500,000—its outlay costs of manufacturing the machine.

The Brazilian subsidiary will not agree to a transfer price of more than $800,000. At a price of $800,000, the Brazilian subsidiary's incremental operating income from purchasing and selling the milling machine will be $0 ($1,000,000 – $200,000 – $800,000).

The Swiss subsidiary will not agree to a transfer price of more than $700,000. At a price of $700,000, the Swiss subsidiary's incremental operating income from purchasing and selling the milling machine will be $0 ($950,000 – $250,000 – $700,000).

Any transfer price between $700,000 and $800,000 will achieve the optimal actions determined in requirement 1. For prices in this range, Anita Corporation will be willing to sell, the Brazilian Corporation willing to buy, and the Swiss subsidiary not interested in acquiring the machine.

Where within the range of $700,000 to $800,000 that the transfer price will be set depends on the bargaining powers of the Anita Corporation and the Brazilian subsidiary managers. Anita Corporation's main source of bargaining power comes from the threat of selling the machine to the Swiss subsidiary. If the transfer price is set at $700,000, then

Anita's operating income, $700,000 – $500,000	$200,000
Brazilian subsidiary's operating income, $1,000,000 – $700,000 – $200,000	$100,000
Overall operating income of Anita and subsidiaries	$300,000

Note that the general guideline could be used to derive the minimum transfer price.

23-32 (cont'd)

$$\begin{pmatrix} \text{Minimum} \\ \text{transfer price} \end{pmatrix} = \begin{pmatrix} \text{Additional } \textit{incremental} \text{ costs} \\ \text{per unit incurred up} \\ \text{to the point of transfer} \end{pmatrix} + \begin{pmatrix} \textit{Opportunity} \text{ costs} \\ \text{per unit to the} \\ \text{supplying division} \end{pmatrix}$$

$$= \$500,000 + \$200,000 = \$700,000$$

Anita's opportunity cost of supplying the machine to the Brazilian subsidiary is the $200,000 in operating income it forgoes by not supplying the machine to the Swiss subsidiary. Note that competition between the Brazilian and Swiss subsidiaries means that the transfer price will be at least $700,000.

3. Consider the optimal transfer prices that can be set to minimize taxes (for Anita and its subsidiaries) (a) for transfers from Anita to the Brazilian subsidiary and (b) for transfers from Anita to the Swiss subsidiary.

(a) Transfers from Anita to the Brazilian subsidiary should "allocate" as much of the operating income to Anita as possible, since the tax rate in Canada is lower than in Brazil for this transaction. Therefore, these transfers should be priced at the highest allowable transfer price of $700,000 to minimize overall company taxes.

Taxes paid:

Anita, 0.40 ($700,000 – $500,000)	$ 80,000
Brazilian subsidiary, 0.60 ($1,000,000 – $700,000 – $200,000)	60,000
Total taxes paid by Anita Corporation and its subsidiaries on transfers to Brazil	$140,000

After-tax operating income:

Anita, ($700,000 – $500,000) – $80,000	$120,000
Brazilian subsidiary ($1,000,000 – $700,000 – $200,000) – $60,000	40,000
Total after-tax operating income for Anita Corporation and its subsidiaries on transfers to Brazil	$160,000

(b) Transfers from Anita to the Swiss subsidiary should "allocate" as little of the operating income to Anita as possible, since the tax rate in Canada is higher than in Switzerland for this transaction. Therefore, these transfers should be priced at the lowest allowable transfer price of $500,000 to minimize overall company taxes.

Taxes paid:

Anita, 0.40 ($500,000 – $500,000)	$ 0
Swiss subsidiary, 0.15 ($950,000 – $500,000 – $250,000)	30,000
Total taxes paid by Anita Corporation and its subsidiaries on transfers to Switzerland	$30,000

After-tax operating income

Anita,($500,000 – $500,000) – $0	$ 0
Swiss subsidiary ($950,000 – $500,000 – $250,000) – $30,000	170,000
Total net income for Anita Corporation and its subsidiaries on transfers to Switzerland	$170,000

From the viewpoint of Anita Corporation and its subsidiaries together, overall after-tax operating income is maximized if the machine is transferred to the Swiss subsidiary (after-tax operating income of $170,000 versus after-tax operating income of $160,000 if the machine is transferred to the Brazilian subsidiary). Note that the corporation and its subsidiaries trade off the lower overall before-tax operating income achieved by transferring to the Swiss subsidiary with the lower taxes that result from such a transfer. Hence (a) the equipment should be manufactured by Anita and (b) it should be transferred to the Swiss subsidiary at a price of $500,000.

4.   As in requirement 2, the Brazilian subsidiary would be willing to bid up the price to $800,000, while the Swiss subsidiary would only be willing to pay up to $700,000. Anita Corporation acting autonomously would like to maximize its own after-tax operating income by transferring the machine at as high a transfer price as possible. As in requirement 2, the price would end up being at least $700,000. Since the taxing authorities will not allow prices above $700,000, the transfer price will be $700,000. At this transfer price, the Swiss subsidiary makes zero operating income and will not be interested in the machine. Hence Anita Corporation will sell the machine to the Brazilian subsidiary at a price of $700,000.

The answer is not the same as in requirement 3 since, acting autonomously, the objective of each manager is to maximize after-tax operating income of his or her own company rather than after-tax operating income of Anita Corporation and its subsidiaries as a whole. Goal congruence is not achieved in this setting.

Can the company induce the managers to take the right actions without infringing on their autonomy? This outcome is probably not going to be easy.

One possibility might be to implement a dual pricing scheme in which the machine is transferred at cost ($500,000), but under which Anita Corporation is credited with after-tax operating income earned on the machine by the subsidiary it ships the machine to (in this example, $170,000 of net income earned by the Swiss subsidiary). A negative feature of this arrangement is that the $170,000 of after-tax operating income will be "double counted" and recognized on the books of both Anita Corporation and the Swiss subsidiary.

Another possibility might be to evaluate the managers on the basis of overall after-tax operating income of Anita Corporation and its subsidiaries. This approach will induce a more global perspective, but at the cost of inducing a larger noncontrollable element in each manager's performance measure.

23-34 (40–50 min.) **Utilization of capacity.**

1.

	Super-chip	Okay-chip
Selling price	$60	$12
Direct materials	2	1
Direct manufacturing labour	28	7
Contribution margin per unit	$30	$ 4
Contribution margin per hour ($30 ÷ 2; $4 ÷ 0.5)	$15	$ 8

Because the contribution margin per hour is higher for Super-chip than for Okay-chip, CIC should produce and sell as many Super-chips as it can and use the remaining available capacity to produce Okay-chip.

The total demand for Super-chips is 15,000 units, which would take 30,000 hours (15,000 × 2 hours per unit). CIC should use its remaining capacity of 20,000 hours (50,000 – 30,000) to produce 40,000 Okay-chips (20,000 ÷ 0.5).

2.   Options for manufacturing process-control unit

	Using Circuit Board	Using Super-chip
Selling price	$132	$132
Direct materials	60	2
Direct manufacturing labour (Super-chip)	0	28
Direct manufacturing labour (Process-control unit)	50	60
Contribution margin per unit	$ 22	$ 42

Overall Company Viewpoint

Alternative 1: No Transfer of Super-chips

Sell 15,000 Super-chips at contribution margin per unit of $30	$450,000
Transfer 0 Super-chips	0
Sell 40,000 Okay-chips at contribution margin per unit of $4	160,000
Sell 5,000 Control units at contribution margin per unit of $22	110,000
Total contribution margin	$720,000

Alternative 2: Transfer 5,000 Super-chips to Process-Control Division. These Super-chips would require 10,000 hours to manufacture, leaving only 10,000 hours for the manufacture of 20,000 Okay-chips (10,000 ÷ 0.5)

Sell 15,000 Super-chips at contribution margin per unit of $30	$450,000
Transfer 5,000 Super-chips to Process-Control Division	0
Sell 20,000 Okay-chips at contribution margin per unit of $4	80,000
Sell 5,000 Control units at contribution margin per unit of $42	210,000
Total contribution margin	$740,000

CIC is better off transferring 5,000 Super-chips to the Process-Control Division.

3. For each Super-chip that is transferred, two hours of time (labour capacity) are given up in the Semiconductor Division, and, in those two hours, four Okay-chips could be produced, each contributing $4.

$$\begin{array}{c}\text{Minimum transfer price}\\ \text{per Super-chip}\end{array} = \begin{array}{c}\text{Incremental cost}\\ \text{per unit to}\\ \text{the point of transfer}\end{array} + \begin{array}{c}\text{Opportunity cost per}\\ \text{unit for the}\\ \text{Semiconductor Divisio}\end{array}$$

$$= \$30 + \$16$$

$$= \$46 \text{ per unit}$$

If the selling price for the process-control unit were firm at $132, the Process-Control Division would accept any transfer price up to $50 ($60 price of circuit board – $10 incremental labour cost if Super-chip used).

However, consider what happens if the transfer price of Super-chip is set at, say, $49, and the price of the control unit drops to $108. From CIC's viewpoint:

	Using Circuit Board	Using Super-chip
Selling price	$108	$108
Direct materials	60	49
Direct manufacturing labour	50	60
Contribution margin per hour	$ –2	$ –1

Process-Control Division will not produce any control units. From the company's viewpoint, the contribution margin on the control unit if the Super-chip is used is:

Selling price	$108
Direct materials	2
Direct manufacturing labour (Super-chip)	28
Direct manufacturing labour (process-control unit)	60
Contribution margin per unit	$ 18

The contribution margin per unit from producing Super-chips for the process-control unit exceeds the contribution margin of $16 from producing 4 Okay-chips, each yielding a contribution margin of $4 per unit. Hence the Semiconductor Division should transfer 5,000 Super-chips as the following calculations show:

Alternative 1—No transfer (and, therefore, no sales of process-control units)

Sell 15,000 Super-chips at contribution margin per unit of $30	$450,000
Sell 40,000 Okay-chips at contribution margin per unit of $4	160,000
	$610,000

23-34 (cont'd)

Alternative 2—Transfer 5,000 Super-chips.

Sell 15,000 Super-chips at contribution margin per unit of $30	$450,000
Sell 20,000 Okay-chips at contribution margin per unit of $4	80,000
Sell 5,000 control units at contribution margin per unit of $18	90,000
	$620,000

Therefore, if the price for the control unit is uncertain, the transfer price must be set at the minimum acceptable transfer price of $46.

4. For a transfer of any amount between 0 and 10,000 Super-chips (which require 2 hours each to produce), the opportunity cost is the production of Okay-chips (which require 1/2 hour each). In this range, the relevant costs are equal to the transfer price of $46 established in part 3.

If more than 10,000 Super-chips are transferred, the opportunity cost becomes the sale of Super-chips on the outside market. Now the minimum transfer price per Super-chip becomes

Incremental cost per Super-chip up to the point of transfer + Opportunity cost per Super-chip to the Semiconductor Division = $30 + ($60 − $30) = $60, the market price

At this transfer price, it is cheaper for the Process-Control Division to buy the circuit board for $60, since $10 of additional direct manufacturing labour cost is saved.

The Semiconductor Division should at most transfer 10,000 Super-chips.

Internal Demand	Transfer
0-10,000	$46
10,000-25,000	60

CHAPTER 24
PERFORMANCE MEASUREMENT, COMPENSATION, AND MULTINATIONAL CONSIDERATIONS

24-2   The five steps in designing an accounting-based performance measure are:
1.   Choosing the variable(s) that represents top management's financial goal(s).
2.   Choosing definitions of the items included in the variables in Step 1.
3.   Choosing measures for the items included in the variables in Step 1.
4.   Choosing a target against which to gauge performance.
5.   Choosing the timing of feedback.

24-4   Yes. Residual income is not identical to ROI. ROI is a percentage with investment as the denominator of the computation. Residual income is an absolute amount in which investment is used to calculate an imputed interest charge.

24-6   Definitions of investment used in practice when computing ROI are:
1.   Total assets available.
2.   Total assets employed.
3.   Working capital (current assets minus current liabilities) plus other assets.
4.   Stockholders' equity.

24-8   Special problems arise when evaluating the performance of divisions in multinational companies because
   (a)   The economic, legal, political, social, and cultural environments differ significantly across countries.
   (b)   Governments in some countries may impose controls and limit selling prices of products.
   (c)   Availability of materials and skilled labour, as well as costs of materials, labour, and infrastructure may differ significantly across countries.
   (d)   Divisions operating in different countries keep score of their performance in different currencies.

24-10   Moral hazard describes contexts in which an employee is tempted to put in less effort (or report distorted information) because the employee's interests differ from the owner's and because the employee's effort cannot be accurately monitored and enforced.

24-12   Measures of performance that are superior (measures that change significantly with the manager's performance and not very much with changes in factors that are beyond the manager's control) are the key to designing strong incentive systems in organizations. When selecting performance measures the management accountant must choose those performance measures that change with changes in the actions taken by managers. For example, if a manager has no authority for making investments, then using an investment-based measure to evaluate the manager imposes risk on the manager and provides little information about the manager's performance. The management accountant might suggest evaluating the manager on the basis of costs, or costs and revenues, rather than ROI.

24-14 When employees have to perform multiple tasks as part of their jobs, incentive problems can arise when one task is easy to monitor and measure while the other task is more difficult to evaluate. Employers want employees to intelligently allocate time and effort among various tasks. If, however, employees are rewarded on the basis of the task that is more easily measured, they will tend to focus their efforts on that task and ignore the others.

24-16 (30 min.)   **Return on investment; comparisons of three companies.**

1.   The separate components highlight several features of return on investment not revealed by a single calculation:
  (a) The importance of investment turnover as a key to income is stressed.
  (b) The importance of revenues is explicitly recognized.
  (c) The important components are expressed as ratios or percentages instead of dollar figures. This form of expression often enhances comparability of different divisions, businesses, and time periods.
  (d) The breakdown stresses the possibility of trading off investment turnover for income as a percentage of revenues so as to increase the average ROI at a given level of output.

2.   (Filled-in blanks are in bold face.)

	Companies in Same Industry		
	A	**B**	**C**
Revenue	$1,000,000	$ 500,000	**$10,000,000**
Income	$ 100,000	$ 50,000	$ **50,000**
Investment	$ 500,000	**$5,000,000**	$ 5,000,000
Income as a % of revenue	**10%**	10%	0.5%
Investment turnover	**2.0**	**0.1**	2.0
Return on investment	**20%**	1%	1%

Income and investment alone shed little light on comparative performances because of disparities in size between Company A and the other two companies. Thus, it is impossible to say whether B's low return on investment in comparison with A's is attributable to its larger investment or to its lower income. Furthermore the fact that Companies B and C have identical income and investment may suggest that the same conditions underlie the low ROI, but this conclusion is erroneous. B has higher margins but a lower investment turnover. C has very small margins (1/20th of B) but turns over investment 20 times faster.

24-16 (cont'd)

<u>I.M.A. Report No. 35</u> (p. 35) states:

"Introducing revenues to measure level of operations helps to disclose specific areas for more intensive investigation. Company B does as well as Company A in terms of income margin, for both companies earn 10% on revenues. But Company B has a much lower turnover of investment than does Company A. Whereas a dollar of investment in Company A supports two dollars in revenues each period, a dollar investment in Company B supports only ten cents in revenues each period. This suggests that the analyst should look carefully at Company B's investment. Is the company keeping an inventory larger than necessary for its revenue level? Are receivables being collected promptly? Or did Company A acquire its fixed assets at a price level that was much lower than that at which Company B purchased its plant?"

"On the other hand, C's investment turnover is as high as A's, but C's income as a percentage of revenue is much lower. Why? Are its operations inefficient, are its material costs too high, or does its location entail high transportation costs?"

"Analysis of ROI raises questions such as the foregoing. When answers are obtained, basic reasons for differences between rates of return may be discovered. For example, in Company B's case, it is apparent that the emphasis will have to be on increasing turnover by reducing investment or increasing revenues. Clearly, B cannot appreciably increase its ROI simply by increasing its income as a percent of revenue. In contrast, Company C's management should concentrate on increasing the percent of income on revenue."

24-18 (10-15 min.) **ROI and RI.**

$$ROI = \frac{\text{Operating income}}{\text{Investment}}$$

$$\text{Operating income} = ROI \times \text{Investment}$$

[No. of menhirs sold (Selling price – Var. cost per unit)] – Fixed costs = ROI × Investment

Let X = minimum selling price per unit to achieve a 20% ROI

1. $10,000 (X - \$300) - \$1,000,000 = 20\% (\$1,600,000)$
    $10,000X = \$320,000 + \$3,000,000 + \$1,000,000 = \$4,320,000$
    $X = \$432$

2. $10,000 (X - \$300) - \$1,000,000 = 15\% (\$1,600,000)$
    $10,000X = \$240,000 + \$3,000,000 + \$1,000,000 = \$4,240,000$
    $X = \$424$

24-20 (25 min.) **Financial and nonfinancial performance measures, goal congruence.**

1.   Operating income is a good summary measure of short-term financial performance. By itself, however, it does not indicate whether operating income in the short run was earned by taking actions that would lead to long-run competitive advantage. For example, Summit's divisions might be able to increase short-run operating income by producing more product while ignoring quality or rework. Harrington, however, would like to see division managers increase operating income without sacrificing quality. The new performance measures take a balanced scorecard approach by evaluating and rewarding managers on the basis of direct measures (such as rework costs, on-time delivery performance, and sales returns). This motivates managers to take actions that Harrington believes will increase operating income now and in the future. The nonoperating income measures serve as surrogate measures of future profitability.

2.   The semi-annual installments and total bonus for the Charter Division are calculated as follows:

Charter Division Bonus Calculation
For Year Ended December 31, 2003

January 1, 2003 to June 30, 2003

Profitability	(0.02) ($462,000)	$ 9,240
Rework	(0.02 × $462,000) – $11,500	(2,260)
On-time delivery	No bonus – under 96%	0
Sales returns	[(0.015 × $4,200,000) – $84,000] × 50%	(10,500)
Semi-annual installment		(3,520)
Semi-annual bonus awarded		$ 0

July 1, 2003 to December 31, 2003

Profitability	(0.02) ($440,000)	$ 8,800
Rework	(0.02 × $440,000) – $11,000	(2,200)
On-time delivery	96% to 98%	2,000
Sales returns	[(0.015 × $4,400,000) – $70,000] × 50%	(2,000)
Semi-annual installment		6,600
Semi-annual bonus awarded		$ 6,600
Total bonus awarded for the year		$ 6,600

24-20 (cont'd)

The semi-annual installments and total bonus for the Mesa Division are calculated as follows:

Mesa Division Bonus Calculation
For Year Ended December 31, 2003

January 1, 2003 to June 30, 2003

Profitability	(0.02) ($342,000)	$ 6,840
Rework	(0.02 × $342,000) – $6,000	0
On-time delivery	Over 98%	5,000
Sales returns	[(0.015 × $2,850,000) – $44,750] × 50%	(1,000)
Semi-annual bonus installment		$10,840
Semi-annual bonus awarded		$10,840

July 1, 2003 to December 31, 2003

Profitability	(0.02) ($406,000)	$ 8,120
Rework	(0.02 × $406,000) – $8,000	0
On-time delivery	No bonus—under 96%	0
Sales returns	[(0.015 × $2,900,000) – $42,500] which is greater than zero, yielding a bonus of	3,000
Semi-annual bonus installment		$11,120
Semi-annual bonus awarded		$11,120
Total bonus awarded for the year		$21,960

3.   The manager of the Charter Division is likely to be frustrated by the new plan as the division bonus is more than $20,000 less than the previous year. However the new performance measures have begun to have the desired effect—both on-time deliveries and sales returns improved in the second half of the year while rework costs were relatively even. If the division continues to improve at the same rate, the Charter bonus could approximate or exceed what it was under the old plan.

The manager of the Mesa Division should be as satisfied with the new plan as with the old plan as the bonus is almost equivalent. However, there is no sign of improvements in the performance measures instituted by Harrington in this division; as a matter of fact, on-time deliveries declined considerably in the second half of the year. Unless the manager institutes better controls, the bonus situation may not be as favourable in the future. This could motivate the manager to improve in the future but currently, at least, the manager has been able to maintain his bonus without showing improvements in the areas targeted by Harrington.

24-20 (cont'd)

Ben Harrington's revised bonus plan for the Charter Division fostered the following improvements in the second half of the year despite an increase in sales
- increase of 1.9 percent in on-time deliveries.
- $500 reduction in rework costs.
- $14,000 reduction in sales returns.

However, operating income as a percent of sales has decreased (11 to 10 percent).

The Mesa Division's bonus has remained at the status quo as a result of the following effects
- increase of 2.0 percent in operating income as a percent of sales (12 to 14 percent).
- decrease of 3.6 percent in on-time deliveries.
- $2,000 increase in rework costs.
- $2,250 decrease in sales returns.

This would suggest that there needs to be some revisions to the bonus plan. Possible changes include:

- increasing the weights put on on-time deliveries, rework costs, and sales returns in the performance measures while decreasing the weight put on operating income.
- a reward structure for rework costs that are below 2 percent of operating income that would encourage managers to drive costs lower.
- reviewing the whole year in total. The bonus plan should carry forward the negative amounts for one six-month period into the next six-month period incorporating the entire year when calculating a bonus.
- developing benchmarks, and then giving rewards for improvements over prior periods and encouraging continuous improvement.

24-22 (25 min.) **RI, EVA.**

1.

	Truck Rental Division	Transportation Division
Total assets	$650,000	$950,000
Current liabilities	120,000	200,000
Investment (Total assets – current liabilities)	530,000	750,000
Required return (12% × Investment)	63,600	90.0~
Operating income before tax	75,000	16
Residual income (Optg inc. before tax – Reqd. return)	11,400	70,

2. After-tax cost of debt financing = $(1 - 0.4) \times 10\% = 6\%$
   After-tax cost of equity financing = 15%

   $$\text{Weighted average cost of capital} = \frac{\$900,000 \times 6\% + 600,000 \times 15\%}{\$900,000 + 600,000} = 9.\text{(}$$

Required return for EVA 9.6% × Investment (9.6% × $530,000; 9.6% × $750,000)	$50,880	$72,000
Operating income after tax 0.6 × operating income before tax	45,000	96,000
EVA (Optg inc. after tax – Reqd. return)	(5,880)	24,000

3. Both the residual income and the EVA calculations indicate that the Transportation Division is performing better than the Truck Rental Division. The Transportation Division has a higher residual income ($70,000 versus $11,400) and a higher EVA [$24,000 versus $(5,880)]. The negative EVA for the Truck Rental Division indicates that on an after-tax basis the division is destroying value—the after-tax economic return from the Truck Rental Division's assets is less than the required return. If EVA continues to be negative, Burlingame may have to consider shutting down the Truck Rental Division.

24-24 (20–30 min.) **ROI, RI, measurement of assets** (CMA, adapted).

The method for computing profitability preferred by each manager follows:

Manager of	Method Chosen
Bristol	Residual income based on net book value
Darden	Residual income based on gross book value
Gregory	ROI based on either gross or net book value

Supporting Calculations:

Return on Investment Calculations

Division	Operating Income / Gross Book Value*	Operating Income / Net Book Value*
Bristol	$94,700 ÷ $800,000 = 11.84% (3)	$94,700 ÷ $370,000 = 25.59% (3)
Darden	$91,700 ÷ $760,000 = 12.07% (2)	$91,700 ÷ $350,000 = 26.20% (2)
Gregory	$61,400 ÷ $500,000 = 12.28% (1)	$61,400 ÷ $220,000 = 27.91% (1)

Residual Income Calculations

Division	Operating Income – 10% Gross BV	Operating Income – 10% Net BV*
Bristol	$94,700 – $80,000 = $14,700 (2)	$94,700 – $37,000 = $57,700 (1)
Darden	$91,700 – $76,000 = $15,700 (1)	$91,700 – $35,000 = $56,700 (2)
Gregory	$61,400 – $50,000 = $11,400 (3)	$61,400 – $22,000 = $39,400 (3)

*Net book value is gross book value minus accumulated depreciation.

The biggest weakness of ROI is the tendency to reject projects that will lower historical ROI even though the prospective ROI exceeds the required ROI. RI achieves goal congruence because subunits will make investments as long as they earn a rate in excess of the required return for investments. The biggest weakness of residual income is it favours larger divisions in ranking performance. The greater the amount of the investment (the size of the division), the more likely that larger divisions will be favoured assuming that income grows proportionately.

24-26 (20 min.) **Multinational performance measurement, ROI, RI.**

1(a) Dundas' ROI for 2003 $= \dfrac{\$765,000}{\$4,500,000} = 17\%$

1(b) Lyon Division's 2003 ROI in French francs $= \dfrac{3,600,000 \text{ francs}}{20,000,000 \text{ francs}} = 18\%$

1(c) We can't tell which division earned a better ROI because Lyon's return may have been helped by greater inflation in France and a weakening franc.

2.   To make RI comparable, we need to make the following conversions for the Lyon Division

Operating assets at December 31, 2002 rate $= \dfrac{20,000,000 \text{ francs}}{4 \text{ francs per dollar}} =$ $5,000,000

Convert operating income into dollars at the average exchange rate prevailing during 2003 when operating income was earned equal to

$\dfrac{3,600,000 \text{ francs}}{4.5 \text{ francs per dollar}} = \$800,000$

2003 RI for Lyon in dollars $= \$800,000 - 15\% \times \$5,000,000 = \$50,000$

2003 RI for Dundas $= \$765,000 - 15\% \times \$4,500,000 = \$90,000$

On a comparable basis, after adjusting for inflationary and currency differences, Dundas has the higher residual income.

3.   Lyon's 2003 ROI calculated in dollar terms $= \dfrac{\$800,000}{\$5,000,000} = 16\%$

Both the ROI and the residual income calculations indicate that after removing the effects of any differences in inflation rates between the two countries, the Dundas Division has performed better than the Lyon Division in 2003 (ROI of 17% versus 16% and residual return of $90,000 versus $50,000).

Even after adjusting for inflation differences, the relative performance of the two divisions in 2003 is inadequate for making the decision about which manager to promote to the vice-president's position. The economic performance of the divisions must be distinguished from the performance of the managers of those divisions. For example, the poorer performance of the Lyon division in 2003 relative to the Dundas Division may be attributable to the more difficult business environment in Lyon. Recall that the economic, legal, political, social, and cultural environments differ significantly across countries as does the availability and costs of inputs such as materials and labour. Furthermore, promotion to the vice-president's position should not be based on the performance of the divisions in 2003 alone. The decision should consider the performance history of the two managers over the most recent few years.

24-28 (40-50 min.) **ROI performance measures based on historical cost and current cost.**

1. ROI using historical cost measures:

Calistoga : $\dfrac{\$130,000}{\$340,000}$ = 38.24%

Alpine Springs : $\dfrac{\$220,000}{\$1,150,000}$ = 19.13%

Rocky Mountains : $\dfrac{\$380,000}{\$1,620,000}$ = 23.46%

The Calistoga Division appears to be considerably more efficient than are the Alpine Springs and Rocky Mountain Divisions.

2. The gross book values (i.e., the original costs of the plants) under historical cost are calculated as the useful life of each plant (12) × the annual depreciation:

Calistoga   : 12 × $ 70,000 = $ 840,000
Alpine Springs : 12 × $100,000 = $1,200,000
Rocky Mountains : 12 × $120,000 = $1,440,000

Step 1: Restate long-term assets from gross book value at historical cost to gross book value at current cost as of the end of 2002.

$$\text{Gross book value of long-term assets at historical cost} \times \dfrac{\text{Construction cost index in 2002}}{\text{Construction cost index in year of construction}}$$

Calistoga: $ 840,000 × (170 ÷ 100) = $1,428,000
Alpine Springs: $1,200,000 × (170 ÷ 136) = $1,500,000
Rocky Mountain: $1,440,000 × (170 ÷ 160) = $1,530,000

Step 2: Derive net book value of long-term assets at current cost as of the end of 2002. (Assume estimated useful life of each plant is 12 years.)

$$\text{Gross book value of long-term assets at current cost at the end of 2002} \times \dfrac{\text{Estimated useful life remaining}}{\text{Estimated total useful life}}$$

Calistoga: $1,428,000 × (2 ÷ 12)   = $ 238,000
Alpine Springs: $1,500,000 × (9 ÷ 12)   = $1,125,000
Rocky Mountains: $1,530,000 × (11 ÷ 12) = $1,402,500

24-28 (cont'd)

Step 3: Compute current cost of total assets at the end of 2002. (Assume current assets of each plant is expressed in 2002 dollars.)

Current assets at the end of 2002 (given) + Net book value of longterm assets at current cost at the end of 2002 (Step 2

Calistoga: $200,000 + $ 238,000 = $ 438,000
Alpine Springs: $250,000 + $1,125,000 = $1,375,000
Rocky Mountains: $300,000 + $1,402,500 = $1,702,500

Step 4: Compute current-cost depreciation expense in 2002 dollars.

Gross book value of long-term assets at current cost at the end of 2002 (from Step 1) × (1 ÷ 12)

Calistoga: $1,428,000 × (1 ÷ 12) = $119,000
Alpine Springs: $1,500,000 × (1 ÷ 12) = $125,000
Rocky Mountains: $1,530,000 × (1 ÷ 12) = $127,500

Step 5: Compute 2002 operating income using 2002 current-cost depreciation.

$$\text{Historical-cost operating income} - \left(\begin{array}{c} \text{Current-cost} \\ \text{depreciation in} \\ \text{2002 dollars (Step 4)} \end{array} - \begin{array}{c} \text{Historical-cost} \\ \text{depreciation} \end{array} \right)$$

Calistoga: $130,000 – ($119,000 – $ 70,000) = $ 81,000
Alpine Springs: $220,000 – ($125,000 – $100,000) = $195,000
Rocky Mountains: $380,000 – ($127,500 – $120,000) = $372,500

Step 6: Compute ROI using current-cost estimates for long-term assets and depreciation.

Operating income for 2002 using 2002 current-cost depreciation (Step 5)

Current cost of total assets at the end of 2002 (Step 3)

Calistoga: $ 81,000 ÷ $ 438,000   = 18.49%
Alpine Springs: $195,000 ÷ $1,375,000   = 14.18%
Rocky Mountains: $372,500 ÷ $1,702,500   = 21.88%

	ROI: Historical Cost	ROI: Current Cost
Calistoga	38.24%	18.49%
Alpine Springs	19.13	14.18
Rocky Mountains	23.46	21.88

24-28 (cont'd)

Use of current cost results in the Rocky Mountains Division appearing to be the most efficient. The Calistoga ROI is reduced substantially when the ten year old plant is restated for the 70% increase in construction costs over the 1992 to 2002 period.

3.   Use of current costs increases the comparability of ROI measures across divisions operating plants built at different construction cost price levels. Use of current cost also will increase the willingness of managers, evaluated on the basis of ROI, to move from divisions with assets purchased many years ago to divisions with assets purchased in recent years.

24-30 (25 min.) ROI, RI, ROS management incentives.

1. If Mason Industries uses return on investment to measure the Jump-Start Division's (JSD's) performance, Grieco may be reluctant to invest in the new plant because, as shown below, return on investment for the plant of 19.2% is lower than JSD's current ROI of 24%.

Operating income for new plant	$480,000
New investment	$2,500,000
Return on investment for new plant	19.2%

Investing in the new plant would lower JSD's ROI and, hence, limit Grieco's bonus.

2. The residual income computation for the new plant is as follows:

$$\text{Residual income} = \text{Income} - (\text{Imputed interest} \times \text{Investment})$$

Investment $\underline{\$2,500,000}$	
Operating income	$ 480,000
Charge for funds (Investment, $2,500,000 × 15%)	375,000
Residual income	$ 105,000

Investing in the new plant would add $105,000 to JSD's residual income. Consequently, if Mason Industries could be persuaded to use residual income to measure performance, Grieco would be more willing to invest in the new plant.

3. Return on Sales (ROS) $= \dfrac{\text{Operating income}}{\text{Sales}} = \dfrac{480,000}{2,400,000} = 20\%$

If Mason Industries uses ROS to determine Grieco's bonus, Grieco will be more willing to invest in the new plant because ROS for the new plant of 20% exceeds the current ROS of 19%.

The advantages of using ROS are (a) that it is simpler to calculate and (b) that it avoids the negative short-run effects of ROI measures that may induce Grieco to not make the investment in the new plant. Grieco may favour ROS because she believes that eventually increases in ROS will increase ROI and RI.

The main disadvantage of using ROS is that it ignores the amount of investment needed to earn a return. For example, ROS may be high but not high enough to justify the level of investment needed to earn the required return on an investment.

24-32 (30 min.)   **Relevant costs, performance evaluation, goal-congruence.**

This problem illustrates the dysfunctional behaviour that could be motivated by arbitrary allocations of corporate overhead to profit-conscious divisional managers.

1.   Without the $800,000 in sales from the low-margin product line in the Andorian Division, the second-quarter operating statements (in thousands) will be:

	Andorian	Orion	Tribble	Total
Net sales	$1,200	$1,200	$1,600	$4,000
Cost of sales	450	540	640	1,630
Divisional overhead	150	125	160	435
Divisional contribution	600	535	800	1,935
Corporate overhead	288	288	384	960
Operating income	$ 312	$ 247	$ 416	$ 975

2.   The company is worse off as a result of dropping the low profitability line of products because it has lost $100,000 in contribution margin from the dropped product line with no reduction in corporate overhead. Total operating income decreases from $1,075,000 in the first quarter to $975,000 in the second quarter.

3.   The Andorian Division manager's performance evaluation measure (divisional operating income) is higher ($312,000 in the second quarter versus $300,000 in the first quarter) as a result of dropping the low-profitability product line. The Andorian Division manager is able to show a $12,000 higher operating income because the $100,000 in lost contribution margin from the dropped product line is more than offset by the $112,000 reduction in corporate overhead that is charged to the Andorian Division. Andorian Division sales are now only 30% of corporate sales rather than the previous 41.7% of sales (so 30% of total corporate overhead costs of $960,000 equal to $288,000 are allocated to the Andorian Division in the second quarter, whereas 41.7% of $960,000 equal to $400,000 are allocated to the Andorian Division in the first quarter).

4.   The easiest solution is to not allocate fixed corporate overhead to divisions. Then, the problem of dysfunctional behaviour will not arise. But central management may want the division managers to "see" the cost of corporate operations so that they will understand that the corporation as a whole is not profitable unless the combined divisions' contribution margins exceed corporate overhead. In this case, an allocation basis should be chosen that is not manipulable or under the control of division managers. It must also have the property that the action taken by one division does not affect the corporate overhead allocations that get made to the other divisions (as occurred in the second quarter for the company).

24-32 (cont'd)

In general, a lump sum allocation based on, say, budgeted net income, or budgeted assets, rather than an allocation that varies proportionately with an actual measure of activity (such as sales or actual net income) will minimize dysfunctional behavior. The allocation should be such that managers treat it as a fixed, unavoidable charge, rather than a charge that will vary with the decisions they take. Of course, a potential disadvantage of this proposal is that managers may try to underbudget the amounts that serve as the cost allocation bases, so that their divisions get less of the corporate overhead charges.

24-34 (30-40 min.) **ROI, RI, investment decisions.**

1.

	$\dfrac{\text{Revenues}}{\text{Total Assets}}$ ×	$\dfrac{\text{Operating Income}}{\text{Revenues}}$ =	$\dfrac{\text{Operating Income}}{\text{Total Assets}}$
2002			
Newspapers	0.939	0.239	0.224
Television	2.133	0.025	0.053
Film Studios	0.635	0.121	0.077
2001*			
Newspapers	1.023	0.200	0.205
Television	2.222	0.022	0.048
Film Studios	0.640	0.137	0.088

*Not Required

The Newspaper Division has a high ROI because of its high income margin. The Television Division has a low ROI despite a high investment turnover because of its very low income margin. The Film Studios Division has a low ROI despite a reasonably high income margin because of its low investment turnover.

2. Although the proposed investment is small, relative to the total assets invested, it earns less than the 2002 return on investment (0.224) [or the 2001 return on investment (0.205)] (All dollar numbers in millions):

$$\text{2002 ROI (before proposal)} = \frac{\$1{,}100}{\$4{,}900} = 0.224$$

$$\text{Investment proposal ROI} = \frac{\$ 30}{\$200} = 0.150$$

$$\text{2002 ROI (with proposal)} = \frac{\$1{,}130}{\$5{,}100} = 0.222$$

Given the existing bonus plan, any proposal that reduces the ROI is unattractive.

3. Residual income for 2002 (before proposal, in millions):

	Operating Income		Imputed Interest Charge		Division Residual Income
Newspapers	$1,100	–	$588 (0.12 × $4,900)	=	$ 512
Television	$ 160	–	$360 (0.12 × $3,000)	=	$(200)
Film Studios	$ 200	–	$312 (0.12 × $2,600)	=	$(112)

24-34 (cont'd)

4. Residual income for proposal (in millions):

Operating Income		Imputed Interest Charge		Residual Income
$30	–	$24 (0.12 × $200)	=	$6

Investing in the fast-speed printing press will increase the Newspaper Division's residual income. Hence, if Kearney is evaluated using a residual income measure, Kearney would be much more willing to adopt the printing press proposal.

24-36 (25 min.) Ethics, manager's performance evaluation.

1a. Variable manufacturing cost per unit = $2

Fixed manufacturing cost per unit = $9,000,000 ÷ 500,000 = $18

Revenues, $20 × 500,000	$10,000,000
Variable manufacturing costs, $2 × 500,000	1,000,000
Fixed manufacturing costs, $18 × 500,000	9,000,000
Fixed marketing costs	400,000
Total costs	10,400,000
Operating income	$ (400,000)

1b. Variable manufacturing cost per unit = $2

Fixed manufacturing cost per unit = $9,000,000 ÷ 600,000 = $15

Revenues, $20 × 500,000	$10,000,000
Variable manufacturing costs, $2 × 500,000	1,000,000
Fixed manufacturing costs, $15 × 500,000	7,500,000
Fixed marketing costs	400,000
Total costs	8,900,000
Operating income	$ 1,100,000

2. Jones's behaviour is not ethical. Professional managers are expected to take actions that are in the best interests of their shareholders. Jones's action benefited himself at the cost of shareholders. Jones's actions are equivalent to "cooking the books," even though he achieved this by producing more inventory than was needed, rather than through fictitious accounting. Some students might argue that Jones's behaviour is not unethical—he simply took advantage of the faulty contract the board of directors had given him when he was hired.

3. Asking distributors to take more products than they need is also equivalent to "cooking the books." In effect, distributors are being coerced into taking more product. This is a particular problem if distributors will take less product in the following year or alternatively return the excess inventory next year. Some students might argue that Jones's behaviour is not unethical—it is up to the distributors to decide whether to take more inventory or not. So long as Jones is not forcing the product on the distributors, it is not unethical for Jones to push sales this year even if the excess product will sit in the distributors' inventory.